JESUS WINS!

ELIZABETH VIERA TALBOT

Pacific Press®
Publishing Association

Nampa, Idaho | www.pacificpress.com

Cover design by Gerald Lee Monks
Cover illustration by Darrel Tank
Inside design by Aaron Troia
Edited by Aivars Ozolins

The author assumes full responsibility for the accuracy of all facts and quotations as cited in this book.

Portions of this material are based on previously published books of the author and are not otherwise cited.

All of the words appearing in italics in the Bible texts are the author's emphasis.

You can obtain additional copies of this book by calling toll-free 1-800-765-6955 or by visiting http://www.adventistbookcenter.com.

Library of Congress Cataloging-in-Publication Data

Names: Talbot, Elizabeth Viera, author.
Title: Jesus wins! / Elizabeth Talbot.
Description: Nampa : Pacific Press Publishing Association, 2019.
Identifiers: LCCN 2019016080 | ISBN 9780816364497 (hardcover : alk. paper)
Subjects: LCSH: Devotional calendars—Seventh-Day Adventists.
Classification: LCC BV4811 .T36 2019 | DDC 242/.2—dc23 LC record available at
   https://lccn.loc.gov/2019016080

June 2019

TABLE OF CONTENTS

INTRODUCTION

Yes, *Jesus wins*! He already achieved victory at the cross! Through His sacrifice, He triumphed on our behalf—that's why there is a cross with a kingly crown on the cover of this book. Not only is Jesus victorious in the cosmic battle between good and evil, but He also triumphs individually in each person's heart who accepts His sacrifice in our place. When we trust in Christ's merits for our personal eternal salvation, everything changes, including the way we view our past, our present, and our future—for God offers us His forgiveness, His assurance, His peace, His presence, and His joy.

This devotional book is based on passages from the four Gospels and Acts, and a few verses from Revelation—to remind us how the story ends. It is designed to motivate the daily study of the Scriptures, for these testify of Jesus. It is my prayer that each devotional will take you directly to the Bible, inspiring you to continue studying that day's topic while the Holy Spirit anoints your reading and impresses upon your heart the message you need for that day. This devotional book does not follow the order of the biblical narrative; instead, each month concentrates on a different aspect of God's grace. These devotionals also include an additional feature—a response line at the bottom of each day. Please use that space to write a thought, a prayer, or a verse or to draw something that comes to your mind. Respond in any way that will stay with you throughout the day as you take a hold of God's Word for your own life. May you bask in His grace at all times and in all circumstances.

I dedicate this devotional book to all of you who, over the years, have reminded me of God's outrageous and flamboyant grace when I needed it most. You know who you are. In my life—in rainy and sunny days, in joy and pain, in health and sickness, in seasons of assurance and periods of emotional turmoil—I have discovered that the love of God is more than enough, and His grace is more than sufficient. May the assurance of His victory at the cross fill your heart with hope and wholeness as we eagerly await His return. He has promised that He will come back for us! Until that blessed day, may His sacrificial triumph ever remind us how the story ends: *JESUS WINS!*

ACCEPTING
HIS LOVE

HIS VICTORY

"These things I have spoken to you, so that in Me you may have peace. In the world you have tribulation, but take courage; I have overcome the world."

—John 16:33

I had heard the story before and I knew the ending, but it still gripped me every time my dad told it in a sermon. The story was about a boy who loved and admired the main hero in a book series. He had just bought the latest volume and realized that this book was very different! Unlike the previous books, this time his hero was being beaten and seemed to be losing! Not very far into the book, the boy couldn't take it anymore and, holding his breath, went straight to the last chapter. With trembling hands, he turned to the last page and read the last paragraph. And there, in the last sentences of the story, he discovered that, despite the many seeming defeats, his hero was the victor after all, and the villain was destroyed. Now that he knew the ending, he was at peace and went back to the place where he had left off and continued reading the book. This time, having new information, whenever the villain seemed to be winning, the boy would say aloud, "If he knew what I know—if he just knew what I know!"

Jesus has told us the end of the story: He has overcome! Furthermore, He highlighted the contrast of two realities: Himself and the world. *In Him* we may have peace, yet *in the world* we will have tribulation (verse 33). After informing the disciples of their impending personal failure (verse 32), Jesus proclaims that "in Him" they may have peace. Every day we face the choice of which reality to empower: the world and its troubles, which are sure to come, or the love and inward peace that we may find *in Jesus*, focusing on His already-attained victory on the cross. As in the case of the introductory story, it makes a world of difference to know how the story ends. When we face sickness, death, loss, and various troubles, let's remember that evil is a conquered enemy. When I posted a photo of my dad's hand in mine, to announce his passing, I added the phrase that is now the title of this devotional book: *Jesus Wins!* Jesus' victorious love is the basis of our faith!

My Response: _____

HIS LOVE

"For God so loved the world, that He gave His only begotten Son,
that whoever believes in Him shall not perish,
but have eternal life."

—John 3:16

I had barely opened the door of my second-floor condo when I was shocked by the sight of a big snake! I instinctively jumped back and ran out. Later I called my neighbors and the department of animal control, and someone came and got the reptile out of my place. But it took me many months to get over the trauma.

This experience reminds me how Jesus used a snake to teach us about salvation and love. Snakes have a way of getting our attention, but that's not the reason why Jesus reminded Nicodemus of an ancient experience with these animals as a visualization of Himself and how God loved the world so much that He sent His Son to die. In this first extended dialogue in John's Gospel, Jesus is explaining God's love and salvation to a teacher of the law. Nicodemus, judging by the signs Christ was doing, starts with an impressive assertion about Jesus having come from God (John 3:2). But Jesus does not engage in reciprocal flattery; instead, He tells Nicodemus that he must be born again (verses 5, 7). When Nicodemus misinterprets Jesus' words, the Savior resorts to the history of Israel. He alludes to an event recorded in Numbers 21:4–9, when venomous serpents started biting the Israelites after God had withdrawn His protection due to their unbelief. God instructed Moses to make a bronze snake and place it on a pole. Whoever looked at it would be saved. And Jesus, explaining the gospel to Nicodemus, says: "As Moses lifted up the serpent in the wilderness, even so must the Son of Man be lifted up; so that whoever believes will in Him have eternal life. For God so loved the world" (John 3:14–16). Yes, God's unfailing love is so amazing that He provided the Antidote for His sinful children. Jesus is heaven's greatest Gift! As much as we enjoy healthy love in this world, it is still stained by our sin and shortcomings. Yet God's love for us is perfect and unfailing, and we can always count on it! For God so loved you . . . that He gave His Son!

My Response: _____

HIS DESCRIPTION

To Him who loves us and released us from our sins
by His blood . . . to Him be the glory and the dominion
forever and ever. Amen.

—Revelation 1:5, 6

I was overwhelmed, standing at the end of the main street of the ancient city of Ephesus, with its amazingly well-preserved ruins and its magnificent amphitheater. I envisioned travelers crowding through the city in the time when John wrote the book of Revelation. I also visited the island of Patmos, where John received the *unveiling* of Jesus. I tried to imagine how John must have felt on this island, about fifty miles southwest of Ephesus, being shown the final chapter of the world's history and the indisputable announcement: Jesus Wins!

In light of the revelations he received, how would John introduce Jesus to the audience? There are two verbs in John's opening description of Jesus that we will focus on, because they give us assurance from the very beginning of this book. "Grace to you and peace, from Him who is and who was and who is to come, and from the seven Spirits who are before His throne, and from Jesus Christ, the faithful witness, the firstborn of the dead, and the ruler of the kings of the earth. To Him who *loves us* and *released us* from our sins by His blood" (Revelation 1:4, 5). Let's start with the phrase: "who *loves* us" (verse 5). This *present* tense verb reminds us of the ongoing love of Jesus Christ for us, right now and forever. The original meaning is continuous: He loves us and keeps loving and loving and loving us. Then comes the second phrase: "And *released* us from our sins by His blood" (verse 5). In the original Greek, the past tense of the verb "to release" is what is called an aorist participle, which means a completed action in the past. Therefore, here we find two verbs that describe the relationship of Jesus with us: He loves us, continuously and unceasingly, and He has purchased our freedom on the cross. These two verbs form the core of the everlasting gospel. Many have not experienced real, unconditional love in this world, yet God's message changes that. The last chapter of the world's history starts with the reminder that Jesus *loves us,* and that He has *freed* us. These two realities will sustain us every day until we see Him face to face!

My Response: _____

HIS CONQUEST

*"The time is fulfilled, and the kingdom of God is at hand;
repent and believe in the gospel."*

—Mark 1:15

As the Olympics, the World Cup of soccer is a much-awaited world-wide event involving many countries, represented by their national teams. In 1978, Argentina hosted the Cup, and the national team won the trophy. I will never forget this victory. I was in high school, and the country ground to an absolute stop for three days in order to celebrate this momentous event. Even though the victory had been won by the able athletes, all of us had won; their triumph was ours, the victory belonged to the whole country! They were our representatives!

Mark opens his book by stating, "The beginning of the gospel [good news] of Jesus Christ" (Mark 1:1). The Greek noun *euangelion* is translated into English as "good news" or "gospel"—a term that comes from the Old English *godspell*, which means "good news." This term was used when messengers came from the battlefield, announcing that the king had fought on behalf of his subjects and had won; the messengers who brought the good news were called *evangelists*. The Greek term was used in the Greek translation of the Old Testament (LXX) to announce God's ultimate deliverance of His people:

> How lovely on the mountains
> Are the feet of him who brings *good news*,
> Who announces peace
> And brings *good news* of happiness,
> Who announces salvation,
> And says to Zion, "Your God reigns!"
> (Isaiah 52:7).

When Jesus proclaimed, "The time is fulfilled and the kingdom of God is at hand; repent and believe in the *gospel*" (Mark 1:15), He was announcing that the good news of God's victory through Jesus was about to be revealed. It is highly significant that Mark chose this term to introduce his book about Jesus. Jesus has won the battle on our behalf! Don't ever let fear of the future, or anything else, take away the joy of your salvation. Jesus, our Representative and Substitute, has conquered in our place! Rejoice!

My Response: _____

HIS KINGSHIP

"Where is He who has been born King of the Jews?"
—Matthew 2:2

Whether in the tombs and treasures of Egypt or Buckingham Palace in the United Kingdom; whether in ancient kingdoms or modern monarchies, one common thread runs throughout history: the splendor and grandeur that surrounds kings and queens. I have visited many such majestic buildings, and I have always marveled at the beauty and riches in honor of mortal men and women. And I wonder about the contrast between earthly royalties and Jesus, the King of kings, who walked on this earth two thousand years ago. Who would pay Him homage?

Matthew shocks his audience by narrating the visit of the Magi. The story starts by placing Jesus in the territory and tribe of the Davidic kings, hence the clarification that this is Bethlehem of Judea, where David was born: "Now after Jesus was born in Bethlehem *of Judea*" (Matthew 2:1). At that time, Herod was the king (verses 1, 3), and these wise men went straight to his palace in Jerusalem, perhaps expecting the new King to be born in the royal family. But they were in for a surprise! They spoke to King Herod about another *King of the Jews*, thus introducing tension between the two kings from the very beginning of the story. Herod clearly understood that their inquiry was related to the Messiah (see verse 4). It is a notable fact that the Magi used the title "King of the Jews" instead of "our King," which indicates that they were Gentiles. Evidently, Matthew included this story to highlight the inclusivity of Jesus' mission (see Jesus' command to make disciples of *all nations*, Matthew 28:19). Yet what I find most fascinating about the title "King of the Jews" is that the only other use of it in Matthew is found in the story of the trial and crucifixion of Jesus (Matthew 27:11, 29, 37), and once again, it is spoken by Gentiles. It was the legal charge placed on the cross by Pilate: "This is Jesus the King of the Jews" (verse 37). The One who loved us to the point of death has revealed to us how the story ends: *Jesus Wins!* He will return, as the King of kings, to take us home. Until then, let's honor Him and invite Him to be the King of our lives, reigning in our hearts!

My Response: _____

HIS MAJESTY

They rejoiced exceedingly with great joy. . . . They fell
to the ground and worshiped Him.
—Matthew 2:10, 11

I have happy childhood memories in South America of leaving my shoes outside my bedroom so that the wise men would leave me gifts as they passed by. Sometimes, just for fun, children would leave straw and water for the camels. The story of the Magi has been celebrated in many Latin American countries on January 6 as the feast of Epiphany, highlighting how God reached out to all nations with the good news of the Savior's birth.

Matthew contrasts the Magi, who have come to worship (2:2), with Herod the king and all the people of Jerusalem, who are troubled by the news (verse 3). As the dignitaries from the East followed God's guidance and arrived to where the Child was, they "rejoiced exceedingly with great joy" (2:10). The language is lush and flamboyant as Matthew describes a super-joyful occasion, fit for a king (see a similar phrase used in 1 Kings 1:40). I love that the Greek word for "great" is mega! Even now, I believe that those who follow God's leading towards a greater revelation of Jesus experience mega joy, which is above whatever circumstances we find ourselves in. When they arrived to the place where the Child was found, "they fell to the ground and worshiped Him" (verse 11). The original language says that they prostrated themselves, which means completely falling to the ground. What a scene! Non-Jews were worshiping Jesus when the rest of Israel was not! These were distinguished and learned people, who had traveled from afar and had even been granted an audience with Herod the Great. Now they are giving homage to a baby in a humble home. God has a way of turning our world upside down! They even brought Him expensive gifts, as was the custom to honor a king (Matthew 2:11, compare with 1 Kings 10:2). In Jesus, God has given us the Greatest Gift! We will joyfully worship Jesus throughout eternity, showing him our gratitude and honor. Let's start today! For "Worthy is the Lamb that was slain to receive power and riches and wisdom and might and honor and glory and blessing" (Revelation 5:12).

My Response: _____

HIS INFLUENCE

This is the disciple who is testifying to these things and wrote these things, and we know that his testimony is true.

—John 21:24

D*on Quixote*, the seventeenth-century classic of Miguel de Cervantes, and the Broadway musical, *Man of La Mancha*, showcase a woman of shady reputation named Aldonza. In the novel, the mad knight sees her through the eyes of grace, and calls her Dulcinea, which means sweet. Yet, she rejects this new identity, because she is more than aware of who she really is. However, in the end, the influence of his love, and the way he views her, completely changes her into a sweet and reputable woman. Many believe that Cervantes wrote this work during the time of the Inquisition as a veiled spiritual allegory of the gospel.

John, the disciple, was not known for his sweetness. He had such a bad temper that Jesus nicknamed him and his brother James, *Boanerges*, which means "Sons of Thunder" (Mark 3:17). I don't think I would have chosen *him* . . . but Jesus did. The "thunder" brothers wanted the best place in the upcoming kingdom (see Mark 10:35–45) and came up with the idea of sending fire from heaven on a Samaritan village that didn't show Jesus hospitality (see Luke 9:51–55). But John, along with the other disciples, were *ordinary people* who were exposed to Jesus' *extraordinary grace*.* Jesus treated them with love, and His grace changed them. This selfish and angry disciple became known as the disciple of love. He doesn't even use his own name in his Gospel but identifies himself as "the disciple Jesus loved" (John 13:23; 19:26; 21:7; 21:20). In their last dinner together, John was reclining on Jesus' bosom, as close to Him as possible (John 13:23, 25). Jesus' love had influenced and captured him. John chose to accept the extraordinary love of Jesus, and this became the guiding principle in his ministry. John uses the word *love* fifty-seven times in his Gospel, and fifty-two times in his letters; one hundred nine times in total! (compare with Matthew's seventeen times, Mark's eight times and Luke's nineteen times). If you are struggling with a character trait that God needs to work on, bask in the grace of Jesus, and let His love and grace influence you from inside out.

My Response: _____

———————

* For an additional study of the twelve disciples, see Elizabeth Talbot and Aivars Ozolins, *Jesus 101: Radical Discipleship* (Nampa, ID: Pacific Press®, 2016).

HIS KNOWLEDGE

"When you were under the fig tree, I saw you."

—John 1:48

Have you ever been surprised by how much someone knows you? I went to preach at a church in central California and spent the whole weekend there; we had a fantastic time studying the Scriptures together. A couple of ladies, whom I had never met, approached me and told me that they knew me since I was one year of age. I was startled! They went on to explain that they were teenagers in a local church in Argentina, where my dad was the pastor. I had turned one year old in that church! They knew me and they knew my family! It's a small world!

Nathanael was more than surprised by Jesus' knowledge of him! After Jesus had called Philip to follow Him (see John 1:43), Philip found Nathanael and excitedly announced: "We have found Him of whom Moses in the Law and also the Prophets wrote—Jesus of Nazareth, the son of Joseph" (verse 45). But Nathanael was less than impressed; his prejudice against Nazareth didn't let him see beyond the stereotype: "Can any good thing come out of Nazareth?" (verse 46). Instead of arguing, Philip invited him to come and see for himself. Before Nathanael could utter a word, Jesus said to him, "Behold, an Israelite indeed, in whom there is no deceit!" (verse 47). Can you imagine Nathanael's mind racing, wondering how He knew him? Jesus had revealed that He *really* knew him and stated that Nathanael was "Israel" without the "Jacob" part, without the deception, dishonesty, treachery, and trickery associated with the patriarch Jacob. "Nathanael said to Him, 'How do You know me?' Jesus answered and said to him, 'Before Philip called you, when you were under the fig tree, I saw you' " (verse 48). I am speechless, and so was Nathanael. This revelation made a profound impact on him, and from his heart came his confession: "Rabbi, You are the Son of God; You are the King of Israel" (verse 49). God knows us intimately. When you opened this book this morning, He saw you. When you cried yourself to sleep last night, He saw you. He knows your joys, your sadness, your dreams, your trials. No need to hide anything from Him. He knows everything about you and He loves you!

My Response: _____

HIS CREATION

As many as received Him, to them He gave
the right to become children of God.

—John 1:12

My maternal grandparents lived in a large farmhouse where I loved to visit them. It was in a different country, so I went there for summer vacations. Soon I found out that there were other young people living there and, as I grew up, I realized that these young people were foster kids, some with learning disabilities, others with difficult upbringings who needed a nurturing place to live. They found a safe home with my grandparents, and some of them became like their own children, until adulthood. We all need a safe place, a home where we belong.

John announces that the Word of God was the active Agent through which everything was created (John 1:3). He Himself was Life (verse 4), He didn't just *give* life but He *was* Life. And following the order of Creation, John talks about light; he says that the Word was life, and that life became "the Light of men" (verse 4). And when the Light appeared, the darkness did not understand it (verse 5). God was about to redeem His creation, and the story of redemption starts at *the beginning*. John goes on to say that Jesus "was the true Light which . . . enlightens every man" (John 1:9). Every person, at some level, has the chance to accept or reject the Light. Then we learn that when the Light came to His own home, those at home did not receive Him! How sad! Home is supposed to be your own place, where everybody knows your name. The Word, the Life-Giver, and Light Bearer "was in the world, and the world was made through Him, and the world did not know Him. He came to His own, and those who were His own did not receive Him" (verses 10, 11). This is the bad news, but there is also good news. Some *did accept* the Light. And to those who received Him by believing in Him, He gave a gift: a new status—children of God. Those who believe in Him are *given* that right (verses 12, 13). Have you ever been rejected by your own family, by your own home? God invites you to join the heavenly family. No one can take you away from Him. You become a child, born of the will of God. You have a home. And your Father knows your name.

My Response: _____

His Family

*"For whoever does the will of My Father who is in heaven,
he is My brother and sister and mother."*
—Matthew 12:50

I thank God for the parents He chose for me. When I sit in front of their tombstone, my heart is filled with gratitude for their godly lives. When my parents retired, they came to live in the same state where I reside. After my mother passed away, my father spoke with me about the future, knowing that his well-being would be so important to me. I had been working in ministerial capacities for almost fifteen years, and he said to me that if I were asked to minister in another state and felt it was a call from God, I should go even if that meant leaving him behind in California. I never had to cross that bridge, yet I was so blessed to have parents who placed the priorities of the kingdom of God above themselves.

As Jesus was ministering, His family came to talk with Him. Mark gives us an inside look at their motive: "When His own people [kinsmen, family] heard of this, they went out to take custody of Him; for they were saying 'He has lost His senses' " (Mark 3:21). Jesus didn't have brothers and sisters who fully understood His mission, at least not at first. Some members of His family did later become influential leaders of the Christian community. When His mother and siblings arrived where He was speaking, "Someone said to Him, 'Behold, Your mother and Your brothers are standing outside seeking to speak to You.' But Jesus answered the one who was telling Him and said, 'Who is My mother and who are My brothers?' " (Matthew 12:47, 48). What a strange question, especially since His family was standing outside! Jesus was not renouncing His family; He was stating His priorities. Jesus stretched out His hand towards the disciples and went on to explain that those who do the will of His Father are His true family (verses 49, 50). Even the closest of human relationships wouldn't take priority over the kingdom's mission. If you have relatives who do not understand your calling and purpose, be encouraged because when you become a follower of Jesus, you also become part of His family on earth. You have brothers and sisters, and *His* Father is *your* Father.

My Response: _____

HIS GIFT

"If you knew the gift of God . . . you would have asked Him,
and He would have given you living water."

—John 4:10

I don't know how to describe severe loneliness, other than to say that it is like a dark chill that cuts through your heart. I remember the time when I was starting my postgraduate studies in Europe and had just arrived in a city where I would be meeting with my dissertation supervisor. I didn't know anyone in that town and I was planning to spend many days there to study and research. I felt overwhelmed by so many things: the academic tasks, the unfamiliar place, the lack of human contact, and the fact that I didn't know a single person in that area. I will never forget the dark loneliness I felt and the relief I found for it in God's acceptance and intimate knowledge of my soul.

The Samaritan woman that Jesus encountered in John 4 was all alone. She was surrounded by people, yet had no real female friends that would risk being seen with her at the well. In Bible times, fetching water was the women's daily task, and they usually went in groups (that's why if someone wanted to find a wife, they went to the well). But this woman was filled with shame. She came to the well by herself at noon, so that no one would ask her anything. Yet there was more to her loneliness: in Israel a woman normally couldn't initiate divorce, which meant that the five husbands she had been married to had rejected her by serving a certificate of divorce. And at the present time, she was being rejected in the worst way by a man who didn't even have the decency to marry her. Furthermore, in the first century a woman divorced more than three times was considered an outcast. This is why I love the way this story starts: "He *had* to pass through Samaria" (John 4:4). The need was not geographical, because there were other roads. Jesus *had* to come in order to offer this lonely soul His *gift* of eternal life (verse 10). He *had* to tell her that He was the Messiah, and that He knew everything about her and still accepted *her*. His gift was for her! No wonder this encounter changed her life. And His gift is for you and me as well!

My Response: _____

His Determination

"Is it not written, 'My house shall be called a house of prayer for all the nations'?' But you have made it a robbers' den."

—Mark 11:17

Parents contend for their children's well-being; they even fight with an attacker when a child's safety is at stake. A woman, whose car was stolen with her little child inside, fought the attacker and hung on to the car's rear bumper while the man was driving away. She wouldn't let go; her child was more important to her than her own life. She appeared in the news with both hands bandaged due to the injuries she sustained, but she was happily holding her child.

Jesus was determined to defend *all* His children from religious, economic, and ethnic abuses. The temple had become a fruitless institution, just like the fig-less tree (Matthew 21:18–22). It was time to do something about it, so Jesus cleansed the temple from the business-like environment and the merchants in the court of the Gentiles. Just in case anyone missed what He was doing, Jesus began to teach them what this was all about. "Is it not written, 'My house shall be called a house of prayer for all the nations'? But you have made it a robbers' den" (Mark 11:17). Mark quotes more fully than the other Gospels the citations from the Scriptures that Jesus used to explain His actions and in doing so helps us interpret the heart of the matter. The first part of the teaching of Jesus comes from Isaiah 56:7; Mark includes the words "for all the nations" from that passage. Jesus was protecting the original intention for which the temple was designed: everyone was welcome to come to pray and worship the God of heaven and earth. But the religious leaders of the day, with no regard for "all the nations," had taken the only place where non-Jews could worship and turned it into a shady marketplace. No foreigner could be at peace with God in that noisy place, and Jesus was defending them! Just like a zealous mother defends her children, Jesus is determined to defend the right of everyone to come as they are to receive His blessing! *All seekers* are welcome in His Presence. Jesus fought so hard for us on the cross that His hands and feet sustained irreversible injuries!

My Response: _____

HIS ANOINTING

The Holy Spirit descended upon Him . . . , and a voice came out of heaven, "You are My beloved Son, in You I am well-pleased"
—Luke 3:22

My parents always went out of their way to communicate their love and support for me. Recently, I found a note inside a book that they gifted to me, expressing their love and parental pride, which means so much now that both of them have passed away. My mother left a memories chest for me, in which she had kept mementos from various stages of my life. It contains things like my little red gloves from when I was a one-year-old and a feather I wore on my hat as a child. I thank God for my parents, who lavished me with love and approval.

Jesus received the affirmation of His Father's love and approval from the very beginning of His public ministry. Luke is the only Gospel writer to report that after His baptism, Jesus was *praying* when the Holy Spirit descended upon Him in the form of a dove, and a Voice from heaven was heard (Luke 3:21, 22). Prayer is an important, recurring theme for Luke.* The Holy Spirit is another recurring Lukan theme, both in his Gospel and in Acts. Two foundational events occur at the time of Jesus' baptism: the Holy Spirit descends upon Jesus to empower Him for His redeeming mission, and God declares the Sonship of Jesus, along with God's love and approval of Him. The identity of Jesus as the Son of God and the presence of the Holy Spirit had been pronounced since His birth (Luke 1:32, 35), but at this time He was being empowered for public ministry as the divine Agent for the redemption of humankind. God Himself now confirms what the angel Gabriel had announced to Mary (Luke 1:35). Three times a Voice was heard from heaven, affirming the ministry of Jesus (see Luke 3:22; 9:35; John 12:28). In Jesus, Heaven gave it all. His identity and mission would become the only source of salvation for humankind, which He achieved through His sacrifice. Now we are to proclaim what He has done, until He comes back. And for this task, God promises the same two realities for us: in Christ, we are God's beloved children, and He empowers us for His mission through the Holy Spirit. Praise be to God!

My Response: _____

---

* For examples, see Luke 5:16; 6:12; 9:18; 22:32; 23:34.

His Sonship

"This is My beloved Son, in whom I am well-pleased."
—Matthew 3:17

It is such a blessing to have godly parents. My parents were a constant source of support for me, which they manifested in so many ways, lavishing me with unconditional and unwavering love. I still remember when I graduated with my first master's degree. My dad had been diagnosed with stomach cancer and was about to have a major surgery. Still, he insisted on attending my graduation, in spite of his failing health, because he knew how much his presence meant to me. Now that they are no longer alive, I like to re-read the notes of encouragement that my parents used to send me, telling me of their love and support.

God made sure Jesus knew of His support and love. After Jesus' baptism, we find one of the most amazing scenes in the New Testament, one in which the Trinity is manifested. The Spirit comes upon Jesus, and a Voice from heaven speaks, asserting God's view of Jesus in a heavenly revelation of His identity: "This is My beloved Son, in whom I am well-pleased" (Matthew 3:17; see also 12:18; 17:5). In the Jewish Scriptures (Old Testament), Israel is called the "son of God" (for example, Exodus 4:22, 23; Hosea 11:1). The Davidic kings of Israel were also called "sons of God" (for example, Psalm 2:7). Now Jesus, the ultimate King of Israel, is identified as *the* Son of God. And God asserts His Sonship and the fact that the Father "delights" in Him. Right after this assertion, the status of Jesus as God's Son will be challenged by the devil ("*If you are the Son of God . . .*" Matthew 4:3–6), who tempts Jesus to use His divine power for His own benefit. When a person accepts Jesus as their Savior, they become beloved in the Beloved. In Him, we are the beloved children of God: "See how great a love the Father has bestowed on us, that we would be called children of God" (1 John 3:1). Even our final reunion with God is portrayed with these divine words: "I will be his God and *he will be My son*" (Revelation 21:7). Through the Sonship of Jesus, we too become children of God. When we are in Jesus, we know with certainty God's view of us: we are His beloved children, and He delights in us!

My Response: _____

HIS SACRIFICE

"I lay down My life so that I may take it again. No one has taken it away from Me, but I lay it down on My own initiative."
—John 10:17, 18

You may have heard the name of Salman Kunan, a retired Thai Navy officer who volunteered to help in the rescue that captured the world's attention in June–July 2018. Twelve boys and their soccer coach were trapped in Thailand's Thum Luang cave. Kunan lost his life while delivering oxygen to them during the rescue mission. He was a hero. Sources say that when he realized that the oxygen level in the cave was low, he left his own oxygen equipment and tried to swim back without it, knowing that it would be difficult to make it. In selfless love, he made the choice to save those thirteen lives by giving up his.

Jesus' sacrifice was His own choice. The fact that He was laying down His life for His sheep is repeated four times in this short narrative (John 10:11–18). John emphasizes that the sacrifice of Jesus was not an accident or a simple misfortune; it was the plan all along, and He submitted Himself to it voluntarily, in order to save the human race. The Greek original word is often translated as "myself": "I lay it [my life] down *myself*" (verse 18). Frankly, it is a mystery to me that Jesus loved us so much, to the point of not only choosing, but planning ahead to die in our place for our salvation. That's why we find our personal worth at the Cross, as we realize how much we mean to Him. Barclay explains: "Jesus was not helplessly caught up in a mesh of circumstances from which he could not break free. Apart from any divine power he might have called in, it is quite clear that to the end he could have turned back and saved his life. He did not lose his life; he gave it. The cross was not thrust upon him: he willingly accepted it—for us."* Jesus continued to be in control to the very end when He gave up His spirit (John 19:30). It was not the nails that kept Jesus on the cross. It was His love for you and me! He had the power to get down from the cross and avoid additional torture and death. But His love for us was greater than His physical, emotional, and unsurpassed spiritual anguish. Yes, my friend, you are loved *that* much!

My Response: _____

---

* William Barclay, *The Gospel of John*, vol. 2 (Philadelphia: Westminster Press, 1975), 67.

HIS INTIMACY

*"Greater love has no one than this, that one lay
down his life for his friends."*

—John 15:13

F riendship means mutual affection, respect, and honesty. Friends have each other's backs and like each other despite their character defects. I am not talking about acquaintances, but close friends who will take your secrets to their graves. This is what Jesus has chosen to call us: His *friends*. He knows everything about us: the good, the bad, and the ugly. And in spite of His intimate knowledge of us, He has chosen us as His friends.

The ultimate demonstration of the love of Jesus for us was His sacrifice on the cross. Yet many view God as a distant and demanding Master, who treats us as slaves and not as friends. When Jesus commanded His disciples to *love one another,* His love for us was the example: "This is My commandment, that you love one another, just as I have loved you. Greater love has no one than this, that one lays down his life for his friends" (John 15:12, 13). Then he went on to explain the intimacy of this relationship: "No longer do I call you slaves, for the slave does not know what his master is doing; but I have called you friends, for all things that I have heard from My Father I have made known to you. You did not choose Me but I chose you" (John 15:15, 16). F. F. Bruce points out that, "The contrast between the slave and the friend here is not unlike the contrast between the slave and the son in Galatians 4:7. John Wesley, looking back on his conversion in later years, described it as the time when he exchanged the faith of a servant for the faith of a son. Had he expressed himself in Johannine rather than Pauline language, he might have said that he then exchanged the obedience of a slave for the obedience of a friend."* Jesus has chosen us as His friends and has shared His plans with us. Whoever pledges allegiance to Him becomes His intimate friend (verse 14). Many carry the sting of rejection with them. Perhaps you have never been chosen, either for a school sports team or simply as a friend. Yet Jesus, the King of the universe, has died for you and has chosen you for a friend!

My Response: _____

---

* F. F. Bruce, *The Gospel of John: A Verse-by-Verse Exposition* (Grand Rapids, MI: Eerdmans, 1983), 112.

HIS INITIATIVE

*"What man among you, if he has a hundred sheep and
has lost one of them, does not . . . go after the one
which is lost until he finds it?"*

—Luke 15:4

While going through rough times, I once received an encouraging card. The statement on the front caught my attention: "All you need is another card telling you to hang in there . . . ." *Yep, that's all I need,* I thought, as my eyes settled on a little lamb, with sweat dripping from its brow, holding fast to something that wasn't visible on the cover. I opened the card to read the message inside, which has stayed with me until now: "I want to tell you that you are SAFE in HIS grip; and He is not going to let you go." A strong hand was holding the little lamb.

We've all read books and heard sermons that emphasize *our* seeking after God, *our* perseverance, *our* strength, *our* hanging in during the storm and not letting go when we find ourselves at our wit's end. But, as important as all these things are, the Bible's major emphasis is on *God* seeking after us, *His* initiative to go after what was lost, the strength of *His* grip, and *His* hanging on to us when we are weak and exhausted. Our God is a passionate and loving God, who is eager and able to initiate action to find us, and who safely holds us in *His* grip. He is a loving Parent, who *pursues* us with His goodness and grace all the days of our lives (see Psalm 23:6). The parent's grip on the child is the child's security. When the Pharisees and scribes are grumbling because Jesus is receiving sinners (Luke 15:2), the first parable that Jesus tells them is about a shepherd who *goes after* a lost sheep until He finds it (verse 4). Once he has found it, He lays it on his shoulders, rejoicing! (verse 5). God has loved us *before* we loved Him; our love for Him is only a response to His infinite love for us (1 John 4:19). His initiative is our assurance. He is the Shepherd who desperately searches for the lost sheep. "For thus says the Lord GOD, 'Behold, I Myself will search for My sheep and seek them out. As a shepherd cares for his herd in the day when he is among his scattered sheep, so I will care for My sheep and will deliver them from all the places to which they were scattered on a cloudy and gloomy day' " (Ezekiel 34:11, 12). Thank you, Lord!

My Response: _____

HIS SELF-DENIAL

"Do You not answer? See how many charges they bring against You!"
But Jesus made no further answer; so Pilate was amazed.
—Mark 15:4, 5

When the tropical storm Harvey hit southeastern Texas, authorities reported more than thirteen thousand rescues. Unfortunately, some lost their lives. Among them was a woman who, along with her young daughter, had been swept away by high water. While floating in the canal, the mother did everything that she could to keep her daughter alive. When rescuers found them, the daughter was clinging to her mom. The woman did not make it, but her daughter was worth her sacrifice.

The mockery and torture that Jesus suffered was more than we can imagine. "Some began to spit at Him, and to blindfold Him, and to beat Him with their fists, and to say to Him, 'Prophesy!' And the officers received Him with slaps in the face" (Mark 14:65). Before His crucifixion, Jesus endured His disciples' betrayal, the false accusations of the religious leaders, the mockery of the soldiers, the questioning of the authorities, the unjust scourging, the crown of thorns, etc., yet He did not defend Himself. "He kept silent and did not answer" (Mark 14:61). This was in fulfillment of Isaiah's prophecy:

> He was oppressed and He was afflicted,
> Yet He did not open His mouth;
> Like a lamb that is led to slaughter,
> And like a sheep that is silent before its shearers,
> So He did not open His mouth
> (Isaiah 53:7).

It's not that He didn't have anything to say, or that He couldn't prove His innocence. He was not helpless to deliver Himself. No! He voluntarily renounced His rights; He relinquished His life. From His conduct we may learn that we don't always need to defend our rights when a greater purpose is served. We may also learn to surrender to God's will. We may learn humility as well. All these are very valuable. Yet most of all, may we learn and understand that Jesus surrendered His life in exchange for ours. His silence was a loud proof of His love for us!

My Response:_____

HIS PROPOSAL

*"I stand at the door and knock; if anyone hears My voice
and opens the door, I will come in to him and will dine
with him, and he with Me."*

—Revelation 3:20

I heard a touching story, but I don't know its source. A little boy arrived at the pediatrician's office. When the doctor was using the stethoscope on the child's chest, he placed the earpieces in the boy's ears, so that he could listen to the sound of his own heart. Having never heard a heartbeat, the child was startled! Then he asked: "Is that the sound of Jesus knocking on the door of my heart?"

I cherish this endearing and tender picture of Jesus found in Revelation 3:20. He is standing at the door and knocking, desirous to come in. He proposes, to whoever opens the door, the intimacy of a spiritual meal with Him. His offer is particularly touching to me because it is found right after the portrayal of the church in Laodicea, a church that is both lukewarm and self-sufficient (see verses 15–19). Laodicea was one of the wealthiest business centers in the known world, and it was famous for its banking system, black wool industry, and medical school. Therefore, these are used as the background of the counsel to Laodicea: to come to Christ for gold refined by fire, white garments to clothe their nakedness, and eye salve to see (verse 18). The Laodicean church doesn't perceive its own spiritual needs; it believes it is fine as it is. It is neither cold nor hot; it is lukewarm and doesn't realize that it is spiritually wretched, miserable, poor, blind, and naked. After a call to repent, Jesus offers Himself. So far the message has been addressed to the corporate church, the church of Laodicea as a whole. But in this verse, it changes to an individual proposal and appeal: "If *anyone* hears My voice." Even if the group doesn't accept Jesus' offer, the individuals may. Jesus already stands at the door. His initiative precedes our acceptance of Him, yet He doesn't force Himself in. It is the knock and plea of love personified (see Song of Solomon 5:2). He promises to come in and dine in intimacy with anyone who hears His voice and opens the door to Him. The proposed meal is not a hurried one. He yearns to come in! This is the eager plea of the One who gave His life for you and for me!

My Response: _____

HIS STEADFASTNESS

"Or do you think that I cannot appeal to My Father,
and He will at once put at My disposal more than
twelve legions of angels?"

—Matthew 26:53

I recently revisited the National Mall in Washington DC, which includes several monuments, such as the Lincoln Memorial and the Washington monument. When I had been there almost three decades ago, the Martin Luther King Jr. Memorial had not been built, so it was completely new to me. It is a stunning monument. Engraved on the walls of the memorial are several of his amazing quotations, including this one, from 1963: "Darkness cannot drive out darkness, only light can do that. Hate cannot drive out hate, only love can do that."

When Jesus was arrested, Peter drew out his sword to defend Him and he cut Malchus's ear (John 18:10). I am pretty sure Peter wasn't going for the ear, but something more vital. But Jesus ordered him to put the sword away and said: "Or do you think that I cannot appeal to My Father, and He will at once put at My disposal more than twelve legions of angels? How then will the Scriptures be fulfilled, which say that it must happen this way?" (Matthew 26:53, 54). If Jesus wanted to free Himself, He wouldn't have relied on a few disciples with swords. No! He was keenly aware of the supernatural resources available to Him! He was innocent, He had power, and He had other divine resources. And yet He didn't use any of these but restrained Himself in order to follow His Father's will for our redemption. The use of force was not in Jesus' plan. He was unwavering in His resolve to follow the will of God, even if that meant giving up His rights, His power, and His place in heaven. His steadfastness to follow God's plan, walking the path set before Him, is contrasted with His disciples' response to the situation. We too may feel tempted to use force, perhaps not with a sword, but with words, attitudes, hierarchy, power, control, and other forms of coercion in our attempts to subdue our opponents. Yet God is asking us to follow the way of Jesus: the way of love, forgiveness, and humility (see Philippians 2:5–8). God bids us to put away our "swords," for "hate cannot drive out hate, only love can do that."

My Response: _____

HIS KINDNESS

And Jesus seeing their faith said to the paralytic,
"Son, your sins are forgiven."

—Mark 2:5

I t was a very difficult time in my life, and it just so happened that I was about to spend Christmas Day by myself. My loving parents lived on the East Coast while I was in California, and we didn't have money to visit each other. But then something incredible happened! An airline advertised a very inexpensive Christmas fare, but the round trip had to be completed within forty-eight hours. My parents called me to tell me the exciting news that both of them were coming to spend Christmas with me. I was not alone after all! They cared for me deeply.

There was a paralyzed man who suffered greatly and desperately needed to know that someone cared. Four friends brought him to Jesus, but the crowd around the house was so big that they were unable to get in (Mark 2:3, 4). What should they do? Go back? Not these men. Their persistence underscores the dire condition this man was in. They made their way to the roof of the house, since dwellings in Palestine had flat roofs accessible from the outside, but when they got there, they had to make a hole in the roof in order to access the interior of the house. They were so eager to help that they willingly stepped outside their comfort zone and even risked losing their honor. But the sick man was about to receive much more than physical healing. They lowered him through the hole: "And Jesus seeing their faith said to the paralytic, '*Son*, your sins are forgiven' " (verse 5). Did you notice the first words that Jesus uttered? They conveyed His kindness and care for this man! Because of his disability, people would call him cursed by God, yet Jesus calls him *teknon* (Greek) instead, which communicates endearment and is translated as "son" or "child." Apart from addressing his disciples as "children" (Mark 10:24), this is the only time in the Gospel of Mark that Jesus calls a person by this term. This man would also receive forgiveness and healing, but the first kind word he heard was "*son*." No matter how helpless or hopeless we may feel, Jesus kindly addresses us the same way: "Child, your sins are forgiven!"

My Response: _____

HIS FATHERHOOD

"Daughter, your faith has made you well; go in peace."
—Luke 8:48

My parents did whatever was necessary for my well-being. When I was a child, I would get sudden asthma attacks that were life-threatening, and I remember my parents rushing me to the hospital, which was on the other side of town. As my face was turning blue, my dad would flash the car lights so that the other cars would move out of the way, while my mother would frantically wave her arms through the window to signal that this was an emergency. They saved my life many times. I'm sure you would do the same for your children.

It is no surprise that Jairus, an official of the synagogue, fell at the feet of Jesus "and began to implore Him to come to his house; for he had an only daughter, about twelve years old, and she was dying" (Luke 8:41, 42). He was willing to do anything for his daughter's well-being. Jesus agreed and went. But what happens next is surprising. As Jesus is walking toward the house of Jairus, a destitute and sick woman, who has been bleeding for twelve years, interrupts His journey. The daughter of Jairus has a reputable daddy, willing to speak to Jesus on her behalf, but this unclean woman has no respectable male to stand up for her (which was expected in that culture): no father, no husband, no son, no rabbi, no doctor . . . no one. So she, herself, "came up behind Him and touched the fringe of His cloak, and immediately her hemorrhage stopped" (verse 44). Just like that! She received the healing miracle that she had been waiting for during twelve years! But Jesus had more for her. He stopped the multitude, asking who had touched Him. Trembling, she came, fell before Him (verse 47), and explained what had happened. She was now clean, but Jesus did more than just heal her. He publicly reinstated her to society. And there was yet another surprise! "He said to her, 'Daughter' " (verse 8). *Daughter!* This is the *only* story, in all four Gospels, where Jesus addresses a woman directly as His daughter. She was the daughter of Jesus! She was no longer destitute. She had a Father! And you and I are also His children. (1 John 3:1). He has done everything that was necessary to save us!

My Response: _____

His Persistence

*And Jesus said to him, "Friend,
do what you have come for."*

—Matthew 26:50

When we were airing our TV series *Radical Discipleship,** based on stories about the disciples of Jesus, I received a comment from a viewer saying that he didn't believe that Jesus had consented to Judas being His disciple. But even though Jesus could read Judas's heart, He didn't reject him (see Luke 6:13; John 15:16). Instead He exposed him to His grace. Still, I completely understand this viewer's sentiment, as Judas may very well be the most despised man in history; his name is synonymous with heinous betrayal.

The Gospels often note the betrayal of Judas (for examples, see Luke 6:16; John 12:4). Judas was the only one among the disciples who was given a specific function: to be in charge of their funds (John 13:29). Even though appearing pious, he was dishonest and used to pilfer from the money box (John 12:5, 6). He betrayed and sold Jesus for thirty pieces of silver (Matthew 26:14–16). But the way Jesus treated this man is an incredible source of encouragement for me. Jesus constantly showed Judas extraordinary grace and love with a persistence that is hard to grasp. Jesus was constantly trying to win Judas back through specific acts of love. At the last supper of Jesus and His disciples, Judas was given a place of honor, close enough for Jesus to hand him a piece of bread (see John 13:26). Plus, eating with someone was understood as a mark of inclusion. And the last words of Jesus to Judas really touch my heart. Judas was leading the chief priests, the elders of the people, and the crowd to the place where Jesus was, so that they could apprehend Him; Judas gave them a sign: a kiss (see Matthew 26:47, 48). Jesus let Judas kiss Him (verse 49), then said to him, " '*Friend*, do what you have come for.' Then they came and laid hands on Jesus and seized Him" (Matthew 26:50). Really? Friend? How could Jesus call Judas friend? But to the very end, Jesus exposed Judas to His love and grace. He loved him, as He loves us. He knows everything about us—even our motives and darkest secrets. His love does not depend on our goodness, and he will keep pursuing us to the very end!

My Response: _____

His Reinstatement

"Simon, son of John, do you love Me?"
He said to Him, "Yes, Lord, You know that I love You,"
He said to him, "Shepherd My sheep."

—John 21:16

We met in a public place; her eyes betrayed her lack of sleep and weariness of spirit. She had hit bottom, in a downward spiral of substance abuse, feeling helpless and hopeless. As we continued to see each other, over time she started trusting that God had something better for her. Several months later she was offered a position as a university professor. Her strength and confidence were renewed, her spirit flamboyant, and her faith in God fully restored. She became a bright arrow, pointing to a graceful God.

So, is there ministry after failure? Can God use us for His glory after a serious misstep? I am so glad you asked! After the resurrection, Jesus appeared to His disciples a third time by the Sea of Galilee and prepared a breakfast for them (John 21:12–14). They had worked all night but had caught nothing, and Jesus miraculously caused them to catch a large quantity of fish (see verses 1–11). This event is similar to the one narrated in Luke 5, at the beginning of the ministry of Jesus, except that this time it is right after Peter had denied Jesus three times (John 18:25–27; Mark 14:66–72); he no longer has all the answers and his confidence is shattered. As Peter had denied Him three times, now Jesus offers him the opportunity to declare his love for Him three times (John 21:15–17). Peter humbly responds thrice: "You know that I love You" (John 21:15–17). Jesus reinstates Peter's original calling and bids him, "Tend My sheep." Those of us who have tasted Jesus' extraordinary forgiveness in our own lives are called to proclaim His grace boldly.

> I waited patiently for the Lord;
> And He inclined to me and heard my cry.
> He brought me up out of the pit of destruction, out of the miry
>   clay.
> And He set my feet upon a rock making my footsteps firm.
> He put a new song in my mouth, a song of praise to our God;
> (Psalm 40:1–3).

Amen!

My Response: _____

His Hour

Jesus knowing that His hour had come . . . having loved His own who were in the world, He loved them to the end.

—John 13:1

I had imagined this moment for a long time, and now everything was on the line. Several years earlier, I had started my PhD program, and now it was time to defend my dissertation. I flew from Los Angeles to London the day before the defense. My degree, my future, all my efforts, and thousands of dollars, were at stake as I entered the room. It was a court-type setting; the professors sat directly in front of me, the doctoral arbiter between us. The hour had come.

Sometimes we are preparing our whole lives for a specific moment. God had been planning for *His hour* since the foundation of the world. Beginning with the first miracle of Jesus in the Gospel of John, the reader is informed that Jesus knows that His hour will eventually arrive, *"My hour* has not yet come" (John 2:4). We can follow the progression of Jesus towards the cross through the statements about "His hour" (see John 7:30; 8:20; 12:23, 27; 13:1; 17:1). As we move closer to Passover Friday, Jesus becomes aware that His hour has finally arrived; "Now before the Feast of the Passover, *Jesus knowing that His hour had come . . . ."* (John 13:1). John wants us to understand that Jesus is always in control and submitting Himself to the Father. There was a plan, and He was fulfilling it. The hour of His glory would be on the cross; therefore, His *passion* is repeatedly described as His glory (John 12:23; 13:31, 32; 17:1, 4). The eternal clock of heaven sounded the alarm to redeem the human race. Everything had been orchestrated in God's salvific plan: "When the fullness of the time came, God sent forth His Son, born of a woman, born under the Law, so that He might redeem those who were under the Law, that we might receive the adoption as sons" (Galatians 4:4, 5). There is an appointed time for everything (Ecclesiastes 3:1); the birth and death of Jesus had been planned, and He voluntarily submitted to the plan because of His love for you and me. His hour came, He went through it, and He was victorious. Now He invites us to trust His plan, His love, His timing, and the efficacy of His hour.

My Response: _____

His Ownership

"Do not harm the earth or the sea or the trees until we have sealed the bond-servants of our God on their foreheads."
—Revelation 7:2, 3

I n our Jesus 101 ministry, we use a stamp that has our website and other important information. We use it to stamp books and other resources that belong to our ministry. A seal or a stamp is a mark of ownership. That's why when I visit my parents' tomb, I find great comfort reading the verse inscribed on their tombstone: "Do not fear, for I have redeemed you; I have called you by name; *you are Mine!*" (Isaiah 43:1). They rest in Jesus until His second coming, in total assurance because they are His. You and I can live with the same certainty.

When it comes to the future and end-time events, I realize that many people live with fear and utter anxiety. Yet, through the blood of Jesus, we have God's assurance, and He bids us to choose faith over fear. One of those certainties is that *we are His!* Revelation 7 starts with four angels standing at the four corners of the earth, holding back the winds of destruction, until God's servants are sealed (Revelation 7:1). God is in control of *everything!* He decides what He allows and when, and it all serves His redeeming purposes. God sends an angel who is to "stamp" each servant of God before the final troubles come to the earth. A helpful visualization is to imagine a signet ring (used in the first century) that imprints the name of God and the Lamb on the forehead of each one of God's own people. The mark announces to the whole universe, "This one is mine!" It is a symbol for protection and ownership. Throughout the book of Revelation, God's servants, who pledge allegiance to the Lamb, bear His mark of ownership (see Revelation 9:4; 14:1; 22:4). The Holy Spirit testifies to our own spirits that we are His and that we have an inheritance guaranteed by the Lamb (See Ephesians 1:13, 14; 4:30; 2 Corinthians 1:21, 22). In other words, the seal gives the assurance of salvation to those who trust in the merits of Christ. "The Lord knows those *who are His*" (2 Timothy 2:19). Whether you are facing sickness, death, difficulties, challenges, or uncertainties, believe what God is telling you: "You are mine!"

My Response: _____

HIS ASSESSMENT

*"Truly I say to you, this poor widow
put in more than all of them."*

—Luke 21:3

When my husband was a little boy, he used to bring little gifts to his mom, whom he loved very much. He collected shiny papers from the street or food from parties. His mother always received him and his presents with utter appreciation. One time, he decided to bring her ice-cream, which he placed in his pocket and headed home. When he arrived, the ice-cream had melted. She took off his little pants and, before washing the stain, she licked the pocket in front of him and said: "This tastes so good, thank you for bringing me this ice-cream!"

Jesus revealed that God's assessment of our gifts to Him is not dependent on their value or human recognition. God sees the heart, the motive behind the action. Jesus made a strong exhortation against becoming like the hypocritical scribes who walked around in long robes in order to show off their socio-religious status; they also loved the best seats in the synagogues and banquets (see Luke 20:46, 47). Jesus also spoke against their defrauding of widows and their long prayers to impress others (verse 47). That's when Luke narrates that Jesus saw a paradoxical contrast in the temple: "He looked up and saw the rich putting their gifts into the treasury. And He saw a poor widow putting in two small copper coins" (Luke 21:1, 2). Later Jewish material points out that there were thirteen containers in the court of women where offerings could be deposited for the temple treasury. The rich gave impressive amounts; this poor widow gave two *leptas*, the smallest Jewish coin in circulation at the time. But Jesus publicly assessed that she put in "more than all of them" (verse 3). The rich had given from their surplus, but she had given her livelihood (verse 4). When it comes to your response of love to God's infinite love, do not measure your talents, money, energy, time, and resources by comparing them to those of others. God knows your heart and is pleased with your passionate and loving response. Your gifts to His kingdom touch His heart, even if they are like melted ice-cream. He gave *all*, emptying Himself, leaving His place of honor, in order to purchase our salvation. In response, let's bring Him our *all*!

My Response: _____

HIS GENEALOGY

The son of Enosh, the son of Seth,
the son of Adam, the son of God.

—Luke 3:38

Lately, the number of DNA testing companies have grown considerably, reflecting an increasing desire to find our ancestry. There is a renewed interest in establishing one's genealogy. "Genealogy [is] the study of family origins and history. Genealogists compile lists of ancestors, which they arrange in pedigree charts or other written forms. The word *genealogy* comes from two Greek words—one meaning 'race' or 'family' and the other 'theory' or 'science.' Thus is derived 'to trace ancestry,' the science of studying family history."*

Luke provides an extensive genealogy of Jesus, and places it between His baptism (Luke 3:21, 22) and the temptations in the wilderness (Luke 4:1–13). Luke begins this section by stating that Jesus was about thirty years of age when He started His public ministry; thirty was considered the age of full maturity and, therefore, the time when a person could manage adult responsibilities and public office (for examples, see Joseph in Genesis 41:46, and David in 2 Samuel 5:4). While Matthew presents the ancestry of Jesus to Abraham (Matthew 1:2), Luke traces it back all the way to Adam, *son* of God, which is another pointer to the fact that he is trying to depict how the whole human race is included in the plan of salvation (Luke 3:23–38). Using a reverse order, Luke recognizes Jesus as part of the human race, tracing His ancestry back to the first human—Adam, the son of God, thus confirming the divine Source of humankind. We were made in God's image (Genesis 1:26). Don't ever let anybody tell you that you are less than others . . . you are a child of God, created in God's image! In spite of His miraculous birth (Luke 1:35; 3:22), Jesus became one with us, in order to be the Second Adam and to gain the victory for the human race, because the first Adam had failed (1 Corinthians 15:45; Romans 5:19). Jesus was fully God *and* fully human. Are you painfully aware of your failures, of not qualifying as a child of God? Jesus is our Representative, whose obedience and death are ascribed to us. In the *perfect* Son of God, we are accepted as God's own children. Praise be to Jesus, our Savior!

My Response: _____

---

* Encyclopedia Britannica Online, Leslie Gilbert Pine, "Genealogy," last modified Feb. 22, 2017, https://www.britannica.com/topic/genealogy.

HIS EVALUATION

"Do not fear; you are more valuable than many sparrows."
—Luke 12:7

By the time I was six years old, my mother had saved my life many times. She had rescued me when I was drowning in a pool, she had run many miles when I was bleeding to death, and she had taken me to the hospital on several occasions when I couldn't breathe due to an asthma attack, just to name a few. As a kid, I was sure about one thing: I had great value in my parents' eyes. And that realization shaped my view of God as well.

The way God values each one of us should be a source of assurance for our souls. Jesus used images of nature to remind us that God cares for the smallest of flowers and animals, and that we are much more valuable than those. Moving from lesser to greater, Jesus utilized an argument style called *qal wahomer* ("how much more"), assuring His disciples that if God cares for the most insignificant of birds, *how much more* does He care for human beings, created in His image! I love the passage in Luke 12:6, 7: "Are not five sparrows sold for two cents? Yet not one of them is forgotten before God. . . . Do not fear; you are more valuable than many sparrows." In other words, if God knows and cares for these birds, even though five of them are sold for two pennies, then how much more does God care for you! His loving evaluation of us, and what we mean to Him, is a guarantee that He knows us and cares for us. Why fear, if we know that He places such great value on us? The context of this verse is that even when facing persecution, difficulties, and hardship, we shouldn't ever doubt if God cares for us. He is sovereign and His wisdom surpasses our understanding of the situations we face in our lives, yet we can always count on His care for us. We are never forgotten! He knows everything about us; even "the very hairs of your head are all numbered" (verse 7). He knows every hurt, every tear, and every heartbreak; He cares about our afflictions. Don't forget that He valued us so highly that He gave His life to save ours. During difficult days, watch the birds, and remember how God views you. Yes, in God's view, you are much more valuable than many sparrows!

My Response: _____

HIS UNITY

"I in them and You in Me, that they may be perfected in unity,
so that the world may know that You sent Me, and loved them,
even as You have loved Me."

—John 17:23

I have participated in satellite evangelistic series, where many people come together in one area to plan and organize meetings that are televised with the purpose of sharing the gospel of Jesus Christ. One of the most encouraging aspects of these experiences is to watch people, with different backgrounds and unique skills, come together with an evangelistic purpose in mind: to share God's redemption through Jesus and His love for humanity.

In his Gospel, John records a prayer of Jesus that has been called "the High Priestly prayer." In it, He petitions the Father that His followers may become united with an evangelistic purpose: "That they may all be one; even as You, Father, are in Me and I in You, that they also may be in Us, *so that the world may believe that you sent Me*" (John 17:21). Each beloved believer is unique in the eyes of God, and He has not asked us to give up our God-given individuality. The purpose of unity is always to make Jesus known to the world. Jesus continues: "I in them and You in Me, that they may be perfected in unity [Greek: perfected into one], *so that the world may know that you sent Me, and loved them, even as You have loved Me*" (verse 23). The purpose of the unity is not *sameness* but an *evangelistic message*: making Jesus and His love for all known. It is a privilege to be in a group of people whose primary aim is to proclaim the love of God, as manifested in Jesus. By the way, did you realize from this verse that God wants you to know that He loves you? And that the Father loves you as He loves Jesus! Wow! And not only that: He wants you to be with Him for eternity! "Father, I desire that they also, whom You have given Me, *be with Me* where I am" (verse 24). I personalize this verse: "I want *Elizabeth* to be with Me." Place your name there too, because Jesus desires *you* to be with Him! May we be part of a community that is *one* in Jesus, with the purpose of sharing Jesus with the world!

My Response: _____

HIS GOODNESS

*"But I say to you, love your enemies and pray for those
who persecute you, so that you may be sons of your
Father who is in heaven."*

—Matthew 5:44, 45

One of the faith heroes among the Anabaptists was a man named Dirk Willems, born in the Netherlands. Due to his newfound faith and re-baptism, he was condemned and arrested. He was able to escape prison and cross a frozen pond. But a guard, who had noticed his escape, pursued him and fell into the icy waters, yelling for help. Willems knew the price he would have to pay for helping him, yet he could not refuse. He helped his pursuer get out of the freezing waters, which meant that Willems was recaptured and eventually burned at the stake.

God's love for humans motivated the plan of salvation, which meant that Jesus died in our place while we didn't want anything to do with Him. "But God demonstrates His own love toward us, in that while we were yet sinners, Christ died for us" (Romans 5:8). We did not deserve it and we still don't. It is with this understanding that Jesus' followers are empowered to love their enemies and pray for those who oppress them. God's goodness flows into the believers' hearts and spills over into the world, even toward those who make their lives difficult. We are called to love our enemies and not to retaliate (Matthew 5:39, 44). Note that the singular word "enemy" (verse 43) is changed to the plural "enemies" in the next verse (verse 44). The audience of Jesus would have had many different types of enemies: among them the Romans, as political oppressors, and tax collectors, who were considered traitors. Yet, by using the plural with no exceptions, Jesus makes an all-encompassing pronouncement: "Love your enemies and pray for those who persecute you, so that you may be sons of your Father who is in heaven; for He causes His sun to rise on the evil and the good, and sends rain on the righteous and the unrighteous" (verses 44, 45). A practical way of loving our enemies is to pray for them, imitating our heavenly Father, whose goodness provides the sun and the rain on those who worship him and those who don't. May the love that Jesus has bestowed upon us overflow towards our fellowmen, even for those who persecute us.

My Response: _____

TRUSTING
HIS PROVISION

HIS LIGHT

"I am the Light of the world."

—John 9:5

I had an unforgettable experience while visiting New Zealand to speak at a women's retreat. I was hoping to find some time between my speaking engagements to visit the Waitomo Glowworm Caves. Thanks to the kindness and efforts of my hosts, we made it. In a little boat, we entered a very dark cave; the guide asked us to be completely silent. We quietly sat there in the dark as excitement started to fill my heart. I had heard about the light-emitting worms inhabiting these caves, yet nothing prepared me for the sight of them! As the boat turned into the larger section of the cave, thousands of tiny bright lights appeared as if we were looking at a star-filled night sky. Because of the surrounding darkness, the lights shone much brighter than I had imagined. And once again, I felt amazed at the beauty of God's creation!

There is something about darkness that makes the light shine even brighter! In one of His revealing "I am" statements in the Gospel of John, Jesus announces: "I am the Light of the world" (John 9:5). Jesus then proceeds to heal a blind man, who ends up seeing both physically and spiritually, and is the only person in this Gospel to *worship* Jesus. The words the blind man uses referring to Jesus highlight his progression towards spiritual sight: he calls Jesus a man (verse 11), then a prophet (verse 17), "from God" (verse 33), et cetera, and finally, he believes in Him and worships Him (verse 38). On the other hand, the Pharisees, who thought they could see, end up being *blind* (verses 39–41), and declare themselves disciples of Moses and not of Jesus (verse 28). They call Jesus "a sinner" (verse 24) and put the formerly blind man out of the synagogue in the name of Moses and Sabbath keeping. Sometimes, spiritual darkness can be found even in religious circles. We are blind if anything or anyone other than Jesus becomes the object of our worship, even if it is something religious, as in the case of these Pharisees. Only Jesus provides peace. He is the Light that illumines our minds, dispels our doubts and fears, and holds our future. He is the Light of the world and the Light of our lives!

My Response: _____

His Touch

Jesus stretched out His hand and touched him, saying, "I am willing; be cleansed." And immediately his leprosy was cleansed.
—Matthew 8:3

My friend Steve was going through an emotionally difficult time when he decided to focus his energy on helping others. He founded a ministry called "Hugs for HumanKIND," going out several times a week to meaningfully engage with people living on the streets, showing interest in their lives, helping them, or simply listening to what they wanted to share. When appropriate, he gives them a real hug, which most of them have not experienced in years. Many of them have not had a healthy human touch in a long time, and they are pleasantly surprised and thankful to be the recipients of this type of kindness.

In the first century, leprosy was a disease that rendered its victims unfit for society. A leper was considered unclean and untouchable (see Leviticus 13, 14) and would be forced out of his village. A leper had to carry the stigma of a horrendous and contagious disease. Therefore, the leper who comes to Jesus in Matthew 8:1–4 is not even sure if Jesus is *willing* to heal him.

In the Gospels, sometimes Jesus' greatest acts of service on behalf of his fellow human beings go unnoticed because we concentrate on the miracles of healing and resurrection. In this event, we should notice Jesus' attitude towards the sick person: "Jesus stretched out His hand and *touched him*" (Matthew 8:3). He touched the untouchable! During His life on earth, the Son of God never became unclean or defiled by diseases; instead, He brought life and health. He provided healing for the body, mind, and soul. In this case, Jesus' *touch* showed his willingness to reach out to the unclean and the marginalized. You may not have leprosy, but you may be struggling with an addiction, a sin, a dark past, an unhealthy relationship, or anything else that brings shame to your life or to the life of a loved one. May this story give you the assurance of Jesus' willingness to *touch* the dark areas of our lives and provide healing where there is sickness. Jesus' touch demonstrates both His love and compassion!

My Response: _____

HIS NOURISHMENT

Jesus said to them, "I am the bread of life; he who comes to Me will not hunger, and he who believes in Me will never thirst."

—John 6:30

Have you ever been hungry, in real need of food? The closest I got to that was when I came to the United States, many decades ago. It was hard to find jobs at first, and we were dependent on a church that gave us a weekly box of food, containing bread, cheese, rice, beans, et cetera. One day, when I opened the refrigerator, I found only some bread and cheese, nothing else. I am grateful that God sustained and blessed us. Little by little, things got easier and better.

Bread was a big concern in the first century; many people worked for it daily. When Jesus performed the miraculous feeding of the multitude (John 6:1–13), people interpreted that the awaited prophet like Moses (see Deuteronomy 18:15) had arrived: "This is truly the prophet who is to come into the world" (John 6:14). People wanted to make sure that He was the awaited One, so they asked Him to do another sign, that they might believe in Him (see John 6:30, 31). They alluded to manna: God had provided water and food for them in the wilderness through Moses. Was Jesus going to prove Himself by doing the same? Jesus explained that He was the true Bread from heaven, who provides life-giving nourishment to the world (verses 32, 33). Back in Exodus 16, God had sent manna, and Israel had collected it every day because it was perishable food. Only on the sixth day were they to collect for the Sabbath, on which they rested to remember their divine Provider. But the true Bread from heaven, to which manna pointed, provides permanent and on-going nourishment. "I am the bread of life; he who comes to me will not hunger, and . . . will never thirst" (verse 35). In John, this is the first emphatic "I am" statement, followed by a metaphor for Jesus' identity. Human hearts are always searching for nourishment, though sometimes in the wrong places. But Jesus satisfies our thirst and hunger permanently. In Him we find salvation, assurance, joy, meaning, purpose, and real nourishment. He fills our souls; He is our All in all. Lord: give us this day our daily Bread! Jesus!

My Response: _____

HIS SUSTENANCE

"It is not Moses who has given you the bread out of heaven, but it is My Father who gives you the true bread out of heaven."
—John 6:32

When my husband was growing up, there were eight members in his immediate family. His parents were very hospitable, therefore there were always many needy people sitting at the table along with them. They were not wealthy, yet somehow there was always enough food for them and their visitors. His siblings always point out that even though they never saw the food multiply, they are sure God frequently and miraculously increased the food so all could be fed.

In his Gospel, John records a lengthy and insightful interaction between Jesus and the people that took place after the feeding of the five thousand (John 6:26–58). Having been miraculously fed, the crowd now asks Jesus to perform another sign, that they may believe in Him. They said: "Our fathers ate the manna in the wilderness" (verse 31). It was God who had given them the manna, sustaining them in the wilderness, day after day, for forty years. I really like the story of the manna, which is recorded in Exodus 16; please take a moment to read it. Perhaps I would have been among the anxious ones who tried to collect more than one day's supply, not sure if God would provide for the following day. . . . Would I have trusted enough to rest on the seventh day, celebrating my Provider's faithfulness towards His children? Back to John 6, Jesus revealed that the manna was pointing to Him, who was the true Manna that came down from heaven from God. The material provision in the wilderness was pointing to the spiritual Sustenance that we have in Jesus. The first was perishable, but the latter is eternal nourishment. Jesus said: "I am the living bread that came down out of heaven; if anyone eats of this bread, he will live forever; and the bread also which I will give for the life of the world is My flesh" (verse 51). God lovingly provides for all our needs, physical and spiritual. Let's trust His faithfulness towards us, casting our anxieties at the foot of the cross. "He who did not spare His own Son, but delivered Him over for us all, how will He not also with Him freely give us all things?" (Romans 8:32).

My Response: _____

HIS OMNISCIENCE

*This took place to fulfill what was spoken
through the prophet.*

—Matthew 21:4

To follow our ministerial calling, we decided to move to another town, where our income would be considerably lower. Wondering how we would be able to afford house payments with the reduced income, we decided to explore a new home community. As we got there, we both got the impression to pause and pray. We inquired about a house that we really liked and calculated what our house payment would be. I left the place with tears of thanksgiving, for the payment was less than half of our previous house payment, and we could easily afford it. But, of course, God knew that ahead of time!

We can rest in God's pre-knowledge and pre-provision for every situation. During Jesus' triumphal entry into Jerusalem, we are made aware of His complete knowledge about, and provision for, the situation ahead. Jesus sent two disciples: "Go into the village opposite you, and immediately you will find a donkey tied there and a colt with her; untie them and bring them to Me" (Matthew 21:2). Jesus gave specific instructions as to what they were to say if questioned. This is the only time that Jesus rode an animal. He always walked, yet for these last few miles He needed a colt in order to enact a particular prophecy. Matthew indicates that the prophecy was from Zechariah 9:9 (with Isaiah 62:11): "This took place to fulfill what was spoken through the prophet: 'Say to the daughter of Zion, "Behold your king is coming to you, gentle, and mounted on a donkey, even on a colt, the foal of a beast of burden" ' " (Matthew 21:4, 5). Some scholars suggest that Jesus had prearranged for this animal, but even if that's the case, the point still stands. Jesus knew the prophecy; He planned the enactment of the fulfillment of that particular prophecy; He knew where to find the animal; and He gave specific instructions to His disciples. Every part of Jesus' ministry followed a divine plan, even in the smallest details. Rest assured that God knows and provides for everything that you and I need for our salvation and our daily lives. He certainly goes *ahead* of us!

My Response: _____

HIS CHILDREN

*"From whom do the kings of the earth collect customs
or poll-tax, from their sons or from strangers? . . .
the sons are exempt."*
—Matthew 17:25, 26

O ne of the highlights during my trip to the Holy Land was the visit to the beautiful Sea of Galilee, which Jesus and His disciples navigated so many times. There is a fish named *Chromis Simonis* in honor of Simon Peter. It has a large mouth, big enough to hold a *statēr*, which is a silver coin worth four drachmas—one shekel. The background to our text today is a story about the miraculous provision of a *statēr* in the mouth of a fish in order to pay the temple tax.

The story takes place in Capernaum. Tax collectors asked Peter "Does your teacher not pay the two-drachma tax?" (Matthew 17:24). Peter answered affirmatively. The tax in question was the temple tribute, which every twenty-year-old-and-above Jewish male was expected to pay. There were some exceptions though; priests, for instance, did not have to pay it. The temple tax was based on the instructions found in the Law (see Exodus 30:11–16). It was half a shekel per person and was used to maintain the temple. Later, in the house, Jesus and Peter had a very interesting conversation that reminds us of our identity as children of God. "Jesus spoke to him first, saying, 'What do you think, Simon? From whom do the kings of the earth collect customs or poll-tax, from their sons or from strangers?'" (verse 25). Peter answered that the earthly rulers collect tribute from strangers, not from their own children. In this metaphoric saying, God is the king, and Jesus and His followers are the sons. In response, Jesus concluded, "then the sons are exempt" (verse 26), meaning that He and His followers were not subject to the tribute for their Father's House. The temple and its sacrificial system would soon become obsolete when its services would find their fulfillment in the sacrifice of Jesus. Still, not to offend the Jewish authorities needlessly, Peter would encounter a divine provision by catching a fish that had a *statēr* in its mouth, the equivalent of one shekel and enough to pay the temple tax for both Jesus and Peter (verse 27). We are not strangers! We are *children* of the king, and He provides everything we need.

My Response: _____

HIS INTERVENTION

"Do not worry about how or what you are to say; for it will be given you in that hour what you are to say."

—Matthew 10:19

I had to chuckle when I read the comment on Matthew 10:19 in my study Bible: " 'Do not worry about . . . what you are to say.' Not to be used by preachers as an excuse for lack of sermon preparation!"* As I started studying this topic, I found similar exhortations in other academic commentaries. But even though this verse seems to have been misused, it contains a most important promise of Jesus.

When we get to this verse, Jesus has already addressed the persecution and opposition that His followers would encounter when they would be handed over to courts and synagogues (Matthew 10:17). And now Jesus expands this to include the highest levels of society and authority: "You will even be brought before governors and kings for My sake, as a testimony to them and to the Gentiles" (verse 18). Even these unplanned and perhaps unpleasant meetings with authorities and dignitaries would be used by God as missionary endeavors, to witness about Jesus to unbelievers.

Jesus went on to discuss that in some of these critical circumstances, a verbal witnessing would be necessary. And this is where Jesus asserts that *our Father*, whom we trust to provide for our daily and basic needs (Matthew 6:25–34), would also provide the words we are to speak in such a crisis. This is a most assuring promise: no matter the social status or intellectual capabilities of the followers of Jesus called to witness in this manner, God will intervene and provide a Divine Resource. "For it is not you who speak, but *it is* the Spirit of your Father who speaks in you" (Matthew 10:20). Therefore "do not worry about how or what you are to say; for it will be given you in that hour" (verse 19). Jesus says that we shouldn't be anxious about our witnessing, even at the highest levels of authority. We will be talking about Jesus, and the Father intervenes by giving His Spirit for such situations. Yes, God provides our food and clothing (Matthew 6:25–34), and He also provides our words when we give our testimony of Jesus (Matthew 10:18–20). Therefore "do not worry" and trust the Spirit's intervention.

My Response: _____

---

* Kenneth L. Barker, ed. et al. *Zondervan NASB Study Bible* (Grand Rapids, MI: Zondervan, 1999), 1382.

HIS RESPONSE

"It is written, 'Man shall not live on bread alone, but on every word that proceeds out of the mouth of God.' "
—Matthew 4:4

In my youth, each summer we used to spend our annual vacation camping on the beach. Several of my relatives got together, and we formed a small tent village. One of my uncles designed a large handmade tent; all our tents could fit inside his. He secured several iron poles under the tarp, creating a large living area. I still remember when a storm hit one time, and we all ended up under this sturdy tent, with the large poles. It was strong, and it didn't fall.

When we are hit by a storm of temptation, our core beliefs are tested, and will determine if our tent stands or falls. When Jesus was tempted by the devil in the wilderness (Matthew 4:1–11), He answered the adversary with Scriptural words. The devil tempted Jesus to doubt His *position, provision, protection, and plan.* "*If* You are the Son of God . . ." (verses 4, 6). Jesus had heard a Voice from heaven affirming that He was the Son of God (Matthew 3:17). Now, with conditional clauses, His adversary wanted Him to doubt His personal position in God's kingdom. By the way, later while hanging on the cross, He was tempted in the same manner: '*If* You are the Son of God, come down from the cross" (Matthew 27:40). Second, would He trust God to provide for what He needed, or did He have to step in and provide for Himself (Matthew 4:3)? Thirdly, did He need to test God's protection of Him, or was He sure that God was with Him (verses 5, 6); was God really in control of His life? And lastly, the devil tempted Jesus to bypass the cross and follow a different plan (verse 9), as if salvation could have been achieved any other way. To all these temptations, Jesus responded with truths from the Bible. We can learn from this narrative that there are four poles of belief that will keep our spiritual tent standing when a storm of temptation hits: (1) You are a child of God and He loves you; (2) God will provide for all your needs, physical and spiritual; (3) God is in complete control, and nothing can happen that He doesn't allow for your own growth and salvation; and (4) He has a detailed plan for your life. Amen!

My Response: _____

HIS GARMENT

*"I advise you to buy from Me . . . white garments so that
you may clothe yourself, and that the shame of your
nakedness will not be revealed."*

—Revelation 3:18

I had an idea for a visual aid to make my sermon memorable. In order to illustrate the point of the parable of the marriage feast and the man who was found without the festal garment (see Matthew 22:1–14), I brought large, white plastic bags to church for everyone to wear. There were more than one thousand people there. It was quite a sight to see the entire audience completely dressed in white. In the skit that followed, the one person dressed in black was taken outside of the venue, for his refusal to wear the provided garment.

This parable is not the only place in the Bible where God makes it clear that our own spiritual "clothing" is not good enough to qualify us for heaven. Throughout the Bible, sin is represented as a *clothing crisis*. It started with Adam and Eve who, having sinned, realized that they were naked (Genesis 3:7). Instead of running back to God to ask for forgiveness and the restoration of God's covering over them, they decided to sew fig leaves together and made themselves coverings, which were not acceptable to God. Time after time, God offers the garments of salvation that He has prepared for us (for examples, see Isaiah 61:1–4, 10, 11; Zechariah 3:1–5). In the Gospels, parables such as the one found in Matthew 22 make the same point. Even in Luke 15:22, when the prodigal son returns, the first order of the father is to bring out the "best robe" and put it on him. In the last book of the Bible, God's plea is that the church of Laodicea buys from Him white garments (Revelation 3:18), so that their nakedness may be covered. The sad part is that Laodicea is proud about their many spiritual blessings and wealth; they don't realize their need. They say: "I am rich, and have become wealthy, and have need of nothing," and God responds: "You do not know that you are wretched and miserable and poor and blind and naked" (Revelation 3:17). God's solution is to give us His garment of righteousness, which He purchased at the high price of the blood of Jesus. Accept His generous offer. The robe of salvation is *not* found in our own closets; it is only provided by Him!

My Response: _____

HIS PROVISION

"Your Father knows what you need before you ask Him."
—Matthew 6:8

When my dad passed away, a deep sadness came upon me. I didn't fully understand all the levels of grief I was experiencing. A friend sent me an article that greatly helped me; it explained how when we lose our final parent, we grieve on three additional levels: when we lose our first parent, we place our energy on the parent that we have left, but when the second parent dies, we grieve both parents anew. Second, for the first time we are orphans. Third, the generation before us is gone, therefore we are the next to face our mortality. Being an orphan brought a new, personal level of grief. And immediately all the Bible verses that referred to God as our *Father* had a new and intimate meaning for me.

Jesus introduced His followers to a new and intimate way to relate to God: He is *our Father*. He said that unbelievers try to impress God by mere repetitions (Matthew 6:7), but His disciples should not. Several times in the Sermon on the Mount, Jesus talks about God as the disciples' Father (see 5:16, 45, 48; 6:1, 4, 6, 8, 9, 14, 15, 18, 26; 7:11). This has become personal for me. When addressing God as *our Father*, I am not talking to a distant god, but to One who loves and cares for me. And by using the first person plural possessive pronoun, I am part of the community of God's children. The Lord's Prayer is divided into two main parts: one contains three statements about God, and the other contains three petitions for His provision. "Hallowed be Your name. Your kingdom come. Your will be done" (Matthew 6:9, 10). *Your, Your, Your.* Our perspective is aligned with God's when our focus is on Him, recognizing the holiness of His name, and desiring His kingdom to be established and His purposes fulfilled. Then, we acknowledge our dependency on Him, requesting daily provision for our physical needs, as well as forgiveness for our sins and deliverance from temptations (see verses 11–13). All of this is preceded by Jesus' reminder that *our Father* knows what we need even before we ask Him (verse 8). We are the beloved children of God. We delight in providing for our children. How much more *our Heavenly Father* delights in providing for us!

My Response: _____

His Supply

"Give us this day our daily bread."

—Matthew 6:11

Daily bread is a basic need, which is not met in some areas of the world at this time. ADRA (The Adventist Development and Relief Agency) gives this staggering information on their website: "Hunger and malnutrition kill more people each year than AIDS, malaria, and tuberculosis combined. Today, nearly one billion people in the world are hungry, and food is insecure."* Having enough daily food is still a major concern today, as it was in biblical times.

Hunger and thirst were the first obstacles that Israel faced after crossing the Red Sea. Immediately after the Israelites sang the flamboyant song of redemption (Exodus 15:1–21), God revealed Himself to them as their Provider, healing the bitter waters at Marah (Exodus 15:22–27) and giving them bread from heaven, eventually called manna (Exodus 16:4, 5). The manna would rain down from heaven daily, except on the Sabbath of the Lord (which was the reminder of God's provision for their spiritual as well as physical needs). "The LORD said to Moses, 'Behold, I will rain bread from heaven for you; and the people shall go out and gather *a day's portion every day*' " (verse 4). In the first century, most people depended on their daily wages for their daily bread, which was an important part of their diet, as exemplified by the miraculous feedings. Physical bread was also a metaphor for spiritual nourishment, evident in Jesus' answer to the tempter, quoting Deuteronomy 8:3: "It is written, 'Man shall not live on bread alone, but on every word that proceeds from the mouth of God' " (Matthew 4:4). When teaching His disciples how to pray, Jesus included the request for daily bread (Matthew 6:11). We may ask God to supply our daily physical, emotional, and spiritual needs as well: "Give us this day our daily *peace*," "our daily *trust*," "our daily *faith*," "give us this day our daily *joy*." God is eager to supply all our needs. Most importantly, the manna also foreshadowed Jesus, who is *the* real Manna: "I am the living bread that came down out of heaven" (John 6:51). Oh, Lord, give us a daily and abundant revelation of Jesus and His grace!

My Response: _____

---

* "Hunger & Nutrition," *ADRA*, accessed April 9, 2019, https://adra.org/impact-areas/hunger-nutrition/.

HIS BEAUTY

*"Observe how the lilies of the field grow. . . .
I say to you that not even Solomon in all his glory
clothed himself like one of these."*
—Matthew 6:28, 29

My mother loved nature. While driving, we might stop repeatedly just to marvel at a bird's nest or a flower that she had spotted on the roadside. We usually vacationed in nature; she saw God's glory in the vibrancy and beauty of creation. A few weeks before her passing, I was sitting on her bedside, and we talked about her memorial service—instead of her pictures, she wanted me to display her photos of birds she had taken, which we did. She truly rejoiced in the beauty of nature, which declares God's love, care, and provision for His creatures.

When God created the world, He wanted His creatures to be surrounded by beauty: "The LORD God planted a garden toward the east, in Eden; and there He placed the man whom He had formed. Out of the ground the LORD God caused to grow every tree that is pleasing to the sight and good for food" (Genesis 2:8, 9). Can you imagine God planting trees *pleasing* to the sight, so that His children would delight in the surrounding beauty? I was amazed by this detail. We do the same for our babies, surrounding them with color and beauty. All the beauty in the world was created for our happiness and as a witness to His glory. He designed the fragrance of fields, the splendor of flowers, and the songs of birds. All for us! "The heavens are telling of the glory of God; And their expanse is declaring the work of His hands" (Psalm 19:1). All of nature speaks of God's passionate love for us. From the beginning, He surrounded us with beauty, and when we rebelled against Him, He died to pay our ransom and to restore us to the beauty of Paradise. Jesus exhorts us to observe the splendor of the flowers: not even Solomon, the wealthy king, dressed like them. And He reasons with us: if God so clothes the flowers of the fields that only last a day or so, will He not take care of us, His beloved children? Of course, He will! God has done all that was needed for our eternal salvation and for our present sustenance. Cast your fear and anxiety aside! Enjoy His gift of beauty that tells of His constant provision for us.

My Response: _____

HIS REMEDY

"Seek first His kingdom and His righteousness,
and all these things will be added to you."
—Matthew 6:33

A married couple was discussing their financial future and making plans, figuring out what they could afford. Without their knowledge, their young child overheard their conversation. A few hours later they noticed that their son had a worried look on his face and they inquired about it. He went on to tell them his understanding of their private conversation. Consequently, he was very anxious and worried that they might not be able to provide for him. They embraced him and assured him that there was nothing to fear, and that they would provide for his every need. I wonder how often God has seen a worried look on my face?

Many of us are prone to anxiety. Jesus addresses this topic in the Sermon on the Mount, making three imperatives, usually translated as "do not worry" (Matthew 6:25, 31, 34). He explains the futility of worrying and offers a remedy for it. He begins by addressing the anxiety about our basic, legitimate daily needs: food and clothing (verse 25). He demonstrates how our Heavenly Father provides for His creation, by feeding the birds (verse 26) and clothing the flowers (verse 28). Jesus also points out the uselessness of worrying: "And who of you by being worried can add a single hour to his life?" (verse 27). How true! And still we do! He continues with a contrast between believers and unbelievers: Gentiles worry about these basic needs, but His followers have a Heavenly Father who knows their needs. He then offers a remedy for anxiety: seek God's kingdom as the ultimate priority and trust His faithfulness to provide for our needs. "Seek first His kingdom and His righteousness, and all these things will be added to you." (verse 33). Simple, right? Well, I need to be reminded many times a day of this simple, yet profound, cure for anxiety. Finally, Jesus expands his "do not worry" imperative beyond basic needs—to fears about the future (verse 34). Do not be anxious about tomorrow. Stay in the present, in today. God is in charge; God is in control; He knows what we need. Relax. God's faithfulness is the remedy for our anxiety. Woo-hoo!

My Response: _____

HIS BELOVED

*"Let us rejoice and be glad and give the glory to Him,
for the marriage of the Lamb has come and His bride
has made herself ready."*

—Revelation 19:7

A few years ago, we celebrated my parents' fiftieth wedding anniversary, and it was a most joyful occasion. At the entrance of the hall where the festivities were taking place, there were various exhibits displayed, including wedding gifts and my mother's wedding dress. In the photos of the wedding, my mother looks truly stunning, and my father has a sparkle in his eyes as they are leaving the church, as if saying, "She is all mine from this day forward!"

Can you imagine what we will feel when we finally meet our heavenly Bridegroom, who gave His life for us? Can you imagine how eager Jesus is to take us home? In order to fully savor the Scriptural metaphor of marriage relating to the final union of Jesus with His church, Dr. Ranko Stefanovic helps us understand a wedding in the first century: "The Hebrew wedding usually began with the betrothal at the house of the bride's father, where the groom paid the dowry. The two were, afterwards, considered husband and wife. The groom then returned to his father's house to prepare the place where he and his bride would live. During that time the bride stayed at her father's home preparing herself for the wedding. When both the place and the bride were ready, the bridegroom would return to take the bride to his father's house where the wedding ceremony was to take place (cf. Matthew 25:1–10)."* Yet, unlike in regular weddings, in this final wedding, the Lamb who is the Bridegroom, does *everything* for the bride: He becomes the dowry, giving up His own life for her. He washes the bride clean. He provides the white dress. He does everything! The bride just loves Him back because He first loved her, and pledges allegiance to her Beloved. Check out all that He has done to make sure the bride is ready: "Christ also *loved* the church, and *gave Himself up for her, so that He might sanctify her, having cleansed her by the washing of water with the word, that He might present to Himself the church in all her glory*" (Ephesians 5:25–27). You are loved! Jesus can't wait to take you home!

My Response: _____

---

* Ranko Stefanovic, *Revelation of Jesus Christ,* 2nd ed. (Berrien Springs, MI: Andrews University Press, 2009), 553.

His Willingness

"How much more will your Father who is in heaven give what is good to those who ask Him!"

—Matthew 7:11

When I was growing up, my parents made many sacrifices for me, so that I could have a good education and everything I needed. Many of us can relate to this because children become their parents' priority, even to the point of denying themselves essential things in order to provide for their children. This begins from the moment the children are born and often continues even after the parents are gone, as many plan to provide an inheritance for their adult children.

Jesus used this closest of human relationships (between a parent and a child) to teach us about God's willingness to give us all the good things that we need. "Ask, and it will be given to you; seek, and you will find; knock, and it will be opened to you" (Matthew 7:7). This famous saying of Jesus contains three synonymous imperatives: ask, seek, and knock, followed by three assurances: "It will be given . . . you will find . . . it will be opened." God, as the heavenly Father who is faithful and willing to provide for His children, had been introduced in the previous chapter (Matthew 6:25–34). Now Jesus encourages His followers to an ongoing mindset of trust in God's ability to surpass even the goodwill of earthly parents towards their children. Jesus uses a typical Jewish argument style called *qal wahomer* ("from lesser to greater"), showing that if the lesser is true, *how much more* is the greater true. If earthly parents, being sinful, know how to give good gifts to their children, how much more is our heavenly Father willing to give us the good things we need (verse 11). Jesus refers to the unthinkable scenario of a parent denying their child the typical Galilean meal (bread and fish) (verses 8, 9), and replacing it with something harmful (stone and snake). If parents can't fathom that option, why should we mistrust the willingness of our Heavenly Father? As we mentioned previously, (February 4), in Paul's words: "He who did not spare His own Son . . . how will He not also with Him freely give us all things? (Romans 8:32). Let's trust the willing heart of Him who gave Himself for us.

My Response: _____

HIS INVITATION

"Follow Me, and I will make you fishers of men."
—Matthew 4:19

One of my most significant experiences in the Holy Land was a boat ride on the Sea of Galilee. It felt surreal to be on the same lake that Jesus and His disciples so often crossed. And it was a treat to see fishermen at their trade, throwing the nets, just as it was done two thousand years ago. It was absolutely amazing to watch! Who would have thought that this daily task of catching fish would become a metaphor for evangelism?

Matthew narrates the call of the first four disciples as Jesus is walking by the Sea of Galilee, in fulfillment of the previously quoted Isaiah's prophecy (Matthew 4:15, 16). Simon, who is identified as Peter, and his brother Andrew are casting a net, "for they were fishermen" (verse 18). And Jesus extends to them what must have been a surprising invitation: "Follow Me" (verse 19). It was a rabbinic custom to have pupils follow their master, learning from him. But what is striking about Jesus' invitation is that He is the One initiating the relationship, not the other way around as was the habitual practice. Moreover, Jesus takes their occupation as fishermen and uses it as a metaphor for their future endeavors; they will be fishers of human beings! (verse 19; see Matthew 13:47, 48). I am so thankful that Jesus' call comes with the assurance that He will equip His disciples for the task: "Follow Me, and *I will make you* fishers of men" (Matthew 4:19). He provides what is necessary to evangelize. Going on from there, Jesus called James and John. All four of them responded immediately and decisively. They left everything (nets, boat, father; see verses 20, 22). God calls each one of us, in the midst of our ordinary tasks, and invites us to follow Him and become fishers for His kingdom. Most of us won't be asked to leave our occupations, but to rearrange our priorities. Discipleship is a reversal of values in light of Jesus' redemptive mission. May we share the amazing grace that we have found in Jesus, recognizing that He equips us for this call. It's all His grace: the salvation, the call, and the equipping. Be assured of His provision as you excitedly share the gospel!

My Response: _____

HIS FORTITUDE

After they had preached the gospel to that city and had made many disciples, they returned to Lystra and to Iconium and to Antioch, strengthening the souls of the disciples, encouraging them to continue in the faith.

—Acts 14:21, 22

The Gospel of Jesus is the favorite topic of discussion at the Talbot family reunions. My brother-in-law, Jorge, is a retired physician and an avid student of the Bible. We often talk about the miraculous fortitude God provided for His gospel martyrs, such as John Huss, who sang while being burned at the stake. Singing while flames are consuming the body is physically impossible, yet God honored the gospel on their lips, by providing miraculous strength.

Today's text portrays Paul strengthening and encouraging disciples in his missionary endeavors. But what is remarkable is that two verses before, "Jews came from Antioch and Iconium . . . they stoned Paul and dragged him out of the city, supposing him to be dead. But . . . he got up and entered the city" (Acts 14:19, 20). How could Paul be so uplifting and encouraging, and how could he continue preaching the gospel with gladness, just after being stoned and left for dead? Paul himself tells of some of his trials: "Five times I received from the Jews thirty-nine lashes. Three times I was beaten with rods, once I was stoned, three times I was shipwrecked. . . in dangers from rivers . . . dangers from robbers . . . dangers from my countrymen, dangers from the Gentiles . . ., dangers in the wilderness . . . dangers on the sea" (2 Corinthians 11:24–27). And the list continues: hunger, thirst, cold, et cetera. How could he experience these circumstances and yet go on preaching and encouraging others? When we accept the good news that Jesus died in our place, God provides assurance for our eternal future, and He also miraculously provides all that is necessary for the present, including fortitude, mental and emotional strength to live a life for his glory, even in the midst of adversity and pain. When Paul asked for his "thorn in the flesh" to be removed, the Lord told him: "My grace is sufficient for you, for power is perfected in weakness" (2 Corinthians 12:9). And the same answer is true for us. God provides His grace for every aspect of our lives. He truly provides for all our needs through Jesus.

My Response: _____

HIS EAGERNESS

"Now, will not God bring about justice for His elect who cry to Him day and night, and will He delay long over them?"
—Luke 18:7

I've often seen parents defend and protect their children, and I am astounded at the way God placed this instinct in the animal kingdom. I recently watched a clip of two videographers filming a little bear cub. They must have been a bit too close because all of a sudden you can see the mother bear charging towards them and hitting the camera, responding to a perceived threat to her cub. The videographers survived the attack, but I am sure that they will never again underestimate the parental protective instinct found in nature.

The Bible often showcases God's eagerness to defend and avenge His children, faithfully protecting them. Jesus told a parable about God's willingness and readiness to aid His chosen ones, and about not becoming discouraged and persisting in prayer with the expectation of God's prompt intervention on our behalf (Luke 18:1–8). How vital it is to have a healthy view of God's eager disposition towards us! The parable contains two main characters: a notoriously wicked judge, who has complete disregard for God and his fellowmen, and a destitute widow, who is in peril and in need of legal protection from an opponent. The wicked judge does not help her at the beginning, but after a while gives in, and provides the legal protection she needs, because he is weary of her persistence, which she portrays in spite of the unrighteous character of the judge. In a classic argument of lesser to greater (*qal wahomer*), Jesus concludes: if such a wicked and heartless judge finally gives justice to the persistent widow, *how much more* will God bring justice, avenging and vindicating His own, who cry out to Him day and night! In other words: "Do you hear what the judge, corrupt as he is, is saying? So what makes you think God won't step in and work justice for his chosen people, who continue to cry out for help? Won't he stick up for them? I assure you, he will. He will not drag his feet." (Luke 18:6–8, *The Message*). Trust God's eagerness to save, protect, and act on your behalf! He will not fail you!

My Response: _____

HIS BLOOD

*"Say to the owner of the house, 'The Teacher says,
"Where is My guest room in which I may eat the
Passover with My disciples?" ' "*

—Mark 14:14

During a difficult season, I visited my valued mentor. He took me back to Israel's history; and we read Exodus 14:13, 14: "But Moses said to the people, 'Do not fear! Stand by and see the salvation of the LORD which He will accomplish for your today. . . . The LORD will fight for you while you keep silent." God's power to deliver His people was revealed through the Passover Lamb and the dividing of the sea. My mentor reminded me to trust that the battle is the Lord's!

When Jesus was about to surrender His life to redeem the world, He planned to eat the last Passover meal with His disciples (Mark 14:12–16). In a combination of practical arrangements and divine prescience, Jesus gave His disciples explicit instructions to find a guest room to eat the Passover together. They were to follow a man with a pitcher of water (verse 13); an unusual sight, given that mostly women carried jars of water. The owner of the house was simply to be told, "The Teacher says, 'Where is My guest room in which I may eat the Passover with My disciples?' " (verse 14). The word "Passover" is mentioned four times in this short narrative. Can you imagine Jesus' thoughts as they prepared for the meal that was a memorial of deliverance and redemption, instituted back in Exodus 12:21–27, which symbolized His own death? The Israelites slayed the Passover lamb and applied the blood on the lintel and the two doorposts of the house, and the angel of destruction did not smite them, as they were thus covered. They were delivered by the blood of the Lamb. Later they encountered the Egyptians, while trapped by the sea, and once again they were reminded that the battle was the Lord's. On their way to the Promised Land, they were reminded that God was the Provider of water and bread. The battle was the Lord's! Back in Jerusalem, as Jesus was eating the meal, He explained to His disciples that it represented His body and His blood. Our Passover Lamb, Jesus, has been sacrificed! (1 Corinthians 5:7). He has delivered us! Now, will we trust Him to provide what we need as we journey to the Promised Land?

My Response: _____

HIS ENDURANCE

About midnight Paul and Silas were praying and singing hymns of praise to God, and the prisoners were listening to them.

—Acts 16:25

During particularly hard times in my life, God often blesses me with a song that becomes my companion through that specific trial. When my father was diagnosed with cancer for the last time, I was blessed with the song "God Wants to Hear You Sing,"* which I listened to over and over. It highlights that God loves to hear our songs when everything is fine, but that we truly bless God's heart when He hears us sing His praises in the midst of sufferings, just as Paul and Silas did.

It is fascinating to understand the circumstances that Jesus went through in the Gospel of Luke, and the parallel experiences of His followers in the book of Acts. Both Jesus and His followers were baptized by the Spirit for public ministry, performed many miracles, endured all kinds of trials and tribulations, and were persecuted and killed. Jesus endured the kind of sufferings and death that none of His followers would ever taste, because He carried the penalty of our sins and transgressions. Yet His disciples were given strength and patience from above to endure many trials. Sometimes God removes the trial, other times He gives us perseverance and a song of praise in the midst of tribulation. This was the case with Paul and Silas in Philippi. The first convert in Europe, named Lydia, was baptized in this city. When Paul exorcised a fortune-telling spirit from a slave girl, he and Silas were put in jail after being struck with many blows (Acts 16:23). For security and punishment purposes, they were placed in the inner prison and their feet were fastened in stocks (verse 24). Yet God provided a way for them to witness about Jesus: they were singing and praising God in the middle of the night (verse 25). Other prisoners were listening, as was probably the jailer himself. When a great earthquake occurred, they had the opportunity to tell the jailer about salvation through Jesus, and he and his family were baptized. If you are suffering today, ask God to give you a song of praise in the night. Your *test* will become your *testi*mony! And God will use it for His salvific purposes!

My Response: _____

---

* "God Wants to Hear You Sing" by Greater Vision.

His Plenty

They all ate and were satisfied.

—Mark 6:42

I was a church youth leader when our group decided to participate in a large community event of serving a holiday meal for homeless people in downtown Los Angeles. Thousands of people ate until they were completely full, and still there were plenty of leftovers, which is very unusual for there are more than forty thousand unsheltered, homeless individuals in this city. Oh, that this abundance could be theirs every day!

There is a fascinating section found in Mark 6–8, and we will spend a few days in it. It relates to the feeding of the five thousand and the feeding of the four thousand. The narrative starts with Jesus teaching a large crowd in a desolate place, and it gets quite late; it is time to eat (Mark 6:34, 35). The disciples could only find five loaves of bread and two fish (verse 38), and they brought these to Jesus. The crowd sat down in groups of fifties and hundreds, as the people had in the wilderness with Moses (Exodus 18:21). Jesus then multiplied the bread. There are four verbs that the reader will re-encounter later in the bread plot: Jesus *takes* the bread, *blesses* it, *breaks* the loaves, and *gives* them to the disciples, who give the bread to the crowd. "They all ate and were satisfied, and they picked up twelve full baskets of the broken pieces. . . . There were five thousand men who ate the loaves" (verses 42–44). The cultural setting of this event is found in the words and numbers used. The numbers five and twelve were representative of the Jewish culture: five was the number of the books in the Law (Torah), and there were twelve tribes in Israel. In this story, there are five loaves of bread, five thousand men fed, and twelve full baskets left, one per tribe. Even the Greek word used for baskets is *kophinos*, associated with the Jews. God's people were fed, satisfied, and had leftovers. But there was more to this enacted teaching, which we will study in the next few days. For now, let's notice that God has no lack of resources, whether for our daily needs or for our eternal salvation. He has no limitations, and His grace is plentiful! He can do immeasurably more than all we ask or imagine (Ephesians 3:18–20)!

My Response: _____

HIS BREAKTHROUGH

"Yes, Lord, but even the dogs under the table
feed on the children's crumbs."

—Mark 7:28

When I was a little girl, I was saving for a bicycle. My dad, who was a church administrator, my mom, and I went to the mountains, where a woman, who owned a hotel far away from any local church, was waiting to give her tithes and offerings. We arrived and sat at a table. She started to divide money into little designated piles: evangelism, tithes, church budget, et cetera. I was sure there would be a pile for me too! When the money ran out, I yelled in utter desperation: "And for my bicycle?!" How could there be so much for the church and nothing for me?

Have you ever wondered if there is enough for you? I have. In the time of Jesus, some wondered whether there was enough for them, because they were labeled as outsiders. The feeding of the five thousand (in Mark's narrative clearly pointing to the Jewish culture) had left the crowd *satisfied* through the multiplication of the *bread* (Mark 6:34–44). Mark 7:24 finds Jesus in Tyre and Sidon, which was a pagan territory that carried a long history of antagonism toward the people of Israel (see 1 Kings 16:31, 32). A Gentile woman, of the Syrophoenician race, asks Jesus for mercy for her daughter. Jesus tells her a riddle, about being *satisfied* with *bread*, the two pivotal words in the preceding feeding of the five thousand. "And He was saying to her, 'Let the children be *satisfied* first, for it is not good to take the children's *bread* and throw it to the dogs' " (Mark 7:27). The woman responds to the riddle and does not ask for the children's *bread*, nor for the first place. She asks for the humble place of a little dog that feeds from the children's crumbs (verse 28). Jesus commends her for her answer and grants her request. She was more insightful than the disciples, who had not yet grasped the inclusivity of Jesus' mission. Many scholars consider this story the *breakthrough* event in this Gospel, followed by the next miraculous feeding that will occur in a Gentile context (Mark 8:1–9). There was *enough bread* for her, for them, and for us to be *satisfied*, no matter where we come from, or where we have been.

My Response: _____

His Satisfying

And they ate and were satisfied; and they picked up seven large baskets
full of what was left over of the broken pieces.

—Mark 8:8

As humans, we seem to be prone to exclusivity, whether on the basis of color, gender, race, religion, or any number of other categories. I have recently learned about the life of the extraordinary mathematician Ramanujan. He went through hard times, due to his race, until he was recognized for his educational endeavors in England. In 1918, he became the first person from India to be elected as Fellow of Trinity College, Cambridge. He died at the age of thirty-two.

It is hard to be accepted into a group when you are considered an outsider. The disciples had difficulty understanding that Gentiles were invited to God's kingdom. After the feeding of the five thousand, where the insiders were fed *bread* and were *satisfied* (Mark 6:34–44), and after the breakthrough riddle with the Syrophoenician woman, where Jesus talked about being *satisfied* with *bread* (Mark 7:24–30), Jesus feeds the four thousand. This is the feeding of the others (Mark 8:1–10); the numbers and the word used for "basket" have changed. This time Jesus starts with seven loaves (verse 5). Once again, we encounter four verbs: Jesus *takes* the bread, *gives thanks*, *breaks* the loaves, and *gives* them to the disciples to give to the people (verse 6). "And they ate and were *satisfied*; and they picked up *seven* large baskets full of what was left over of the broken pieces. About four thousand were there" (verses 8, 9). The numbers have changed from five and twelve in the feeding of the Jews, to seven and four, for the outsiders. The number four is used for the whole earth (four corners); and in the non-Jewish/Gentile geographical setting, seven symbolizes the seven pagan nations displaced by the Israelites in the land of Canaan (see Acts 13:19; Deuteronomy 7:1). The word for baskets is different (*spuris*), befitting of a Gentile audience. They were also *satisfied* and there were *seven baskets* left. If you have felt the pain of being labeled as an outsider, may you know that Jesus wants *you* to be fed and be *satisfied* as well. Tomorrow we will discover what the bread was pointing to!*

My Response: _____

---

* See tomorrow's devotional for the conclusion of the bread plot in Mark.

HIS UNVEILING

And He was saying to them, "Do you not yet understand?"
—Mark 8:21

The 2012 tornado season in the United States turned deadly. Stephanie Decker was at home with her two children when the first tornado hit Henryville, Indiana. With no time to take them to the shelter, she covered them with her own body. The flying debris broke seven of her ribs, and her legs became casualties of the second tornado that hit a few minutes later, but her children didn't suffer as much as a scratch. In the interviews, she was smiling because it was all worth it!

After the feeding of the five thousand, the breakthrough with the Syrophoenician woman, and the feeding of the four thousand (events that we have reviewed for the last three days), it was now time for the *unveiling* of the *bread riddle*. To make sure the hearers and readers do not miss the connection between the two feedings, Mark adds a summary of Jesus: " 'Having eyes, do you not see? And having ears, do you not hear? And do you not remember, when I broke the five loaves for the five thousand, how many baskets [*kophinos*] full of broken pieces you picked up?' They said to Him, 'Twelve.' 'When I broke the seven for the four thousand, how many large baskets [*spuris*] full of broken pieces did you pick up?' And they said to Him, 'Seven.' And He was saying to them, 'Do you not yet understand?' " (Mark 8:18–12). Obviously, there was enough bread for Jews and for non-Jews, for the insiders and the outsiders. And there were leftovers for each group, emphasized by the numbers and words befitting the respective cultural settings. But what, exactly, did the bread symbolize? Towards the end of this Gospel, the full mystery of the ongoing bread riddle is unveiled, using the verbs that had been present in the narrative of both feedings: "While they were eating, Jesus *took* bread, and when he had *given thanks*, he *broke* it and *gave* it to His disciples, saying. 'Take it; *this is my body*' " (Mark 14:22, NIV). Jesus here revealed the fact that He would die for all; He gave up His life so that we could be assured of life eternal. And both feedings confirmed that His sacrificial victory was for *all* who believe in Him. And who, exactly, are *all*? Oh, yes! *All!*

My Response: _____

HIS BESTOWAL

*They were amazed and astonished, saying, ". . . how is it that we each
hear them in our own language to which we were born?"*
—Acts 2:7, 8

I wanted to make sure my message would be properly understood
even though the audience in the convention center had come from
many different countries. The night before the event, I met with the
coordinator of the translators in order to go over some of my key points.
The translation in different languages, transmitted via headset radio system, was of utmost importance as many in the audience were not fluent
in English. I believe that the Holy Spirit anointed their words; otherwise
I would not have been able to communicate the Word.

At the end of His earthly ministry, Jesus promised His disciples that
they would receive "power from on high," in order to proclaim the good
news of Jesus to the world (Luke 24:46–49). And the followers of Jesus
waited for the promise to be fulfilled. They were all together on the day
of Pentecost "and suddenly there came from heaven a noise like a violent
rushing wind. . . . And there appeared to them tongues as of fire distrib-
uting themselves, and they rested on each one of them. And they were
all filled with the Holy Spirit and began to speak with other tongues, as
the Spirit was giving them utterance" (Acts 2:2–4). Jews and proselytes,
pilgrims from other nations, each heard the disciples speak in their own
language! Can you imagine the amazed audience, each hearing the gospel in their own dialect? Many scholars interpret this event as the reversal of the curse of Babel, when humans mistrusted God and thought to
outsmart Him by building a tower to reach the heavens. God confused
their language, and they could no longer understand each other (Genesis
11:1–9). Now in Acts, the opposite happened. The Spirit was bestowed
on the Christian community, and everyone understood their message!
God equipped His followers, providing everything they needed in order
to share Jesus with others. And the Holy Spirit is bestowed upon us,
equipping us for service and providing what is needed. The Spirit will
enable you to share Jesus with others! Trust His power and don't be
afraid to be used by God!

My Response: _____

His Endowment

With a leap he stood upright and began to walk; and he entered the temple with them, walking and leaping and praising God.

—Acts 3:8

Have you ever received more than you could have imagined? We were celebrating my birthday with my family. After a nice dinner, I opened the gifts. One of the gifts was a little yellow toy car, which I really liked because I had wanted to buy a similar real car. There were envelopes attached to the bumper of the car. When I opened them, I found checks inside, amounting to a large sum that was enough to trade my used car and buy the new car I needed. I was speechless!

In Acts 3, there was a man who received much more than he could have imagined. He was handicapped since birth and had been begging for a living: "A man who had been lame from his mother's womb was being carried along, whom they used to set down every day at the gate of the temple which is called Beautiful, in order to beg alms of those who were entering the temple" (verse 2). Peter and John were going to the temple at the hour of prayer, and the man was asking for alms. Peter looked at him and said, "Look at us!" (verse 4). Surely, the beggar looked at them immediately, probably expecting a sizeable gift, only to have his hopes shattered by Peter's opening words: "I do not possess silver and gold" (verse 6) Oh, really? "But what I do have I give to you: In the name of Jesus Christ the Nazarene—walk!" (verse 6). Wait, what? This was much more than he imagined! He could walk! And that was the first gift he received in the name of Jesus! But there was more! For the first time in his life, he *entered the temple*, experiencing God like never before! There were nine gates that led into the inner courts, and a lame person wouldn't have gone further than the court of the Gentiles. The name of Jesus became his *passport* to enter the temple, "walking and leaping and praising God" (verse 8). I am amazed at how God is able to provide more than what we ask or expect. And His greatest endowment is our immediate access to the presence of God through the name of Jesus (Hebrews 10:19–22), no matter how emotionally and spiritually handicapped we have been all our lives.

My Response: _____

HIS COURAGE

"And now, Lord, take note of their threats, and grant that Your bond-servants may speak Your word with all confidence."
—Acts 4:29

Martin Luther had arrived at Worms. The Reformer had expected a scholarly debate about the content of his books, but instead Eck, an official of the Archbishop of Trier, opened the proceedings by asking Luther to acknowledge the authorship of his books and to recant his position. Luther was taken by surprise, and even though he corroborated his authorship, he asked for time to consider the recantation request. A delay of one day was granted. Did he lose his confidence for a few hours? Was it a debate technique? Whatever the reason for his request, Luther surrendered to God, and the next day he asserted in front of the council that he could not retract in light of the Scriptural evidence, come what may.

After their arrest for speaking about salvation through Jesus Christ, Peter and John were commanded by the council "not to speak or teach at all in the name of Jesus" (Acts 4:18). The two disciples responded: "we cannot stop speaking about what we have seen and heard" (verse 20). Then they were threatened and released (verse 21). And they went to their own people and prayed an amazing prayer. When we pray for God to provide what we need while we're going through dire circumstances, we usually think of asking God to remove the trial, to provide for our physical needs, or to send people who will comfort us. But they prayed for God to provide . . . *confidence*; they prayed for courage to continue proclaiming the Word of God! "And now, Lord, take note of their threats, and grant that Your bond-servants may speak Your word with all confidence" (verse 29). We can request the same, especially when we are under oppression or going through difficulties due to our belief in Jesus. God responded with a miraculous manifestation of His Spirit: "the place where they had gathered together was shaken, and they were all filled with the Holy Spirit and *began* to speak the word of God with *boldness*" (verse 31). God will give us courage when we meet opposition to the gospel. This is a divine provision that we are sure to receive!

My Response: _____

HIS RESOLUTION

*The word of God kept on spreading; and the number of the
disciples continued to increase greatly in Jerusalem.*

—Acts 6:7

I am keenly aware of the need to understand the cultural anthropol-
ogy and sociology reflected in the Bible. Background commentaries
help us understand the customs and social history at play, and how
various social groups interacted in the ancient Mediterranean world.
For example, in the New Testament we see that during the infancy of
the Christian church there were relational problems among groups, and
how God provided timely resolutions.

Paul clearly points out that we are all equal at the foot of the cross:
"For all of you who were baptized into Christ have clothed yourselves
with Christ. There is neither Jew nor Greek, there is neither slave nor
free man, there is neither male nor female; for you are all one in Christ
Jesus" (Galatians 3:27, 28). It seems so clear, yet Luke, who was Paul's
traveling companion, reports in the book of Acts that the apostles had to
deal with claims of discrimination at the very start of the believing fellowship. The Christian community was growing, and a complaint arose
on the side of the believing Greeks that the widows from their group
were being overlooked in the daily serving (Greek *diakonia*) of food (Acts
6:1). The apostles did not dismiss their claim, but instead sought a reso-
lution. God provided wisdom to His disciples, who selected *deacons* to
minister in this task. The first deacons were filled with the Spirit, and
they were of Hellenistic (Greek) background (verse 5), which meant that
God provided leaders with whom the complaining group could identify. Right after their selection, we find today's devotional text, one of
six such progress reports about how the word of God kept spreading
and the numbers of believers increased. Conflicts often threatened the
growth of the first century church (as in Acts 15), yet God provided wise
leaders who prayed for heavenly guidance and whose priorities were
the spreading of the good news, and the salvation of the people. Let's
pray for our leaders and communities, that no conflict may have the
power to hinder the proclamation of the gospel.

My Response: _____

His Disclosure

"Take courage, it is I; do not be afraid."

—Matthew 14:27

I don't like ocean cruises because the ship moves too much for my taste. My first cruise was on a very large ship to Mexico. In the middle of the night, it started rocking uncomfortably, and I left the room, looking for the reason. I peeked outside—there was no wind, and the sky was cloudless, filled with bright stars. The only person I found at that time of the night was a man who was cleaning the windows of the shops. With anxiety in my voice, I asked him: "Why is this ship moving so much?" "Because we are in the ocean!" he responded. "But this a big ship!" I said. He answered: "But this ocean is bigger!" I will never forget it!

In Matthew 14:24, we find the disciples in the middle of a storm on the lake, again! (see Matthew 8:24). This time they are by themselves, without Jesus. "The boat was already a *long distance from the land, battered* by the waves; for the wind was *contrary*" (verse 24). Adverse circumstances, to say the least. Sounds familiar? In the fourth watch of the night (which meant 3:00–6:00 A.M.), Jesus came to them (verse 25). They had been battling the storm all night while Jesus had been praying. Knowing their difficulty and distress, He joins them. And we are matter-of-factly told that he was "walking on the sea" (verse 25). Excuse me?! Matthew, what do you mean? Well, I just love that God is not bound by anything, He decides *what* to do and *when* to do it. When they "saw Him walking on the sea, they were terrified, and said 'It is a ghost!' And they cried out in fear" (verse 26). There was a common belief at the time that evil spirits resided under the waters. They can't explain what is happening, therefore they are terrified. That is usually the case with us as well when we don't understand what we are experiencing. But then they hear a Voice that they are well-acquainted with: "Take courage, it is I; do not be afraid" (verse 27). Jesus discloses who He is! The Greek original reads *egō eimi*, which means "I AM," and it was Yahweh's name in the Greek Old Testament (see Exodus 3:14). This disclosure was enough for them, and it's enough for us. The great "I AM" still comes to our aid in the middle of the storm. Take courage!

My Response: _____

FOLLOWING HIS GUIDANCE

HIS PATH

He said to them, "What are these words that you are exchanging with one another as you are walking?"

—Luke 24:17

Life is a journey into ever deepening understanding. Many years ago, as I was going through painful transitions in my life, I realized that the longest journey a person may take is only a few inches long: from the head to the heart. And it is often pain that exposes us to deeper perceptions of reality, especially about God's will for our lives. Our brokenness has a purpose, and we are not alone in this journey. God is always with us, inviting us to choose His path instead of ours.

One of the themes of the Gospel of Luke is about journeys. Everyone is on the move! But these are not just geographical travels; they are journeys of perception. And the journey to the village of Emmaus is no exception. The distance is approximately seven miles (Luke 24:13), and on the way the two disciples are discussing all "these things" that had happened, including the report of the women, which the men had deemed *nonsense* (verses 11, 12, 14, 22–24). "While they were talking and discussing, Jesus Himself approached them and began traveling with them" (verse 15). This is so like Jesus! He comes and meets us where we are; He joins us in our journey in order to invite us to trust Him, His way, and His will. In the Gospels, sight and blindness are usually associated with spiritual insight, or lack thereof, regarding the mission and identity of Jesus. In this case their eyes don't recognize Jesus (verse 16). Sometimes our tears block our view of Jesus, and our mistaken perceptions delay our joy. In order to help them in their journey, Jesus asked them a question, which He already had the answer for: "What are these words that you are exchanging with one another as you are walking?" (verse 17). God listens when we tell Him about our version of the story. Then He lovingly and graciously invites us to trust His path for us; unlike us, He sees all things from a heavenly viewpoint. Jesus had just died and had victoriously resurrected, on their behalf, but they didn't understand. He walked with them on their journey of understanding, and He won't abandon us on ours.

My Response: _____

HIS INTERPRETATION

Then He opened their minds to understand the Scriptures.
—Luke 24:45

I have a mug that I really like because it inspires me. It was sent to me by my dear friends Mirta and Alan. It reads: "Just when the caterpillar thought the world was over, it became a butterfly." So many times, circumstances seem final to us, but from heaven's viewpoint it is not an end but a beginning, filled with newness and meaning. For the believer in Jesus, there are no dead-ends in this world, not even death, because in Christ we will have eternal life.

It all seemed done and final for the two travelers on their way to Emmaus. They tried to explain the finality of the situation to the stranger who had joined them: "The chief priests and our rulers delivered Him to the sentence of death, and crucified Him. But we were hoping that it was He who was going to redeem Israel" (Luke 24:20, 21). They sounded defeated; their dreams were a thing of the past. They didn't know that they were talking to the risen Christ. Their finite interpretation rendered them helpless and hopeless, but this was not an end but a most glorious beginning. Jesus had told them many times that the Crucifixion would not be the end. But it felt like the end to them. Have you ever felt like that? Your marriage is on the rocks; your job is gone; a friendship just ended. That's it! It is hard to imagine that there is anything good left, that God, in fact, has the ability to turn all things for the good of those who love Him (Romans 8:28). Yet from the viewpoint of Jesus, it was completely different. He explained that it was necessary for Christ to die and rise again, and that His plan had been revealed in the Law and the prophets (Luke 24:26, 27, 44). He *opened* their minds to understand the Scriptures. The verb "to open" had been used for Jesus opening the ears of the deaf and the eyes of the blind. Now their minds were open to understand the good news. This was not the end! No! On the contrary, Jesus had opened a new glorious beginning for all! If you are facing an end, trust God's ability to create a new beginning. Sin was supposed to be the end for us, but it wasn't because a Savior came. Trust in Him! He will see you through!

My Response: _____

His Sheep

"He who enters by the door is a shepherd of the sheep. . . .
and the sheep hear his voice, and he calls his own sheep
by name and leads them out."

—John 10:2, 3

My parents fully trusted and rested in the arms of their heavenly Shepherd—in sickness and in health, in difficulties and in abundance, as well as when facing death. That's why my homily at my dad's memorial service was entitled "Rest Assured," based on Psalm 23. Jesus said that His sheep hear His voice (John 10:3), and I am certain that my parents will recognize their Shepherd's voice on the resurrection morning and will follow Him throughout eternity.

One of the most outstanding features of Psalm 23 is that in the first part (verses 1–3) David talks *about* His Shepherd, in the third person singular: *He* is my shepherd; *He* makes me lie down; *He* leads me; *He* restores my soul; *He* guides me. But when he enters the dark valley of the shadow of death, he switches to the second person singular and begins talking in a prayer *with* God: "I fear no evil for *You are with me*" (verse 4). The presence of his divine Shepherd was his antidote against fear. Later on, there was a prophecy, written many years after David's death, that clearly pointed to the upcoming Messiah, a descendant of David, who would come to shepherd God's people: "Then I will set over them one shepherd, My servant David, and he will feed them; he will feed them himself and be their shepherd" (Ezekiel 34:23). When Jesus, the awaited Davidic king, came to live and die for us, He identified Himself with the metaphor of the Good Shepherd who would give His life for His sheep (John 10:2–4, 11, 14). And the antidote against fear continues to be the presence of our Shepherd! I particularly love the fact that He calls us, *"His own sheep"* (verses 3, 14), for we belong to Him! I don't know what you are needing right now, but He does. Perhaps you need a safe place to rest; and your heavenly Shepherd offers that. Or maybe you are wounded and in need of restoration; your Shepherd provides that as well. Or maybe you are facing the valley of death and need assurance of eternal life; your Shepherd guarantees that through His merits! Whatever your needs, *rest assured* in *your* Shepherd's arms.

My Response: _____

HIS ABUNDANCE

"I came that they may have life, and have it abundantly."
—John 10:10

I was attending a worship service in a local church and inadvertently stepped into a youth group Bible study. There I saw a video that made a profound impact on me. It was a real-life video showing how the sheep know the shepherd's voice. There were many sheep and different people tried calling them, but the sheep didn't attempt to move. But then the camera captured their shepherd calling them, with the same sounds as the previous callers, and this time all the sheep came running to him. It was amazing!

Jesus said that the sheep know the voice of their shepherd, the one who has their best interests in mind (John 10:2–4). Over the years, I have collected some information about sheep because they are a commonly used scriptural metaphor to describe the people of God in need of His guidance and provision.* In doing so, I have learned that in general sheep are very helpless animals. They can't find food or water instinctively; they need protection from predators; they can easily drown if they try to drink from deep water; and they can't sleep if there are tensions in the flock. Sheep are absolutely and completely dependent on the shepherd to provide everything for them, including a peaceful place, a green pasture, quiet waters, et cetera. The sheep don't know where they are; they just need to follow their shepherd. As in Psalm 23, the abundance of the shepherd's provision may be visualized in terms of a flock finding food, rest, and comfort in nurturing pastures and restful waters. Jesus announced that He came to give His sheep an abundant life! (verse 10). But the sheep's abundant life would come through the death of the Shepherd: "I am the good shepherd; the good shepherd lays down His life for the sheep" (John 10:11). This is an emphatic "I am" statement of Jesus as *the* Good Shepherd, highlighting that He is the *Only One* who is able to provide for all that we need, and that he paid the high price with His blood for our abundance. May we be keenly aware of our need for the Shepherd: for His guidance, provision, healing, restoration, permanent love, and death, which gives us eternal life.

My Response: _____

---

* See information on this topic in my book: Elizabeth Talbot, *I Will Give You Rest* (Nampa, ID: Pacific Press®, 2015), 78.

HIS LEADING

The Lamb in the center of the throne will be their shepherd, and will guide them to springs of the water of life.

—Revelation 7:17

Public transportation was the main way we got around when I was a little girl. One evening, we thought we had boarded the right bus but soon realized that we were in an area that we didn't recognize, and it was getting dark. We got off the bus and found ourselves in a dangerous part of town. I had no idea where we were; all I could do was hang on to mom's hand and follow her lead. As we walked, we kept reciting Psalm 34:7. Finally, she led us to a residential area and found a way to get us home. I had fully expected her to lead us to safety. She was my mom!

Today we discuss a picture of Jesus that has brought comfort to countless people in distress. Those who have washed their robes and made them white in the blood of the Lamb, find themselves before the throne of God, who spreads His tent or tabernacle over them (Revelation 7:15). The Greek word for *tabernacle* is the same word that was used in the Greek Old Testament for the tent of meeting in the wilderness (see Exodus 26:13). All the evils that God's own suffered on this earth are no more. We are reminded of their blissful eternal existence: "They will hunger no longer, nor thirst anymore; nor will the sun beat down on them, nor any heat" (Revelation 7:16; compare with Isaiah 49:10 and 25:8). What follows is one of the most comforting pictures of Jesus: "For the Lamb in the center of the throne will be *their shepherd*, and will guide them to springs of the water of life; and God will wipe away every tear from their eyes" (Revelation 7:17). In a striking expansion of the role of the Lamb, the Lamb now becomes *their eternal Shepherd*! He has provided for their salvation, and He will supply whatever else they need forever and ever. He guides them to springs of water; He leads them to places of rest. Jesus Himself announced that He was the good Shepherd (John 10:11). In Revelation 7, the Lamb becomes the Shepherd for eternity! He provided for our salvation and will lead us to safety. If you find yourself in a difficult place today, just don't let go of His hand; He will lead you and restore your soul!

My Response: _____

HIS REPORT

"Go and report to John . . .: the lepers are cleansed . . . the dead are raised up, the poor have the gospel preached to them."

—Luke 7:22

As I write this devotional, there have been two mass shootings in the United States in the last two weeks. Many people lost their lives in these disastrous events. In the midst of personal and corporate tragedy, many may ask, "Where is God in all of this?" Sometimes the effect of unbearable and unexplainable pain in our lives may translate into doubts in our minds and darkness in our hearts. What answer does Jesus provide for us in moments like these?

Jesus had been healing the sick, raising the dead, and proclaiming the good news. And John the Baptist, who had devoted his public ministry to proclaiming the arrival of the *Expected* One, is now sitting in his dark and smelly cell, alone and in pain. He has a question for Jesus: "Are You the Expected One, or do we look for someone else?" (Luke 7:19). Wow! Obviously, John was struggling with his own *expectations* about the Coming One, unlike the way in which Jesus was carrying out His ministry. Perhaps the same is happening to you today, and you are wondering about Jesus and His intervention in your life: "Are You the Expected One, or do we look for someone else?" (verse 20). The emphasis on "the Expected One," or "the Coming One" is repeated in both verses (verses 19, 20). Drawing from several verses in Isaiah, especially Isaiah 61:1, Jesus answered by sending John a report about His salvific activity: the blind received sight, the lame walked, the dead were being raised, and the *gospel* was being preached to the poor. All of these were proofs, enacted parables of His redemptive purposes. That was the report to be given to John; that was the evidence of who Jesus was and is. Even though all of us can witness about God's miraculous intervention in our lives, we often aren't able to explain pain, tragedy, and the reason why God allows certain things. During those times, let's cleave to the core evidence that God has provided through Jesus: His salvific deeds in the plan of redemption. Someday we will understand all things. Until then, let's cling to the cross and trust.

My Response: _____

HIS SILENCE

"The kingdom of heaven suffers violence
and violent men take it by force."

—Matthew 11:12

A s a child, I listened to the Mission Spotlight stories, and it seemed that God's children never had to experience pain, because their houses were always shielded from disasters, and their lives were protected from violent attacks. But as I grew older, life challenged that concept. In the second half of his book about John the Baptist,* Gene Edwards imagines John's agonizing thoughts in Herod's dark prison, as he realizes that Jesus is not coming to deliver *him*, even though He has the power to do so. He ponders the paradox of Jesus helping many, but not *all*.

There is often a temptation to ignore the painful biblical accounts in which God seems to be silent. John the Baptist wrestled with a God who wasn't meeting his expectations. You can read his questions and the tribute Jesus gave to him, in Matthew 11:1–15. We could accept his doubts as trials, but it gets harder when we are faced with John's senseless beheading (narrated in Matthew 14:1–12 and Mark 6:14–29). We are told that when Herod heard of Jesus, he thought that He was John the Baptist risen from the dead (Mark 6:16), because Herod had a remorseful conscience. That's when we find out that, having been incarcerated for denouncing Herod for taking his brother's wife, John was killed in the mindless craze of out-of-control entertainment at a royal banquet (Mark 6:17–29). Herod is so taken by the dance of Herodias's daughter, that he promises the girl up to half of the kingdom (verse 23). Prompted by her evil mother, she asks for the head of John the Baptist (verses 24, 25). Even though Herod is grieved by the request, he grants it because of his oath; his pride and his reputation are at stake before his guests (verse 26). They bring John's head on a platter (verse 28). Wicked people ended the life of God's highly esteemed prophet, yet God was silent. In His sovereignty, God often did not prevent the death of His prophets and martyrs, and He definitely did not stop the death of His Son on our behalf. When we don't understand the silences of God, we are invited to trust His plans, His viewpoint, His wisdom, and, overall, His love.

My Response: _____

---

* Gene Edwards, *The Prisoner in the Third Cell* (Auburn, ME: The Seedsowers, 1991).

HIS IMPERATIVE

*"Get behind Me, Satan! . . . for you are not setting your mind
on God's interests, but man's."*
—Matthew 16:23

In one class of my master's degree in organizational behavior, I was reproved by a substitute professor, and it changed my life. We were studying Kohlberg's Moral Developmental Model, and she challenged me because of a comment I made. I realized that she was right, and that my view of God needed realignment. This reprimand was a pivotal moment for me, and it provoked a reassessment of my understanding of God's will for humankind.

Peter had just made a ground-breaking confession about Jesus being the Son of God (Matthew 16:16), and Jesus said that this understanding was given to Peter by His Father in heaven. Only a few verses later, things had changed dramatically. Jesus was revealing that it was imperative for Him to go to Jerusalem, suffer many things, be killed, and be raised on the third day (verse 21). "That He must go . . ." (verse 21) uses the Greek verb *dei* which means that "it is necessary." Jesus *had* to go through this (see also Luke 24:26). The suffering of Jesus was an absolute necessity in order to achieve His redemptive plan. Peter cannot reconcile this perspective with his preconceived ideas of what the Messiah was to achieve. Taking Jesus aside, he "began to rebuke Him, saying 'God forbid it, Lord! This shall never happen to You' " (Matthew 16:22). Using a double negative (translated as *never*), Peter tries to impress upon Jesus that this is *not* the way. In doing so, Peter has taken Satan's position, trying to divert Jesus from the cross (see Matthew 4:1–11). Jesus recognizes the intention of the enemy and utters a stern reprimand: "Get behind Me, Satan!" (Matthew 16:23; see Matthew 4:10); and goes on to explain that Peter's mind is not set on the things of God but on the things of humans (verse 23). At that moment, Peter had become a stumbling block for the redemptive act of Jesus. In our spiritual walk, we must also surrender to God's interests instead of ours. God is more interested in our salvation than in our comfort. Let's trust God's viewpoint of what is necessary in our lives for His redemptive purposes.

My Response: _____

HIS IMMUTABILITY

Jesus said to them, "Truly, truly, I say to you, before Abraham was born, I am."

—John 8:58

There are days that feel completely out of control. I remember one such day when I was a child and we lived in Buenos Aires. One morning there was a fire at the Church Publishing House, and my dad rushed to help. After a few hours, he came back, showered and left for the office. He returned an hour later and told us that he had been held at gunpoint, his car was stolen, and he had been kidnapped. Later the robbers dropped him off in a remote place, and he walked home.

Much more happened that day, yet even on days like that, God is still on His throne and our salvation is still assured. He is eternal, constant, unchangeable, and in complete control. He does not get bogged down by the things that overwhelm us, nor is He fearful, neither is He rushed nor late. He has been there from eternity and will be there for eternity. The immutability of God is our security and anchor in times of distress; and His love for us is our guarantee. You might not be battling a fire or being held at gunpoint, but you might be battling cancer or find yourself in an oppressive situation. During these difficult seasons in our lives, we find comfort in focusing on who God is, what He has done for us, and how His Presence is always with us. The eternal God of the mountaintop is also the God of the valleys. The Gospel of John starts by stating Jesus' eternal preexistence: "In the beginning was the Word, and the Word was with God, and the Word was God" (John 1:1). Later, in a controversy with the Jews, Jesus Himself asserted His preexistence: "Before Abraham was born, I am" (John 8:58). He didn't say "I was" but "I am," which echoes the powerful name of God's immutability and sovereignty as revealed to Moses in Exodus 3:14: "I AM WHO I AM." Be assured that the eternal and unchangeable God of the universe is also your Redeemer and Deliverer. He guides us through the valley of the shadow of death; and He secured our eternal life on the cross. "For this God is our God for ever and ever; he will be our guide even to the end" (Psalm 48:14, NIV). Amen!

My Response: _____

HIS STRATEGY

After being warned by God in a dream, he left for the regions of Galilee,
and came and lived in a city called Nazareth.

—Matthew 2:22, 23

Have you ever had an experience of finding something wonderful at an unexpected and despised place? Featured in countless magazines and on TV shows, the story of the Paraguayan orchestra of Cateura has warmed my heart. Amidst mountains of trash, the children living in the now-famous Cateura slum could have never imagined that one day they would become internationally known musicians. Someone had the amazing idea of creating instruments out of trash and the unlikely orchestra was born, which has now performed all over the world.*

There are five fascinating infancy narratives in Matthew, each one built around an Old Testament prophecy. This is quite important for Matthew, who points out that Jesus fulfills the Old Testament Messianic prophecies. By the way, this is the core reason why the Old Testament is so important to us: it contains the DNA of Jesus, giving us information about the appointed Deliverer who would come. The last of the infancy narratives, found in Matthew 2:19–23, is puzzling and unexpected. God communicates with Joseph through two dreams, the first of which starts with a divine command to leave Egypt and go into the land of Israel "for those who sought the Child's life are dead" (verse 20, compare with Exodus 4:19). After being warned in a second dream not to go to Judea due to the reign of Archelaus (Herod's son), Joseph took his family to Galilee, to the city of Nazareth. This was a small, obscure town, with a bad reputation, which becomes obvious from Nathanael's comment when introduced to Jesus of Nazareth in John 1:45, 46: "Can any good thing come out of Nazareth?" Nazareth is not mentioned in the Old Testament at all. It was a small town, estimated to have had less than five hundred inhabitants in the first century A.D. Why would God choose such a town for Jesus, the Galilean Messiah? Well, God is an *expert* in creating beauty out of ashes and deliverance in unexpected places. When someone hints that God may not be able to use you and your circumstances for His glory, remember Nazareth.

My Response: _____

---

* For information, go to www.landfillharmonicmovie.com.

HIS PROPHECY

"This is the Moses who said to the sons of Israel,
'God will raise up for you a prophet like me.' "

—Acts 7:37

While preaching at a camp meeting, I experienced a great blessing through a gospel quartet. They gave me one of their CDs, which contained a song entitled "Bible Story."* The main line of the song has stayed with me until now: "He will make a Bible story out of you!" Yes! Out of you and me. The biblical characters were flawed, yet God used them throughout redemption history as His spokespeople and leaders. Of course, He is able to *make a Bible story out of you too*!

Before he was killed, Stephen, the first Christian martyr, preached a sermon mentioning many people who had become "Bible stories": Abraham, Jacob, Joseph, Moses, Joshua, David, and Solomon (Acts 7). We could have many devotionals just from this sermon. It is fascinating! False witnesses had charged Stephen with altering the customs handed down by Moses (Acts 6:14). Now, in his last discourse, Stephen detailed the story of Moses at length (7:20–39), including Moses murdering an Egyptian and having to flee, becoming an alien in Midian, and spending forty years in the wilderness before the Lord called him to finally deliver Israel from Egypt. Moses had tried to liberate Israel in his *own* way: "And he supposed that his brethren understood that God was granting them deliverance through him, but they did not understand" (verse 25). He was educated in the Egyptian culture, became a murderer and a fugitive, and *still* God made a Bible story out of him! "This Moses whom they disowned . . . is the one whom God sent to be both a ruler and a deliverer" (verse 35). He became a symbol of the upcoming Deliverer of the world, and God used him to utter one of the most significant prophecies about Jesus, found in Deuteronomy 18:15, which Stephen referred to: "The Lord your God will raise up for you a prophet like me from among you . . . you shall listen to him." Let God make you a powerful witness of Jesus, no matter how flawed your life has been or how many detours you've taken. In human history, there is only One character who is perfect: Jesus! And all the Bible stories point to Him!

My Response: _____

---

* Lyrics by Scott Kryppayne, "Bible Story," *It Goes Like This*, Spring Hill: 2003, compact disc.

HIS STIRRING

*"Do you understand what you are reading?" . . . "Well,
how could I, unless someone guides me?"*
—Acts 8:30, 31

A particular comment that the Jesus 101 ministry received from a Muslim man caught my attention: "The way I heard about you guys is a long story. I was having a girlfriend who was a Muslim just like me and from the same tribe too . . . she was convincing me about the Christian faith, and I was not listening to her, but now I decided to download this Jesus 101 app to learn and know more about Christianity." What exactly stirs a person's heart to seek to know Jesus?

God is personally involved in guiding people to the Savior. It is a divine initiative that creates divine appointments, reaching out to all types of groups, encouraging seekers to respond to the Spirit's promptings. God sent Peter to explain the gospel to Cornelius, who was a Gentile (Acts 10), and He sent Ananias to minister to Paul, a zealous Jew, who had encountered the risen Jesus on the way to Damascus (Acts 9). It is God's initiative to guide and send appointed guides to explain Jesus to a wide variety of people. Acts 8 is no exception. "An angel of the Lord spoke to Philip saying, 'Get up and go south to the road that descends from Jerusalem to Gaza' " (Acts 8:26). This was a desert road towards Gaza, one of five cities of the Philistines. It seemed an unlikely territory for evangelism. But God knew that someone needed guidance to accept Jesus. It was an Ethiopian man, a treasurer of Candace, queen of the Ethiopians (Nubia). *Kandake* was the title of the queen mother who performed secular activities for the king. This man was far away from home, but he had come to worship in Jerusalem. Was he a Gentile, a proselyte, or a Jew? Luke doesn't say much about him, other than the fact that he was a eunuch, which would have excluded him from the inner temple courts. Yet he wanted to know more and was reading Isaiah the prophet. God sent Philip to guide him in this process, and we will study their encounter tomorrow. In the meanwhile, may you be assured that it is God Himself who stirs human hearts to seek Him and to accept Jesus. And He takes the initiative to guide us in this process!

My Response: _____

HIS PROVIDENCE

Then Philip opened his mouth, and beginning from this
Scripture he preached Jesus to him.

—Acts 8:35

The person who picked me up from the airport at the European country where I had come to preach that weekend had been a supporter of our ministry for a few years and had arranged for this special event to take place. When I asked him how he found out about Jesus 101 in the first place, I was speechless! He told me how one day he was listening to an internet broadcast, when suddenly the programming was interrupted, and our program came on. He was about to turn it off, but lingered for a few seconds, got interested in the Scriptural topic, and the rest is history. I don't believe this was a coincidence but a providential event.

We often hear such testimonies about how people throughout the world discover our media ministry. I am convinced that God is always at work behind the scenes. Some call these events *coincidences*, but I believe otherwise. In Acts 8, the story is told of the Ethiopian man who was a court official of the queen of the Ethiopians (verse 37). He had gone to Jerusalem to worship and was on his way back, reading in his chariot from the prophet Isaiah. Suddenly, Philip ran up next to the chariot and asked him if he understood what he was reading (verse 30). He was reading Isaiah 53! This chapter is called the "proto-gospel," because it is the prophecy about the suffering Servant, explaining the death of Jesus on our behalf. The man needed someone to explain this prophecy, and Philip, filled with the Spirit, was right there, ready to preach Jesus to him from this very Scripture (verses 30–35). The Ethiopian official could have called Philip's presence a *coincidence*, but we know better; because in the first four verses of the story we are told how God, in His providence, had orchestrated this meeting. Philip was given divine direction to take this particular road (verse 26), and to go up to this specific chariot (verse 29). God is always providentially guiding our lives, and He desires our ultimate redemption. If you truly desire to do God's will, you can be assured that He will providentially and clearly provide the guidance you need.

My Response: _____

HIS CALLING

"Go, for he is a chosen instrument of Mine, to bear My name before the Gentiles and kings and the sons of Israel."

—Acts 9:15

The way God guides us in our life purpose is as real as it is enigmatic. God doesn't give us the whole map, but instead guides us one step at a time. Consider the way God guided the prophet Elijah (see 1 Kings 17). First, Elijah told the king that it wouldn't rain for a few years; then God guided him to the brook Cherith, where he could drink and was fed by ravens. Then the brook dried up, and God sent him to the house of a widow in Sidon, outside of Israel's territory; then . . . Well, you get the picture. Elijah received instructions one step at a time.

When the risen Jesus met Saul on the way to Damascus, He gave him instructions only for the next step: "Get up and enter the city, and it will be told you what you must do" (Acts 9:6). Jesus didn't show him a map of the next ten years; neither did He disclose all the epistles that he, as the apostle Paul, would write, or the churches he would visit. After his encounter with the risen Christ, Saul discovered that he couldn't see, so he was led to Damascus. In this story, God guided another man through a vision. His name was Ananias, and we don't know much about him (he is mentioned again in Acts 22:12). Ananias got instructions for the next step as well: "Get up and go to the street called Straight, and inquire at the house of Judas for a man from Tarsus named Saul, for he is praying, and he has seen in a vision a man named Ananias come in and lay hands on him" (Acts 9:11, 12). God sent two visions: one to Ananias, and another one to Saul. Ananias answered something like, *Are you sure? I've heard about this man . . . the harm he has done to your followers and the purpose of his visit to Damascus . . .* Then the Lord disclosed to Ananias that He had chosen Saul to bear His name to Gentiles, kings, and Israelites (verse 15). Ananias went to Saul, laying his hands on him and calling him, "brother Saul." And the rest is history, as Paul began to proclaim Jesus. The same God who designed the plan for your salvation, is the One who promises to guide you in your calling. And He will do it *one step at a time.*

My Response: _____

HIS OMNIPOTENCE

And behold, an angel of the Lord suddenly appeared and a light shone in the cell; and he struck Peter's side and woke him up, saying, "Get up quickly." And his chains fell off his hands.

—Acts 12:7

I was attending a graduate class in a business setting when the professor asked us to share some impactful experiences. One of my classmates simply said: "I saw my guardian angel." We all wanted to know more about it. She went on to tell us about a horrific car accident she was involved in, and how, having seen her bloody face in a mirror, she panicked. Then a man with a peaceful voice came to her window, calmed her down, and stayed with her until help arrived. When she inquired about the man who had helped her, no one had seen him.

When we find ourselves in situations that are completely out of our control, let's remember that God is omniscient and omnipotent. He knows what we don't know and will guide us according to His sovereign will. In His power and might, He is able to remove any obstacles if and when He sees fit. Peter experienced this firsthand in the book of Acts. The first disciple to be put to death was James, the brother of John (Acts 12:2). When Herod saw that this pleased the Jews, he arrested Peter as well (verse 3). He held him in prison with maximum security and precautions, assigning four quaternions (of four soldiers each) to guard him. The church was praying for Peter, and God, in His sovereignty, chose to intervene. "On the very night when Herod was about to bring him forward, Peter was sleeping between two soldiers, bound with two chains, and guards in front of the door were watching over the prison" (verse 6). I am astonished at the level of security, with soldiers, chains, and guards; and startled at the notion that Peter was sleeping under those circumstances. And just like that, an angel of the Lord came to the cell, light filled the place, he woke up Peter, the chains fell off, Peter got dressed, put on his sandals and cloak, they passed the first and second guards, and the iron gate opened by itself (verses 7–11). And Peter was free. God is omnipotent to save us and to deliver us from trials, according to His sovereign will. Let's trust Him!

My Response: _____

HIS WILL

*When Peter came to himself, he said, "Now I know for sure
that the Lord has sent forth His angel and rescued me
from the hand of Herod."*

—Acts 12:11

V isiting the Garden of Gethsemane was one of the most profound experiences of my life. As I walked among the olive trees, I remembered the Savior's prayer: "Father, if You are willing, remove this cup from Me; *yet not My will, but Yours be done*" (Luke 22:42). Being there, in the very place where Jesus surrendered to His Father's will in order to save me . . . well, it was more than I can describe in words. And God did answer Him, because He always does. Yet it was not His will to remove that cup, because there was no other way to save us.

When Peter was imprisoned by Herod, the church kept praying fervently for him (Acts 12:5). I would assume they had also prayed for James, but God, in His sovereign will, allowed James to become the first of the twelve disciples to taste martyrdom; yet He miraculously set Peter free. When the angel brought him out of the jail, Peter thought he was seeing a vision (verse 9); yet soon he found himself on the street and realized what had happened. He rushed to the house of Mary, the mother of John Mark, where many were gathered praying for him. He wanted to let the believers know that their prayer had been answered positively! When the servant-girl recognized Peter and ran in to announce that he was at the door, the skeptical response she received was: "You are out of your mind!" (verse 15). They were so surprised that God had answered their prayer that they couldn't believe it! *You are crazy!* they said. Peter explained how the Lord had delivered him (verse 17) and asked them to report it to others. Then Peter went away; we are not told where. His last appearance in the book of Acts is in chapter 15.

God always answers prayer, yet not always as we expect. Sometimes He says yes, no, no for now, yes for now, or wait. Prayer is not for us to twist God's arm, but it is the way we submit to His sovereign will. God will work *all* things for the good of those who love Him (Romans 8:28). Yes, *all* things, even the painful events in our lives, when His answer was not the one we were expecting.

My Response: _____

HIS PERMISSION

After they came to Mysia, they were trying to go into Bithynia,
and the Spirit of Jesus did not permit them.

—Acts 16:7

Years ago, I tried to start a group with the purpose of studying and sharing the gospel. Many people got together to talk about the plan, location of the meetings, et cetera. But things were not happening as expected. It truly felt as if we were forcing something that God was not approving. And it never took off. It's confusing when we want to do something good, to advance God's kingdom, and God seems to prevent it. It simply doesn't work out. Over the years, I have realized that just because something is good doesn't necessarily mean that it is God's will for that time, place, or set of circumstances.

Sometimes the Spirit of God guided Paul away from his plans, even preventing him from preaching the gospel in a particular area. In Acts 16, during his second missionary journey, Paul arrived to Derbe and Lystra. After going through the churches that had already been established in that area, "They passed through the Phrygian and Galatian region, *having been forbidden by the Holy Spirit to speak the word in Asia*" (verse 6). If you look at an ancient map, it looks reasonable that they would want to go west, towards Ephesus. But God prevented them. F. F. Bruce explains: "Paul's missionary journeys display an extraordinary combination of strategic planning and keen sensitiveness to the guidance of the Spirit of God, however that guidance was conveyed—by prophetic utterance, inward prompting, or the overruling of external circumstances."* Then they tried to go north, into Bithynia, "and the Spirit of Jesus *did not permit them*" (verse 7). Eventually, Paul received a vision to cross over into Macedonia (verses 9, 10). It is crucial to submit ourselves to God's guidance; and that even includes our good plans that seem so obvious to us. It is essential to remember that He is our Creator, Savior, and Lord. He knows where, when, and how the preaching of the gospel will be most effective. We can trust Him, who gave His life for the whole world, to open the doors for Jesus to be lifted up, that He may draw all people to Himself!

My Response: _____

---

* F. F. Bruce, *The Book of the Acts,* NICNT (Grand Rapids, MI: Eerdmans, 1988), 306.

HIS WISDOM

"Therefore having overlooked the times of ignorance, God is now declaring to men that all people everywhere should repent."
—Acts 17:30

The archeological sites of Athens are extraordinary. The Aeropagus Hill is of special significance to me because that's where Paul delivered his famous sermon, recorded in Acts 17:22–31. At the place from where it is believed Paul addressed the men of Athens with the good news of Jesus, there is a bronze plaque with the Greek text of Paul's sermon inscribed on it. More than two thousand years later, we continue to seek divine wisdom, as Paul did, to find a *point of contact* with diverse audiences throughout the world that do not know about Jesus Christ.

Athens was a cultural center, showcasing high levels of art, sculpture, literature, oratory, philosophy, et cetera that continue to influence our modern world. Renowned philosophers, such as Socrates and Plato, had shared their thoughts and ideas there. Yet this is not what caught Paul's attention when he got to Athens. "Now while Paul was waiting for them [Silas and Timothy] at Athens, his spirit was being provoked within him as *he was observing the city full of idols*" (Acts 17:16). It wasn't the masterpieces that stirred the soul of Paul. It was the idols and temples. He started proclaiming the gospel everywhere, to all who would listen: in the synagogue, at the marketplace, and dialoguing with the Epicurean and Stoic philosophers (verses 17, 18). Eventually they took him to the Areopagus, the center of religious and moral discussions, and Paul pro claimed the gospel there. Yet notice that he did not start with pointing out everything they were doing wrong! He started by calling them "very religious in all respects" (verse 22). He went on to say that he noticed the objects of their worship and the altar "To an Unknown God" (verse 23). The Greeks did not want to displease their gods by accidentally ignoring one they might not know about. In this Paul received wisdom from God, finding a *connection point* to proclaim Jesus to them as the unknown God. He even quoted their own poets! Let's ask God for wisdom to find a *point of contact* to share the grace of Jesus with our friends and loved ones who do not know Him.

My Response: _____

His Illumination

There was the true Light which, coming into the world, enlightens every man.

—John 1:9

As our tour bus was passing the opera house in Vienna, our guide told us the sad story of its two architects. Sicardsburg and van der Nüll designed this world-acclaimed landmark building of Vienna. However, their design fell under harsh criticism by both the press and the emperor. It is believed that the unkind comments led van der Nüll to commit suicide. Sicardsburg died about ten weeks later. Neither of them was alive when the opera house opened.

When we base our identity and purpose in life on people's opinions about us, we are bound to lose our way. There is only one true Light, Jesus Christ, who illumines our way and reminds us who we are. He is the source of life for all human beings: "In Him was life, and the life was the Light of men" (John 1:4). In Greek, as in English, both "life" and "Light" are preceded by a definite article: *the* life was *the* Light. Not just *a* light but *the* only true Light. *Life* is one of John's key themes, including the concepts of eternal life (John 3:16), and abundant life (John 10:10). He uses the word thirty-six times in his Gospel, more than any other New Testament book. In Christ was life; He is the Light that illumines our path. Jesus, as the Light, is available to the whole human race; "every man" (John 1:9) has the opportunity to accept the Light. Unfortunately, not everyone will. The world was made through Him, yet when He came, the world did not receive Him (verses 10, 11). "But . . ." Oh, how I thank God for this *but*! "*But* as many as received Him, to them He gave the right to become children of God." (verse 12). Yes! That is who we are. Children of God! And our identity and life purpose are found only in Him. When *who we are* is rooted in Christ, we are no longer guided by public opinion nor motivated by people-pleasing, or fear about the future. Jesus is our Light, who guides our steps to eternal life. He paid our price on the cross, and therefore, we can live with assurance and purpose, because in Him is life. Let the true Light guide your mind and your heart and illumine your path today!

My Response: _____

HIS REVITALIZATION

And when the doors were shut . . . for fear of the Jews,
Jesus came and stood in their midst and said to them,
"Peace be with you."

—John 20:19

I was astonished to see the high-water mark on the wall. In June 2013, in the beautiful German city of Passau, the flood waters reached the highest level in more than five hundred years. Due to the rising waters in the three rivers, the Danube, the Inn and the Ilz, this section of the old city, with its beautiful architecture and tourist attractions, was underwater up to the third floors of its buildings. It was a tragedy! Then I saw photos of the residents of the town coming together in order to rebuild their city. It was amazing! When I visited Passau in 2018, it was as beautiful as ever. How does God guide us in rebuilding our lives after tragic events?

The crucifixion of Jesus was the darkest moment for His disciples. From their perspective, the pounding of each nail and the eventual death of their beloved Master had totally crashed their dreams for the redemption of Israel. Yet from heaven's perspective, the exact same events were the ones that secured eternal salvation for all! Jesus had taken upon Himself the punishment of our sins, and He rose from the dead on the third day! In the evening, the disciples were gathered with doors shut for fear of the Jews. They didn't know how to begin to rebuild their shattered lives! What could possibly revitalize their minds and hearts for them to go on? That's when Jesus showed up and stood in their midst. His first words to them were: "Peace be with you" (John 20:19). After a tragic event, when God is rebuilding our lives, it is helpful to understand the way in which Jesus, after His death, revived the hearts of the disciples with His *presence*, His *peace*, His *revelation*, His *joy*, and His *purpose* (verses 19–21). He personally came and stood among them to reveal Himself in a new way and to speak peace. They rejoiced seeing Jesus in this new light, as He reminded them of His purpose for them: "As the Father has sent Me, I also send you" (verse 21). When tragedy strikes, we won't always understand, but God will guide us with His presence, peace, joy, and purpose; and He will always reveal Himself to us in a new and deeper way.

My Response: _____

HIS ADEQUACY

Jesus said to him, "I am the way, and the truth, and the life; no one comes to the Father but through Me."
—John 14:6

After a long day of travel, we arrived in Budapest to start a short river cruise vacation on the Danube river. As we were boarding the ship, my husband had an accident; he fell on a metal sheet and cut his hand very badly. It was obvious that he would need urgent care, but we didn't know where to go or what to do. The ship's personnel called a doctor. We waited until a young physician arrived. After examining his hand, she said that he would need stitches. Then she said: "Do not worry, I will do everything that is needed right here in your room." And she did! We were so thankful and relieved!

It is difficult when we don't understand what is going on, and when we don't know the way forward. When Jesus was talking about going away to prepare a place for His followers and coming back for them, His disciples didn't really understand and one of them asked Him a question: "Thomas said to Him, 'Lord, we do not know where You are going, *how do we know the way*?' " (John 14:5). This is a question that reverberates through the hallways of human history. Have you ever asked this important question: *How do we know the way?* Whether we need guidance for eternal salvation or are searching for the next step in our spiritual life, the response of Jesus applies to all of us. "Jesus said to him, 'I am the way, and the truth, and the life; no one comes to the Father but through Me' " (verse 6). Jesus said that He is everything! He is the way forward; He is the only path that leads to heaven. He embodies the truth of the gospel, the self-revelation of God Himself; He is our life and He is more than adequate to meet all of our needs, for He not only shows us the way, but He is the Way! He is all that we need. We can trust in His sufficiency! In the words of the Budapest doctor: *Do not worry, I will supply everything that is needed!* Like Thomas, sometimes we feel completely lost and without answers. Jesus calls us to follow Him, for He will take us safely to our heavenly home. He not only knows the way, but He is the Way! Trust the Way!

My Response: _____

HIS HELPER

*"I will ask the Father, and He will give you another Helper,
that He may be with you forever. . . . I will not
leave you as orphans."*

—John 14:16, 18

I am sure it was providential. In my own morning devotionals this week, I kept bumping into the story of the spies who went to survey the Promised Land that God had already promised to them (Numbers 13; 14). Their report highlighted the size of the giants; not the power of God. Only Joshua and Caleb, who had a "different spirit" (Numbers 14:24), kept trying to bring the congregation to choose faith over fear. But the people chose to focus on the giants instead. I say this was providential because one of my relatives received a not-so-good report from their doctor. And we have a choice: to focus on the giants or on the power of God to guide us through this.

When we face giants in our lives, it is imperative to remember who we are in Christ: we are children of the living God, bought with the blood of Jesus, heirs of an eternal inheritance with Him. We are not *orphans*; we are not on our own, facing insurmountable obstacles. We are His, and Jesus promised: "I will not leave you as orphans" (John 14:18). The One who has purchased our eternal salvation, has also made Himself responsible for us. He has provided unlimited resources for His beloved children on earth. Wouldn't you do the same if your children needed help? Jesus promised that the Father would send "the Spirit of truth" (verse 17). This member of the Trinity comes to guide us to all truth, and the core Truth is Jesus, whom He comes to glorify and explain (see John 16:13, 14). He is called, *Helper* (John 14:16). The Greek word here is *paraklētos*, which in English may be translated as Comforter, Encourager, Advocate, or One who comes alongside to help. Jesus Himself is called *paraklētos* as well (1 John 2:1). God has sent divine Helpers: Jesus as the Savior and the Spirit as the Comforter. We are *not* alone. The giants of sin and death have already been conquered by Jesus on the cross. And He has made every provision to empower and comfort His children on earth, no matter what they are facing. Our God is much greater than the giants we face, therefore let's not focus on the size of the giants but on the power of our God.

My Response: _____

HIS PURSUIT

Nicodemus, who had first come to Him by night, also came, bringing a mixture of myrrh and aloes.

—John 19:39

C. S. Lewis describes his surrender to God's incessant pursuit: "You must picture me alone in that room at Magdalen, night after night, feeling, whenever my mind lifted even for a second from my work, the steady, unrelenting approach of Him whom I so earnestly desired not to meet. That which I greatly feared had at last come upon me. In the Trinity Term of 1929 I gave in, and admitted that God was God, and knelt and prayed: perhaps, that night, the most dejected and reluctant convert in all England."* Within two years he became a Christian. God doesn't give up on us, or on our loved ones, even when there isn't any evidence that we are accepting His efforts to reach us. Unrelenting in His pursuit, He guides our souls.

The name of Nicodemus is found in three accounts in the Bible, all in the Gospel of John. First, Nicodemus sought to meet Jesus by night (John 3:1–21), and even though he didn't publicly acknowledge Him, the seed of the gospel had been placed in his heart. The second is found in John 7:50, when Nicodemus, a ruler of the Jews, dissuaded the Pharisees from apprehending Jesus. The third and last account is found in John 19:39, when Nicodemus brought spices for the burial of Jesus. Three years had gone by, and the gospel seed finally showed its fruit. This was the process: "Too proud openly to acknowledge himself in sympathy with the Galilean Teacher, he [Nicodemus] had sought a secret interview. In this interview Jesus had unfolded to him the plan of salvation and His mission to the world, yet still Nicodemus had hesitated. He hid the truth in his heart, and for three years there was little apparent fruit . . . he had in the Sanhedrin council repeatedly thwarted the schemes of the priests to destroy Him. When at last Christ had been lifted up on the cross, Nicodemus remembered the words that He had spoken to him in the night interview on the Mount of Olives, 'As Moses lifted up the serpent in the wilderness, even so must the Son of man be lifted up' (John 3:14); and he saw in Jesus the world's Redeemer."† Praise God! He does not give up on us!

My Response: _____

---

* C. S. Lewis, *Surprised by Joy* (New York: HarperCollins, 1955), 266.
† Ellen G. White, *The Acts of the Apostles* (Mountain View, CA: Pacific Press®, 1911), 104.

HIS TIMETABLE

*"For the resurrection of the dead I am on
trial before you today."*

—Acts 24:21

I was delighted to receive a call to ministry. For the previous fifteen years I had been working in the business world and was now considering leaving it all behind in order to enter ministry. But the call was to a part-time position, with only a possibility of a full-time position in the future. Was I supposed to leave my career, my full salary, and my seniority for a part-time job with no guarantees? Well, when we are certain that God is guiding us, we need to surrender to His timetable. I took the position and waited. . . . A few months later, I became a full-time minister.

When we read about Paul's powerful testimony in the book of Acts, we see an intrepid preacher, boldly proclaiming the gospel. He did this over and over again, explaining the prophecies about Jesus, His death, and His resurrection. In Caesarea, Paul witnessed in front of Governor Felix (Acts 24:10–21). Felix did not find anything in Paul worthy of death, and, "he gave orders to the centurion for him [Paul] to be kept in custody and yet have some freedom." (verse 23). But as time passed by, every now and then Felix would call Paul, "and heard him speak about faith in Christ Jesus" (verse 24). Can you imagine Paul's thoughts? *When will God let me get out of here? I am testifying about Jesus! I want to go to other cities!* Yet more time went by. And Felix had some ulterior motives too: "At the same time too, he [Felix] was hoping that money would be given him by Paul; therefore he also used to send for him quite often and converse with him" (verse 26). Well, that's great. But for how long? What was God's timetable for this gospel preacher? Now, the startling part: "*After two years had passed,* Felix was succeeded by Porcius Festus, and wishing to do the Jews a favor, Felix left Paul imprisoned" (verse 27). Excuse me? Two more years? Why did God allow that? Well, Paul would get the privilege of testifying about Jesus to Festus, to King Agrippa II, and his sister Bernice (Acts 25; 26), before heading to Rome. God's schedule is definitely not ours. We can trust that the One who died to save us, will also guide us to the places, and the timing, that best serve His salvific purposes.

My Response: _____

HIS PATTERN

*So that you may know the exact truth about
the things you have been taught.*

—Luke 1:4

One of my relatives needed an orthopedic doctor urgently, and someone suggested a specialist who had made an impact on her because of his excellent skills and Christian witness. The artwork on the walls of his office was all about grace and salvation by faith. When the doctor was done with the examination, he handed us a little card and asked that we read the text aloud. "If you confess with your mouth Jesus as Lord and believe in your heart that God raised Him from the dead, you will be saved" (Romans 10:9). I was amazed at his passion to share Jesus!

This is God's pattern of sharing the gospel with the world: each person sharing Jesus and His grace in their place of employment, study, or in their social circles. Luke is a case in point. As far as we can tell, Luke was a physician (see Colossians 4:14), and at some point, he became enamored with salvation through Jesus. He started traveling with Paul (see Acts 16:10) and became one of his closest companions (Philemon 24). And this doctor, who had a keen interest in the historical events in the life of Jesus and His followers, ended up writing the most words in the New Testament, included in his two books (the Gospel of Luke and Acts). Luke had an amazing command of the Greek language and put it to good use in writing about Jesus. Showcasing great cultural sensitivity, Luke wrote about the way and inclusivity of salvation, utilizing radical parables of grace, such as the prodigal son, and the Pharisee and the publican (Luke 15; 18), not found in any other Gospel. His interest in investigating eyewitnesses' reports about Jesus is evident from the start (see Luke 1:1–4). "It seemed fitting for me as well, having investigated everything carefully from the beginning, to write it out for you in consecutive order, most excellent Theophilus; *so that you may know the exact truth about the things you have been taught*" (Luke 1:3, 4). Let's ask God to guide us in using our skills and talents to share salvation by faith in Jesus, right now, wherever we are; becoming part of the "chain of witnesses" in the history of salvation!

My Response: _____

HIS RESOURCES

"Where are we to buy bread, so that these may eat?"
This He was saying to test him, for He Himself
knew what He was intending to do.

—John 6:5, 6

I was a youth leader for several years. Two or three times a year, I organized trips for our group; approximately thirty of us would travel together in large vans. I used to scout the complete trip ahead of time, taking photos, finding restrooms and markets to buy ice and water, planning the food for the whole group, et cetera. Well, you get the picture. I was the girl with the map and calculator in hand, planning every detail to make sure everything was under control. As the years went by, I realized that in life I would need much more than calculators.

Philip is the pragmatic disciple, who makes the comments that I would have made. He seems to worry about details, wanting to make sure there are no surprises. One time, Jesus was encouraging His disciples, telling them not to worry, that He would come back for them and that they were to believe in Him (John 14:1–3). Philip answered: "Lord, show us the Father, and it is enough for us" (verse 8). *Jesus, I want to see for myself, then I will be OK.* I can totally relate!

But Jesus wanted Philip to realize that maps and calculators are not enough to navigate life nor to assure us of our salvation. Once a great crowd followed Jesus and He found a perfect opportunity to demonstrate this. John writes that Jesus asked Philip, "Where are we to buy bread, so that these may eat?" (John 6:5). This was only a test, because Jesus already had in mind the miracle of the feeding (verse 6). This is the moment when Philip is supposed to respond: *Lord, You know, but I don't.* Instead, he pulls out his calculator and gives Jesus a financial report: "Two hundred denarii worth of bread is not sufficient for them, for everyone to receive a little" (verse 7). We, like Philip, need to learn to focus on Jesus and trust in His plan, instead of our skills and solutions. He who accomplished salvation for us, that which was impossible for us to do, also has ample resources to meet all the challenges that we could possibly face in life. And just as with the miraculous feeding, He always has a plan. Let's trust Him and His guidance!

My Response: _____

HIS REMAKING

*"Reach here with your finger, and see My hands;
and reach here your hand and put it into My side;
and do not be unbelieving, but believing."*

—John 20:27

I n her book* about letting God bring His newness into our lives after we have experienced a bitter disappointment, Lysa TerKeurst offers insightful phrases to remember, such as: "If I want His promises, I have to trust His process;" "God isn't ever going to forsake you, but He will go to great lengths to remake you;" and one of my favorites: *"What if disappointment is really the exact appointment your soul needs to radically encounter God?"**

Thomas was utterly disappointed. His expectations about Jesus and the upcoming kingdom had been completely shattered, and he refused to believe, even when the other disciples were telling him that they had seen the risen Jesus! His devastation was clear: "Unless I see in His hands the imprint of the nails, and put my finger into the place of the nails, and put my hand into His side, I will not believe" (John 20:25). When we find ourselves at the end of our rope, God offers to remake us, bringing newness out of the dust. We live in a sinful world that is sure to disappoint us, either through a discouraging medical diagnosis, the death of a loved one, unexpected spousal infidelity, et cetera. That's when God does His miraculous work by not only guiding us through the painful process, but also remaking us and bringing newness to our battered souls. That's what happened to Thomas: Jesus revealed Himself to him in a new way (verse 27), and Thomas responded with the most profound confession about the divinity of Jesus found in the Gospels: "Thomas . . . said to Him, 'My Lord and my God!' " (verse 28). Later, Thomas was part of the group of disciples that saw the risen Lord at the Sea of Galilee (John 21:1, 2) and witnessed a miraculous catch. And I am excited to tell you that Thomas is mentioned among the disciples who gathered in the upper room (Acts 1:13), as the newly formed Christian community was about to start its public ministry with the baptism of the Holy Spirit! Yes, God is an expert at revealing His radical grace to us in moments of bitter disappointment.

My Response: _____

---

* Lysa TerKeurst, *It's Not Supposed to Be This Way* (Nashville, TN: Nelson Books, 2018), loc. 767, 777, Kindle.

HIS AID

And yet Elijah was sent to none of them
[many widows in Israel], but only to Zarephath,
in the land of Sidon, to a woman who was a widow.

—Luke 4:26

Mount Carmel was a very impressive site. There is an imposing statue of Elijah triumphantly raising a sword after his showdown with the prophets of Baal. God had sent fire from heaven in response to His servant. And this is the way we like to see God's prophets: strong, victorious, and assured. But what about when they became weak, discouraged, and depressed? Did God still guide them then?

Jesus mentioned Elijah in His Sabbath-morning sermon in Nazareth: "There were many widows in Israel in the days of Elijah, when the sky was shut up for three years and six months . . . and yet Elijah *was sent* to none of them, but only to Zarephath, in the land of Sidon, to a woman who was a widow" (Luke 4:25, 26). Giving an example of the inclusivity of God's grace, Jesus pointed out that during this period of drought, God *sent* Elijah to the house of a widow in Sidon, outside of the land of Israel. It was in this house that the continuous miracle of the never-ending flour and oil occurred (1 Kings 17). Elijah even raised the widow's son from death! God first guided His prophet there and then back to Israel, where the final showdown occurred on Mount Carmel (1 Kings 18), and rain came upon the land. God always aided Elijah in everything, even giving him specific instructions where to go and what to do to represent Him to the people. Yet after God showed Himself strong against the prophets of Baal, Elijah became afraid of Jezebel, the evil queen. Exhausted, he became depressed and even suicidal (1 Kings 19:1–4). Yet God did not abandon him. He sent a heavenly messenger, who brought him food! Elijah slept, ate, and walked until he got to Horeb, where God revealed Himself to him in a still, small Voice. There was more for him to do, and God would be his Aid and his Guide, as He had always been. The God of the mountaintop is also the God of the valleys. His grace is sufficient for us, and in our weakness we're still in His grip. He is our Savior and, as He did on the cross, He comes to our aid at our lowest point, doing for us what we can't do for ourselves.

My Response: _____

HIS BENEFIT

The people on the island who had diseases
were coming to him.

—Acts 28:9

Having grown up outside of the United States, I didn't know the meaning of Murphy's Law. I learned later that it is the *principle* that whatever can go wrong, will go wrong and usually at the worst time. It is credited to Edward Murphy, Jr., who was an aerospace engineer, born in 1918, and who actually had a totally different meaning for it. He had originally stated the principle that you need to imagine the worst possible scenario in order to prevent it or prepare for it.

Today I want to tell you that our God is much more powerful than Murphy's Law, and that He can turn even a worst-case scenario into a blessing for His people and into honor for His name. Perhaps you, or someone you love, have been in a progression of calamities, thinking, "What else can go wrong?" If you are, please read Acts 27; 28. Paul started his sea journey to Rome with a violent storm that lasted many days. The wind took them away from their course, and they were shipwrecked, having to swim to land. Whew! At least he made it! Who cared if they were on the wrong island? At least they were alive! They ended up in Malta, and the natives of the island kindled a fire for the castaways (Acts 28:1). Paul, probably bruised and exhausted, started gathering sticks for the fire, and a snake bit him! Seriously? It must have been known as venomous because the people were expecting Paul to swell up and die. What else could possibly go wrong? Well, they thought that he must really be a bad person, because even though he survived the storm, now he was getting justice through the viper (verses 3–6). When he survived, they changed their minds and thought he was a god! (That's how volatile popular opinion is.) Yet God turned all these tragedies into blessings for the people of Malta through the presence of Paul, who stayed on the island for three months, performing many miracles of healing and surely sharing the gospel with them as well. Tragedies are not more powerful than God! He will turn difficulties into a spiritual benefit for your soul. That's what He did on the cross: when sin tragically ruined everything, He stepped in and bestowed His grace upon us!

My Response: _____

HIS FOREKNOWLEDGE

"From now on I am telling you before it comes to pass, so that when it does occur, you may believe that I am He."

—John 13:19

When it comes to guidance in a particularly difficult process, we look for the most knowledgeable and well-informed guides. For example, as my parents went through cancer treatments, we looked for experts in their specific fields: doctors who could give accurate diagnoses and prognoses. Even though no human being is omniscient, an informed forecast of the possible outcome and progress of the disease was of the utmost importance.

God has complete foreknowledge of the future. Furthermore, He has communicated to us the great events of redemption history ahead of time. In this way, God has revealed His sovereignty, and His preknowledge throughout the ages. This principle is explained in Isaiah 48:3–6. These verses make plain God's pattern of revealing major redemptive events *before* they happened, so that when He acted, His people would recognize that it was He who had acted. Jesus spoke in similar terms, and His foreknowledge was another *proof* of His divine identity and of His submission to a prior plan. Before these events happened, He spoke of His own sacrifice and the one who would betray Him (see John 13:18, 19). The purpose of this foretelling revelation was to help His disciples to believe in Him as the great "I am" (Greek *egō eimi*; verse 19), as they surveyed the events in retrospect. Barclay explains: "Jesus knew what was happening. He knew the cost and he was ready to pay it. He did not want the disciples to think that he was caught up in a blind web of circumstances from which he could not escape. He was not going to be killed; he was choosing to die. At the moment they did not, and could not, see that, but he wanted to be sure that a day would come when they would look back and remember and understand."* We can definitely entrust our circumstances, and our future, to the One who, with complete *foreknowledge*, chose to die for us. He knows our past, present, and future. He knows what is to come hereafter and has already revealed that He is coming back for us! Hallelujah!

My Response: _____

---

* William Barclay, *The Gospel of John*, vol. 2 (Philadelphia: Westminster Press, 1975), 143.

His Reclamation

"Go! For I will send you far away to the Gentiles."

—Acts 22:21

I like the term *reclamation*. It means to recover something that was considered waste in order to put it to a good use. Many of us, having made wrong choices or taken the wrong path, have gone through times of spiritual reclamation. God doesn't abandon us, even when we make wild decisions and take crazy detours. Furthermore, God can turn our mistakes into purpose and use our brokenness for His glory. And all of this is possible because, on the cross, Jesus paid for our transgressions and iniquities, and, in addition, he purchased the right to bless us with healing and peace (see Isaiah 53:5).

The Bible does not skip over the dark times of the heroes of faith. On the contrary, it gives detailed accounts of their failures, which is one of the pointers to the inspired truthfulness of the Bible, written not to boost the egos of men, but to highlight the power of God's love and grace. The conversion of the apostle Paul (previously Saul) is narrated three times in the book of Acts (Acts 9; 22; 26). In Acts 22 and 26, Luke records Paul's own words and testimony. What is amazing to me is that Paul never sugarcoats his own story. He doesn't hide his detours or his bloodthirsty religious practices. When he speaks in front of the Jews in Jerusalem, he really tells it like it was: "I persecuted this Way to the death, binding and putting both men and women into prisons. . . . And when the blood of . . . Stephen was being shed, I also was standing by approving, and watching out for the coats of those who were slaying him" (Acts 22:4, 20). Paul could have lived the rest of his life in seclusion and shame due to the atrocious things he had done. But God had reclaimed his life, providing a new purpose for him, and his previous life became part of his testimony about God's grace in his life. He now had a calling: to preach Jesus to the Gentiles! (verse 21). The gospel teaches us that the blood of Jesus paid for our sins and shame in full. Through His sacrifice, He provided salvation and a new life for us that has purpose and meaning. No need to hide! Go and tell of God's amazing grace and guidance in your life!

My Response: _____

BELIEVING HIS SALVATION

HIS SIGNAL

*"This is My blood of the covenant, which is poured out
for many for forgiveness of sins."*
—Matthew 26:28

I was working at a church when I received an unexpected request.
A synagogue was inviting their Christian neighbors to help serve
in their Passover celebration. Soon I learned that several members
of my church went every year to perform these duties and decided to
join them. It was a memorable experience for me. I discovered that the
festivities, when seen through Christian eyes, were truly pointing to the
Lamb of God, who was sacrificed for our redemption.

Jesus and His disciples were discussing how to prepare for the Passover (Matthew 26:17–19). This was a memorial of redemption established
when God delivered Israel out of slavery in Egypt. The symbolic meal is
explained in detail: "Go and take for yourselves lambs according to your
families, and slay the Passover lamb. You shall take a bunch of hyssop
and dip it in the blood which is in the basin, and apply some of the blood
that is in the basin to the lintel and the two doorposts; and none of you
shall go outside the door of his house until morning. For the LORD will
pass through to smite the Egyptians; and when He sees the blood on the
lintel and on the two doorposts, the LORD will pass over the door and will
not allow the destroyer to come in to your houses to smite you" (Exodus 12:21–23). The blood on the doorposts would be the signal to pass
over that house. In subsequent years, as the Passover was celebrated,
they were to recite the story, called the *Haggadah,* which contained many
symbols, including bread and cups. While eating, Jesus took bread and
modified the *Haggadah.* Instead of saying, "This is the bread of afflic-
tion," He said, "Take, eat; this is My body" (Matthew 26:26), and He took
the cup and said, "This is My blood of the covenant which is poured out
for many for forgiveness of sins" (verse 28). Jesus is our Passover Lamb,
who was sacrificed for our redemption (see 1 Corinthians 5:7). Unfortunately, many people live in fear of the judgment. Whenever we become
anxious about this topic, we should revisit the Passover story and ask
God to remind us that we are covered by Jesus' blood!

My Response: _____

HIS WASHING

"If I do not wash you, you have no part with Me."

—John 13:8

I was touched by a video clip as a sermon illustration about grace. Two young children start playing in the mud; at first, they have just a few stains on them, but eventually become covered with mud. At that moment, the camera captures their frowning father coming towards them. The children freeze, knowing that they are in trouble. But the father, with a hose in hand, starts washing the children with water. They all have a great time, and the children end up clean.

Washing guests' feet was the task of the servants, and it was done before a meal, as visitors came in from walking the dusty roads. At the last gathering of Jesus and His disciples, no one had performed that task. When the meal was on its way, Jesus got up to wash the disciples' feet. The timing of His action emphasizes the importance of what Jesus was about to teach them. When Jesus got to Peter, the disciple was more than embarrassed: "He came to Simon Peter. He said to Him, 'Lord, do *You* wash *my* feet?" (John 13:6). In the original Greek, the words *You* and *my* are next to each other, highlighting the paradox. Jesus responded: "What I do you do not realize now, but you will understand hereafter" (verse 7). In this explanation, Jesus revealed that He was not only performing the function of a servant, but that this was an enacted parable of salvation. There was a profound significance that they would only understand after His death and resurrection. He was truly submitting Himself as the Servant, in order for them to be cleansed from their sins. Peter objected: "Never shall You wash my feet" (verse 8). This is when Jesus confirms that this is a symbol of something deeper: "If I do not wash you, you have no part with Me" (verse 8). He was the only One who could wash him clean. Peter then said: "Lord, then wash not only my feet, but also my hands and my head" (verse 9). Both of Peter's responses are still used by people now, claiming that either what Jesus did for us is unnecessary, or that what He did is not enough. But Jesus has washed our sins away at the cross; and that was both necessary and sufficient!

My Response: _____

HIS SUFFICIENCY

The Lord turned and looked at Peter. And Peter remembered the
word of the Lord . . . "you will deny me three times."
—Luke 22:61

A couple of decades ago I used to belong to a vocal group called Opus 7, which was founded by a friend of mine, Dr. Ariel Quintana. One of the songs we sang and recorded kept repeating a phrase that is more than appropriate for today's topic: "His arms are *long enough* to save you . . . His heart is big enough to love you . . . His grace is more than sufficient." Is it really? Is His sacrifice sufficient for the worst of the worst among us? Murderers? Terrorists? Betrayers?

The juxtaposition of Peter and Judas has always caught my attention. The betrayals of Peter and Judas are narrated back-to-back, as in one breath (see Matthew 26:69–27:10; Luke 22:47–62). And yet, the end of each of their earthly stories is so different: Judas would hang himself, while Peter would become a powerful preacher of the gospel. When Judas saw that Jesus had been condemned, he felt remorse, returned the thirty pieces of silver, and exclaimed: "I have sinned by betraying innocent blood" (Matthew 27:4). Peter, when he remembered Jesus' prophecy about his own betrayal, "wept bitterly" (Matthew 26:75; Luke 22:62). Jesus extended grace to both of them, calling Judas "friend" (Matthew 26:50) and dealing tenderly with Peter (Luke 22:31–34, 61). Both Peter and Judas betrayed Jesus and both felt remorse; however, there was a huge difference between the two and where each of them ended up. The main difference between the two was that Peter chose to believe that God's grace was enough, and that Jesus' blood was sufficient to cover his sin; as far as we know, Judas did not. Do we believe that Jesus' sacrifice was sufficient for our sin? Yes, that sin that you are thinking about! Yes! His arms are *long enough* to reach us, and His blood is more than sufficient to cover us. Jesus has supplied more than a sufficient ransom for each human being, because the provision of forgiveness precedes repentance and draws the sinner to ask for what is already offered freely. Place your trust in His sufficiency and not in your insufficiency. When we accept His sacrifice, we know how our story ends.

My Response: _____

HIS INNOCENCE

Pilate said to them, "Take Him yourselves
and crucify Him, for I find no guilt in Him."

—John 19:6

The gospel is not about *fairness* but *grace*. The One who was not guilty was condemned to die, and all of us who are guilty have been gifted with eternal life. My friend Steve Trapero, who is a talented graphic designer, created for me a large poster entitled *The Great Exchange*. On one side of it, one can see two hands bringing a gift-wrapped box that has a skull on it, symbolizing death. On the other side, there are two nail-pierced hands bringing the gift of life: Romans 6:23 is written on that box. The poster portrays the exchange.

The apostle Paul often discusses the fact that Jesus, being innocent, was condemned as guilty, and that the guilty ones are considered righteous in His name. Such is the case in 2 Corinthians 5:21: "He made Him who knew no sin to be sin on our behalf, so that we might become the righteousness of God in Him." The four Gospels also allude to this paradox in the way the authors narrate the events surrounding the death of Jesus. For example, one of the thieves on the cross clearly states that they are guilty but Jesus is innocent: "We indeed are suffering justly, for we are receiving what we deserve for our deeds; but this man has done nothing wrong" (Luke 23:41). The Righteous One was condemned. Another such striking contrast is made when Pilate, according to their custom to release a prisoner at Passover, offers to release Jesus, but the crowd chooses Barabbas instead. Barabbas was a murderer and a rebel (see Luke 23:19; Mark 15:7). And what I find extremely insightful is that Barabbas means "son of Abba" or "son of the father." This "son of the father" was guilty and should have been condemned, and yet he was released. But the "Son of the Father," Jesus, who was innocent, was crucified instead. Three times Pilate clearly stated that he found no guilt in Jesus (John 18:38; 19:4, 6), yet Jesus died in the place of the guilty. If you know yourself guilty of condemnation, accept the paradox of the gospel and be set free. We have His eternal life, because He died our death. Thank you, Jesus!

My Response: _____

HIS HUMANITY

Jesus, knowing that all things had already been accomplished, to fulfill the Scripture, said, "I am thirsty."

—John 19:28

Twenty years ago, I was part of a group of ministers led by Dr. Kiemeney, who designed "CrossWords," a weekend evangelistic series for young adults. The series was repeated in more than one geographical area, and it invigorated young adult ministries in the local churches involved. I still remember the large banners announcing the event. The series was based on the seven sayings of Jesus on the cross. The tagline for CrossWords was: "A dying man's last words are revealing."

As He hung on the cross, Jesus knew that all Scripture was being fulfilled. Aside from the spiritual burden that He was carrying, which we can't fully understand, Jesus also felt physical pain. His dry mouth needing relief, He said: "I am thirsty" (John 19:28). Someone gave Him vinegar with a sponge. Even this very detail is fulfillment of prophecy, as recorded by the psalmist: "For my thirst they gave me vinegar to drink" (Psalm 69:21). John reports that the sponge was attached to a branch of hyssop, which I believe is a significant detail because at the time of the Exodus, the Israelites dipped twigs of hyssop in the blood of the Passover lamb to mark the lintels and doorposts of their houses (see Exodus 12:22). Jesus is now dying as the fulfillment of the Passover Lamb. At the time of the writing of John's Gospel, some early Christians became entangled in Gnosticism, which was a heretical teaching that Jesus was only a spirit without a real human body, and that He was human only in appearance and therefore couldn't experience physical suffering on the cross. John's report that Jesus was thirsty highlights that He was fully human, as well as fully God. We can trust Jesus to be compassionate with us because He became human. The author of Hebrews emphasizes that Jesus fully understands us: "For we do not have a high priest who cannot sympathize with our weaknesses, but One who has been tempted in all things as *we are*, yet without sin. Therefore let us draw near with confidence to the throne of grace, so that we may receive mercy and find grace to help in time of need" (Hebrews 4:15, 16).

My Response: _____

His Request

*Jesus was saying, "Father forgive them; for they
do not know what they are doing."*

—Luke 23:34

Most people recognize the name of Nelson Mandela, who was president of South Africa from 1994 to 1999 and received numerous honors, including the Nobel Peace Prize. The world was stunned when, having been imprisoned for twenty-seven years for his objections to apartheid, he emerged from his cell with words of reconciliation and forgiveness instead of revenge. Almost three decades of captivity and torture did not alter Mandela's focus on healing and peace.

The Word of God, who had created the world, had become flesh and had come to His own in order to redeem them (John 1:1–14). Now, hanging between two criminals, He was being crucified by those whom He had come to save (Luke 23:33–37). The persistence of Jesus in His redemptive mission, in the midst of such dire circumstances, stands in contrast to the mockery, torture, and humiliation that His opponents are exerting on Him. Practicing what He had taught His followers—to pray for the ones who mistreat us (see Luke 6:28), Jesus turned to God with a request: "Father, forgive them; for they do not know what they are doing" (Luke 23:34). That Jesus would call God "Father" as He was being crucified, portrays the intimate relationship that Jesus maintained with His Father until the very end. Jesus appealed to their ignorance, as He was becoming a guilt offering on their behalf (see Leviticus 5:17–19; Isaiah 53:10). Jesus had a burden for the eternal salvation of His adversaries, not for His own suffering. And He interceded not only for those who eagerly prosecuted and killed Him, but also down the centuries for you and me, offering forgiveness for our sins. Ellen White explains: "That prayer of Christ for His enemies embraced the world. It took in every sinner that had lived or should live, from the beginning of the world to the end of time. Upon all rests the guilt of crucifying the Son of God. To all, forgiveness is freely offered, 'Whosoever will' may have peace with God, and inherit eternal life."* And that, my friend, is the extremely good news of the gospel!

My Response: _____

---

* Ellen G. White, *The Desire of Ages* (Mountain View, CA: Pacific Press®, 1940), 736.

HIS INHERITANCE

"Jesus, remember me when You come in Your kingdom!"
—Luke 23:42

Have you ever seen a person suddenly become a millionaire? It is hard to explain the emotions that instant wealth brings to a person. I watched on TV as a woman won one million dollars and I witnessed the instantaneous flamboyant celebration that followed. Can you imagine the thoughts and feelings of a person who goes from poor to rich in a matter of seconds? But something even greater happened to the thief on the cross.

Just when we thought that the story of the prodigal son was only a parable (Luke 15:11–32), we find a real-life prodigal, an undeserving evildoer, who will request his share of the inheritance. He is being crucified next to Jesus, and Luke records his shocking request: *May I have part of the inheritance?* In other words: "Jesus, remember me when You come in Your kingdom!" (Luke 23:42). On what basis should Jesus remember *him* in His kingdom, and give *him* an inheritance? First of all, the criminal calls Christ by His name: *Jesus*. He did not call Him "Rabbi" or "Lord" like most people did during His ministry. He called Him "Jesus," a name that recalls that "Yahweh saves" (see Matthew 1:21). The second part of his request is, "remember me." In the Jewish Scripture this type of request was usually addressed to Yahweh. When the LORD *remembered* somebody, it was about acting on behalf of them within the framework of His covenant. (see Judges 16:28; 1 Samuel 1:11). This is about Jesus acting on his behalf. Thirdly, the sentence "when You come in Your kingdom," shows that this criminal had come to believe that the Crucifixion was not the end of Jesus; there was His kingdom beyond the cross. The charge against Jesus placed on the cross was a fulfillment of prophecy. But would Jesus even hear this *prodigal son's* shocking request for an inheritance? Jesus answered: "Truly to you I say today with Me you will be in paradise" (Luke 23:43, Greek-English Interlinear NT). On the spot, Jesus assured him of a heavenly inheritance, which at that moment He was securing for him. We can live with the same assurance of eternal life, which is our inheritance in Christ! (Hebrews 9:15).

My Response: _____

HIS QUALIFICATION

"Truly to you I say today with Me you will be in paradise."
—Luke 23:43*

A preacher was accompanying a celebrity on a trip to the Middle East. On arrival, the security was tight as the bodyguards surrounded the luminary. At one point the preacher had fallen behind and tried to rejoin the group. He explained to the guards that he was part of the group, but to no avail. Then, from a distance, the celebrity noticed that the preacher was missing and turned around, announcing in a loud voice, "He is *with me!*" Immediately the tight circle of security parted, and the preacher was able to walk in, just because he was *with him.*

The shocking response of Jesus to the thief on the cross applies to each one of us. The above rendition of Scripture reflects the original Greek word order. Let's notice four elements in our text: "today," "you will be," "paradise," and "with Me." In this devotional, we will look at the second and the fourth elements, while tomorrow we will address the first and the third. *You will be.* The assurance Jesus gives to the evildoer is in the second person singular and in the future tense, and it is a *sure* promise. It's not *you might be*, but *you will be.* This man was totally undeserving, yet there was a future for him. His presence with Jesus in His kingdom was not a *possibility* but a *reality.* This is the radical difference that separates the biblical gospel from a pseudo gospel. The false gospel offers the *possibility* of salvation; but the real gospel gives the *assurance.* Yet this man does not qualify! Why would he be there? That's where the other element comes in. *With Me.* In Greek, the weight of the content is in the middle of the sentence, and "with Me" is in that spot, at the very center. Jesus was saying to him, "You will be in Paradise *because* you are with Me. I am the One who qualifies! And you get in *with Me!*" If you know yourself unqualified for heaven, cling to this promise of Jesus to the thief on the cross. I like to imagine myself one day walking the streets of gold, and other people objecting to me being there. "What are you doing here?" they will wonder. Well . . . I can't wait for Jesus to turn around and in a sweet but thunderous voice announce, "She is with Me!"

My Response: _____

---

* J. D. Douglas, *The New Greek-English Interlinear New Testament*, 4th rev. ed. (Carol Stream, IL: Tyndale House, 1993).

HIS PROMPTNESS

"Quickly bring out the best robe and put it on him."

—Luke 15:22

Something that touches my heart, in the parable of the prodigal son and the loving father (Luke 15:11–32), is the immediacy with which the father covers the son's shamefulness. He doesn't say "I told you so," nor does he expect to hear a list of deeds the son plans to do to atone for himself. No! The father gives the order to act swiftly and immediately: "*Quickly* bring out the best robe and put in on him" (verse 22). Wouldn't you do the same for your wayward child?

Likewise, during His dialogue with the real-life prodigal (Luke 23:40–43), Jesus answers with the eagerness of a parent responding to a desperate child. But, unlike the father of the prodigal, Jesus couldn't run to meet the evildoer and embrace him; He could only speak to him because His hands and feet were nailed to the cross. This undeserving son had requested Jesus to remember him in His kingdom (Luke 23:42). In today's devotional, we will look at the two other words in Jesus' answer: "today," and "paradise." "Truly I say to you, *today* . . ." (verse 43). Jesus didn't want this man to wait until His Coming to find out what his fate would be. The evildoer could have the assurance of salvation *that day*, at that very instant. No anxiety or uncertainty; just assurance. Can you imagine that? In Luke, the word *today* highlights the immediacy of the assurance of salvation (see Luke 4:21; 19:9). Jesus was saying: "Quickly, bring out the robe of My righteousness and put it on him! Today!" And what was this immediate assurance about? ". . . *with Me* you will be in *paradise*" (verse 43).* Paradise! The place where God had created His children! The same place they had lost back in Genesis 3! This is the *only* instance that Jesus utters the word *paradise* (same Greek word as in Genesis 2 and 3 in the LXX). At this very moment, Jesus was opening up a way back home for His children. Neither He nor the thief would go to paradise that day, but the thief was given the ultimate assurance. Jesus was responding immediately, promising *paradise* to His undeserving son! If you utter the same prayer, making the request that the thief made, you will receive the same assurance. And you will receive it *today*!

My Response: _____

---

* J. D. Douglas, *New Greek-English Interlinear New Testament*, 4th rev. ed. (Carol Stream, IL: Tyndale House, 1993).

His Abandonment

"My God, My God, why have you forsaken me?"
—Matthew 27:46

Throughout my life, I was assured of the ever-present help of my parents. I was on a pastoral retreat, with other ministers, in one of the National Parks of the United States. Something went terribly wrong, and I experienced food or water poisoning that turned life-threatening within two hours. After the paramedics came to that beautiful and remote hotel, they told me that I had to remain there for a few days to regain my strength. Everyone in my group was leaving, and I would have to stay there alone. Within a few minutes, my parents had packed and were on their way to me and stayed with me until I was strong enough to travel. I never felt abandoned by them, not even in the darkest and most difficult circumstances.

As close as our human relationships may be, it is impossible for us to fully understand the intimacy that exists between Jesus and His Heavenly Father. This is why the crucifixion narrative, found in Matthew 27:46, in which Jesus asks *why* God had abandoned Him, seems such a mystery to us. About the ninth hour (3:00 P.M.), which was the time of the evening sacrifice, Jesus cried out the words recorded in Psalm 22:1. I am absolutely amazed that He who was called Immanuel (Matthew 1:23), "God with us," was now agonizing about *why* God had abandoned Him. The "El" in Immanu-*El*, is the same God as in "*Eli, Eli* . . . My God, My God" (Matthew 27:46). It is striking that Jesus had such a deep awareness of the loss of God's intimate presence in His hour of darkness, that He called Him "God" (the only time in Matthew), instead of "Father" as He regularly did. Furthermore, I am amazed that Jesus, in His time of utter distress and in the midst of His desolation, used the first-person possessive pronoun, "*my* God," still holding on to His trust in God as His God. Jesus was the Sin Bearer, the Representative and Substitute of the human race. He felt the abandonment of His Father as our sin was placed upon Him. If you ever wonder if God has forsaken you due to wrong choices and sin, remember that Jesus was abandoned in your place so that you may never be. God will never cast you out! He will never leave you, nor forsake you!

My Response: _____

HIS CULMINATION

He said, "It is finished!" And He bowed His head
and gave up His spirit.

—John 19:30

My dissertation supervisor, Professor Andrew Lincoln, was the president of the British New Testament Society and continues to be a prominent New Testament scholar. At his suggestion, I attended conferences in the United Kingdom and have distinct memories of different sessions and distinguished scholars that I met during those meetings. I particularly remember one plenary session because it ended in a most unusual way. The last slide of the PowerPoint presentation had one single word on the screen: *tetelestai*, which in Greek means "it is finished!" It was clear that the presentation had concluded.

Yet when it comes to our salvation, for some reason, we seem to be less sure about what this phrase means. John tells us that Jesus knew, at His dying moment, that all the things He had come to do were accomplished, His work on earth was finished, and His mission was fulfilled. The Greek word expressing completion is, you guessed it, *tetelestai*. Jesus was dying, "knowing that all things had already been accomplished [*tetelestai*]" (John 19:28). Jesus then uttered the loud cry that would pronounce His mission completed. It was not a victim's agonizing cry of pain; it was a Victor's shout of triumph: "It is finished!" (verse 30). And yes, in Greek it is that word: *tetelestai*. Jesus was announcing it to the whole universe: It is done! It is accomplished! It is finished! It is completed! In the mediating role that Jesus would fulfill in heaven, He would be presenting His shed blood on our behalf; His sacrifice, as our ransom, had been accomplished. "It is finished" contains the same root word as the one utilized in Genesis, when the creation was completed (see Genesis 2:2; LXX). There is nothing that we must add to complete our redemption. It is finished and perfect. No "and," "but," or "plus" to be added. We are saved by *His blood plus nothing*. The redemption of the human race was accomplished two thousand years ago. This is how Christians are to spell redemption: d-o-n-e. Oh my soul, rejoice! *Tetelestai!*

My Response: _____

His Resurrection

"He is not here, for He has risen, just as He said."
—Matthew 28:6

I t was the Easter weekend worship service and it was time for the children's story. Many children went up to the platform, and the children's pastor handed each of them a plastic Easter egg, but they were not to open it until she told them to. I was wondering what the lesson was about. When she gave the signal, all the children expectantly opened their eggs at the same time. I could see confusion and disappointment in their faces. "Are you surprised?" she asked and then added, "They are empty! And so was the tomb of Jesus!" I never forgot that visual aid.

When the two Marys came to the tomb, they were more than surprised! They must have been terrified, because the first thing the angel said to them was "Do not be afraid" (Matthew 28:5), and then he added "I know that you are looking for Jesus who has been crucified" (verse 5). "The One who was crucified" would forever become the identity of Jesus, yet the crucified One had risen from the dead! "He is not here, for He has risen" (verse 6). Amazing news! That the tomb was *empty* would become a core proclamation of the Christian church. Two elements are present in the explanation that follows: "He is not here, for He has risen, *just as He said.* Come, *see* the place where He was lying" (verse 6). First, Jesus had risen, as He had told them ahead of time; He had made specific predictions about His death and resurrection (Matthew 16:21; 17:23; 20:19; see also 26:32), but His disciples had not understood. Second, the angel invited the women to see the place where He had been lying, which is significant because these two women had been present when the body of Jesus was placed inside the tomb and the large stone was rolled against its entrance (Matthew 27:59–61). Following this, the angel commissions these women as the first proclaimers of the astonishing news of resurrection. They are to tell the disciples that He is risen and let them know that He will meet with them in Galilee (Matthew 28:7), *just as He said* ahead of time (see Matthew 26:32). Yes! Our God was wounded for our transgressions, dying for our sins. But He is now alive and is coming soon to take us with Him (Matthew 24:30, 31), *just as He said!*

My Response: _____

His Announcement

*"Go to My brethren and say to them, 'I ascend to My Father
and your Father, and My God and your God.' "*

—John 20:17

Visiting Magdala was one of the most impactful experiences of my life. We visited this ancient site, including the oldest excavated synagogue in Galilee. Aside from the archeological park, the location includes the Magdalena Institute, which was inspired by the encounter of Mary Magdalene with Jesus. One of the many objectives of the Institute is to support women who are seeking spiritual healing and renewal. This center of *applied archeology* made a profound impact on me.

Luke mentions that seven demons went out of Mary of Magdala, and that she became part of the group of women who were with Jesus (see Luke 8:1–3). The Gospels place her at the crucifixion scene. On resurrection morning, she came to the tomb, and when she saw that the stone had been rolled away, she went to get Peter and John (see John 20:1–18). She stood outside of the tomb weeping, as she had not heard the news of Jesus' resurrection. When asked about the reason for her weeping, she said, "Because they have taken away my Lord, and I do not know where they have laid Him" (verse 13). She wanted the body of her Lord to be appropriately taken care of! This was *her* Lord, who had healed and restored her! Through her tears she saw a man and, thinking He was the gardener, asked him about the location of the body. Then she heard Jesus calling her name: "Mary!" (verse 16). Can you imagine the tenderness of His voice and the joy of her heart?! She appears to have been the first person to see the risen Christ, perhaps because she needed Him most! Jesus commissioned her to take a message to His disciples, and that's why she has been called the apostle to the apostles. His announcement contains a reference to Him going to the Father and Jesus' personal identification with His disciples as His brothers: "I ascend to My Father and your Father, and My God and your God" (verse 17). Mary joyfully announced to them; "I have seen the Lord!" (verse 18). Jesus is always close to us, in all places and situations. In our grief, He reveals Himself to us as the risen Christ! And He knows each one of us by name!

My Response: _____

HIS WORDS

*And they remembered His Words, and returned from
the tomb and reported all these things.*

—Luke 24:8, 9

I still have my preaching notes for the eightieth anniversary of the Alhambra SDA Church in California. The title of the sermon was "Remember the Future." It is so important to reflect about how God has guided us in the past because that's where we find assurance for what is to come. When we look back at our own lives, we become aware of how God has been with us all along. And when it comes to our salvation, we find certainty for the future only when we look back to the Cross.

The women came to the tomb early on Sunday. The stone that covered the entrance of the tomb had been rolled away, and they did not find Jesus' body (Luke 24:1–3). They were bewildered, especially because they had seen, with their own eyes, how the body of Jesus was laid in the tomb (see Luke 23:55). As they were confused and perplexed, two angels came to them (Luke 24:4, 23) and announced that Jesus was alive! "Why do you seek the living One among the dead? He is not here, but He has risen. *Remember* how He spoke to you while He was still in Galilee, saying that the Son of Man must be delivered into the hands of sinful men, and be crucified, and the third day rise again" (verses 5–7). The angels told them that they should pause and look back to what Jesus had spoken to them (see Luke 9:22, 44), "and they [the women] *remembered* His words" (Luke 24:8). They recalled Jesus' prophecies about His own death and resurrection. The women went from perplexity to clarity by *remembering* Jesus' words. *Remembering* Christ's words is a heavenly remedy for anxiety and worry. The same Jesus who foretold His own death and resurrection, also prophesied His own victory (see Luke 21:27; 22:69). Whenever we become bewildered by circumstances that we don't understand, recalling Jesus' words brings insight and peace. If you ever become anxious about your salvation or the end of the world, *remember* His words on the cross to the thief who asked to be remembered in His kingdom: "You shall be with Me in Paradise" (Luke 23:43).

My Response: _____

His Appearance

He showed them both His hands and His side. The disciples then rejoiced when they saw the Lord.

—John 20:20

I keep a cherished photo on my iPhone. When my mom realized that the end of her life was approaching, she wanted to go buy her "final property," as she called it. So, my parents and I headed to the cemetery. They found a spot that they liked and purchased it. Both of them stood on their future tomb, and I took the photo that I now cherish. She passed away two weeks later. I can't imagine the joy that I will experience when I see them again, completely restored, with their cancer-free and glorified bodies.

I can't start to fathom the rejoicing of the disciples that day. Some of them had witnessed the crucifixion of Jesus. They saw His agony, the nails puncturing His hands and feet, and the spear piercing His side. On the evening of the resurrection day, Jesus miraculously appeared to His disciples. John observes that, on that occasion, the doors were shut for fear of the Jews. "Jesus came and stood in their midst and said to them, 'Peace *be* with you' " (John 20:19). Even though this is still a common Jewish greeting today, on that occasion it carried all the weight of Jesus' promise of His peace (see John 14:27). Which is quite remarkable, taking into consideration that they all had abandoned Him and were worthy of reproach and condemnation. Instead, Jesus greets them with His *peace*, and shows them His hands and His side. When they recognized Him, the disciples were flabbergasted, beside themselves with joy! Jesus had prophesied this moment: "Therefore you too have grief now; but I will see you again, and your heart will rejoice, and no one will take your joy away from you" (John 16:22). Now they were beholding their risen Lord, and no one could take their joy away! For a second time, Jesus pronounced His blessing of peace upon them and then commissioned them, giving them the Holy Spirit (see John 20:21, 22). Jesus was the Firstborn of the dead (Revelation 1:5), which guarantees that our loved ones, who died in Him, will rise too. On that day, our grief will be turned into indescribable joy!

My Response: _____

His Pronouncement

"Blessed are they who did not see, and yet believed."
—John 20:29

More than two decades ago, I was working in the business world. I was sharing Bible studies with a coworker when I realized how difficult it is for the human mind to believe that which can't be seen. We got to the study of the virgin birth of Jesus, and he said something like: "Really . . . who is going to believe that?" Spiritual things are spiritually discerned, which means that God has left quite a bit of room for faith: "the conviction of things not seen" (Hebrews 11:1).

When Jesus appeared to His disciples after the resurrection, Thomas wasn't present at that reunion (John 20:24). The other disciples were excited to tell him, "We have seen the Lord!" (verse 25), but Thomas was skeptical. He was a loyal but pessimistic disciple (see John 11:16; 14:5). To him, the cross was only what he had expected (John 11:16). Now he is demanding visual and kinesthetic proof (Luke 20:25); he will believe only when he can see and touch Jesus. No one in the entire New Testament makes a greater demand in order to believe. This is why Thomas became the epitome of unbelief. Sight, not faith! One of the great drawbacks of unbelief is that our joy is delayed! Thomas could have been rejoicing with the rest; but, because he refused to believe, he had to wait. Eight days later Jesus appears again and says to Thomas: "Reach here with your finger, and see My hands; and reach here your hand and put it into My side; and do not be unbelieving, but believing" (verse 27). Wow! Thomas must have been speechless for a while before he said, "My Lord and my God!" (verse 28). This is the most profound confession in all four Gospels; nobody had ever addressed Jesus like this. Thomas made a leap of faith and came to believe that Jesus was God (John 1:1). Jesus responded with His last beatitude: "Because you have seen Me, have you believed? Blessed are they who did not see, and yet believed" (Luke 20:29). Jesus pronounced a blessing upon us! Believing because of seeing would no longer be available; faith would be the only way because Jesus was ascending to heaven. Remember that God always leaves room for faith and blesses us when we believe!

My Response: _____

HIS NECESSITY

"Was it not necessary for the Christ to suffer these things and to enter into His glory?"

—Luke 24:26

We don't always need what we think we do, and we often do need what we think we don't. I have watched children try to talk their parents into buying toys and candy. You have probably heard a child say: "Daddy, I *need* this!" Of course, we smile at such a statement, but I wonder how often we sound exactly like that to God. I believe that when David penned Psalm 23:1, "The LORD is my shepherd, I shall not *want*," it wasn't that he didn't *want* or wish for anything, but that he had come to believe that God would provide whatever he actually needed.

In Luke 24:19–24, two disciples on their way to Emmaus explain to Jesus why their hopes and wishes had been shattered. Let me point out to you four obstacles that left them confused about their previous expectations. These are also obstacles in our minds. (1) *Limited perception:* they say that Jesus was a prophet, mighty in deed and word (verse 19). But Jesus was so much more than that! He was the Messiah! He was and is God! The Savior of the world! But they didn't perceive that. (2) *Finality:* the two disciples shared how Jesus had been sentenced to death and crucified (verse 20). Jesus had told them many times that the cross would not be the end, but it felt like the end to them. Their pain didn't allow them to remember the words of Jesus that He would rise again. (3) *Regret:* "But we were hoping that it was He who was going to redeem Israel" (verse 21). Hoping? Sound familiar? "I was hoping that . . . ." Well, Jesus had just redeemed the world! But their regrets didn't allow them to understand nor celebrate. (4) *Unbelief.* They had received a firsthand report from the women, who proclaimed that Jesus had resurrected and that the tomb was empty. But they didn't believe because they didn't see. These four obstacles had marred their perception. They thought they *needed* a military leader who would establish an earthly kingdom. Jesus responded with what they *really needed:* "Was it not *necessary* for the Christ to suffer these things . . . ?" (verse 26). Yes, it was! His sacrifice is what we *really need*!

My Response: _____

His Sign

*"No sign will be given . . . but the sign of
Jonah the prophet."*

—Matthew 12:39

D o miracles produce real faith? This is a question that many religious groups have tried to answer till this day; there is even an ongoing dialogue about it on the internet. Yet the biblical account reports that after experiencing God's miraculous deliverance through the Red Sea (Exodus 14) and the supernatural provisions of food and water (Exodus 16), Israel still questioned if God was with them (Exodus 17:7). This was the case many times in the Bible stories. In light of these events, we ask: is there anything that can produce real faith in Jesus?

Having described several miracles of Jesus, Matthew recounts how the scribes and Pharisees came to Him asking for a sign (Matthew 12:38). Signs and miracles had legitimized the ministry of some of the Old Testament prophets, such as Moses and Elijah. But Jesus could read the hearts of His inquirers and knew that they had mocked and misinterpreted even His exorcisms (see Matthew 12:24). Jesus answered: "An evil and adulterous generation craves for a sign; and yet no sign will be given to it but the sign of Jonah the prophet; for just as Jonah was three days and three nights in the belly of the sea monster, so will the Son of Man be three days and three nights in the heart of the earth" (Matthew 12:39, 40). Jonah was a reluctant prophet who had tried to run away from God's call to proclaim His grace to Nineveh. It was a pagan city, which later became the capital of Assyria, whose populace eventually repented from their ways when Jonah finally preached to them. But the prophet himself was in dire need of God's grace. While on his rebellious journey, he ended up in the belly of a fish for three days, pleading with God in prayer. We find the heart of the gospel in the plea of Jonah: "Salvation is from the LORD" (Jonah 2:9). In a remarkable parallelism, Jesus announces to the Pharisees and scribes that His sacrifice on the cross would be the only *sign* that they would have about His identity and mission. If we are to avoid skepticism and desire to guard ourselves against unbelief, we must ask God for a daily revelation of Jesus' sacrifice for us. That's *the* only convincing sign!

My Response: _____

HIS TRUTH

"You will know the truth, and the truth will make you free."
—John 8:32

Hiroo Onada was a soldier who refused to give himself up when the Japanese emperor surrendered in 1945. He stayed in the jungle, hiding for twenty-nine years, long after World War II had ended. He only surrendered when, in March 1974, his former commander flew to where Onada was and reversed his orders from 1945. Can you imagine hiding and surviving in the jungle for almost thirty years after the war was over? How about us? Are we living with the joy of salvation that Jesus achieved for us, or are we still under the yoke of fear?

There are two radically different types of Christians today: *enslaved* and *redeemed*! And you can usually tell the difference right away! It is sad to see so many Christians still hiding in the "religious jungle," barely surviving two thousand years after the loud cry of Jesus, "It is finished," reverberated throughout the universe (John 19:30). In the Gospel of John, "truth" is closely associated with the person of Jesus (see John 1:14, 17). Jesus announced that He is the Truth: "I am the way, and the truth, and the life; no one comes to the Father but through Me" (John 14:6). Back to John 8, Jesus was talking to the Jews who supposedly believed in Him: "If you continue in My word, then you are truly disciples of Mine; and you will know the truth, and the truth will make you free" (verse 31, 32). But the listeners of Jesus reminded Him that they were Abraham's descendants! Completely disregarding their current oppression under the Romans and dismissing their past bondage in Egypt and Babylon, they claimed that they had never been enslaved to anyone. How could they be set free? (verse 33). This is where Jesus clearly states that freedom is not found in your ancestry, pedigree, or religious system. Sin is an *equal opportunity* oppressor, and Jesus is the only answer: "Everyone who commits sin is the slave of sin. The slave does not remain in the house forever; the son does remain forever. *So if the Son makes you free, you will be free indeed*" (verses 34–36). The war has been won; Jesus is victorious. Do not be enslaved by fear but rejoice! He makes us free indeed!

My Response: _____

HIS REACH

Jesus, the Messiah, the son of David, . . . David was the father of Solomon by Bathsheba who had been the wife of Uriah.
—Matthew 1:1, 6

I was sitting with a young adult, talking about her future. She asked me if God could bless her even though she had not done everything according to what God wanted her to do: "Can God bless me with a good marriage even if I have not done things God's way?" I responded with the story of Bathsheba, the woman with whom David committed adultery and then killed her husband, Uriah the Hittite. God blessed them with a son named Solomon (2 Samuel 11; 12), who became the king to succeed David and was the wisest man in the history of the world. Why would God have blessed *them* with this son? And even more shockingly, why would this woman be included in Jesus' lineage?

Great question! As a matter of fact, we can expand our query to: what was Matthew thinking when he, contrary to the customs of the day, decided to include four foremothers in Jesus' genealogy in the first chapter of this Gospel? The four women mentioned in Matthew 1:3–6 are Tamar (Genesis 38), Rahab (Joshua 2; 6), Ruth (the book of Ruth), and the wife of Uriah (Bathsheba), who became David's wife after his adultery and homicide (2 Samuel 11; 12). Tamar was a Canaanite who posed as a prostitute to get pregnant by her father-in-law because the kinsman-redeemer provisions had not been fulfilled. Rahab was a prostitute from Jericho in Canaan. Ruth came from Moab, and Bathsheba was the wife of a Hittite. Wouldn't you have chosen someone like Sarah or Rebekah? The four unlikely women in Matthew 1 were not considered purebred Israelites. They even have questionable reputations! This is Matthew's way of proclaiming that the reach of Jesus' ministry would supersede all expectations! God's salvation cannot be boxed in by a particular pedigree or social status. We are all unworthy of His salvation and yet we are included, blessed, and assured. Whenever we are weighed down by our past mistakes or discouraged by our background, let's remember these women and rejoice! We are invited and we are included!

My Response: _____

HIS BRIDGE

"You will see the heavens opened and the angels of God ascending and descending on the Son of Man."

—John 1:51

While on a guided kayaking tour, we decided to explore the jungle. We were going to kayak for a while and then hike to a beautiful waterfall. However, due to heavy rain the day before, the current had turned rough. When we needed to cross the river, being amateur kayakers, we could not do so without a bridge. But our guide found a solution to the problem. He tied a rope to a tree on one side of the river, kayaked across and tied the other end of the rope to another tree. The whole group was able to cross over on foot. One by one, we got waist deep into the water and, holding on to the rope, crossed over safely.

Abandoning his prejudice and realizing that Jesus had seen him under the fig tree before they met, Nathanael recognizes that Jesus really knows him (see John 1:48). He makes one of the most profound confessions about Jesus in all of the New Testament, declaring Him, both, "the Son of God" and the "King of Israel" (verse 49). Jesus responds, "Because I said to you that I saw you under the fig tree, do you believe? You will see greater things than these" (verse 50). What could be greater than the realization that Jesus knows us intimately? Oh, I'm so glad you asked! His redemption ministry! "Truly, truly, I say to you, you will see the heavens opened and the angels of God ascending and descending on the Son of Man" (verse 51). This is an allusion to Genesis 28:12, in which, having cheated his brother of their father's blessing, Jacob is fleeing for his life. Feeling separated from his loved ones and his God, he stops to sleep at a certain place. "He had a dream, and behold, a ladder was set on the earth with its top reaching to heaven; and behold, the angels of God were ascending and descending on it" (verse 12). In that dream, the LORD had assured Jacob of His presence. Now Jesus is revealing to Nathanael that He is the true Ladder across the sin-created chasm; His redeeming ministry is the *bridge* between heaven and earth. If, like Jacob, you have ever taken a detour, remember that in Jesus, God offers you a bridge to Himself.

My Response: _____

HIS CONCERN

And Jesus said to her, "Woman, what does that have to do with us? My hour has not yet come."

—John 2:4

In some places of the world, weddings are not just an occasion for one evening. Instead, celebrations continue over several days. I attended a wedding like that, which lasted a whole week. It was a wonderful family reunion, filled with joy and with much work, too, because most of the food came directly from the family's farm. The hosts went to great lengths to ensure that the guests had plenty of food and drink available, which was a very important part of their hospitality.

There was a wedding taking place in Cana (John 2:1), the home of Nathanael (John 21:2), which was not far from Nazareth, where Jesus grew up. The mother of Jesus (not identified by name) was there and seemed to have had some level of responsibility in the preparations for the festivities, appearing in an active role only here and at the cross in this Gospel. For the first time in His public ministry, Jesus and His disciples were appearing at a public event together. By attending this wedding, Jesus endorsed this divinely ordained institution (see Genesis 2:22–25). These celebrations used to take up to seven days, and in this instance the host ran out of wine, which was a huge breach of social etiquette and general expectations for three reasons: it disturbed the merriment, it was a sign of lack of hospitality, and the host could be liable, as the bridegroom's family was legally required to supply wine for the whole week. The mother of Jesus, used to relying on her Son for help and resources, came to Him in this time of need. Yet she discovered that much had changed since she last saw Him: He had started His public ministry, He had been baptized with the Holy Spirit, and He had been to the wilderness, tempted by the devil. And now a group of disciples follow Him. Jesus said: "Woman. . . My hour has not yet come" (John 2:4). Jesus didn't address her as "mother," which highlights that even family ties were now subject to His redemptive identity and mission. Jesus was aware of, and provided for, their temporary needs (see tomorrow's devotional), yet His most prominent concern was, and continues to be, the plan of redemption.

My Response: _____

His Timing

"Every man serves the good wine first . . . but you have kept the good wine until now."

—John 2:10

There are two fascinating dimensions to God's timing, expressed by two Greek words: *chronos* and *plērōma*. *Chronos* is the time that never stops but keeps flowing, like in "chronometer." *Plērōma* is the completion of all the variables that must come together to make things complete. "But when the fullness (*plērōma*) of the time (*chronos*) came, God sent forth His Son" (Galatians 4:4). As in a pregnancy, not only is time going by, but there is an evident growth of the baby inside the womb. Both fullness and time must converge for a healthy birth. It's the same in spiritual matters; that is why God's timing is so different from ours.

When the mother of Jesus came to Him at Cana, informing Him that the hosts had run out of wine, Jesus answered, "Woman . . . My *hour* has not yet come" (John 2:4). Jesus knew that more variables had to come in place in order for His *hour* to be fulfilled. In this Gospel, the *hour* for Jesus is the cross, and throughout the narrative the approximation to His *hour* is developed (see John 2:4; 7:30; 8:20; 12:23, 27; 13:1). That's when His glory would be fully revealed. In Cana, Jesus performs the first public miracle, turning water into wine. John narrates seven *signs* in his Gospel, of which this is the first (John 2:11); he doesn't call them miracles, but *signs*, revealing a deeper understanding of the identity of Jesus through each one of them. When the master of the banquet tasted the new wine, he said "Every man serves the good wine first . . . but you have kept the good wine until now" (verse 10). Being that the stories of Jesus in John have a second, more profound meaning, it's not surprising that many scholars believe that this miracle was an enacted parable, similar to the old and new wine metaphors (see Matthew 9:17), about the new order that Jesus introduced, replacing the old order of ceremonial laws (see the purification jars mentioned in verse 6) with the newness of His mission and sacrifice. Jesus patiently waited for His hour to achieve salvation for us. And He invites us to trust His timing in our lives.

My Response: _____

HIS LIBERATION

*And when the days for their purification according to
the law of Moses were completed, they brought Him
[Jesus] . . . to present Him to the Lord.*

—Luke 2:22

W hen in Egypt, I spent almost two weeks navigating the Nile
river. I was dumbfounded by the magnificent structures built
during the time of Pharaohs: numerous imposing temples and
striking tombs, such as the pyramids at Giza. Looking at the ancient buildings, I got a glimpse of the power and wealth of those rulers of old. I tried
to imagine what it must have been like to watch the showdown between
the gods of Egypt and the God of Israel during the ten plagues and to
witness God's miraculous redemption through the blood of the lamb.

Baby Jesus, the firstborn of Mary, was presented to the Lord, "Every
firstborn male that opens the womb shall be called holy to the Lord"
(Luke 2:23). The firstborns were dedicated to the Lord; this practice came
from the time when God delivered Israel from Egypt. God had sent a
message to Pharaoh: "Israel is My son, My firstborn. So I said to you, 'Let
My son go that he may serve Me'; but you have refused to let him go.
Behold, I will kill your son, your firstborn" (Exodus 4:22, 23). Because
Pharaoh refused to let Israel go, the firstborns of Egypt died in the tenth
plague, but God spared the firstborns of Israel through the blood of the
Passover lamb sacrificed in their place (Exodus 12:21–27). From there on,
the firstborns of humans and animals belonged to the Lord (see Exodus
13:12–16), and they were presented to Him for sacred service and were
redeemed back, since the Levites now served in place of the firstborns
of Israel (see Numbers 3:11–13; 8:17, 18). As Baby Jesus was presented
to the Lord that day, the priest did not realize that this was *the* ultimate
Firstborn, whose blood had been foreshadowed by the Passover lamb
in Egypt. "Christ our Passover has been sacrificed" (1 Corinthians 5:7).
Jesus would die so that we may be set free. If you ever become discouraged and afraid for your eternal salvation, remember the blood of Jesus
that was poured out in your place, so that you may be redeemed! Live in
the assurance of His abundant sufficiency!

My Response: _____

HIS VASTNESS

"For my eyes have seen Your salvation, Which You have prepared in the presence of all peoples, A light of revelation to the Gentiles, And the glory of Your people Israel."

—Luke 2:30–32

When I was twelve years old, my family was about to move to the United States for one year in order for my dad to complete his graduate studies. In preparation for this new life, I got baptized, sealing my commitment to Jesus the day before our departure. When we made it to Michigan, I was delighted to see the ground covered with snow! But when school began, I realized that having come from another country, I was different and therefore not very popular and not always accepted by my peers. It was painful.

This was the experience of many new Christians in the first century. When the Gentiles began to accept the gospel, they found out that many of the Jewish Christians were not too welcoming of their new fellow believers. Luke, who penned the most words of all writers of the New Testament, is careful to emphasize that the salvation that Jesus offers has a vast reach for all peoples, regardless of any cultural barriers. In his Gospel, Luke includes several unique stories that highlight the inclusivity of God's salvation through Christ. One of these stories is about Simeon, a godly man to whom the Holy Spirit had revealed that he would not die without having seen the Lord's Anointed (Luke 2:26). When Simeon saw Baby Jesus, he sang a song that is named after its first words in Latin: "Nunc Dimittis" (see Luke 2:29–32). This was a shocking song for a Jewish audience, because it spoke about the salvation offered to both Gentiles and Jews. Today, the followers of Christ are called to be the champions for the elimination of barriers between different groups of people. At the foot of the cross we are all on level ground—all equally undeserving yet saved by the grace of God. Isaiah prophesied about the amplitude of God's salvation:

> Enlarge the place of your tent;
> Stretch out the curtains of your dwellings . . .
> Lengthen your cords
> And strengthen your pegs.
> For you will spread abroad to the right and to the left
> (Isaiah 54:2, 3).

My Response: _____

HIS CREDENTIALS

"You search the Scriptures because you think that in them you have eternal life; it is these that testify about Me."
—John 5:39

F. F. Bruce's book cover reads: "In Jesus the promise is confirmed, the covenant is renewed, the prophecies are fulfilled, the law is vindicated, salvation is brought near, sacred history has reached its climax, the perfect sacrifice has been offered and accepted, the great priest over the houschold of God has taken his seat at God's right hand, the Prophet like Moses has been raised up, the Son of David reigns, the kingdom of God has been inaugurated."*

God does not ask us to believe without evidence. Jesus Himself referred to the different witnesses that testified of Him: John, the forerunner; Jesus' own miraculous works; the Father's testimony; and finally, the witness of the Scriptures (John 5:31–47). Jesus unequivocally explained that these (the Old Testament) authenticated His identity and mission. The sad part was that while the Jewish leaders were meticulous students of the Scriptures, they rejected Jesus. They kept the Ten Commandments, observed the Sabbath, prayed, tithed, et cetera, but they dismissed Jesus! (see verses 45–47). Interpreting all the Scriptures (the Law, the Prophets, and the Psalms) in light of Jesus and His sacrifice has eternal consequences! "The sacred writings . . . give you the wisdom that *leads to salvation through faith which is in Christ Jesus.*" (2 Timothy 3:15). The Bible points us to Jesus as our only Hope, Assurance, Substitute, Sacrifice, High Priest, King, Lord, and Savior. Jesus is our *All in all.* It is only through Him that we have eternal life! Every sermon and Bible study should be centered at the cross of Jesus. "The sacrifice of Christ as an atonement for sin is the great truth around which all other truths cluster. In order to be rightly understood and appreciated, every truth in the Word of God, from Genesis to Revelation, must be studied in the light that streams from the cross of Calvary. I present before you the great, grand monument of mercy and regeneration, salvation and redemption,—the Son of God uplifted on the cross. This is to be the foundation of every discourse given by our ministers."†

My Response: _____

---

* F. F. Bruce, *New Testament Development of Old Testament Themes* (Grand Rapids, MI: Eerdmans, 1994), book jacket text.

† Ellen G. White, *Gospel Workers* (Washington, DC: Review and Herald®, 1915), 315; emphasis added.

HIS ACCURACY

[He] was restored, and began to see everything clearly.
—Mark 8:25

In my teens, I experienced a strange condition: for no apparent reason my pupil would dilate, causing blurry vision that would last for several hours. I had a brain scan to find out if I had a tumor. I went to an ophthalmological institute, where they thoroughly studied my eyes but could not find anything wrong. Years later I discovered that if my asthma medication got on my hands, and if I happened to rub my eyes, it caused my pupils to dilate!

Mark chronicles an unusual miracle not recorded by any other Gospel writer. It is a two-step enacted teaching used to introduce the greatest revelation of all time. A blind man was brought to Jesus, and after laying His hands on him, Jesus asked Him: "Do you see anything?" (Mark 8:23). The man could see something, but not clearly: "I see men, for I see them like trees, walking around" (verse 24). He could see something, but it was partial sight. "Then again He laid His hands on his eyes; and he looked intently and was restored, and began to see everything clearly" (verse 25). Through His miracles, Jesus did not just offer physical healing but also taught deeper spiritual truths. Interestingly, right after this two-step miracle, the true reality of Jesus' identity and mission is revealed, also in two steps. This miracle contains three unparalleled elements. First, Jesus asks the blind man about the effectiveness of the healing. Second, the blind man responds saying that he can see, but not accurately. Third, Jesus lays hands on him for a second time, and from then on, the formerly blind man can see clearly. In the section that follows (Mark 8:27–31), the disciples say that many think that Jesus is a prophet, and that they believe He is the Messiah. But their answer is like the sight of "trees walking." It was a limited understanding and not yet clear sight. Jesus went on to reveal that He was also the suffering Son of Man, who would be killed and rise three days later (verse 31). Just like them, when we accept the necessity of His death, we start seeing Jesus accurately; His grace becomes real to us. Let's ask God for a daily revelation of His infinite love, manifested at the cross, that we may see clearly!

My Response: _____

HIS DECLARATION

*"I tell you, this man [the tax collector] went to his house
justified rather than the other."*

—Luke 18:14

What makes us fit for the kingdom of God? We all want to qualify, but what does that mean? Are we supposed to offer a résumé as for a job? When I arrived in the United States thirty-five years ago, I applied for a job, and they tested my typewriting skills. I was feeling pretty comfortable until I started typing and realized that this was an electric typewriter, which I had never used. Instead of typing one letter with a push of a key, I would get ten! It was a disaster. Do you ever feel like that when thinking about your qualifications for the kingdom?

Jesus told a story about this (Luke 18:9–14). Two men came to the temple to pray; one was a Pharisee, and the other was a tax collector. The Pharisee was thankful, mainly for his own deeds and not so much for God's: "God, I thank You that I am not like other people; swindlers, unjust, adulterers, or even like this tax collector" (verse 11). He fasted twice a week and paid tithes for everything (verse 12). He was a hard-praying, Sabbath-keeping, always grateful, church-going person; in other words, he was a great example. On the other hand, the tax collector stood some distance away. He didn't have a list, of good stuff he was proud of or of bad stuff he avoided, to present. He couldn't even look up to heaven; instead, he beat his chest and said, "God, be merciful to me, the sinner!" (verse 13). And then Jesus makes a startling declaration, turning their world upside down (or is it the right side up?): "This man [the tax collector] went to his house justified rather than the other; for everyone who exalts himself will be humbled, but he who humbles himself will be exalted" (verse 14). The tax collector, not the Pharisee, went home justified! How is this possible? Well, the question is not *What* but rather *Who qualifies us for the heavenly kingdom.* Jesus does. We are justified by grace, through faith in His perfect life and death on our behalf. Paul summarized it well: "For all have sinned and fall short of the glory of God, being justified as a gift by His grace through the redemption which is in Christ Jesus" (Romans 3:23, 24).

My Response: _____

His Suffering

And He began to teach them that the Son of Man must suffer many things and be rejected by the elders and the chief priests and the scribes, and be killed, and after three days rise again.

—Mark 8:31

A pivot is a shaft or a pin on which something turns, but the word may also refer to a person, a thing, or a factor having a major or central role, function, or effect.* Thus, we speak of pivotal moments, events, words, and decisions that change the course of our lives. Today's devotional text represents a pivotal disclosure in the Gospel of Mark and in the history of redemption.

The first half of this Gospel highlights the authority of Jesus. Everyone is asking: "Who is this?" And the obvious answer, in light of His mighty works, is that Jesus is the authoritative Son of God, who has power over everything, including nature, demons, disease, and death. From Mark 1:1 to 8:30 everyone is in awe of Jesus, because He is the awaited Christ who has come with power and might! But then comes the pivotal verse that changes everything. For the first time, Jesus discloses to His disciples the prophecy of His sufferings: He must suffer many things, including rejection and death, and He will rise again after three days (see Mark 8:31). This is the first of three predictions of His death, which we call the *passion predictions* (Mark 8:31; 9:31; 10:33). This was the purpose for which He had come, and there it was, exposed for the world to see clearly for the first time. This was the shocking news, the truth beyond logical comprehension: Jesus had come to die—not just to show love or power—but to suffer to the point of death. He had come to be our Savior, and His death on our behalf becomes *the pivotal event* that changes the course of our lives as well. He was the "Suffering Servant," prophesied in Isaiah 53. Please place your name in the blank spaces. "Surely he took up _____'s pain and bore _____'s suffering . . . But he was pierced for _____'s transgressions, he was crushed for _____'s iniquities; the punishment that brought ____ peace was on him, and by his wounds ____ is healed" (Isaiah 53:4, 5; NIV, author's paraphrase). Yes! You are loved *that* much!

My Response: _____

---

* *Merriam-Webster*, s.v. "pivot (n.)," accessed April 11, 2019, https://www.merriam-webster.com/dictionary/pivot.

HIS RANSOM

"For even the Son of Man did not come to be served,
but to serve, and to give His life a ransom for many."

—Mark 10:45

I remember my anticipation as I walked into the classroom. It was the first day of class with this New Testament professor. But little did I know how this class, focused on the four Gospels, would change my life and my ministry. Without introduction, the professor started to read: "You know that those who are recognized as rulers of the Gentiles lord it over them; and their great men exercise authority over them. But it is not this way among you, but whoever wishes to become great among you shall be your servant; and whoever wishes to be first among you shall be slave of all. For even the Son of Man did not come to be served, but to serve, and to give His life a ransom for many" (Mark 10:42–45).

His reading made a profound impact on my mind. For some reason I had never paid much attention to the larger context of this key verse of the Gospel of Mark (10:45). Jesus teaches his disciples that they should not be lording it over people. His words came in response to an argument that broke among the disciples because James and John had been seeking the best positions in the upcoming kingdom, the nature of which they clearly did not understand. These clueless disciples, guided by their selfish hearts, were prideful and power-hungry, yet Jesus, the tender, loving Jesus, always showed them a better way by His own example. On that particular day, the Master taught His followers that the way of the kingdom of God is radically different than the world's authority structure. Servants are considered great, and slaves are counted as first. And Jesus, God in the flesh, is not only our example but, most importantly, our Savior. After three predictions of His death in this Gospel (8:31; 9:31; 10:33), Jesus clearly and unequivocally announces that He did not come to be served but to serve humanity. And not only that! He would give His life as a *ransom* for many! Yes, we have been *ransomed* for the high price of the blood of the Son of God! And the "many" includes you and me! Now that our ransom has been paid, we are free to love and to serve.

My Response: _____

CELEBRATING HIS VICTORY

HIS COMING

*"They will see the Son of Man coming on the clouds
of the sky with power and great glory."*
—Matthew 24:30

I was standing on the Mount of Olives, and the view virtually took my breath away. There is a Jewish cemetery there, with thousands of tombs overlooking the temple. Some scholars believe that the earliest burials there date back three thousand years. Certainly, the cemetery was already there during the Second Temple period and the time of Jesus. I find it fascinating that Jesus decided to deliver His discourse about His second coming and the end times from this place, overlooking the temple and this oldest and most important Jewish cemetery.

Jesus was on the Mount of Olives when His disciples came to ask Him about the destruction of the temple (Matthew 24:1, 2), His coming, and the end of the age (verse 3). The Mount of Olives is mentioned in a prophecy found in Zechariah 14:4: "In that day His feet will stand on the Mount of Olives, which is in front of Jerusalem on the east; and the Mount of Olives will be split in its middle from east to west by a very large valley." Now Jesus is on the Mount of Olives, in front of this ancient cemetery, overlooking the magnificent temple, and he chooses this specific place to discuss the destruction of the temple and, most importantly, the signs and the event of His Coming. At this time, the disciples were not able to distinguish between the two events; both probably seemed the same to them. After mentioning persecution, wars, pseudo-prophets, et cetera, Jesus reveals how this age of pain will end with His second coming! The Greek word for His coming is *parousia*; it is used three times in this discourse (Matthew 24:27, 37, 39) and not at all in the other Gospels. *Parousia* became the blessed hope of Christians in all ages. In the New Testament, the word "hope" is used in the sense of "assurance," not in the English sense of "I *hope* this happens" but with the certainty that it will happen. When I visit my parents' tomb, I often imagine what that cemetery will look like on the morning of the resurrection, the day of Jesus' second coming. I can't wait! Jesus promised it, and therefore, it is a sure thing!

My Response: _____

HIS REDEMPTION

"When these things begin to take place, straighten up and lift up your heads, because your redemption is drawing near."

—Luke 21:28

When I was a young girl, we were blessed to have a good-sized backyard with several fruit trees in the city of Buenos Aires. I eagerly awaited summer time, when I would be able to play with my friends and eat the delicious figs, avocados, and sweet grapes. As an adult, I discovered that my anticipation of summer was actually a parable that Jesus told about His second coming.

During His ministry, Jesus prophesied things to come, both in their immediate future and in His second coming. In the last days, there would be signs in the sun, moon, stars, and the sea (Luke 21:25–27). Jesus mentioned two strikingly opposite responses to these signs: some would faint from *fear* of the things that are coming, yet Jesus admonishes us to *straighten up and lift up our heads* because our redemption is drawing near. Then He tells the parable of the trees and the summer: "Behold the fig tree and all the trees; as soon as they put forth leaves, you see it and know for yourselves that summer is now near. So you also, when you see these things [attesting signs] happening, recognize that the kingdom of God is near" (verses 30, 31). When leaves appear on the trees, we start looking forward to summer! Jesus exhorts us to choose faith over fear and to lift up our heads when we see the signs of His coming because our *redemption* is drawing near! I find a calm assurance in the terms "Redeemer" and "redemption," because in the Old Testament (LXX) these terms related to the *release of a person* or property on *payment of a ransom*. Redemption is the recovery of the human race through the high price that Jesus paid for us on the cross! The ransom has been paid, and He is coming back to take us home! Jesus said: "They will see the Son of Man coming in a cloud with power and great glory" (verse 27). Christ is coming back for us as a parent who paid the ransom for His kidnapped children and is coming to deliver them! I am eagerly awaiting that blessed day! In the meanwhile, choose *faith over fear*! Our redemption is near!

My Response: _____

HIS ARRIVAL

"At midnight there was a shout, 'Behold, the bridegroom! Come out to meet him.' "

—Matthew 25:6

When I married my husband, my three close friends were my bridesmaids. They planned a special, intimate time just for the four of us before the wedding. It was so beautiful and meaningful! I remember everything about it. At the wedding, they readily took care of every detail, including some unexpected situations that arose. I am so thankful for my bridesmaids, who made our wedding extra special.

After the discourse of Jesus about His glorious second coming, Luke records three parables that address being ready for His coming, because we don't know the hour. The second parable (Matthew 25:1–13), referred to as the parable of the ten virgins, talks about a longer than anticipated delay of the bridegroom. In the first century, and even now in some Palestinian villages, the bridesmaids, after a day of festivities, leave the bride at night and go out with torches to meet the bridegroom. They bring him to the bride, and then the joyful procession escorts the bride to the groom's house. It was common for the groom to be delayed, and therefore the maids had to be prepared, having extra oil for their torches. In this parable, as the groom delays longer than expected, all ten virgins fall asleep. Then at midnight the shout is heard: "Behold, the bridegroom!" There is one other occasion in Matthew where the word *bridegroom* is used (Matthew 9:15); in both cases it refers to Jesus. When the bridegroom arrives, only half of the them are ready (as is the case with the men in the fields and the women at the mill; see Matthew 24:40, 41). The foolish maids who are lacking oil to light the way for the groom go out to buy some, but it is too late. The time for getting ready is over, and they miss the procession and the festivities. The parable ends with the exhortation of Jesus: "Be on the alert then, for you do not know the day nor the hour" (Matthew 25:13). This is the time for persistent, joyful spiritual preparedness and watchfulness. "Blessed are those who are invited to the marriage supper of the Lamb" (Revelation 19:9). Let's not become weary of waiting for His arrival. Be assured of the *certainty* of His coming!

My Response: _____

HIS GOSPEL

*"This gospel of the kingdom shall be preached in the
whole world as a testimony to all the nations,
and then the end will come."*

—Matthew 24:14

Being part of a generation that was born without social media, I continue to be amazed at the way the whole world can be reached with the touch of a button. As our ministry is growing, I was curious to find out where, geographically, people are watching our videos. It was a sobering moment when consulting one of our internet video program hosts, I saw a world map with areas of our audience highlighted in shades of blue. I was stunned to see that areas of blue spanned the globe. Matthew 24:14 immediately came to my mind.

Jesus explained in general terms to expect difficult times, including false messiahs and pseudo-prophets, as well as wars, rumors of wars, betrayals, hate, famines, earthquakes, and lawlessness (Matthew 24:5–12). These things sound like our daily news, don't they? As a result, some will be misled, others will fall away and the love of many will grow cold, but Jesus says this will not yet be the end (verse 6). The good news is greater than the bad news: "This gospel of the kingdom shall be preached in the whole world as a testimony to all the nations, and *then the end will come*" (verse 14). The phrase, "then the end will come" stands in contrast to the previous phrase "is not yet the end" (verse 6), highlighting that the wars, famines, and earthquakes do not usher in the end, but that the fulfillment of the gospel commission does. The scope of the proclamation is clearly delineated in the phrase "in the whole world." It literally means all the inhabited earth. The focus of the preaching is the *gospel* (verse 14; see Revelation 14:6). The word translated as "gospel/good news" was used secularly as the victory cry that the heralds brought from the battlefield. We are to herald Jesus' victory over evil, which He achieved through His perfect life, death, and resurrection. Hence the title of this devotional book: "Jesus Wins!" As important as the *signs* of the end may be, these are not to be our core proclamation; the *gospel* of Jesus Christ is the focus of our mission. May Jesus' sacrifice be preached to all the nations, and then the end will come!

My Response: _____

HIS STRENGTH

And there was war in heaven, Michael and his angels
waging war with the dragon. The dragon and his angels
waged war, and they were not strong enough.
—Revelation 12:7, 8

Several years ago, I was invited to join a radio ministry called *Voice of Prophecy*. My boss at the time, Elder Kinsey, often spoke about today's devotional text with great passion. He frequently shared the great assurance found in the understanding that in the war waged against Michael and His angels, the dragon (Satan) and his angels *were not strong enough!* How important it is to remember that the devil *cannot* prevail! He is not strong enough! Jesus wins!

John reveals who this dragon is: "And the great dragon was thrown down, the serpent of old who is called the devil and Satan, who deceives the whole world" (Revelation 12:9). He rebelled against God and took with him a considerable number of accomplices (verse 4). They made war against Michael, the leader of the armies of heaven. The next verse clarifies that this name refers to Jesus Christ Himself: "Now the salvation, and the power, and the kingdom of our God and the authority of His Christ have come" (see verses 10, 11). It was at the cross that the rule of Satan was completely overthrown; and those who follow Jesus overcome the devil *because* of the blood of the Lamb (verse 11). In the great controversy between good and evil, the adversary of God still inflicts pain and suffering, yet he is a defeated foe. Jesus is the ultimate Victor and will intervene and eradicate evil, as well as rescue His own (see Daniel 12:1). The dragon and his angels *were not strong enough* against our Savior and King. His sacrifice is our assurance! "The death of Christ upon the cross made sure the destruction of him who has the power of death, who was the originator of sin. . . . It is through the efficacy of the cross that the angels of heaven are guarded from apostasy. Without the cross they would be no more secure against evil than were the angels before the fall of Satan. Angelic perfection failed in heaven. Human perfection failed in Eden, the paradise of bliss. All who wish for security in earth or heaven must look to the Lamb of God."*

My Response: _____

---

* Ellen G. White, "What Was Secured by the Death of Christ," *Signs of the Times*, December 30, 1889, par. 4.

HIS JUBILATION

*And they sang a new song before the throne. . . . and no one
could learn the song except the one hundred and forty-four thousand
who had been purchased from the earth.*

—Revelation 14:3

Through the years, I have been part of, and have directed, several vocal groups and choirs. I remember a particular event when our choir performed songs of a very well-known composer in a large auditorium. What made this performance extra special was the fact that the composer himself was actually playing the piano and directing the choir. We joyfully sang with all our hearts, grateful for the privilege of performing in the presence of the maestro.

Yet this jubilant occasion, or any other this world may offer, does not come close to the celebration we will experience as we gather around the victorious King of the universe! In the only narrative in the book of Revelation that mentions Mount Zion, the Lamb is standing on this very place that had foreshadowed the deliverance of God's people all along. But He is not alone; the victorious Lamb is surrounded by His own, those who have "His name and the name of His Father written on their foreheads" (Revelation 14:1). One hundred forty-four thousand is the number of spiritual Israel, mentioned in Revelation 7:4. The redeemed, excited and exceedingly joyful, start singing a new song in front of the throne. This is our song, for no one else can sing it! In contrast to other worship scenes in Revelation, where the heavenly beings join in praise, this particular song can only be sung by the one hundred forty-four thousand. Why is that? The answer follows in the text itself: "No one could learn the song except the one hundred and forty-four thousand *who had been purchased from the earth*" (Revelation 14:3). That's why! We are the only ones who can sing the song of redemption that tells the story that no one else can tell. And we will sing our hearts out! The Lamb reigns! Jesus wins! This picture of the victorious Lamb and all of us around Him, gratefully celebrating His triumph, reminds us that pain, cancer, abuse, broken vows, and death are temporary situations, and that soon Jesus will take over and all the hurts and pain of this earth will be no more. Amen!

My Response: _____

HIS OUTCOME

"And I saw another angel flying in midheaven, having an eternal gospel to preach to those who live on the earth."
—Revelation 14:6

I've learned that I can't control most circumstances that occur around me, and that usually *the outcome is not in my hands.* My only real option is to submit to God's wisdom and control of all the situations in my life. Yet the *final outcome* of the world's history, and of my personal story, has already been revealed, and it is good news! The Greek noun *euangelion* is translated into English as "good news" or "gospel." As discussed earlier, this term and its equivalent Hebrew term were used when messengers came bearing good news from the battlefield to the people anxiously waiting within the city walls. You could hear the messenger from afar, crying out in a loud voice: *Good news! Our king has won!*

This is why it is so important that after John's vision of the victorious Lamb, standing on Mount Zion, surrounded by the redeemed (Revelation 14:1), God reveals that He is sending three final messengers who are carrying the *good news, the everlasting gospel* (Revelation 14:6), crying in a loud voice that Jesus has, in fact, won the battle between good and evil. In summary, each one of the angels announces an aspect or angle of the eternal good news. The first angel invites the whole earth to *worship* the Creator God and to pledge allegiance to the One who made the heavens and the earth. This angel announces that the hour of His judgment has come (verse 7), which for the believers is really good news because their sins have already been paid for at the cross, so they do not fear the judgment. The second angel announces that the opposing satanic system has collapsed (verse 8). Babylon has fallen! The capital city of the evil system is no more! *Finito!* Done! Jesus wins! And the third bearer of good news reminds everyone that God knows His own, and that you are safe if you trust in Jesus, the Lamb of God, and bear His mark (Revelation 14:9–12). It is true that uncertainties surround us, yet one thing is guaranteed: *the outcome is assured!* On the cross, Jesus paid our price, evil and pain have been defeated, and God's children have been reconciled with Him. Yes! Satan loses, and Jesus wins!

My Response: _____

HIS RESOLVE

*"He who overcomes will inherit these things, and I will be
his God and he will be My son."*

—Revelation 21:7

My dad was preaching, and my mother was in the back of the church taking care of me, a baby at the time. Unexpectedly, a man came running into the sanctuary, snatched me from the seat, and took off. But by the time the man got to his pickup truck my mother was there, too, and jumped into the passenger side. He drove to a building my mom didn't recognize, where they were greeted by a radio announcer, congratulating the man who was holding me. It turned out that the first person to show up to the radio station with a baby, won a pretty sizable prize. My mother, not knowing what was going on, was determined to be where I was, no matter what, until she got me back. After all, I am *her daughter!*

God didn't let go of His kidnapped children either! He was willing to do whatever was needed to get them back. When Adam and Eve, the children of God, chose to leave the moral umbrella of their heavenly Father and follow the deceiver (Genesis 3:1–8), God immediately and passionately expressed His resolve to get them back, no matter the cost (Genesis 3:15). This is what we call the covenant. The whole Bible is the story of how God ransomed His kidnapped children.* When we get to the new earth, the covenant will be fulfilled and the consequences of sin will be no more: no more death, crying or pain (see Revelation 21:4). Can you imagine that? God wins in the universal battle between good and evil, and He gets His children back. The ultimate reality for us, who trust in the Lamb's sacrifice to the end, will be that we will receive the *divine sonship*: "I will be his God and he will be *My son*" (verse 7). We are, in fact, children of God. God will be with us, and we will be with God. Reunited! Forever! Oh, what a day that will be! God Himself will announce the completion of this final reality (verse 7). Yes! You are a child of the King! And His victory is yours because you are an heir with Christ. "See how great a love the Father has bestowed on us, that we would be called children of God; and such we are" (1 John 3:1). Let no one convince you otherwise!

My Response: _____

──────────

* For a study on this topic, see Elizabeth Talbot, *Surprised by Love* (Nampa, ID: Pacific Press®, 2010).

HIS SOLUTION

"The one who sows the good seed is the Son of Man."
—Matthew 13:37

Some counterfeit items look so similar to the real thing that it takes an expert to tell them apart. Years ago, I got a nice purse of a famous brand which prominently displayed its logo in multiple places. I showed it to a friend who knew much more about purses than I did. Having examined my new bag, she told me: "It's not real, it's a counterfeit." It definitely looked real to me, and I asked her why she thought so. "Because," she said, "this particular brand never places stiches over their logo." Only an expert could tell.

In this parable only told by Matthew, we receive an answer to two very frequently asked questions: "Why is there is evil in this world?" and "What is God going to do about it?" The answer to the first is: "Because an enemy has done this!" (verse 28); and the second: "He will eradicate it at the end of times, once and for all (verses 30, 40–42)." The parable compares the kingdom of heaven to a situation found in a field. A man sowed *good seed*, but an enemy came and sowed tares (weeds, Greek *zizania*) among the wheat (verses 24, 25). This type of agricultural undermining attack, often used as revenge, was punishable by Roman law. Time went by, and when the wheat grew and was bearing grain, the weeds became noticeable (verse 26). When the landowner's workers offered to remedy the evident problem by gathering the weeds, the master asked them not to, not because they couldn't tell them apart, but because they might "uproot the wheat with them" (verse 29). The roots were intertwined, and the landowner cared too much about the wheat. Jesus explained this parable in great detail (verses 36–43) and highlighted that "the one who sows the good seed is the Son of Man, and the field is the world . . . and the enemy who sowed them [the tares] is the devil" (verses 37–39). This is the great controversy between good and evil in one parable. Jesus explains that at the end of the world, He will do away with evil once and for all. Yes! Evil will eventually be fully destroyed. This is a source of assurance for Christ's followers. Jesus tells us how it will all end! And Jesus wins!

My Response: _____

HIS TENDERNESS

When Jesus then saw His mother, and the disciple
whom He loved standing nearby, He said to His mother,
"Woman, behold, your son!"

—John 19:26

Visiting the ancient city of Ephesus was one of the most amazing experiences of my life. I was absolutely baffled when we got to the ancient city and saw the magnificent remains of so many buildings, the library, and the huge amphitheater. We also visited the traditional site of Mary's house, a few miles away. At first, I was confused, because we were in Turkey, and the mother of Jesus lived in Israel. That's when I remembered that Jesus entrusted His mother to John, the beloved disciple, who eventually became an elder in the church of Ephesus.

John records three last sayings of Jesus on the cross that are not recorded by the other Gospel writers. The first one is addressed to His mother and the beloved disciple. It is amazing to me that in the midst of His physical and even greater spiritual distress, Jesus thinks of His mother. She had been visited by the angel Gabriel, and when she became pregnant out of wedlock, she endured much ridicule. She had witnessed how the Jewish leaders rejected Jesus and had felt much pain because of it. She had kept in her heart the prophecies about Him, and now she was standing by the cross of her beloved Son. And Jesus honors His earthly mother by making sure that she is taken care of. Amazing! May we treat our own mothers with such care and tenderness. Perhaps because the brothers of Jesus had not yet believed that He was the Savior (see John 7:5), Jesus felt the need to entrust His mother to the beloved disciple: "When Jesus then saw His mother, and the disciple whom He loved standing nearby, He said to His mother, 'Woman, behold, your son!' Then He said to the disciple, 'Behold your mother!' From that hour the disciple took her into his own household" (John 19:26, 27). The concern of Jesus for His mother, who had been divinely chosen to bring Him into this world, is another reminder of His gentle heart, which experienced love in addition to pain and always showed tender care. At the cross, the tenderness of Jesus was offered to each one of us as well. His victorious love is our assurance.

My Response: _____

HIS ACCOMPLISHMENT

*"And behold, a severe earthquake had occurred,
for an angel of the Lord descended from heaven and . . .
rolled away the stone and sat upon it."*

—Matthew 28:2

It was time for my dad and I to choose the words to be engraved on my mother's tombstone. We chose the text of Isaiah 43:1, "Do not fear, for I have redeemed you; I have called you by name; you are Mine!" Both of us were comforted by God's assurance of redemption, His tender reminder that He knows each of us by name, and that we are His! A few months later, my dad was sleeping in Jesus under the same tombstone. Both of my parents passed away with the assurance that Jesus had accomplished their eternal life through His death.

Matthew's narrative of the resurrection is the most dramatic of all four Gospels. He adds unique details that become visualizations of the salvific work of Jesus. For example, Matthew mentions that the earth shook when Jesus died, opening the tombs (Matthew 27:51, 52), and that there was also a great earthquake (*seismos megas*) when the angel of the Lord descended on the resurrection morning (John 28:2). "An angel of the Lord . . . rolled away the stone *and sat upon it*" (verse 2). The angel *sat on the stone* of Jesus' tomb! As if saying, with defiant body language: *any questions, anyone? Jesus has conquered death!* Yes, Jesus' death had triumphed over death, and now Jesus Himself had risen, and the stone placed on the tomb to guard it became the angel's stool . . . I love it! Countless times, when facing problems that were greater than my abilities to solve them, I pictured the angel sitting on the stone! God sits on our problems, in total control. But there is one more *shaking* in this scene: "The guards *shook* for fear of him and became like dead men" (verse 4). How paradoxical is that? The men who had been placed to guard Jesus' body were now shaking and becoming like dead bodies, while the One who had been dead was now alive! If you, or someone you love, have to face the valley of the shadow of death, remember Jesus' accomplishment: victory over death! I can't wait to see my parents again on resurrection morning; the angel will remove their tombstone and *sit on it!*

My Response: _____

HIS IDENTITY

The record of the genealogy of Jesus the Messiah,
the son of David, the son of Abraham.

—Matthew 1:1

I asked the cemetery representative if they would allow me to bring a key and bury it along with my father and mother. As an only child, it was extremely difficult to lose both of my parents in a short time. As the place was opened to lay the remains of my father next to my mother's, I placed the key in their grave. Jesus said that he has the keys of death (Revelation 1:18). He will be the next one to open my parents' tomb and will see the key I placed there because I believe He will fulfill His resurrection promise. Praise God! His promises are everything!

Matthew starts his Gospel announcing that Jesus is the long-awaited Deliverer, who was promised throughout the Jewish Scriptures (Old Testament). By using the title "Messiah" (Matthew 1:1), which is "*Christos*" (Christ) in Greek and means "the Anointed One," Matthew reminds us that Jesus comes as the fulfillment of the covenantal promises of God. This theological title of Jesus as the awaited Anointed One appears several times in this Gospel, even in the first chapter (1:1, 16, 17, 18). Matthew also mentions that Jesus is the descendant of David and Abraham (1:1), both pivotal names in God's covenant with Israel (2 Samuel 7:16) and with all the nations of the earth (Genesis 12:3). He repeats the same two important names (David and Abraham) at the end of his genealogical introduction (Matthew 1:17).

Matthew will allude to the Old Testament prophecies several times. On some occasions, he will use what we call a prophetic formula in which he starts the verse by stating: "This took place to fulfill what was spoken by the Lord through the prophet" (for example, 1:22; 2:15). Surely, Jesus is the fulfillment of God's promises to send a Deliverer. It is difficult for us to grasp how much this would have meant to Matthew's predominantly Jewish audience, which had awaited the promised Messiah for centuries. For us, this verse is a reminder that God is truly faithful to His promises, and that as He fulfilled His promise in Jesus' first coming, He will do it again in Jesus' second coming! You can count on that!

My Response: _____

HIS PROMISE

"Do not let your heart be troubled; believe in God,
believe also in Me. . . . I will come again and receive you to Myself,
that where I am, there you may be also."
—John 14:1, 3

When David was running for his life, God provided a loving and supportive friend: King Saul's son, Jonathan. It was an unlikely friendship, because Jonathan would have been the natural successor to his father, yet he knew that David had been chosen by God to be the king of Israel. Instead of feeling jealous, Jonathan loved David, and they became best friends. Jonathan seemed certain that David would be king one day and asked him to preserve his descendants when he did (1 Samuel 20:15–17). And so, this covenant and promise was secured between these two unlikely friends. When David became king over all of Israel, just as Jonathan had predicted, he kept his promise (2 Samuel 9:1–13). David did not exterminate Jonathan's descendants, as was the custom of the time; a son of Jonathan, Mephibosheth, who was crippled in both feet, was brought to David, and from then on Mephibosheth ate at the king's table regularly as one of David's sons.

In biblical history, God has always been faithful to His promises. He is the ultimate promise keeper. Jesus has told us the end of the covenant story: He wins! And He is coming back for us, that we may eat at His table eternally. When His disciples had received incomprehensibly bad news (John 13:33, 36), Jesus reassured them by directing their thoughts to the end of the story. The imperative "Do not let your heart be troubled" (John 14:1) could be translated as "Stop being distressed." They were anxious, and Jesus gave them the reason not to be. He was going ahead of them, opening the path, and preparing their home. Even though they would be going through some troublesome days, the remedy for their downcast souls was, and continues to be, to believe in His promise. Jesus reassured them that His Presence would continue with them for eternity! He said: "that where I am, there you may be also" (verse 3). We should focus on the end of the story: Jesus wins! And we are, and will be, with Him forever, just as He promised!

My Response: _____

HIS RETURN

*"This Jesus, who has been taken up from you into heaven,
will come in just the same way as you have
watched Him go into heaven."*

—Acts 1:11

We all want to know that things will be OK. We want the assurance that the ending will turn out all right. Have you ever watched a movie twice, read a book for a second time, or watched a previously played sports game for which you already knew the final score? Then you have experienced an anxiety-free activity, especially when the game, movie or book ended on a very positive note. When we know the outcome ahead of time, there is no point in worrying or fretting.

This is why the book of Acts *begins at the end*. After Jesus died to save the human race and rose from the dead, He presented Himself alive to His disciples for forty days (see Acts 1:3). During this time, He explained to His disciples many things regarding the kingdom of God. After commissioning them to be His witnesses in Jerusalem, Judea, Samaria, and even to the remotest parts of the earth (verse 8), Jesus ascended to heaven. He was lifted up, a cloud received Him, and He was out of their sight (verse 9). Notice that the disciples kept looking upwards *intently* (verse 10); some suggest that they might have expected the cloud to dissipate and to see Jesus again, as had happened on the Mount of Transfiguration. But instead they saw two men in bright clothing, heavenly messengers, who told them that this same Jesus, who had been taken up from them, was sure to come back in the same manner as they had watched Him go into heaven (verse 11). So, in the book of Acts, before we are told about their baptism of the Holy Spirit and how they spread throughout the world, proclaiming the good news of salvation and eventually experiencing tribulations, persecution and even martyrdom, the first thing we (and they) find out is the final outcome: Jesus *will come back*! It is not just a possibility but a sure thing. And the assurance of His return kept them free from fear and anxiety during the dark and difficult days that followed. The same is true for us. In this world we might be going through pain and tribulations, yet we know the outcome ahead of time. He *will come back* for us! Hallelujah!

My Response: _____

HIS OBJECTIVE

*"God raised Him up again, putting an end to the agony of death,
since it was impossible for Him to be held in its power."*

—Acts 2:24

I recently returned from a ministerial trip that spanned multiple countries and included various speaking engagements. By God's grace it was a success as everything had worked as planned. And it involved a lot of logistical planning and coordination with different church entities in various countries: airline tickets, hotels, meals, local transportation, media, equipment, luggage allowance, translators, et cetera. These things usually do not happen by chance . . . every detail was carefully planned and carried out.

The sermon Peter preached on the day of Pentecost clearly reveals that God had predesigned a detailed plan for our redemption. Peter explained that even the infilling of the followers of Jesus by the Holy Spirit had been prophesied in the Old Testament (Acts 2:14–20). Then he continued to proclaim who Jesus was and how He had fulfilled the prophecies found in the Jewish Scriptures. The sermons preached by Peter and others recorded in the book of Acts always point to the fact that the Old Testament prophecies about the upcoming Messiah were fulfilled in the ministry, life, death, and resurrection of Jesus. And that even though humans put Him to death, it was in fact God's preordained plan of redemption that was being realized. "This *Man, delivered over by the predetermined plan and foreknowledge of God,* you nailed to a cross by the hands of godless men and put *Him* to death. But God raised Him up again, putting an end to the agony [literally, *birth pains*] of death. . ." (Acts 2:23, 24). It was God's objective and predetermined plan to reverse the consequences of sin, including pain and death, through Jesus' victory on our behalf. His plan was successful and did not happen by chance. It was a detailed, *predetermined* plan. Death could not hold Jesus in its grip. And we can live with the assurance of His absolute victory for us, knowing that death will not be victorious over His followers either. In addition, we are invited to joyfully surrender to and trust God's *predesigned* plan for our lives.

My Response: _____

HIS PREVAILING

So the word of the Lord was growing
mightily and prevailing.

—Acts 19:20

The controversy between good and evil is real. Evil spirits are active in bringing fear, pain, and destruction, as well as being obstacles to the spreading of the good news. And I thank God that I am assured that He is infinitely more powerful than Satan, so that the followers of Jesus can rest in the assurance of His protective power. I travel very often, and when I get to my hotel room, the first thing I do is to kneel down and ask God to take over that place by the power of the blood of Jesus, and not to allow any evil forces or influences in my room, no matter what has happened there before my stay. "Greater is He who is in you than he who is in the world" (1 John 4:4). Jesus always prevails.

When Paul arrived at Ephesus, God was performing mighty miracles of healing and exorcism through him (Acts 19:11, 12). Seeing this, some tried to exorcise evil spirits by invoking the name of "Jesus whom Paul preaches" (verse 13), as if it were a magic spell or an incantation formula. Seven sons of a Jewish chief priest named Sceva tried to do this. "And the evil spirit answered and said to them, 'I recognize Jesus, and I know about Paul, but who are you?'" (verse 15). The evil spirit overpowered the impostors, and they had to flee that house (verse 16). We don't face the forces of darkness on our own and we don't take evil for granted. Yet all evil spirits recognize and are conquered by the power of the name of Jesus, and they know the names of those who belong to Jesus, because His mighty and complete protection covers us. This event became widely known in Ephesus. "And the name of the Lord Jesus was being magnified" (verse 17). It resulted in many who practiced magic renouncing their sorcery and publicly burning their incantation scrolls, valued at fifty thousand drachmae (pieces of silver) because of the power they were thought to possess. It is at this point that Luke (the author of Acts) makes the fifth *report of progress* in this book: "The word of the Lord was growing mightily and *prevailing*" (verse 20). Yes! Jesus prevails over evil! At the cross He overcame evil for good! Be assured that the name of Jesus protects you!

My Response: _____

HIS CAUSE

"Take courage; for as you have solemnly witnessed to My cause at Jerusalem, so you must witness at Rome also."

—Acts 23:11

It's amazing that God is triumphant and His cause advances even in the midst of the most disheartening of circumstances. For example, consider what happened to Joseph back in Genesis 37. The sons of Jacob stripped Joseph of his colorful tunic, sold him to the Ishmaelites for twenty shekels of silver, and he was taken to Egypt to Potiphar's house. Yet God was triumphant in the midst of this tragedy, and Joseph became a ruler of Egypt, second only to Pharaoh. God used him to save the lives of many people and to preserve the race through which the Messiah would come. I am amazed that "God causes *all things* to work together for good to those who love God, to those who are called according to His purpose" (Romans 8:28).

Paul was in trouble, as he had often been, but this time he was seized in the temple in Jerusalem. After telling the Jews the story of his conversion and the calling he received from God (Acts 22), he then appeared before the council (Acts 23). But a great dissension occurred between the Pharisees and Sadducees about Paul being a Pharisee, "on trial for the hope and resurrection of the dead!" (Acts 23:6), and the commander ordered Paul to be taken away by force and brought into the barracks, because he was afraid that Paul would be torn to pieces (verse 10). The following night, the Lord Himself stood by Paul's side, as He had done at other pivotal times in his ministry when his circumstances looked disheartening. The Lord said: "Take courage; for as you have solemnly witnessed to My cause at Jerusalem, so you must witness at Rome also" (verse 11). No doubt this meant so much for Paul and sustained him on his journey to Rome, which took a long time and was filled with perils, trials, and opportunities to witness. God used this difficulty in Jerusalem to spread the gospel further, and His cause was advanced in that way. We don't always understand how God can turn *all things* for good and for His glory, yet we can fully trust His ability to do exactly that. After all, the cross looked as if it were the greatest defeat, and yet it was His greatest triumph!

My Response: _____

His Dependability

*"Therefore, keep up your courage, men, for I believe God
that it will turn out exactly as I have been told."*

—Acts 27:25

I had just finished preaching from the book of Ruth, on the topic of
the *Go'el*, the kinsman-redeemer, which is my favorite theme, as it
relates to Jesus in the whole Bible. A scholar came up to me at the end
and said: "And Jesus is not the type of *Go'el* who removes His sandal!"
It was a clever observation because, in the book of Ruth, the closest relative that could redeem Naomi and Ruth refused to do so, signifying his
decision by removing his sandal according to the custom of the time (see
Ruth 4:7, 8). Then Boaz, the second kinsman-redeemer in line, bought
the land and married Ruth. Jesus, the ultimate Redeemer, never refuses
to act on our behalf; he never *removes His sandal*. We can always trust His
word and depend on His presence, His promises, and the efficacy of His
sacrifice for us.

Everything around us constantly changes: including people, circumstances, economy, and relationships. But there is something you can
always depend on: God with us, Immanuel. He is the same yesterday,
today, and tomorrow. He is always there, His word is reliable, and so
is His assurance of salvation through the blood of Jesus. You can depend on it! In the book of Acts, Paul learned to depend on God's words
through thick and thin. When they were at sea, in the middle of a fierce
and devastating storm that would cause a shipwreck, God sent an angel
with a message for Paul: "Do not be afraid, Paul; you must stand before
Caesar . . . God has granted you all those who are sailing with you" (Acts
27:24). Paul absolutely believed the message and spoke to the men in
the ship: "There will be no loss of life among you, but only of the ship"
(verse 22). He had no proof of this other than God's word, and that was
enough for him. "And so it happened that they all were brought safely to
land" (verse 44). God has promised that believers in Jesus will be saved
through His sacrifice on the cross. He has also promised to be with us
every day, until the end of this world. You can depend on Him! His
promises are reliable, His victory is assured, and His sacrifice is more
than sufficient!

My Response: _____

HIS RECREATION

On either side of the river was the tree of life, bearing twelve kinds of fruit, yielding its fruit every month; and the leaves of the tree were for the healing of the nations.

—Revelation 22:2

Have you ever received much more than you expected? I was in the middle of a long international trip when, having finished a speaking engagement, I had to stay a few extra days in a hotel to work on a project before heading to the next country. My hosts graciously paid for the additional nights. Wondering where I would be eating during the few extra days, I went to the reception desk. That's when I was notified that my hosts had prepaid for all of my daily meals at a restaurant. Wow! I was pleasantly surprised and so grateful!

We can't even start to grasp what awaits us in eternity! Even our best imagination fails us when it comes to God's heavenly surprise for His children. The last book of the Bible ends with a scene of redeemed humanity returned to the tree of life. We have come full circle, and God has recreated the earth! The tree that God planted in the beginning in Paradise is back. Remember how Jesus promised Paradise to the criminal on the cross (see Luke 23:43)? Well, here we are, standing by the tree of life. John utters the seventh and last beatitude in this book: "Blessed are those who wash their robes, so that they may have the right to the tree of life, and may enter by the gates into the city" (Revelation 22:14). The expression of "washing their robes" has already been explained in Revelation: "They have washed their robes and made them white in the blood of the Lamb" (Revelation 7:14). The blessed ones have the right to the tree of life, a symbol of immortality, because they have washed their robes in the blood of the Lamb, accepting the ransom He paid. "The tree of life in the new Jerusalem symbolizes eternal life free of death and suffering. . . . Once again human beings will share in the gift of eternal life that Adam enjoyed before sin entered the world. All that was lost through Adam is now regained through Christ."* Praise the Lord! Be encouraged! Jesus has purchased a suffering-free eternal reality for us!

My Response: _____

---

* Ranko Stefanovic, *Revelation of Jesus Christ*, 2nd ed. (Berrien Springs, MI: Andrews University Press, 2009), 604.

His Bride

The Spirit and the bride say, "Come." And let the one who hears say, "Come." And let the one who is thirsty come.
—Revelation 22:17

I am sure you've heard marriage vows before; perhaps you've even uttered them yourself at your wedding ceremony. We promise to be faithful to each other, in sickness and in health, for richer or poorer, and so on. Then the final sentence: " 'Til death do us part." Wonderfully, with our heavenly Bridegroom, it is the exact *opposite*! His death is what reunites us and guarantees our eternal life with Him!

The Bible teaches that there will be a new earth, where God will dwell with His people, His bride, forever: "And I saw the holy city, new Jerusalem, coming down out of heaven from God, made ready as a bride adorned for her husband. And I heard a loud voice from the throne, saying, 'Behold, the tabernacle of God is among men . . . and they shall be His people, and God Himself will be among them' " (Revelation 21:2, 3). This will be an eternity without pain, sickness, or death! And all of heaven is so excited about us, His bride: "Then one of the seven angels . . . came and spoke with me saying, 'Come here, I will show you *the bride, the wife of the Lamb*' " (verse 9). Yes, there is an eternal future without pain for the people of God. In this sinful world, we see marriage vows and trust being violated, which leaves us brokenhearted. But it is not that way with our heavenly Bridegroom! He is eager to have us home with Him forever. At the end of the book of Revelation, the bride of the Lamb issues a passionate invitation: Come and join us! We, the bride, are so excited that our Bridegroom is at hand that we don't want anyone missing! "The Spirit *and the bride* say, 'Come.' And let the one who hears say, 'Come.' And let the one who is thirsty come; *let the one who wishes take the water of life without cost*" (Revelation 22:17). Oh, yes! It is without cost for us! But it did cost the Bridegroom His life. I can't wait for His hug after all these years of suffering and pain. He is eager to embrace us and to embrace you, and to welcome us to a pain-free eternity. If you are suffering today, may this assured future encourage you. The wedding march is about to begin: Here comes the Groom!

My Response: _____

HIS YEARNING

He who testifies to these things says, "Yes, I am coming quickly."
Amen. Come, Lord Jesus.

—Revelation 22:20

I closely followed the kidnapping of Utah teenager Elizabeth Smart and her ordeal in captivity from June 5, 2002 to March 12, 2003. Since then I have read her book about the nightmare. I was deeply touched by the way Salt Lake City celebrated her homecoming when she was found. The whole town was dressed in ribbons and balloons in Elizabeth's favorite colors: blue and yellow. Businesses stopped advertising their services and products, and placed "Elizabeth, Welcome Home" signs instead. It was a celebration that showcased the longing that characterized the nine-month search for Elizabeth. She was now home!

We are all longing for our heavenly home! And yet sometimes we forget the yearning of our heavenly Father to come back for us. At the end of the book of Revelation, we get the final multi-descriptive portrait of Christ, which repeats some of the descriptions of Jesus that we found at the beginning of the book: "I am the Alpha and the Omega, the first and the last, the beginning and the end" (Revelation 22:13). Jesus was there at the beginning, and He will be there at the end of our earthly story. Jesus is, was, and will be with us! The last words of the risen Christ are recorded in Revelation 22:20: "Yes, I am coming *quickly.*" Do you hear the eagerness, the yearning of a Parent coming back to take His children home? John's answer is also representative of the longing response of all of us—to be with our Redeemer forever: "Amen. Come, Lord Jesus" (verse 20). Yes! Let's add our eager voices together: Amen! Come, Lord Jesus! Come soon! This is the true history of humankind from the beginning to eternity. Jesus is triumphant, and the kidnapper has lost. This is the story of the successful rescue of God's kidnapped children, only possible because a costly ransom was paid for us at the cross. Can you imagine the heavenly signs: "Dear child, Welcome Home!"? I can't wait for our voices to join the two-word cry: Jesus wins! If you are facing pain and trials today, just remember how it ends. Jesus is yearning to embrace you and take you home!

My Response: _____

153

HIS BENEVOLENCE

Opening his mouth, Peter said: "I most certainly understand now that God is not one to show partiality."
—Acts 10:34

As I travel around the world, I am always amazed at how history repeats itself. There are sad chapters in history, when a social, racial, religious, or political group is oppressed by another group which happens to be in power at the time. Unfortunately, when times change, and the tables are turned, frequently the oppressed became the oppressor. This phenomenon is rooted in the core of the human heart, which seeks to exclude others, who are not part of their own group.

In the New Testament, members of the newly-formed Christian community had a hard time understanding that God's benevolence and goodwill was directed towards all individuals, not only those of Jewish background. It was so hard for them to understand God's favor upon the others. The religious people were much harder to convince of the inclusivity of God's love and salvation than the Gentiles were. A case in point is the story of Cornelius and Peter, narrated in Acts 10. Cornelius was a centurion, who had become a *God-fearer*, which means that he worshiped the God of Israel, but had not converted to Judaism and was not ritually circumcised. On the other hand, Peter had been with Jesus during His public ministry. He was a disciple, one of the twelve, and a member of His inner circle of three disciples who witnessed additional divine manifestations. Having been reinstated to ministry after denying his Master, he experienced Jesus' grace and love firsthand. Yet it took a lot to convince Peter that he should step into Cornelius's house. It was much easier for God to convince Cornelius to send messengers to fetch Peter than it was to convince Peter to go with the messengers to Cornelius. Peter saw a vision three times (verses 10–16), which he then interpreted as: "God has shown me that I should not call any man unholy or unclean. That is why I came" (verses 28, 29). God's love challenges our biases. He does not show partiality to color, accent, ancestry, or social status. You are *His beloved child*. Whatever your background or circumstances, He loves you and His victory is for *all*!

My Response: _____

HIS EXCEPTION

"Surely no one can refuse the water for these to be baptized who have received the Holy Spirit just as we did, can he?"
—Acts 10:47

I had the privilege of visiting ancient Caesarea. Built by Herod the Great and named in honor of Caesar Augustus, it is an impressive town on the coast. Several structures, such as the ancient Roman amphitheater and the aqueduct, witness to its flourishing society during New Testament times. It is in this town that a centurion by the name of Cornelius saw a vision of an angel instructing him to send someone to Joppa (a town thirty-eight miles south of Caesarea) to fetch Peter, so that he could explain the gospel to him (see Acts 10:1–8).

Immediately Cornelius sent for Peter, who was staying at Simon the Tanner's house in Joppa. As we discussed yesterday, God had to convince Peter, through visions and the voice of the Spirit, to go with these men (verses 9–20). In Caesarea, Cornelius had gathered his relatives and close friends, and Peter preached the gospel to them. Then God did something out of the usual sequence, astonishing Peter and all his companions. "While Peter was still speaking these words, the Holy Spirit fell upon all those who were listening to the message. All the circumcised believers who came with Peter were amazed, because the gift of the Holy Spirit had been poured out on the Gentiles also. For they were hearing them speaking with tongues and exalting God" (verses 44–46). Then Peter ordered that they be baptized. Wow! You see, with visions and all, Peter wasn't ready to baptize Gentiles into the community, so God got ahead of him. In Acts, the order is *always* as follows: the gospel of Jesus is preached, people are baptized, and the Holy Spirit falls on them, *except* this time. God chose the Gentiles and had to get out of sequence because His own people were not ready to recognize His choice. The Spirit fell on them first, and *then* they were baptized. God loves all and often chooses people who are *outside the box*. If you were left out of the "in" group or were told that you need to change in order for God to love you, may this story convince you that God's love is not subject to human barriers.

My Response: _____

HIS IDENTIFICATION

"Saul, Saul, why are you persecuting Me?"

—Acts 9:4

The persecution of Christians is growing around the globe. I was startled when I read recent reports that highlight that this problem is worse now than at any other time in the past. The Open Doors organization, which serves persecuted Christians worldwide, labels many countries as having "high, very high, or extreme persecution" and keeps adding them to the World Watch List.* This is not just an ancient problem, and we can get involved by praying for oppressed Christians.

The first verse of Acts 9 is astonishing: "Now Saul, still breathing threats and murder against the disciples of the Lord, went to the high priest." Saul, who had been introduced to the reader back at the stoning of Stephen (Acts 7:58), went to Caiaphas to ask for letters of extradition to bring all the followers of Jesus "bound" to Jerusalem (Acts 9:2). This time he was after those who had taken refuge in the city of Damascus, in the province of Syria. This city, located about one hundred fifty miles from Jerusalem, was outside of the Holy Land, and had a large Jewish population. Saul (Hebrew for Paul), had consented to the death of the first Christian martyr (Acts 8:1) and was now persecuting all those belonging to the Way, an identification mentioned many times in Acts (chapters 18, 19, 22, 24). "As he was traveling, it happened that he was approaching Damascus, and suddenly a light from heaven flashed around him; and he fell to the ground and heard a voice saying to him, 'Saul, Saul, why are you persecuting *Me*?' " (Acts 9:3, 4). Notice that the resurrected Christ speaks to Saul, identifying Himself with the persecuted group. He didn't say: "Why are you persecuting *them*?" When Saul asked "Who are You, Lord?" once again Jesus responded, "I am Jesus *whom you are persecuting*" (verse 5). Jesus embodied the persecution of His followers as being done unto Him personally. Jesus continues to identify personally with His oppressed followers; whatever is done to them is being done unto Him. Join me in praying for those who are suffering for their faith in Christ. And if you are going through hardships for His sake, may you know that Jesus identifies personally with you.

My Response: _____

—————————

* Open Doors USA, "World Watch List," http://www.opendoorsusa.org/christian-persecution/world-watch-list/.

HIS SUMMARY

"LOVE THE LORD YOUR GOD WITH ALL YOUR HEART, . . . ALL YOUR SOUL,
. . . ALL YOUR MIND, . . . ALL YOUR STRENGTH."

—Mark 12:30

The newscasters were so emotional that they could hardly talk. My eyes filled with tears too. The body of Sargent Helus, a hero in the mass shooting in Thousand Oaks, California, was being transported by car on the Ventura Freeway. He had given his life trying to save the lives of others. As the procession passed by, everyone stopped in recognition of his ultimate sacrifice. The overpass bridges were crowded with people, as were the side streets; thousands gathered to honor him. We respectfully honor the heroes who freely and lovingly gave their lives.

How can we honor Jesus, who gave His life for us? At the time of Jesus, there were 613 detailed statutes of the Law established, and the religious experts used to argue about which of them was the most important. A scribe asked Jesus: "What commandment is the foremost [first] of all?" (Mark 12:28). Perhaps Jesus would respond with a prioritized list that we all could use. Instead, Jesus summarized the law with one key word: love. Love your God and your neighbor as yourself. The Greek verb is *agapao*, the intrinsically motivated, God-given commitment and devotion, which is the response to His complete, wholehearted love and devotion for us that resulted in His ultimate sacrifice. "We love, *because* He first loved us." (1 John 4:19). Jesus responded with the words of Deuteronomy 6:4, 5, recited daily by devoted Jews, and with Leviticus 19:18. God wants our all: all our heart, all our soul, all our mind, and all our strength (Mark 12:30). And that's what He deserves, because He gave His all! This response of love and devotion is worth much more to Him than anything else we may have or do (verse 33). May we accept more of His love, and therefore love Him more! "That Christ may dwell in your hearts through faith; and that you, being rooted and grounded in *love*, may be able to comprehend with all the saints what is the breadth and length and height and depth, and to know the *love of Christ* which surpasses knowledge, that you may be filled up to all the fullness of God" (Ephesians 3:17–19).

My Response: _____

HIS SPIRIT

After being baptized . . . he saw the Spirit of God descending
as a dove and lighting on Him.

—Matthew 3:16

I was born in a pastor's home and had heard many sermons since my earliest childhood. I still remember my dad's sermon on the mathematical impossibility of the gospel being preached to the whole world before the second coming of Christ. First, he would write on the board some formulas, which included worldwide birth and death ratios, and how it was impossible for the church to catch up with these figures. Then He would add the element of the Spirit of God (as in the time of the first century Christian church) and explain how the divine outcome could not be measured with simple math.

After Jesus was baptized, He came up from the water, the heavens opened, and Jesus saw the Spirit of God descending on Him (Matthew 3:16). Even though Jesus was conceived of the Holy Spirit, and the Spirit was with Him throughout His life, He was now visibly being empowered by the Spirit to fulfill His redemptive mission. The One who would baptize with the Spirit (Matthew 3:11), was now being baptized by the Spirit at the inauguration of His public ministry. The OT prophets had announced that God's chosen Servant would be anointed by the Spirit: "Behold, My Servant, whom I uphold; My chosen one in whom My soul delights. I have put My Spirit upon Him" (Isaiah 42:1; see also Isaiah 11:2). Jesus Himself quoted from Isaiah 61:1 in the synagogue at Nazareth and proclaimed the fulfillment of this prophecy in Him: "THE SPIRIT OF THE LORD IS UPON ME" (Luke 4:18). Jesus promised multiple times to provide the same Spirit to His followers. His disciples were to proclaim the good news of forgiveness of sins in Jesus' name only after being empowered by the Spirit from on high (Luke 24:47–49). We can't measure our ability to do our calling and God-given tasks with our own strength, because we will always become anxious and worried if we do. Those who believe in Jesus have the promise of the Holy Spirit, whose power enables us to proclaim the gospel boldly. Let's ask for a daily filling of God's Spirit!

My Response: _____

HIS DOMINION

And He said to them, "Go!" And they came out.
—Matthew 8:32

I was speechless as I read the headline in the *Telegraph*: "Cannibal tribe apologizes for eating Methodists."* The August 16, 2007 article went on: "A tribe in Papua New Guinea has apologized for killing and eating four 19th century missionaries. . . . Thousands of villagers attended a reconciliation ceremony near Rabaul, the capital of East New Britain province, once notorious for the ferocity of its cannibals." This article was a sobering reminder of the ultimate price paid by dozens of missionaries who ventured into unfriendly regions with the gospel.

Jesus often entered territories where no one else would go. "When He came to the other side into the country of the Gadarenes, two men who were demon-possessed met Him as they were coming out of the tombs. They were so extremely violent that *no one could pass by that way*" (Matthew 8:28). No one could pass there, except Jesus, whose complete dominion over evil forces is highlighted in this account. Jesus had demonstrated power over diseases, nature, and now demons, who immediately recognize Jesus' true identity as "Son of God" (verse 29). The demons, knowing the authoritative power of Jesus over them, request permission to go into a herd of swine, which eventually "perished in the waters" (see verse 32). Jesus' dominion over evil forces is portrayed in one authoritative word: "Go!" And the demons went. And it is striking to me, that with all His power and dominion over the spiritual realms, Jesus does not force His Presence upon the human heart: "They [the whole city] implored Him to leave their region" (verse 34). And He left. The demons implored Jesus for permission to leave, but the people implored *Him* to leave, and He did. Jesus continues to enter the most hopeless of situations where no one else dares to enter, and He continues to be the Healer of all kinds of evil in various forms, bringing peace and hope. Let's give Him dominion over our hearts. "For I am convinced that neither death, nor life, nor angels, nor principalities . . . nor height, nor depth . . . will be able to separate us from the love of God, which is in Christ Jesus our Lord" (Romans 8:38, 39).

My Response: _____

---

* Nick Squires, "Cannibal Tribe Apologizes for Eating Methodists, *Telegraph,* August 16, 2007, 2:59 P.M. BST, https://www.telegraph.co.uk/news/worldnews/1560483 /Cannibal-tribe-apologises-for-eating-Methodists.html.

HIS INTERRUPTION

When the Lord saw her, He felt compassion for her,
and said to her, "Do not weep."

—Luke 7:13

I have referred to this story many times in funerals and memorial services. Oh, how I wish that every one of those gatherings would have been interrupted by Jesus, the way this funeral was. And oh, how thankful I am that it is only a matter of a time until Jesus will interrupt the death of all of His children and will command them to rise! And they will come out of their tombs! I can't wait!

This story takes place in Nain, a village about six miles southeast of Nazareth. Jesus, accompanied by a large crowd, is approaching the village. As they get to the gate, another crowd is coming out in order to bury a young man outside of the city gate, as was the custom. The two crowds meet: an excited crowd (Luke 7:11) and a mourning crowd (verse 12). Can you imagine a widow losing her only source of financial and emotional support? Her whole world came crashing down. This is why it seems strange that Jesus would say to her: "Do not weep" (verse 13). Why shouldn't she weep? All her hopes and dreams had died together with her son; she couldn't imagine life without him. But she didn't realize that Jesus was the Life, victorious over death! Then Jesus does something unimaginable: he touches the untouchable. "He came up and *touched* the coffin; and the bearers came to a halt" (verse 14). Imagine the funeral procession: the woman crying, the coffin holding her precious son, and the crowd accompanying her in the saddest of journeys. Suddenly, Jesus does something totally inappropriate—he touches the casket—and the coffin bearers come to a halt. They hear the voice of Jesus: "Young man, I say to you, arise! The dead man sat up and began to speak" (verses 14, 15). In this story, like in ours, Jesus directs his feelings and actions to the suffering person: the Lord saw *her*, He felt compassion for *her*, He spoke to *her*, and He gave the young man back to *her*. Jesus knows and understands our pain. He has compassion for our grieving hearts. Soon He will interrupt the death sleep of our loved ones, and we will hear His words: Arise! I can't wait for that blessed interruption!

My Response: _____

HIS PERSPECTIVE

*"Our friend Lazarus has fallen asleep; but I go, so that
I may awaken him out of sleep."*

—John 11:11

I distinctly remember the progression of my prayers. My father was very sick with cancer; the doctors had done all they could but now had sent him home to await the inevitable. His faith in Jesus was unshaken, and he was ready. I sent out Facebook messages asking for prayers, that God may grant peace and healing, according to His will. As the days went by, acknowledging that God was imparting supernatural peace, I sent out prayer requests for God's healing *or* for His mercy to let my dad sleep, once and for all. Death came as a relief for two reasons: the evil one could no longer bother him with pain, and my dad's death is temporary, until the resurrection day.

After His apparent delay, following the news of Lazarus's illness, Jesus finally told His disciples: "Let us go to Judea again" (John 11:7). His disciples reminded Him that the Jews had been seeking to stone Him, and Jesus responded by talking about day and night, and light and darkness (verses 8–10). The night symbolizes the absence of Jesus; He is the Light of the world. It was still day—but not for long. Then Jesus made a startling announcement: "Our friend Lazarus has fallen asleep; but I go, so that I may awaken him out of sleep" (verse 11). As usual in this Gospel, they misunderstand what He is saying and respond to His literal words: *OK, then, if he is asleep, he will recover.* Of course, Jesus had spoken of Lazarus's death. Up to the Christian Era, fear of death was paralyzing and widespread. People were terrified by the very thought of death and the unknown surrounding it. When Jesus died and conquered death, He radically changed the way His followers speak about death. It is no longer a terrifying event but a sweet sleep instead. The deceased, including my mother and father, are resting in a sweet sleep, awaiting the resurrection morning when they will hear a loud Voice calling them out of their tombs, just as Lazarus heard (verse 43). What a difference Jesus' perspective makes when a loved one dies! We have assurance because He conquered death!

My Response: _____

HIS COMPASSION

Jesus wept.

—John 11:35

Compassion: "A feeling of deep sympathy and sorrow for another who is stricken by misfortune, accompanied by a strong desire to alleviate the suffering."* I'm sure you have felt it. I have, with tears in my eyes attending a funeral, visiting someone in the hospital, or watching the news. Oh, the pain and sorrow of watching parents say goodbye to their children, or the urgency with which we want to alleviate a loved one's suffering, and the powerlessness we feel at our utter inability to change the circumstances.

But Jesus was not powerless, so why did He weep? Good question! After talking with Mary, Jesus asks where they have laid Lazarus (John 11:28–34). The next verse is the shortest verse of the Bible: "Jesus wept" (verse 35). This Greek verb is different from the verb for *weep* used elsewhere in this story. The others are mourning loudly; Jesus is weeping quietly (This term is used only here in the entire New Testament.) He is moved by everyone's sorrow. He knows what He is about to do, yet He is touched by the suffering of humanity. The Jews interpreted the tears of Jesus as the expression of His love (verse 36), and it was. His tender care for the mourners was evident; but this was not the only reason He cried. Jesus knew that pain was the result of sin; much suffering had been caused by God's enemy. In my favorite book (aside from the Bible), *The Desire of Ages*, we read that at that moment, "He saw that in the history of the world, beginning with the death of Abel, the conflict between good and evil had been unceasing. Looking down the years to come, He saw the suffering and sorrow, tears and death, that were to be the lot of men. His heart was pierced with the pain of the human family of all ages and in all lands. The woes of the sinful race were heavy upon His soul, and the fountain of His tears was broken up as He longed to relieve all their distress."† Yes, Jesus wept for us! Jesus feels compassion and is touched by our suffering, even though He knows that soon He is going to eliminate death, sickness, and evil, once and for all (Revelation 21:4). Be encouraged! Jesus wins!

My Response: _____

---

* *Dictionary.com*, s.v. "compassion (n.)," accessed April 12, 2019, http://www.dictionary.com/browse/compassion?s=t.

† Ellen G. White, *The Desire of Ages* (Mountain View, CA: Pacific Press®, 1940), 517.

HIS LIFE

"Lazarus, come forth." The man who had
died came forth.

—John 11:43, 44

I often go to the cemetery to bring flowers to my parents' tomb and to meditate on the blessings I have received from God through them. They rest in a beautiful section of the park, surrounded by flowers and trees. On special holidays, such as Mother's Day, Christmas, and Thanksgiving, many people come to honor their loved ones. I dare to imagine what that cemetery will look like on the day of the second coming of Jesus. I imagine beautiful scenes of angels reuniting families, just like in some of the paintings I have seen. I can't wait!

As Jesus makes His way to the tomb, the narrator reminds us that Lazarus had been dead for four days (John 11:39). This is an important detail because, unlike the biblical teaching, there was a popular belief that the soul of the dead lingered around the tomb for three days and left for good only on the fourth day. The scene includes a tomb, a stone against it, the sister of the deceased, the fact that four days have gone by, the warning that the body is decomposing, and there might have been a stench (verses 38, 39). As if Jesus had not noticed all these signs of death, He gives the outrageous order: "Remove the stone" (verse 39). Excuse me? Why would anyone want to do that? Perhaps Jesus wants to see His friend one last time . . . but that's not the reason. "Did I not say to you that if you believe, you will see the glory of God?" (verse 40). Believe, Martha! Believe, Elizabeth! Believe, John! Believe! "When He had said these things, He cried out with a loud voice, 'Lazarus, come forth' " (verse 43). Lazarus, come out! Life Himself is calling you! And Lazarus came out! Many say that Jesus called Lazarus by name because otherwise everyone buried in that cemetery would have come out. Life Himself was calling the dead, and death could not resist Life. But this was too big of a sign. "So from that day on they [the council of priests and Pharisees] planned together to kill Him" (verse 53). In the Gospel of John, this is the trigger for the death of Jesus. Jesus gave His life to give Lazarus life. Literally. In more than one sense, Jesus died so Lazarus could live. And He died so that my loved ones and yours may live. He is the Life! Believe!

My Response: _____

ENJOYING
HIS PEACE

HIS KEEPSAKE

"Peace I leave with you; My peace I give to you."
—John 14:27

Most of my life I was afraid of flying. It was so bad that I had to take medication just to get on a plane. I discovered John 14:27, where Jesus promises to give His peace to us. I remember highlighting this text and taking the Bible with me on the plane; I would recite the verse many times when the aircraft encountered turbulence, asking God to fulfill His promise and give me His peace. When it became evident that I would be flying constantly as part of my calling, I had to settle this issue with God. Now, I'm often dozing off as the plane takes off.

The disciples were getting worried because Jesus was talking about leaving them. In John 14, Jesus is comforting their anxious hearts: "Do not let your heart be troubled; believe in God, believe also in Me" (verse 1). His disciples wouldn't become orphans . . . the Helper, the Holy Spirit, would be with them (John 14:16–26). It is then that Jesus makes the most amazing announcement: "Peace I leave with you; My peace I give to you; not as the world gives do I give to you. Do not let your heart be troubled, nor let it be fearful" (verse 27). The word *peace* is repeated twice. This was a common greeting and send-off Jewish expression (*shalom*), but Jesus qualifies it with the possessive pronoun. Jesus was leaving *His peace* with them; this was *His* special gift, a keepsake, that was to remain theirs, permanently. His peace is much greater than the peace the world offers, because the source of His peace is Jesus Himself! If you are anything like me, you know that every morning many thoughts compete for attention. It's easy to lose our inner peace by spinning the wheels in our minds, wasting energy trying to control that which is out of our control. God offers us His peace, which is greater than our own understanding of any situation: "Be anxious for nothing, but in everything by prayer and supplication with thanksgiving let your requests be made known to God. And the *peace of God*, which surpasses all comprehension, will guard your heart and your minds in Christ Jesus" (Philippians 4:6, 7). Jesus paid a high price for it! For "the punishment that brought us *peace* was on him" (Isaiah 53:5, NIV).

My Response: _____

HIS PRIORITY

"You are worried and bothered about so many things; but only one thing is necessary."

—Luke 10:41, 42

T he timing couldn't have been worse. I was trying a new business venture by starting a computer company; we leased our office space, hired employees, and launched the business. One day I got a sharp pain in my knee and suddenly couldn't walk. At the hospital, I was told that my meniscus had been crushed, and I needed immediate surgery. But I had so many things to do! *Who would take care of things? How long would recovery take?* Looking back, I realize that during that time God was training me to trust Him with my anxieties, my future, my bills, and my life. He was teaching me to focus on the *one* thing that is necessary: Jesus!

Martha had good intentions and Jesus counted on her hospitality. The biblical narrative says that "Martha welcomed Him into *her* home" (Luke 10:38). She wanted to make sure everything was taken care of, especially because Jesus was in her house! She definitely needed to make preparations. We are told that she was being distracted about much "service," which in the original Greek language is *diakonia*. How can a church function without deacons and deaconesses? They keep everything running! Well, the issue wasn't really the service. Jesus pointed out that Martha's problem was that she was *worried* and *troubled* about the things she needed to do (see. verse 41). In contrast, we frequently find Mary just sitting at the feet of Jesus and listening to His voice.

When facing challenges most of us go into a problem-solving mode. We try to figure things out and spend quite a bit of energy rehearsing possible scenarios and looking for solutions. Jesus invites us to remember that we are His children. He wants us to learn to focus on who He is and to go to Him as our first resource, resting in His goodness, His love, and His ability to provide for us. Jesus offered the cure for anxiety: many things may be important, but only *one* is necessary: He! His Presence! As we focus on Him—His love, His sufficiency, His peace, His power, His grace—everything else falls into its appropriate place.

My Response: _____

HIS RENEWAL

He said to the man, "Stretch out your hand!" He stretched it out,
and it was restored to normal, like the other.
—Matthew 12:13

The day that I had the emergency meniscectomy on my right knee, I didn't realize that it would take a while before I could walk again. The doctors were not able to extract the meniscus arthroscopically; the incision was large, and I was in need of physical therapy to regain the use of my leg. I remember distinctively how my right leg became very thin compared with the other. It took two months for me to regain enough muscle to be able to stand on the injured leg. Maybe this is why I noticed that the report of Jesus' healing of a man's withered hand (Matthew 12:13) is followed by a description of the extent of the healing: "and it was restored to normal [healthy], *like the other*" (verse 13).

The Pharisees who had challenged Jesus in the grain fields (Matthew 12:1–8) followed Him into the synagogue (12:9–14). There Jesus encountered a man with a withered hand (verse 10). "And they questioned Jesus, asking, 'Is it lawful to heal on the Sabbath?'—so that they might accuse Him." (verse 10). With the exception of the plucking of grain, all the other Sabbath controversies between Jesus and the Pharisees in the Gospels relate to healings and the result of the healings (see Matthew 12:9–14; Luke 13:10–17; 14:1–6; John 5:1–16; 9). From the very beginning of the world, the Sabbath was supposed to point to, and celebrate, the work of Jesus in creating, redeeming, and restoring the human race. Jesus chose the Sabbath day for many of His healing miracles to highlight the redeeming freedom and rest in Him, portrayed in this special day. Jesus responded in the rabbinical style of lesser to greater arguments (*qal wahomer*), followed by a pronouncement: any man would help their sheep if it fell on the Sabbath, "*How much more* valuable then is a man than a sheep! So then, it is lawful to do good on the Sabbath" (Matthew 12:12). Jesus went on to restore the man's hand, to the extent that it was healthy *like the other*. The Sabbath reminds us of the core of the redemption plan: rest and renewal are available for each one of us through the salvific work of Jesus.

My Response: _____

HIS REST

"Come to Me, all who are weary and heavy-laden,
and I will give you rest."

—Matthew 11:28

I posted a picture on my Facebook page and that's when I realized how soul-tired most of the people in my generation really are! It was a photo of an overworked and exhausted young woman who had fallen asleep at her desk, her head resting on top of a pile of unfinished paperwork. Many people commented, relating to this weary person. The caption under the picture encouraged those who were *heavy-laden* to come to Jesus to receive *real rest* (Matthew 11:28–30).

The invitation of Jesus, "Come . . . all who are weary and heavy-laden, and I will give you *rest*" (Matthew 11:28), is as relevant today as when Matthew wrote it down in the first century. Our hearts are worn out in the struggles of life; Jesus knows about this and offers us a remedy. For many years, I have been intrigued by the apparently deliberate juxtaposition found in Matthew 11:28–12:14. First Jesus offers His own rest (Matthew 11:28–30), then proclaims Himself the Lord of the Sabbath, the day of rest, in the next narrative (Matthew 12:8). The invitation of Jesus to rest in Him is unique to Matthew, and it immediately precedes the only two episodes in this Gospel that occur on the *Sabbath*. This intriguing juxtaposition became the topic of my PhD dissertation.* I found very exciting insights during the eight years that I spent in these verses. One of them is that there are 137 occurrences of this particular root word for rest in the Greek Old Testament (LXX), and that in the first five books of the Bible, the term predominantly relates to a *sabbatical rest to the Lord*. Matthew's audience heard Jesus' message loud and clear: "Come to Me, all you who are weary . . . and I will give you the *real sabbatical rest*." Those who heed His invitation now enter into the Sabbath rest in its fullest sense, because they *rest in Him*. Thus, we find the full meaning of the weekly *Sabbath rest celebration* in the identity and mission of Jesus. We were never meant to be overwhelmed by anxiety and fear; we were designed for peace. When we accept the invitation of Jesus, we find *real rest* for our souls. Jesus, calm our anxious hearts!

My Response: _____

———————
* See my book for a sharing version of my findings: Elizabeth Talbot, *I Will Give You Rest* (Nampa, ID: Pacific Press®, 2015).

HIS CARE

*"I am the good shepherd, and I know My own and My own know Me
. . . and I lay down My life for the sheep."*
—John 10:14, 15

It was an unexpected gift from God. I was preparing the outlines for a television series when I reached out to pick up a book I needed. As I opened it, something fell out of the book—sermon notes; however, these were not mine, but my dad's. I was speechless as tears welled up in my eyes, because this was my father's homily that he had preached when I was commissioned to the ministry long ago. The topic was the Good Shepherd, what He has done for us, and His care for His sheep. He then talked about what it means to be called to shepherd God's people. My father has since passed, and I feel so blessed to have found this gift.

Hundreds of years before Jesus was born, Ezekiel prophesied that God would send His Shepherd, a descendant of David, to care for His Sheep. God had entrusted His sheep to religious leaders who had not done their job, and God denounced Israel's shepherds, exposing their transgressions in no uncertain terms. "Woe, shepherds of Israel who have been feeding themselves! . . . You eat the fat and clothe yourselves with the wool, you slaughter the fat sheep without feeding the flock. Those who are sickly you have not strengthened, the diseased you have not healed, the broken you have not bound up, the scattered you have not brought back, nor have you sought for the lost" Ezekiel 34:2–4. God was not happy with the way in which His sheep had been treated: scattered, abandoned, and oppressed; this was not what God had in mind! From there on, He would care for His own sheep: "I Myself will search for My sheep and seek them out. As a shepherd cares for his herd . . . I will care for My sheep and will deliver them . . . I will set over them one shepherd, My servant David [David's descendant], and he will feed them . . . himself and be their shepherd" (Ezekiel 34:11, 12, 23). Jesus fulfilled this prophecy. He laid down His life and lovingly cares for His sheep. If you have been lost, hungry, sick, and oppressed, remember that you now have a Good Shepherd, who is ready to give you peace and to restore your soul (see Psalm 23:3).

My Response: _____

HIS MIRACLE

"Which is easier, to say to the paralytic, 'Your sins are forgiven';
or to say, 'Get up, and pick up your pallet and walk'?"

—Mark 2:9

Stress management was one of the first classes I took in my organizational behavior studies. I found it fascinating and I had to implement the knowledge right away because my car wouldn't start on the day of my final, and I had to borrow another vehicle. After my final exam, another student asked me to assist with his presentation. He connected a little device to my finger and was able to show the whole class how my body was responding to my stress level that day. I became convinced about how closely connected our physical and emotional health are.

Even though the four men brought the paralytic to be healed, the first words of Jesus were, "Son, your sins are forgiven" (Mark 2:5). This was the man's greatest need, so Jesus dealt with it first. We all need to know that we are at peace with God and that we are forgiven; there is no deeper realization for a human being. The scribes started questioning Jesus in their minds because they doubted His authority to forgive sins. The forgiveness of sin was, and is, always the greatest miracle. But it happens on the inside, and therefore they doubted it (verses 6, 7). Jesus asked them "Which is easier, to say to the paralytic, 'Your sins are forgiven'; or to say, 'Get up . . . and walk'?" (verse 9). And before receiving a response, He went on: " '*But so that you may know* that the Son of Man has authority on earth to forgive sins'—He said to the paralytic, 'I say to you, get up, pick up your pallet and go home' " (verse 10, 11). In other words, "Yes! Just get up! I can forgive sins, *and* I can heal you." Both forgiveness and healing are impossible things for mankind to perform, but both are possible for God. He is the Healer of mind, body, and soul. And the man got up, picked up his pallet, and went (verse 12). Are you in desperate need today? Do you need forgiveness? Are you in need of getting up from your mat of depression or inadequate feelings? Are you paralyzed by guilt or shame? His miracle starts in our soul. He offers forgiveness and peace. Our confidence is in the blood of Jesus (see Hebrews 10:19–22). So . . . Get up! Pick up! Go!

My Response: _____

HIS HOLD

*"I give them eternal life, and they shall never perish;
no one will snatch them out of my hand."*
—John 10:28, NIV

On June 7, 2016, a woman and her thirteen-year-old daughter were shopping at a dollar store when a man tried to abduct the girl. As the man was dragging the girl towards the exit her mother did everything she could to save her. Finally, the woman threw herself on top of the child, and the abductor was not able to drag them both. Having let go of the girl, he headed for the exit. He was apprehended in the parking lot by a police deputy. The whole frightening incident was caught on the surveillance camera.

The image of this mother, doing whatever it took to fight off the kidnapper, is the visualization I get when I read today's text. Jesus says with confidence: "no one will snatch them out of my hand" (John 10:28, NIV). This sentence is repeated by Jesus twice in two verses. Having confronted those who didn't believe in Him (verses 24, 25), Jesus explains how secure His sheep really are in His hand, and the Father's hand: "My sheep hear My voice, and I know them, and they follow Me; and I give eternal life to them, and they will never perish; and *no one will snatch them out of My hand*. My Father, who has given them to Me, is greater than all; and *no one is able to snatch them out of the Father's hand*. I and the Father are one' " (verses 27–30). Whoever believes and follows Jesus is eternally secure, just as a sheep is secure in the good Shepherd's hands; just as a child can rest in the arms of a loving Parent. This brings such profound peace to my mind and dissipates my anxiety about the future, the end of the world, eternal life, et cetera. You can rest in the most capable hands in the universe. Even if God's adversary tries to snatch us out of His hand, Jesus and the Father will not let it happen, for they are greater than any power that might threaten God's children. Jesus offers us certainty. In the words of Leon Morris: "No one will snatch them from Christ. It is one of the precious things about the Christian faith that our continuance in eternal life depends not on our feeble hold on Christ, but on his firm grip on us."*

My Response: _____

---

* Leon Morris, *The Gospel According to John*, rev. ed., NICNT (Grand Rapids, MI: 1995, Eerdmans), 463.

HIS POWER

*Then He got up and rebuked the winds and the sea,
and it became perfectly calm.*

—Matthew 8:26

I don't like wind; I particularly don't like storms! I woke up in the middle of the night, in our brand-new home, to an eighty-mile-an-hour wind. After frantic calls to the authorities, I was informed that these were the Santa Ana winds; a "*strong* episode," they said. Strong? *This is a hurricane!*—I thought. It turned out that we had just bought our home in a wind tunnel area. Completely terrified, I invited my husband to pray together. As soon as I finished praying, he fell asleep! Asleep?! Not me; I stayed awake! When he woke up in the morning, he cheerfully announced, "See! You have the gift of prayer—but I have the gift of faith!"

"And behold, there arose a great storm on the sea, so that the boat was being covered with the waves; but Jesus Himself was asleep" (Matthew 8:24). Asleep! How is that possible? Matthew calls this storm a *seismos megas*; a mega shaking, like an earthquake in the lake (verse 24). The disciples run out of options, realizing that they are *powerless* over this particular storm. Then the fishermen turn for help to the Carpenter. They are so desperate that their cry, in Matthew's Greek language, is represented by three single words, that sound something like: "Lord! Save! Perishing!" (verse 25). Have you noticed that our most desperate and heartfelt prayers are usually just one word? "Help!" "Please!" "Really?" "Why?" "Thanks!" They came to Jesus, and their cries woke Him up. "He said to them, 'Why are you afraid, you men of little faith?' Then He got up and rebuked the winds and the sea and it became perfectly (*megalē*) calm." (verse 26). From *mega* storm to *mega* peace. Why were they afraid? Well . . . they were *powerless* over the mega storm. Just like us. A sudden, unexpected storm . . . we do everything we can but it's not working. Our boat (our family, our job, our marriage, etc.) is being overrun by waves. Then we remember that Jesus is in the boat, and we can rest, as he rested in the mega storm. Do you know why? Because we are "*power-less*," but Jesus is "*power-full*." He is our Savior, Lord, and Deliverer. He's our *mega* God!

My Response: _____

His Calmness

The wind died down and it became perfectly calm.
—Mark 4:39

I n 1986 archaeologists found a fishing boat that is believed to date back to the first century A.D. It is now displayed at the Yigal Allon Center at Kibbutz Ginosar and is known as the "Jesus boat." I had the privilege of visiting this site, and it was quite an experience. This fishing boat is twenty-seven feet long, seven and a half feet wide, and approximately four feet deep. Definitely not a very big boat. With thirteen people (Jesus and His twelve disciples), it would have been quite overcrowded in calm waters. But in the storm, it was sinking.

Picture the chaotic scene: fierce winds, waves crashing, the little boat filling up with water. Everyone is fighting for survival, except for One, who is sleeping! In the first century, the sea and other deep bodies of water were considered places where evil and demons resided. Therefore, for the disciples, this was not just a fierce storm; it had strong connotations of evil. This was a *wicked* storm, in the most graphic sense of the word. Mark is the only Gospel writer to tell us that there were "other boats" (Mark 4:36) going through this storm, along with the boat of Jesus and His disciples. Has this ever happened to you? You get hit by an unexpected storm so fierce that you know it has come from the devil himself, and you are under attack? I have. In early Christian art, sometimes the church is depicted as a boat with Jesus in a storm. This visualization helped early Christians under persecution to remember the presence of Jesus with them while going through trials and tribulations. The miracle of the stilling of the sea reminded them of the greater reality of salvation brought about through the saving death and resurrection of Jesus. There are many situations in life that threaten our minds and souls, yet Jesus is with us in the boat. "He got up and rebuked the wind and said to the sea, 'Hush, be still.' And the wind died down and it became perfectly calm" (Mark 4:39). Whether you are in a storm of guilt, shame, persecution, despair, or fear of the future, remember that Jesus has the power to still the storm. His calmness is real and readily available! Jesus, calm our anxious minds!

My Response: _____

His Watchfulness

"Why are you afraid? Do you still have no faith?"

—Mark 4:40

My grandparents lived in a small village, and as a child I loved visiting them. There was a large hospital with a swimming pool next to it, and I used to spend most of my days there because it was such a treat for me. But that section of the country was prone to sudden summer storms that could be quite violent. So, as soon as I would see that the clouds were getting dark, I would start running towards my grandparents' place, which was a couple of miles from the hospital. And I was always certain that my mom would be waiting for me.

The disciples encountered a severe storm, with a "fierce gale of wind," and they couldn't control their boat (Mark 4:37). These experienced fishermen were running out of options; they were sure that they were perishing. Jesus was sleeping in the stern, on the pillow usually found under the coxswain's seat. There is no doubt that the disciples were terrified of the storm, and that's why they woke Him up. Mark tells us that aside from their fear, they were struggling with something else, which is revealed in their rebuke of Jesus: "They woke Him and said to Him, 'Teacher, *do You not care* that we are perishing?' " (verse 38). They were doubting Jesus' personal interest in them, questioning His vigilance and watchfulness over them. Does it matter to you that we are dying? That we have no way out? Do you care? How often this question arises in our minds when we face difficulties that we don't understand. But Jesus is always watchful of His children in the storm. After stilling the tempest, Jesus addressed them: "Why are you afraid? Do you still have no faith?" (verse 40). After all you have witnessed of My power and love, do you still doubt if I care? Do you still wonder if I will act on your behalf? In a storm, we must be absolutely certain of God's care for us, otherwise, what do we have left? An author suggested adding the word "personally" to 1 Peter 5:7 in order to internalize this truth: "Casting all your anxiety on Him, because He *personally* cares for you." He personally cares, never doubt it. And yes! He cared so much, that He died in our place!

My Response: _____

HIS CONTROL

"Who then is this, that even the wind
and the sea obey Him?"

—Mark 4:41

The Sea of Galilee is prone to sudden storms, because it is surrounded by mountains and is approximately 685 feet below sea level. At times, the cool air from the Mediterranean Sea comes down through the mountain passes with fierce force and clashes violently with the hot air of the enclosed lake. I will never forget being on a boat on the same lake where Jesus calmed the storm. We saw fishing nets, we sang songs together, but most of all I imagined Jesus calming the angry waters while the helpless disciples wondered: "Who is this?"

Having addressed the wind and the water, that were by now completely calm, Jesus addressed the disciples: "Why are you afraid?" (Mark 4:40). Well, isn't it obvious? They were afraid because they thought they were perishing; they couldn't control the storm, no matter how hard they tried. We become afraid for the same reasons: we can't stop the phone calls, the medical results, the bad news. We just can't do it! When Jesus stilled the wind and the sea, the disciples were in awe: "They became very much afraid and said to one another, 'Who is this, that even the wind and the sea obey Him?' " (verse 41). Really, *Who is this?* The question "Who is this?" is repeated many times in the first half of Mark's Gospel. The authoritative Messiah is being revealed. This story is the beginning of a crescendo of the power of Jesus. First, His power over nature; next, His control over evil and demons (5:1–20), and the following two stories display His power over disease and death (verses 21–43). But the most striking realization in this Gospel is that Jesus, the powerful Son of God, who controls the wind and the sea, was to be the Servant, submitting His life as a ransom for many (see Mark 10:45). Jesus, the authoritative Messiah, would become the Suffering Servant, and would lay down His power and conquer evil through suffering. The Gospel of Mark is dedicated to understanding this profound juxtaposition: the authoritative Son of God is also the Suffering Son of Man. Jesus is sovereign, and through the cross He gained the crown. Let's submit ourselves to *His control.*

My Response: _____

HIS SECLUSION

"Come away . . . to a secluded place and rest a while."
—Mark 6:31

Sometimes your soul needs to catch up with your mind and body. I had a strong sense that God was asking me to take some time off and concentrate on my PhD dissertation. But I was the senior pastor of a church and things were going well, and there was so much to do . . . yet God seemed to insist. God knew I needed time away from my ministry to be instructed and refreshed. However, requesting leave without pay, to finish my doctoral studies, was one of the hardest things I've ever done, because it went against my personality and my sense of mission.

As the disciples wrap up their mission to the Galilean region, they come to Jesus and joyfully report to Him, "all that they had done and taught" (verse 30). I can imagine how excited they were to recount their experiences. This is the only time in Mark (with the exception of 3:14 in certain manuscripts) that the disciples are called *apostles* (one who is sent). They had been sent on a mission (see Mark 6:7–13) and they had plenty of testimonies to share with Jesus. In response, they receive an imperative from Jesus, which in the Greek original reads: "Come you yourselves privately to a desolate place and rest a little" (Mark 6:30).* This is a command from Jesus that we all need to heed. The mandate of Jesus was to rest in divinely-ordained seclusion, in solitude in an uninhabited place, in contrast to the many people coming and going when they were ministering (verse 31). You don't need to be a professional minister to observe this command. During times of seclusion and solitude, God provides true rest, spiritual nourishment, guidance, revelation, instruction, and much more. Jesus often instructed His disciples privately (for example, see Mark 9:28; 13:3), and He does the same with us. In a culture that celebrates busyness, results, and achievements, let's remember that sometimes less is really more. Overextending ourselves, even in ministry, leaves us depleted of energy and insight. God wants private time with us, to remind us of His love. During times of retreat, He reveals to us the magnitude of His grace, the sufficiency of His sacrifice, and His assurance for the future.

My Response: _____

---

* J. D. Douglas, *The New Greek-English Interlinear New Testament*, 4th rev. ed. (Carol Stream, IL: Tyndale House, 1993).

His Ability

Jesus said to them, "Do you believe that
I am able to do this?"

—Matthew 9:28

When we worry, we're saying, 'God can't.' " says Linda Dillow— "If we are walking in anxiety, we're not walking in faith. We want to be women of faith, yet often *worry* becomes our middle name . . . We're familiar with the small trickle of fear that meanders through our minds until it cuts a channel into which all other thoughts are drained. We *must* conquer this 'God can't' disease."* Do we really believe that God is able to save us, to restore us, and to guide us?

Two blind men followed Jesus, "crying out, 'Have mercy on us, Son of David!' " (Matthew 9:27). Matthew uses the title "Son of David" more than any other Gospel. It is spoken mostly by those requesting mercy, healing, and deliverance. It is rooted in the Old Testament prophecies about a new Davidic Ruler, through Whom God would heal and give rest to Israel (Ezekiel 34:11–15, 23, 24). Blindness was often considered a judgment of God (see John 9:2; Deuteronomy 28:28), and the blind became outcasts, begging for survival (John 9:8). On this occasion, Jesus asks a most intriguing question, unique to this Gospel: "Do you believe that *I am able to do this?*" (Matthew 9:28). They respond, "Yes, Lord" (verse 28), and their eyes were opened (verse 30). It is very helpful to understand that anxiety and worry are often rooted in the belief that God *is not able*, that He doesn't have the power to take care of a particular situation. In the Bible, blindness is a common metaphor for spiritual darkness. God promised of His Chosen Servant:

> "I will appoint you as a covenant to the people,
> As a light to the nations,
> To open blind eyes,
> To bring out prisoners from the dungeon
> And those who dwell in darkness from the prison"
> (Isaiah 42:6, 7).

Let's rest, believing in His ability to save and heal us. Do you believe He is able? Oh, yes! He is able. He is able. I know He is able!

My Response: _____

---

* Linda Dillow, *Calm My Anxious Heart: A Woman's Guide to Finding Contentment* (Colorado Springs, CO: NavPress, 2007), 116.

His Healing

"He Himself took our infirmities and carried away our diseases."

—Matthew 8:17

I had the immense privilege of visiting the synagogue at Capernaum. As I stood there, while we were filming a video for our ministry, I was overwhelmed by the thought that I was walking where Jesus had walked. After we left the synagogue, our guide took us to an excavated site that is believed to have been Peter's house. Once again, it was as if the Bible was coming alive in front of my eyes, as I pictured Jesus entering Peter's house and healing his mother-in-law.

This event (Matthew 8:14–17; see also Mark 1:29–31) is the third healing miracle in this chapter, following the cleansing of the leper (Matthew 8:1–4), and the healing of the centurion's servant (verses 5–13). "When Jesus came into Peter's home, He saw his mother-in-law lying sick in bed with a fever. He touched her hand, and the fever left her; and she got up and waited on Him" (verses 14, 15). The focus of this passage is on Jesus: He saw . . . He touched . . . He cast out the spirits . . . and healed all who were ill (verses 14–17). Touching a person with fever was against the laws of the rabbis, still Jesus touched Peter's mother-in-law, as He had touched the leper. The fever left her immediately, and she served Him (verse 15). A summary verse (verse 16) portrays the inclusivity of Jesus' healing ministry, as He was casting out demons *with a word* (in the same way He had healed the centurion's servant) and *healed all who were ill* (verse 16). But perhaps the most meaningful part of these verses is that Matthew ends this section by proposing that Jesus is fulfilling Isaiah 53:4, which is the prophecy about the ultimate ministry of God's Servant: "This was to fulfill what was spoken through Isaiah the prophet: 'He Himself took our infirmities and carried away our diseases' " (Matthew 8:17). In Isaiah, this sentence precedes the verse that explains that Jesus not only paid the price for our transgressions and iniquities but also purchased the right to bless us with His *peace* and His *healing* (Isaiah 53:5). Is your soul downcast? Is your heart sick due to shame? Jesus paid for your healing with His blood!

My Response: _____

HIS BLESSING

"Blessed are the poor in spirit, for theirs
is the kingdom of heaven."

—Matthew 5:3

Who are the fortunate, happy, and blessed ones? I am sure you have heard this classic story: "A king was suffering from a painful ailment and was told that the only cure for him was to find a contented man, get his shirt, and wear it night and day. So, messengers were sent through the king's realm in search of such a man, with orders to bring back his shirt. Months passed. After a thorough search of the country, the messengers returned without the shirt. 'Did you find a contented man in all my realm?' the king asked. 'Yes, O King, we found one, just one in all the realm.' 'Then why did you not bring back his shirt?' the king demanded. 'Master, the man had no shirt.' "*

In one of the most famous discourses, the Sermon on the Mount (Matthew 5–7), Jesus announces the kingdom's manifesto, highlighting who these blessed ones really are. In nine Beatitudes, Jesus turns the values of the world upside down, starting with today's devotional text: "Blessed are the poor in spirit" (Matthew 5:3). In Judaism, the poor in spirit and the materially poor were closely related concepts (see Luke 6:20), as this is usually the frame of mind of those who are struggling to make ends meet. God has always shown a special concern for the needy and afflicted (see Psalm 9:18). As a matter of fact, the mission of the Messiah, fulfilled in Jesus, was focused on the poor: "The Spirit of the LORD is upon Me, because He anointed Me to preach the gospel to the poor" (Luke 4:18, NKJV; see also Isaiah 61:1). How could the poor and the poor in spirit be called *blessed*, while the world venerated strength and power? The present tense of this particular beatitude is of much importance: "for theirs *is* the kingdom of heaven" (Matthew 5:3). Not *will be* as in other Beatitudes. The poor in spirit not only have a future inheritance but can partake of the blessings of the kingdom *now, in the present*. The poor have no other resource or hope than what is promised by God. And when all we have left is God, that's when we realize that God is more than enough. Yes, we are blessed!

My Response: _____

---

* Paul Lee Tan, *Encyclopedia of 7700 Illustrations* (Rockville, MD: Assurance Publishers, 1979), 272, 273.

HIS VIEWPOINT

*"Rejoice and be glad, for your reward in heaven is great;
for in the same way they persecuted the prophets
who were before you."*

—Matthew 5:12

In my travels, I like to watch how children behave in planes because their perspective usually doesn't match that of adults. Not long ago, I was on a flight that encountered serious turbulence. Some children were really enjoying the air instability; every time the plane went up and down, they made joyful sounds as if they were on a roller-coaster ride. In the meantime, all the adults were anxiously looking around. The presence and care of their parents allowed these children to rejoice when everyone else was worried and anxious.

Faith is trusting a different reality in the middle of the storm, because our Kinsman-Redeemer watches over us and has revealed to us how the story ends. The Beatitudes, spoken by Jesus in the Sermon on the Mount, offer a heavenly viewpoint about the circumstances that we face here on earth. "Blessed are you when people insult you and persecute you, and falsely say all kinds of evil against you because of Me" (Matthew 5:11). Blessed when persecuted, insulted, and falsely accused? He continues: "*Rejoice and be glad* for your reward in heaven is great; for in the same way they persecuted the prophets who were before you" (verse 12). Jesus offers a different perspective. Throughout the ages, the followers of Christ have encountered opposition and discomfort. Even the great men of old, such as Moses, Elijah, David, and Jeremiah, often cried out to God in despair as they faced enemies and foes. Yet they were strengthened by God, trusting that their trials served a greater and divine purpose, and that His presence was with them (take a moment to read their stories in Hebrews 11). Insults and opposition are to be received with rejoicing, for we are called to be witnesses in the redemption history of humankind. Heaven awaits those who have trusted in the merits of Christ, even to the point of extreme suffering. Difficulties and struggles may be part of the storms of this life, yet Jesus has offered us heaven's viewpoint: "In the world you have tribulation, but take courage; I have overcome the world" (John 16:33).

My Response: _____

HIS PEACEMAKING

"Leave your offering there before the altar and go; first be reconciled to your brother, and then come and present your offering."
—Matthew 5:24

We arrived at an inpatient rehab where one of our acquaintances needed to stay for a while, due to alcohol abuse. A sign outside the building had a quotation that made a lasting impact on my mind: "Those who are at war with others are not at peace with themselves."* Later on, I learned that the words are attributed to William Hazlitt, a British writer, who authored many other such quotes.

God took the initiative to reconcile us to Himself, and when we believe in the sacrifice of Jesus on our behalf, we are given true and absolute peace with God: "Therefore, having been justified by faith, we have *peace* with God *through* our Lord Jesus Christ" (Romans 5:1). This is a core principle of the gospel: we didn't earn our peace, but we have peace through Jesus. This is the *vertical* dimension of peace. Having received this divine gift through Jesus, His followers are to allow the overflowing of that peace into their daily affairs with all people (the *horizontal* dimension), becoming peacemakers, as far as it depends on them (see Romans 12:18). In the Sermon on the Mount, Jesus addressed this, pronouncing a blessing over peacemakers: "Blessed are the peacemakers, for they shall be called sons of God" (Matthew 5:9). In this sermon, Jesus makes six pronouncements expanding the meaning of the commandments (Matthew 5:21–48). The first one is about the commandment: "You shall not commit murder" (verse 21), which Jesus expands to include anger against our fellow humans (verse 22). His first illustration on this statement is: "Therefore if you are presenting your offering at the altar, and there remember that your brother has something against you, leave your offering there before the altar and go; first be reconciled to your brother, and then come and present your offering" (verses 23, 24). As God did with us, we are to take the initiative. After we have done our part to share the peace that we have been given, then God will accept and bless our worship. Let's share the peace of Jesus that we have received. *Blessed are the peacemakers, for they shall be called sons of God.* (Matthew 5:9).

My Response: _____

---

* William Hazlitt, *The Collected Works of William Hazlitt,* 12 vols., eds. A. R. Waller and Arnold Glover (London: J. M. Dent & Co.: 1904), 10:280, https://books.google.com/books?id=dS4LAAAAYAAJ&pg.

His Cleansing

"I am willing; be cleansed."

—Matthew 8:3

We don't hear much about leprosy anymore, even though the disease is still around. Yet there are other physical, mental, and emotional conditions that carry a similar social stigma for their victims. Sometimes people end up being known by their misfortune, bad experience, or mistake, instead of their name: There goes the divorcée! Or did you hear about the jailbird? How about the adulteress?! Unfortunately, society in general is quick to judge and marginalize, robbing people of their worth.

It is hard for us to fully understand the impact the story recorded in Matthew 8:2, 3 would have left on the listeners. At the time, leprosy was the most dreaded disease, barring its victims from society because they were considered ceremonially unclean (Leviticus 13; 14). People afflicted by leprosy had to warn others about their misfortune by crying out loud: "Unclean! Unclean!" (Leviticus 13:45). A leper came to Jesus and prostrated himself in front of Him (Matthew 8:2). Somehow, perhaps by witnessing a miracle of Jesus, this man had become convinced that Jesus had the ability to heal him from leprosy: "Lord, if You are willing, You can make me clean" (verse 2). It was all up to Jesus; it was His choice! Would He be willing? In an astounding show of compassion and care, Jesus "stretched out His hand and touched him" (verse 3). Can you imagine the shock? The leper probably had not felt human touch in years! The ritual law stated that if someone touched a leper, they too immediately became ceremonially unclean (see Leviticus 5:3). But not in this case! Instead of Jesus becoming a leper, the leper was cleansed. Jesus had not only the power to heal but also the willingness to do so. He said, " 'I am willing; be cleansed.' And immediately his leprosy was cleansed" (verse 3). Jesus *wanted* to heal this man. When, due to our mistakes, addictions, or the guilt of our sin, we feel separated from our true selves, others, and God, let's remember that Jesus has the power *and* willingness to heal us. Let's come to His feet and ask for healing and peace. He will answer: "I am willing; be cleansed."

My Response: _____

HIS ARGUMENT

"If then you cannot do even a very little thing [add a single hour to your lifespan], why do you worry about other matters?"
—Luke 12:26

Many have shared with me their techniques to combat worry. Some imagine the worst possible scenario, accept it, and seek to improve on it. Others rely on statistics, calculating the chances of getting hit by lightning or dying in a car crash. And still others use calming resources and breathing exercises. But most people find that these methods are not enough. We are a society of worrywarts in need of facing the root of our anxiety.

It has been reported that Kindle's most highlighted Bible text is Philippians 4:6, 7, a passage that addresses anxiety,* showing how our society is struggling with worry. In Luke 12, Jesus addresses our worry and anxiety, mentioning the concept several times. Starting from verse 22, Jesus offers a sequence of arguments against worry: First, those of us who worry about what we will eat and wear have a limited perception of what life is really all about, "For life is more than food, and the body more than clothing" (verse 23). Jesus draws His second argument from nature, utilizing the style of lesser to greater: if God feeds the ravens and clothes the lilies, how much more will He take care of us! Thirdly, Jesus points out the futility and unproductiveness of anxiety, highlighting that we can't add an hour to our lifespan by worrying. If we can't do this "very little thing" through worrying, why do we worry about other matters? (verse 26). The culmination of Jesus' arguments is an alternate way of life to the anxiety-driven struggle to meet one's own needs, and it is based on a simple and powerful awareness: "Your Father knows that you need these things" (verse 30). He is in control. He is graceful to provide. He knows what we need, and He is more than willing to give these things to us. With this understanding, our focus changes to seeking His kingdom, and all these things will be added unto us. God is willing and able to take care of us. We are, thus, set free from self-protecting concerns and can now focus our energies on the gospel propagation. Yes! Jesus sets us free from fear, worry, and anxiety! Woo-hoo!

My Response: _____

---

* Robinson Meyer, "The Most Popular Passages in Books, According to Kindle Data," *Atlantic,* November 2, 2014, https://www.theatlantic.com/technology/archive/2014/11/the-passages-that-readers-love/381373/.

His Submission

And Jesus, crying out with a loud voice, said, "Father, into your hands I commit My spirit." Having said this, He breathed His last.

—Luke 23:46

We find real peace when we surrender to God's plan, even when we don't fully understand His will for us. When I was in my thirties, I went through a series of adverse circumstances that I didn't understand and could not control. These were hard times for me. At the time, I purchased a key ring with an inscription that became my motto as I walked the difficult path. It read: "I don't know the master plan, but I know the Master planned it, and I am included."

I have watched each of my parents submit themselves into God's care, having battled cancer for several years and, finally, facing the end of their lives. As they entrusted themselves into God's keeping in life, so they did in death. When Jesus was facing the end of His life, He committed His Spirit into God's hands, breathed His last, and gave up His Spirit. The Old Testament is often quoted both by Jesus and by the Gospel writers when they describe His final hours. In both Matthew and Mark, Jesus utters words from Psalm 22:1. Luke points out that He also recited the words of Psalm 31:5: "Into Your hands I commit my spirit" (23:46). Luke adds that a darkness fell over the land from noon until 3:00 P.M., which was the time of the evening sacrifice. Some believe that Psalm 31:5 was repeated during the evening sacrifice. Now Jesus Himself, in His prayer to the Father, recites the words of this psalm of confidence. There had been a divine plan, from the foundation of the world, to save you and me. Jesus, the Lamb of God, was to be sacrificed for our sins. As He accomplishes the redemption plan, prophesied in the Scriptures, Jesus commits Himself into His Father's hands. He fully submitted to God's will, just as He had prayed in the Garden of Gethsemane: "Not My will, but Yours be done" (Luke 22:42). Whether in life or in death, there is no safer place than in God's hands. Believing ourselves saved by the sacrifice of Jesus, we now have the privilege of living and/or dying in full submission to His plan and His will. May our words be: "Into Your hands I commit my spirit."

My Response: _____

HIS PLEADING

"His father came out and began pleading with him."

—Luke 15:28

I read that Father's Day was started by Sonora Dodd in 1910. After hearing a sermon about Mother's Day, she told her minister that there should be a day to honor fathers. She wanted to honor her father, a Civil War veteran, who had been a single parent, raising his six children. Originally Sonora had requested June 5, her father's birthday, as the day of the celebration. But the pastors couldn't arrange it fast enough, so they celebrated it on the third Sunday of June, 1910. The day became a national holiday in 1972, when President Nixon signed it into law.*

I was so blessed to have a godly father! He always supported me without smothering me. He really embodied the best qualities of a human being, and I admire him and will be eternally grateful to God for him. But, what does a godly father really look like? Glad you asked. The answer is found in the parable of the prodigal son, and the way the father, representing God, treated both of his sons. The parable was told to answer the Pharisees, who grumbled about Jesus receiving sinners. "A man had two sons," Jesus started the story (Luke 15:11). You know about the younger son, who asked for his share of the estate, squandered it, became impoverished, and returned to his father's household. The merciful father embraced him and killed the fattened calf to celebrate the return of the undeserving son (verses 22–24). That's how our heavenly Father treats us! And Jesus had to die so that He could welcome us back! Back to the story, the older son became angry and didn't want to join the celebration. He didn't agree with his father's acceptance of the prodigal. In response, "his father came out and began *pleading* with him" (verse 28). What kind of a father *pleads* with his complaining son to join the celebration of his brother's return? One who places his love for his children above his own honor. Joel B. Green adds, "Just as the father had run out to meet his younger son, so, again dishonoring himself, he leaves the banquet over which he is host in order to plead with his elder son."† This is our heavenly Father: always welcoming, always pleading. The cross is proof that God loved us more than He loved Himself.

My Response: _____

---

* Wikipedia, s.v. "Sonora Smart Dodd," accessed April 14, 2019, https://en.wikipedia.org/wiki/Sonora_Smart_Dodd#Father's_Day.

† Joel B. Green, *The Gospel of Luke*, 6th ed., NICNT (Grand Rapids, MI: Eerdmans, 1997), 585.

HIS INTENTION

*"These things I have spoken to you so that My joy may be in you,
and that your joy may be made full."*

—John 15:11

Our ministry receives several prayer requests every week through our website (Jesus101.tv) and app (Jesus101). Many individuals request prayers for themselves, to come closer to God and to experience His peace. Some relate stories of how they went away from God, looking for their own path and rejecting His ways. But away from Him they only found darkness and despair, and now they eagerly long to come back to God and to bask in His grace and joy. The amazing news is that God Himself desires that we may be filled with His joy!

In the narrative of the Vine and the branches, Jesus offers us an intimate relationship with Him. He says: "Abide in Me, and I in you" (John 15:4). Also, He explains that only in union with Him we can be fruitful, because apart from Him we can do nothing, and that the purpose of the fruitfulness is to glorify the Father. Then He reveals that this intimate relationship is rooted in His love for us, for in the same way that the Father has loved Him, He loves us; and He bids us to "abide in [His] love." His followers' response to this divine love is to remain in His love, pledging allegiance to Him and His commands (verse 10). And finally, Jesus reveals His intentions for bringing this up to His disciples at the very time when they are grief-stricken: "These things I have spoken to you *so that* My joy may be in you, and that your joy may be made full" (verse 11). He passionately desires that our joy in Him may be complete, full, and overflowing! There is no other gladness that compares with the depth of His joy, even when we are in the midst of pain. In John 14:27, Jesus had introduced His disciples to His peace. Now, He speaks to them of His love and His joy! The word *joy* had been used only once in this Gospel until now, but it is used seven times in these three chapters (John 15–17), just when His disciples need it most! Jesus offers us an intimate relationship with Him, rooted in His love. As we respond to His love, following His ways for us, He permeates us with the fullness of *His* peace, *His* joy, and *His* love.

My Response: _____

HIS TESTIMONY

*They went on stoning Stephen as he called on the Lord
and said, "Lord Jesus, receive my spirit! . . .
do not hold this sin against them!"*

—Acts 7:59, 60

The Greek verb *martureō* means to bear witness or testify. Many Christians lost their lives testifying of their faith in Jesus, and that's why nowadays the word *martyr* is used for a person who dies because of their faith. The death of the martyrs, such as the Czech reformer John Huss who was burned at the stake on July 6, 1415, was characterized by supernatural peace and bold testimony under the direst circumstances. This was also the case with Stephen, the first martyr.

After Stephen's final sermon, his audience "began gnashing their teeth at him" (Acts 7:54), as a prelude to his stoning. Stephen exclaimed: "Behold, I see the heavens opened up and the Son of Man standing at the right hand of God" (verse 56). Not long earlier, Jesus had appeared before the high priest, prior to His crucifixion, and had made a very similar statement: "Jesus said, 'I am [the Christ]; and you shall see the Son of Man sitting at the right hand of power, and coming with the clouds of heaven" (Mark 14:62). Now Stephen was giving testimony that Jesus, in fact, was at the right hand of God! So, they stoned him, just as they had killed Jesus! Stephen gave a testimony of *who* Jesus was and *where* He was! At that moment, Jesus was *standing* at the right hand of God, as a Witness to His witness. Acts 7:56 is the only occurrence of the title Son of Man outside of the four Gospels. I am amazed at the final words of Stephen and how they parallel the statements of Jesus on the cross. Jesus said, "Father, into your hands I commit My spirit" (Luke 23:46); Stephen said: "Lord Jesus, receive my spirit!" (Acts 7:59). Jesus said: "Father, forgive them; for they do not know what they are doing" (Luke 23:34); Stephen said: "Lord, do not hold this sin against them!" (Acts 7:60). You might be called to give a testimony of your faith in Jesus under difficult situations, such as a life-threatening illness, trials, and persecution. Focus on Jesus and be bold, as Stephen was. God will give you His peace, which surpasses understanding!

My Response: _____

HIS CALMING

*"What are you doing, weeping and breaking my heart? For I am ready
. . . even to die at Jerusalem for the name of the Lord Jesus."*
—Acts 21:13

I distinctly remember the day when I ended up in the emergency room. I had been under severe and prolonged stress, and my heart was acting up. I owned a small computer company with specialized software, and we could no longer survive against the competition. The time had come to close its doors, but I had tried so hard to keep it afloat. That day at the ER, I realized that I had to face the inevitable, and that God would give me peace and wisdom to go through it.

God's plan for our lives doesn't always include removing the troubles in our path, but it always involves providing heavenly peace to face the difficulties. God had revealed to Paul that afflictions awaited him in Jerusalem (see Acts 20:22, 23), yet this didn't deter Paul from going there; he was totally at peace with it. He bid farewell to the elders of the church of Ephesus and sailed towards Jerusalem, making several stops. In some places, fellow church members kept telling him not to go to Jerusalem (21:4), yet he kept on his way. When he got to Caesarea, a prophet named Agabus came from the region of Judea. "He took Paul's belt and bound his own feet and hands, and said, 'This is what the Holy Spirit says: "In this way the Jews at Jerusalem will bind the man who owns this belt and deliver him into the hands of the Gentiles" ' " (verse 11). Then everyone started begging Paul not to go to Jerusalem. That's when Paul answered: "What are you doing, weeping and breaking my heart? For I am ready not only to be bound, but even to die at Jerusalem for the name of the Lord Jesus" (verse 13). At that point, they all said: "The will of the Lord be done!" (verse 14). Having preached the gospel, Paul was resolute and at peace to face whatever God would allow. God does not always remove the obstacles in our path, but He will invariably grant a miraculous calm in our souls. God has our best interests at heart; if you are ever in doubt, look back to the cross, at Jesus' resolve to suffer in your place. Trust your Savior to give you peace to go through your most difficult trials, even death. He can be trusted!

My Response: _____

HIS SAFETY

He said, "Stop weeping, for she has not died, but is asleep."
—Luke 8:52

I was looking through Martha's final text messages to me. Her opening words were: "I got the results of the MRI. The tumor has spread in the brain." I was out of the country and texted her back, letting her know that I was praying for a miracle and for the strength and peace which God has promised (John 14:27). She responded: "Amen. Thank you so much." That's the last I heard from her. I was touched by her God-given courage and peace. She died a few days later. But what about the family that she left behind? Can we be at peace when a close relative or friend passes away, and we are left with the pain of their absence? Every time I visit my parents' tomb, I thank God that they are safe in His keeping.

By the time Jesus arrived at Jairus's house, his daughter had died; "they were all weeping and lamenting for her" (Luke 8:52). At that point, Jesus made a surprising declaration: "Stop weeping, for she has not died, but is asleep" (verse 52). Then He took her by the hand and raised her from the dead! (verse 54). Jesus was saying that her death was not permanent but only temporary, like a deep sleep. He made the same assertion about Lazarus's death. When Jesus died, His victory over death was demonstrated by the fact that many who had fallen asleep were raised from the dead (see Matthew 27:52). I find great peace in knowing that my parents are safe in God's keeping. They are not floating around in some kind of limbo, nor are they conscious. They are safely resting in Jesus, awaiting His call. I want to share with you a quotation that is very comforting to me: " 'Precious in the sight of the LORD is the death of His saints' (Psalm 116:15, NKJV). Some may regard this as a strange statement; it is nevertheless true. The servants of God who are now sleeping, are to Him exceedingly precious. So long as time shall last, the influence of their godly life will continue to yield rich fruitage. No longer can the enemy of the human race imperil their welfare; they are safe from his power. Jesus claims them as His own, and on the morning of the resurrection He will bestow upon them the fullness of joy."* Be at peace. Our loved ones are safe in the Savior's keeping!

My Response: _____

---

* Ellen G. White, *Life Sketches of Ellen G. White* (Mountain View, CA: Pacific Press®, 1943), 476.

HIS PARDON

Then He said to her, "Your sins have been forgiven. . . .
Your faith has saved you; go in peace."

—Luke 7:48, 50

We excused ourselves and went to a separate room in the house. As a minister, I was about to anoint a man with oil (as instructed in James 5:14, 15), asking God to heal him, if it was His will, and to provide His peace, no matter the outcome. Privately, he discussed with me things that he had done in his youth, which he knew were against God's will. Then he proceeded to tell me that he was in total peace, because he knew that God had forgiven him his sins through Jesus' sacrifice for him. He passed away a few months later. In complete peace.

There is a direct relationship between God's *pardon* and His *peace*. Many people live their lives carrying a heavy burden of shame and guilt, while God has offered us forgiveness through the merits and in the name of Jesus. Because Jesus suffered in our place, the core proclamation of the Christian church is "repentance for forgiveness of sins . . . in His name" (see Luke 24:47). Yet many choose to live under the shadow of regret and remorse.

In the story found in Luke 7:36–50, we meet two main characters: a Pharisee and a sinner, an immoral woman. The Pharisee had invited Jesus to dine with him, but the sinful woman came to Jesus with an alabaster vial of perfume to anoint His feet. This provoked a dark thought in the Pharisees' mind: "If this man were a prophet He would know who and what sort of person this woman is who is touching Him, that she is a sinner" (verse 39). Jesus then told him a parable of two debtors, highlighting the woman's actions as an act of love in response to the great forgiveness that she had received. Jesus not only accepted her gift of love but also addressed her directly, publicly proclaiming her newly-found wholeness: "Your sins have been forgiven. . . . Your faith has saved you; go in *peace*" (verse 48, 50). Even if you have been a *public* sinner, and everybody knows about it, God's pardon offers you peace and wholeness in the place of shame and despair. He has paid the price of your sin at the cross! Therefore, go in peace!

My Response: _____

HIS AUTHENTICITY

These have been written so that you may believe that
Jesus is the Christ, the Son of God; and that believing
you may have life in His name.

—John 20:31

The reality that I discovered that day far surpassed my expectations! When I visit a new place, I often find that the pictures I've seen before are nicer than the actual site in real life, because pictures are taken from favorable angles, in optimal lighting, using special lenses, and are often photoshopped. But this was not the case when we got to the picturesque Cesky Krumlov, a small Bohemian village in the Czech Republic. The authentic beauty I saw in reality far surpassed the charm that could be witnessed in the photos.

John describes why he decided to write his Gospel. First, he tells us that his purpose is not to have an exhaustive biography of Jesus and His ministry on earth: "Therefore many other signs Jesus also performed in the presence of the disciples which are not written in this book" (John 20:30). Then he unveils his purpose: "*But* these have been written *so that* you may believe that *Jesus is the Christ, the Son of God;* and that believing you may have *life in His name*" (verse 31). Oh, how I love this verse! John wrote his Gospel so that we may believe that Jesus is actually who He says He is! He is the awaited Messiah! The Christ, the Anointed One! The Son of God! John wrote that you may be assured that He is authentic, and that you may believe that you have life in His name. It is not a hoax. The gospel is not a photoshopped, made-up picture of a Savior who *might* give us eternal life. Some Christians believe in a pseudo-gospel, and therefore they don't live with peace and assurance of the future. The pseudo-gospel proclaims the possibility but not the assurance of eternal life through Jesus. Yet the reality that Jesus offers us is greater than we ever imagined! When we believe in Jesus as our Savior, even though we have a sinful nature, we can live with the peace of knowing our eternal destiny is secure, because He carried the penalty of our sin to the cross. Some say it can't be that good! Yet it is *real*, my friend! Jesus is who He says He is, and He has done what He says He has done! Believe! And live in peace, resting in Him!

My Response: _____

HIS ACKNOWLEDGEMENT

"Keep watching and praying that you may not come into temptation; the spirit is willing, but the flesh is weak."

—Mark 14:38

When I was young it sounded simple. It was explained to me that I had two natures: spiritual and carnal, like two lion cubs. The advice I received seemed black and white: I was to feed the spiritual cub and starve the other, that way the spiritual lion would grow more powerful than the carnal one. Simple, right? What I didn't know then was that the two natures would always be at war within me, until Jesus comes. So, how can we be at peace with God?

When Jesus was in Gethsemane, He asked His disciples to keep watch with Him (Mark 14:34). But as the cup of salvation trembled in His hands, the disciples kept falling asleep. When Jesus came back from praying, He addressed Peter: "Simon, are you asleep? Could you not keep watch for one hour? Keep watching and praying that you may not come into temptation; *the spirit is willing, but the flesh is weak*" (verses 37, 38). In the midst of His suffering, Jesus acknowledged the war between the spiritual and carnal natures of His disciples. They had failed Him in His most crucial hour! Can you imagine how Peter must have felt? All of us have moments in which we become painfully aware of our failures, times when the carnal lion seems to be winning, whether in thought or in deed. Perhaps the most honest confession of this inner war came from Paul: "I see a different law in the members of my body, waging war against the law of my mind and making me a prisoner of the law of sin which is in my members. Wretched man that I am! Who will set me free from the body of this death?" (Romans 7:23, 24). Then his response: "Thanks be to God through Jesus Christ our Lord!" (verse 25). When you discover how weak you really are, do not despair. Don't hide from Jesus but run to Him! "There is now no condemnation for those who are in Christ Jesus. . . . For what the Law could not do . . . God *did*: sending His own Son in the likeness of sinful flesh and as an offering for sin, He condemned sin in the flesh" (Romans 8:1, 3). He is the Reason why we can be at peace with God! And He will not abandon us!

My Response: _____

HIS CURE

He said to him, "Do you wish to get well?"

—John 5:6

I have two distinct memories from the archaeological site that is believed to be the Pool of Bethesda (also called Bethzatha). First, the impressive ruins of the pools, much larger than I had anticipated. The second recollection is precious, and I have a video recording of it. Our tour group got together inside the church right next to the twin pools, and we sang "Amazing Grace" a cappella. The sound filled the church, and the words filled my heart because it was such an appropriate song for the location: "Amazing grace, how sweet the sound, that saved a wretch like me. . . ."*

The pool, as described by John, had five porticoes or colonnades. It was an impressive structure. In contrast, its dwellers were most wretched: lame, paralyzed, blind, and suffering from other types of sicknesses (see John 5:3). There was a belief that the waters were stirred supernaturally, and that the first person to get into the pool after the disturbance would get healed. Among the sick there was an extreme case: a man who had been ill for thirty-eight years. That's a very long time! Jesus went to that man, desiring to heal him but not wanting to impose His way. He asked him: "Do you wish to get well?" (verse 6). It seems like a strange question . . . who wouldn't want to get well? But since the man was probably lame, by being well he would have had a hard time adjusting to a new lifestyle after thirty-eight years of total dependence on others. Instead of simply responding affirmatively, the man presents his own understanding of the remedy needed: "Sir, I have no man to put me into the pool" (verse 7). Perhaps Jesus could help him get to it in time. . . . However, Jesus had something better in mind. He doesn't do things the way we do, and He has a thousand resources where we see none. Jesus simply commanded the man to get up and walk, and he did! (verse 8). Many of us have been suffering with emotional and spiritual diseases for decades; trying the same thing over and over again, expecting a different result. Today Jesus comes to us with the ultimate cure. Do you wish to be made well?

My Response: _____

---

* John Newton, "Amazing Grace," 1779, public domain.

HIS UNDERSTANDING

When His own people heard of this, they went out to take custody of Him; for they were saying, "He has lost His senses."

—Mark 3:21

Philip Yancey tells the story of a woman who was experiencing real difficulties. She had made some bad decisions that had led her down a slippery slope into sin. When someone invited her to church, she replied: "I am already feeling bad enough about myself; why would I want to go there?" Confronted by our pain and darkness as a result of abuse, our own sin, illness, or addictions, we often choose to run away from God, thinking that He couldn't possibly understand or accept us.

Yet we can approach Him with the assurance that Jesus knows and understands us. Jesus was born under difficult circumstances. His mother got pregnant before she was married, but people didn't believe the miraculous virgin conception. Furthermore, He was born in poverty and placed in a manger, with no appropriate resources to support Him. And if those circumstances were not enough, the king wanted Him dead, so He lived His early childhood hiding from those who were supposed to protect Him. Are you starting to feel that He may understand you after all? But there is more! When He started His public ministry of preaching and healing, His own *kinsmen*, "went out to take custody of Him; for they were saying, 'He has lost His senses' " (Mark 3:21). Has anyone you care for ever called you crazy? Well, Jesus knows how it feels. Not only that! The religious authorities declared that He was possessed! (verse 22). Even His *church* didn't understand Him! And I could tell you much more about the difficulties and temptations He went through, even before heading to the cross to give His life for the human race that had utterly and completely rejected Him! Yet He loved us so much, with all of our dysfunctional thinking and compulsive behaviors, that He died for us! "For we do not have a high priest who cannot sympathize with our weaknesses, but One who has been tempted in all things as we are, yet without sin. Therefore, let us draw near with confidence to the throne of grace, so that we may receive mercy and find grace to help in time of need" (Hebrews 4:15, 16). Amen!

My Response: _____

AFFIRMING HIS GRACE

HIS MISSION

"It is expedient for you that one man die for the people."
—John 11:50

A close relative told me of the impact a particular lecture had on him many decades ago. In order to visually illustrate the inclusivity of God's grace, the professor took a piece of chalk and started walking all around the room, drawing a straight horizontal line on the walls, doors, windows, the complete circumference of the venue, until everyone in that audience found themselves sitting inside the parameters of the line. "All are included in God's grace" the professor said. How true! Yet so many of us still struggle to believe that we are included.

So what, exactly, qualifies us as recipients of God's grace? After the resurrection of Lazarus, the chief priests and Pharisees got together and planned to kill Jesus (see John 11:47–53). The chief priest, Caiaphas, said to them, "You know nothing at all nor do you take into account that it is expedient for you that one man die for the people" (verses 49, 50). John adds an extremely important note: "Now he did not say this on his own initiative, but being high priest that year, he prophesied that Jesus was going to die for the nation, and not for the nation only, but in order that He might also gather together into one the children of God who are scattered abroad" (verses 51, 52). Caiaphas, unknowingly, had just prophesied what the mission of Jesus was! To die *for* the people! His statement is repeated after Jesus' betrayal: "It was expedient for one man to die *on behalf* of the people" (John 18:14). Jesus died for the human race to undo what Adam and Eve had done. Jesus is the *Second Adam*, whose victorious death on behalf of the human race was even more complete than Adam's utter failure as representative of the race. Paul explains: "So then as through one transgression there resulted condemnation to all men, even so through one act of righteousness there resulted justification of life to all men. For as through the one man's disobedience the many were made sinners, even so through the obedience of the One the many will be made righteous" (Romans 5:18, 19). It's not about what qualifies us, but who qualified *for* us! He died for the people. And that, my friend, includes you!

My Response: _____

His Rescue

"He anointed Me to preach the gospel to the poor. He has sent Me to proclaim release to the captives."

—Luke 4:18

The aftermath of the epic accident of August 5, 2010, when a Chilean mine collapsed, dragged on for sixty-nine days, while the rescuers relentlessly continued their efforts. The thirty-three miners trapped under seven hundred thousand tons of rock could do absolutely nothing to save themselves. Help could only come from above, and it did. On October 12, global audiences in the hundreds of millions, including myself, watched the live TV coverage of the first rescuer arriving at the spot where the miners were trapped. Twenty-four hours later, *all* thirty-three miners and all the rescuers were on the surface.* Two words kept coming up in the interviews that followed: *all* and *joy. All* had been rescued, the healthy and the sick, the strong and the weak. All had been saved through the plan designed from above. And at the end, only pure *joy* remained.

The Gospel of Luke was written to announce a rescue of even greater magnitude! The Savior of the world came down to fulfill Heaven's plan to rescue the world! As you can imagine, Luke's Gospel is filled with joy and excitement as a response to such great news of salvation. Luke narrates his Gospel in a way that makes his point loud and clear: salvation was achieved for *ALL* who would accept it: the fearful, the anxious, the poor, the enslaved, the marginalized, and the destitute. Luke intercalates stories of men and women, Jews and Gentiles, religious people and pub lic sinners. He excitedly announces that Jesus offers salvation for all. If someone says that you don't qualify for salvation because of the color of your skin, your gender, your failures, your past, your family circumstances, or anything else, tell them: "You are right . . . none of us do, that's why the Savior came down to rescue us." If you are buried under an overwhelming burden of sin, anxiety, or fear, remember how Jesus started His Sabbath sermon in his hometown of Nazareth: He reminded us that He came for "the poor," the "captives," "the blind," and "the oppressed" (Luke 4:18). In other words, He came for you and me!

My Response: _____

---

* Richard Pallardy, *Encyclopedia Britannica*, "Chile mine rescue 2010," modified April 11, 2019, https://www.britannica.com/event/chile-mine-rescue-of-2010.

HIS FREEDOM

"TO SET FREE THOSE WHO ARE OPPRESSED,
TO PROCLAIM THE FAVORABLE YEAR OF THE LORD."

—Luke 4:18, 19

My heart was racing excitedly as I was walking the few blocks from my hotel to the Liberty Bell. I was attending some academic meetings in Philadelphia, Pennsylvania, and this was my chance to see what I had heard, and even taught, for years. Let me explain.

When I studied the public discourse of Jesus, recorded in Luke 4, and His reading of Isaiah 61:1, 2 on that occasion, I learned that this quotation of Isaiah alluded to the year of jubilee (see Leviticus 25:8–55). This was the favorable year of the Lord, when once every fifty years all slaves were to be set free, all debts were cancelled, and all property returned to the original owners. On that momentous Sabbath in Nazareth, Jesus was proclaiming that He was fulfilling His role as the real jubilee and ushering in the age of salvation. He was the agent through which the poor, the captives, the blind, and the oppressed were to receive really good news, release, and freedom.

When the United States of America was founded, the dream was that it would be the land of the free. I had been told that Leviticus 25:10 was engraved on the Liberty Bell as a reminder of this fact: "Proclaim a release (or liberty) through the land to all its inhabitants." That's why it is called the *Liberty* Bell. I could barely contain myself as I finally stood in front of the impressive cracked bell, examining every inch of that piece of history. And there it was: "Lev. XXV:X." It was true! Liberty for all was the dream, the promise, and the hope.

If you are carrying a load of guilt and shame from the past, pause now and accept Christ's freedom! Burdens can paralyze us and prevent us from living a life of purpose for the glory of God. Jesus carried our burdens to the cross so that we may live an abundant life! You are one choice away from freedom. The favor of God through Jesus Christ, our jubilee, is ours, even though we don't deserve it!

Accept it today! It is true. We are free! Jesus is our jubilee.

My Response: _____

HIS SCEPTER

*Then I looked, and behold, the Lamb was
standing on Mount Zion.*
—Revelation 14:1

There are no celebrations like the celebrations of freedom and deliverance. In the United States, the Fourth of July, Independence Day, is an occasion of great festivities. But I was amazed when I saw century-old photos of a massive crowd celebrating the Fourth of July, 1918, in Paris. The French were celebrating the official end of the war, expecting a victorious outcome that was still four months away. Thousands of Parisians took to the streets to watch the parade of the American soldiers.

Yet nothing we have experienced on this earth can compare with the joyful celebration of the victory of the Lamb described in Revelation 14. John looks and catches a vivid scene, unparalleled in the final book of the Bible: "Then I looked, and behold, the Lamb was standing on Mount Zion, and with Him one hundred and forty-four thousand, having His name and the name of His Father written on their foreheads" (Revelation 14:1). The number of the complete spiritual Israel that was introduced in Revelation 7:4 is the same number as the group that is now standing with the Lamb on Mount Zion; not one has been lost in the final tribulations. Revelation 14:1 is the only time that Mount Zion is mentioned in the book of Revelation. Throughout the Bible, Mount Zion was the center of the rule of the kingdom of God (see Psalm 2:6; 48:1, 2), and was the place that pointed to the ultimate delivery of His people (Isaiah 52:7; 59:20). Also, in the New Testament Zion represents the final victory of Jesus and those who trust in Him (Romans 9:33; Hebrews 12:22; 1 Peter 2:6). Now the Lamb is *standing* victorious as the triumphant King in Zion, and His very own are with Him forever. The Lamb is triumphant over evil, and we, the redeemed, gather around Him to celebrate, because His victory has purchased our freedom! This portrait of Jesus comforted and sustained the people of the first century and it still comforts us more than two thousand years later when we face difficulties. We know how the story ends: Jesus wins! Start celebrating now!

My Response: _____

HIS LAVISHNESS

"Father, give me the share of the estate that falls to me."
So he divided his wealth between them.

—Luke 15:12

A court official approached the king with a request, "My lord, my daughter is getting married and I don't have money for the wedding. Could you help me, sire, with the expenses?" The king asked, "How much do you need?" The official named what seemed like an astronomical amount. The king granted the request on the spot. Later a confidant of the king asked: "My king, why did you grant this outrageous request?" "This man honored me in two ways: he believed that I am incredibly *wealthy* and astoundingly *generous*," was the king's response.

When Jesus was being friendly with sinners, the Pharisees objected. In response, Jesus told them a story. A wealthy father had two sons; one of them was very good but the other was very bad. The good son was working hard, while the bad one was dreaming about running away. He did not care much about the farm nor the harvest that needed to be gathered. Outrageously, he demanded his inheritance. No doubt, this was extremely insulting to the father because the inheritance was given only after the father had passed away. In effect, he was saying, "Dad, I want you dead." The father, however, displayed amazing patience and generosity. Completely overlooking the insult, he "divided his wealth [From the Greek *bios: livelihood, property, possessions*]" (Luke 15:12). The father in the story represents God. And, thus, we learn from the opening part of the story that our God is incredibly *wealthy* and astoundingly *generous*. He lavishes His wealth of grace upon all of us, sharing His *possessions*, even when we run away from Him and squander it as we see further in the story. Jesus died for us to secure our part of the inheritance, even though we do not deserve it. In Christ, we find indescribable riches: love, grace, acceptance, patience, salvation, et cetera. Our incredibly wealthy God, Jesus Christ, laid down his life for us, and lavishes us with His grace today. "In Him we have redemption through His blood, the forgiveness of our trespasses, according to the *riches* of His grace which He *lavished* on us" (Ephesians 1:7, 8).

My Response: _____

His Patience

*"The younger son gathered everything together and went on
a journey into a distant country, and there he squandered
his estate with loose living."*

—Luke 15:13

There is something really exciting about the anticipation of a journey we are about to embark on. My friend remembers when he was a teenager living in a rural area, how he always wanted to go to the capital city. And when he did get a chance, he was so excited as he rode the train thinking about all the fun things he was planning to do. And naturally, the level of his excitement was directly related to the amount of dispensable money he carried that day.

The younger son, in the story of Jesus, is in that situation (Luke 15:13). He is heading to a country *far away*; he is young, filled with the anticipation of fun, and he has money, lots of it! Finally, he is free to do what he wants. Strangely, his father *seems* to be passive in all of this. Once the inheritance was divided, he does not attempt to prevent his son from going to the far country; he does not interfere in his son's life nor object to the way he is squandering his money. The father is patient. Why patient, we wonder? If there is ever a time to act, it is now! But the father knows that the only way his son can find his way back home is to realize that he has wandered away from home. In order to be found, he has to recognize that he has been lost. Have you ever gone to a distant country? Perhaps right now you may be wandering away from God, your Heavenly Father. And it can happen in little and big things, inside and outside of religious circles. If so, remember: God is a patient Father. Whenever we realize how lost we are, and turn back to Him, we will surely experience the joy of His embrace! (see Luke 15:20–23). The original word used for *far away/distant* (verse 13), is the same word used in the good news shared by Paul: "But now in Christ Jesus you who formerly were *far off* have been brought near *by the blood of Christ*. . . . He came and preached peace to you who were *far away*, and peace to those who were near" (Ephesians 2:13–17). *"Amazing Grace, how sweet the sound, that saved a wretch like me. I once was lost, but now I'm found . . . ."**

My Response: _____

_____

* John Newton, "Amazing Grace," 1779, public domain.

HIS RECEPTION

"While he was still a long way off, his father saw him and felt compassion for him, and ran and embraced him and kissed him."

—Luke 15:20

M any years ago, I was in an antique store, admiring the display of several small items from the first century of the Christian era, when something caught my attention. I came upon a whole section of *signet rings*, instruments of choice to stamp the family's name on important documents. I bought one to use as a visual aid in my talks. The signet ring always reminds me of the grace of God, which is bigger than all of our failures. Let me tell you why.

Jesus was being friendly with sinners, and the religious leaders of the people did not like it. So, they grumbled about it (Luke 15:2). In response to this complaint, Jesus told three parables about *lostness*: one out of a hundred sheep (verses 4–7), one out of ten coins (verses 8–10), and one out of two sons (verses 11–32) all get lost. This is how the third story starts: "A man had two sons. The younger of them said to his father, 'Father, give me the share of the estate that falls to me.' So he divided his wealth between them" (verses 11, 12). And just like that, the younger son left his father, and squandered his estate, becoming impoverished and hungry. "But when he came to his senses" (verse 17), he decided to go back home and work for his father as a hired man. Little did he imagine the reception that awaited him! When he was still far away, his father saw him, ran to him, embraced and kissed him, and said to his servants: "Quickly bring out the best robe and put it on him, and put a ring on his hand and sandals on his feet" (verse 22). These three commands that are recorded are symbolic acts of restoration. The best robe, usually the father's, would immediately cover the son's shamefulness. The ring would once again identify him as part of the family, and if it were a signet ring, it would even give him the authority to attach the family's name to business transactions. The third order is a statement that he was being received as a son, because laborers were not given sandals. If you, or a loved one, have wandered far away from God and decide to come back to Him, you will encounter the same reception!

My Response: _____

His Celebration

"Bring the fattened calf, kill it, and let us eat and celebrate."
—Luke 15:23

Allan Collins is the talented creator of the "silent sermon" sculptures. One of these amazing sculptures is found at La Sierra University in California, entitled *The Glory of God's Grace*. In this sculpture, we see the prodigal son returning home and his father running to meet him. When a contractor was called to adjust the sculpture's base, he wondered what it meant. Once this parable was explained to him, tears filled his eyes, because he had just made his son leave home because of his bad behavior. He was convicted now to go and look for his son and bring him back home.

When the prodigal son had squandered his father's wealth with loose living (Luke 15:13), he wanted to come home. Since he was no longer worthy to be called a son, he planned to work as a servant (verse 19). But his father saw him from afar and ran to him! The sculpture at La Sierra University depicts vividly the passion of the father, running towards his son, as the father's garments seem to be lifted by the wind, exposing his legs, which would have created a shameful situation for an elderly gentleman. Yet the father did not care about his honor; instead he ran, embraced, and kissed the prodigal, restoring him to *sonship* (verses 20–23). But that's not all. He also called for a big celebration: " 'Bring the fattened calf, kill it, and let us eat and celebrate; for this son of mine was dead and has come to life again; he was lost and has been found.' And they began to celebrate." (verses 23, 24). Then we see the older brother, grumbling just like the Pharisees and scribes (verses 28–30, compare with verses 1, 2). The father pleads with him to join the celebration; after all, he is as *undeserving* as the younger son, yet he is in denial. Take a moment to read this fascinating story to the end (Luke 15:11–32). It's packed with celebration and filled with *rejoicing* and *happiness* because that which was lost has been found. Heaven is a place of rejoicing (see verses 7, 10). We will worship Him with exuberant joy when we realize that we are the ones who were lost but are now found! Let's joyfully accept and declare His grace from this day forward!

My Response: _____

HIS PROCLAMATION

"This son of mine was dead and has come to life again."
—Luke 15:24

In his book *What's So Amazing about Grace?*,* Philip Yancey tells the story of a young woman who had run away from home to a big city. Things didn't work out, and she gradually started to spiral down. Now she is broke, sick, and lives on the street. In desperation, she calls her parents but nobody picks up the phone, so she leaves a message that she will be on the bus to her hometown the next day; if they are waiting for her at the terminal, she will get off the bus, but if not, she will ride on. She did not know what to expect, yet she could have never imagined what she saw: her parents, grandparents, uncles, and cousins were all at the terminal, wearing party hats and holding a banner that read, "Welcome home!"

Throughout the Gospel of Luke, we see God declaring that Jesus is *His* Son: "You are *My* beloved Son;" "This is My Son" (Luke 3:22; 9:35). A similar statement is also found in the parable of the prodigal son (Luke 15:11–32), except that this time the son is utterly unworthy. This is the son who demanded the inheritance *before* the death of his parents, in effect rejecting his father and family. Knowing that love cannot exist without freedom, the father "divided his wealth" (verse 12) and gave the younger son his part. Then the young man embarks on a destructive journey, squandering his father's fortune with loose living (verse 13) and prostitutes (verse 30), spiraling down. Later the land experiences a severe famine (verse 14), and he hits bottom. Being hungry, he finds himself a job to feed swine and craves for the pods he is feeding to pigs but is not allowed even that. Have you ever hit bottom? Have you ever felt so lost or know someone who has? Well, you are in for a surprise! When the young man comes back home, he is embraced by a passionate father, wearing a party hat and holding a large "Welcome home" banner! And, most amazingly, the father makes an amazing public proclamation: "this son of *mine*" (verse 24). Yes, this is *my* son! Our Father is not ashamed to call us *His* children! You never stop being your father's child, no matter how lost or undeserving you may be! Come Home! God will embrace you, saying: "You are Mine!" (Isaiah 43:1).

My Response: _____

---

* Philip Yancey, *What's So Amazing About Grace?* (Grand Rapids, MI: Zondervan, 1997).

HIS GENTLENESS

"A battered reed He will not break off,
and a smoldering wick He will not put out."
—Matthew 12:20

Deborah Hall just wouldn't give up. She convinced her husband Ron to join her in volunteering at the local mission, where they met Denver, a tough homeless man who often had outbursts of unfriendly and threatening behavior. However, through Debbie's perseverance and gentleness, God broke down the barriers in Denver's heart and won him over; Ron and Denver became life-long friends. When Debbie died of cancer, Denver gave an emotional testimony at her funeral about the life-changing influence she had on him.

After Jesus healed a man with a withered hand, Matthew reports that He withdrew from there, yet many followed Him, and He healed them (Matthew 12:15). Then Matthew presents another prophetic formula, the longest Old Testament quotation in this Gospel (Matthew 12:18–21). It is the first of four songs in Isaiah about God's coming Servant (Isaiah 42:1–4). This is the only time in the Gospels that Jesus is called God's Servant ("My Servant," Matthew 12:18). It is striking that this passage highlights the gentle and hope-filled ministry of Jesus, particularly for those who are at their wit's end. "A battered reed He will not break off, and a smoldering wick He will not put out . . . and in His name the Gentiles will hope." (Matthew 12:20, 21). A bent reed could no longer be used as a measuring instrument nor to sustain any kind of structure; a smoldering wick had to be replaced in order to serve its purpose. But Jesus refused to give up on people like that. R. T. France explains: "The imagery thus describes an extraordinary willingness to encourage damaged or vulnerable people, giving them a further opportunity to succeed which a results-oriented society would deny them. . . . Here Matthew finds a further portrait of the meek and lowly Jesus who offers a kind yoke and a light burden; the giver of rest to the toiling and heavily loaded (11:28–30)."* Are you in the midst of hopeless circumstances? Jesus is gentle, patient, and kind, and *He is not giving up on you;* you can count on that!

My Response: _____

───────

* R. T. France, *The Gospel of Matthew*, NICNT (Grand Rapids, MI: Eerdmans, 2007), 473.

HIS CLOTHING

He [the king] said to him, "Friend, how did you come in here without wedding clothes?" And the man was speechless.

—Matthew 22:12

In my teens, I went to a boarding school and lived in the dormitory there, far away from home. I decided to join a sewing class but didn't have money to buy the materials. I wanted to make a dress, so I used a pretty set of bed sheets that my mother had given me. I was sure that no one would notice, because the print and color of the fabric were perfect for a summer dress. I was proud to wear it when my parents arrived to visit me. Then I heard my mother's voice from a distance: "Are those your bed sheets?" I could fool everybody except my mom!

The parable of the marriage feast is the last of three parables that portray the unwillingness of God's chosen people to accept Jesus. "The kingdom of heaven may be compared to a king who gave a wedding feast for his son" (Matthew 22:2). All of the original guests pay no attention to the invitation, making excuses and even mistreating and killing the messengers. Then the king chooses to replace the unworthy guests and orders his slaves to go out to the roadways to bring invitees for the feast. "Those slaves went out into the streets and gathered together all they found, both evil and good; and the wedding hall was filled with dinner guests" (verse 10). Even though some scholars disagree, the fact is that the custom of the host supplying the festal robes for the guests is implied, and it would have been necessary in light of the preceding context, where the guests came from the streets (verse 10). When the king finds a man without wedding clothes, he asks why (verses 11, 12). The rejection of the robe that was provided leaves this man without excuse. Perhaps he thought that his own clothing was good enough, but it wasn't. From Genesis to Revelation, humankind is in a clothing crisis. Adam and Eve chose fig leaves (Genesis 3:7), and the members of the Laodicean church did not realize their need for the white robes offered (Revelation 3:17, 18). The robe of righteousness of Jesus, given to us as a gift through His grace, is the only clothing that will be acceptable at the wedding feast of the Lamb. Let's start wearing it now!

My Response: _____

HIS GRACE

For the Law was given through Moses; grace
and truth were realized through Jesus Christ.

—John 1:17

In his insightful article entitled "The Covenants: A Developmental Approach,"* Dr. van Rooyen discusses the process of continuity and discontinuity in the developmental stages of the everlasting covenant that God made with the human race. A phrase that he utilizes in his article has stayed with me for many years and continues to aid my understanding: "The oak is in the acorn, and the acorn is in the oak, yet the tree is not the acorn." I believe that this was the concept that John was conveying from the very beginning of his Gospel.

After the striking revelation that "the Word became flesh, and dwelt [*tabernacled*] among us . . . full of grace and truth" (John 1:14), the Gospel writer expands on what this last sentence means. "For of His fullness we have all received, and *grace upon grace*" (verse 16). Grace is ongoing and never-ending; grace is replaced with more grace and more grace, like the widow's oil and flour, which were never exhausted. This verse is followed by a statement of the developmental nature of the covenant of grace: "For the Law was given through Moses; grace and truth were realized through Jesus Christ" (John 1:17). It's not that there was no grace in the Old Testament because the whole sacrificial system was pointing to a Redeemer. God Himself had given the Law, which embodied His character, that has always been love (see Exodus 34:6; Psalm 86:15). But Jesus is the exact and complete revelation of God's grace, surpassing that of Moses and the prophets (see Hebrews 1:1–3). John emphasizes the expansion of the old with the fullness of the new: the new wine is better than the water of purification (John 2:10); a new birth, not related to ancestry, is needed to enter the kingdom (3:3–5), the Water of Life is greater than the water of Jacob's well (4:13, 14), et cetera. In John 1:17 the Word is given a name for the first time: Jesus Christ. He is the personification and the fullest expression of grace. Through Him we have received unmerited grace, and His grace is our assurance of salvation: grace upon grace! Let's share His grace!

My Response: _____

---

* Smuts van Rooyen, "The Covenants: A Developmental Approach," *Ministry Magazine*, February 2004, https://www.ministrymagazine.org/archive/2004/02/the-covenants-a-developmental-approach.html.

HIS VERDICT

*"He who is without sin among you, let him be
the first to throw a stone at her."*

—John 8:7

Unexpectedly, I found myself in the very place where my mother had told me not to go. My father, then a pastor, was attending workers' meetings in a hotel, and my mom and I had come along. I was a little girl, excitedly playing in the hotel's swimming pool, having been given instructions to stay in the shallow end. But the bottom of the pool was slippery, and I gradually started sliding toward the deep end. I panicked and tried to jump up, but I was drowning and could not reach the surface. In desperation, I made one final attempt, and my mother saw me and rescued me, in spite of the fact that I had ended up on the wrong side.

The adulterous woman ended up exactly where she was told not to go—the deep end. The charge against her is clear: *adultery*, caught "in the very act" (John 8:4). Adultery was one of the three gravest sins for Jews; they would rather die than find themselves caught in idolatry, murder, or adultery. The scribes and the Pharisees came to the temple that day with the Scriptures in one hand and stones in the other and dragged her into the center of the court (verse 3). They wanted to make an example of her, humiliating her in front of everyone. "Now in the Law Moses commanded us to stone such women; what then do you say?" (verse 5; see Leviticus 20:10 and Deuteronomy 22:22–24). There is no doubt that the scribes and Pharisees are shaping the law to fit their intentions, but the truth is that the woman is guilty! Have you ever been guilty and felt condemned by the law? Adultery, lust, pride, gossip, stealing, bad parenting, lying, self-righteousness, et cetera? Yes, you and I are sitting with her in the middle of the court. Only we who have understood the bad news can rejoice with the good news! The verdict Jesus gave is clear: guilty! "He who is without sin among you, let him be the first to throw a stone at her" (John 8:7). Conscience-stricken, they all departed, and Jesus was left alone with her. By His own definition, Jesus was the only One (without sin) who could throw the stones! But He didn't, because He chose to die in her place and in ours. Hallelujah!

My Response: _____

HIS ACQUITTAL

"I do not condemn you. . . . Go. From now on sin no more."
—John 8:11

I was acquitted, not because I was innocent, but because the police officer didn't show up. I had been coming down the mountain into a construction zone. There were many trucks coming and going on the road, and I planned to follow the orange cones that were placed on the road to create a temporary lane. A highway patrol officer thought I was not doing it right, so he pulled me over and gave me a ticket. I decided to challenge this violation in court. But when my name was called, the officer wasn't there, and I was acquitted by default, due to his absence.

When an adulterous woman was brought to Jesus, her accusers came with their Bibles in hand. She had been clearly caught in adultery (John 8:4), and this was their opportunity to kill two birds with one stone: to condemn her and to test Jesus, in order to accuse Him (verse 6). "In the Law Moses commanded us to stone such women; *what then do You say?*" (John 8:5). The trap was cleverly set. Their dilemma was that under the Roman law, the Jews had no power to carry out a death sentences (see John 18:31). So, if Jesus had said, "Go ahead! Stone her!" they could go to the Roman authorities and make a charge against Him. If He had said, "Leave her alone!" they could charge him with breaking the Law of Moses and discredit Him as a rabbi. It was a clever trap. "He who is without sin among you, let him be the first to throw a stone at her," He said (John 8:7). She was guilty, and Jesus was the only One qualified to throw the stone. But He aborted the stoning because a few days later He Himself would take the punishment that she deserved. When He was left alone with her, He said: " 'Woman. . . . Did no one condemn you?' She said, 'No one, Lord.' And Jesus said, 'I do not condemn you, either. Go. From now on sin no more' " (verses 10, 11). Jesus always speaks in the same order. First, "I do not condemn you," then, "Go . . . sin no more." God desires for us to live heathier, more abundant lives, for His glory and for our happiness, yet He never reverses the order. His bidding is always preceded by the good news of acquittal (see Romans 8:1), because He paid the price! Thank you, Jesus!

My Response: _____

HIS APPEAL

"Truly I say to you that the tax collectors and prostitutes will get into the kingdom of God before you."

—Matthew 21:31

There are true followers of Jesus in the most unexpected places. Our ministry, Jesus 101, recently received a wonderful letter from a prisoner describing his response after reading our booklet, "Luke: Salvation for All." "Even though I am incarcerated," he wrote, "my soul has been set free!" He ended his letter with an excited "Woo-hoo!" As I was reading it, it occurred to me that some people in jail are feeling free, while some others in the church pews may actually feel incarcerated. Quite a paradox, isn't it?

Matthew 21:31 is one of the most shocking verses in the New Testament. It's part of the parable of the two sons that Jesus used to respond to the chief priests and elders who questioned His authority (see Matthew 21:23). In the parable, a man appeals to his two sons to go work in the vineyard. The first son responds negatively but later regrets his answer and goes (verse 29). The second son responds positively but then changes his mind and doesn't go (verse 30). Jesus asked them: "Which of the two did the will of his father?" and they answered, "the first" (verse 31). Jesus gave the shocking interpretation: "Truly I say to you that the tax collectors and prostitutes will get into the kingdom of God before you" (verse 31). The most unlikely ones had believed, but the chief priests and elders had not (verse 32). Tax collectors and prostitutes, despised by the religious leaders (see Luke 18:11), were getting to the kingdom *ahead* of the law-abiding, Sabbath-keeping priests and elders. Those who had religious ancestry and pedigree were in peril of being excluded from the kingdom (see Matthew 8:11, 12). In the most literal sense, the last were first, and the first were last. The appeal of Jesus is meant for each one of us, whether we consider ourselves religious or unlikely followers. In the Gospels, the religious folk are always in the gravest danger because they don't recognize their need. Let's respond faithfully to the appeal of Jesus by examining our own hearts and accepting His grace, which none of us deserve.

My Response: _____

HIS GENEROSITY

"When those hired about the eleventh hour came,
each one received a denarius."

—Matthew 20:9

Many years ago, I got a new job. I clearly remember that I started working in the middle of the last quarter of the year. I was very thankful to have this new job, especially because it filled me with purpose and meaning. And I was extremely surprised when my boss announced that I would be getting paid from the beginning of the quarter. I was amazed at his generosity!

There is a surprising parable, found only in the Gospel of Matthew, that highlights God's outrageous generosity. The story is placed between two framing sayings of Jesus about the first becoming last, and the last becoming the first" (Matthew 19:30; 20:16). Explaining these sayings, Matthew records the parable of Jesus about the landowner who hired laborers for his vineyard. "The kingdom of heaven is like" a man who hires workers in the morning and agrees to pay them one denarius for the day and sends them to his vineyard (Matthew 20:1, 2). Then he keeps going back to the marketplace throughout the day, at 9:00 A.M., at noon, at 3:00 P.M., to get more workers, agreeing to pay "whatever is right" (verse 4). We are not told why he needs more and more workers all through the day, yet this was a typical scene during the harvest. But it is surprising that the landowner goes out again to hire at 5:00 P.M., with only one hour left to work. When he asks those workers why they are still there, they answer that no one has hired them (verse 7). It is possible that these were rejected, less desirable laborers, but he still hires them. The law of Moses required employers to pay day laborers at the end of each day (Deuteronomy 24:14, 15). The shocking ending of the parable shows how the *last* group gets called *first* and gets paid full wages! (Matthew 20:9). They each received one denarius even though they had worked only for one hour! Can you imagine their joy? Do you, or someone you know, feel like a reject or less desirable? God invites you into the kingdom, and it's not too late! We are *all* recipients of God's generous salvation! Eternal life is for all who accept, for "some are not more saved than others."*

My Response: _____

---

* France, *Gospel of Matthew*, 751.

HIS PREROGATIVE

"I wish to give to this last man the same as to you."
—Matthew 20:14

An intriguing video clip, entitled "The Good-O-Meter," offers a great illustration about salvation. On Judgment Day, people are lined up, their "life-files" in hand, waiting to step on the scale of the Good-O-Meter to be determined to be either good or bad. Even the person with the most impressive record of good accomplishments is declared "not good enough" and gets quite angry with self-righteous indignation. Finally, one who is obviously unworthy is about to step on the scale when Jesus appears and stands on the scale in his place. Immediately, the Good-O-Meter points to "good enough" and the *unworthy* one is seated with Jesus. The rest of the group shout out indignantly, "It's not fair!" The angel in the final scene responds: "That's why it's called grace!"*

The parable of the generous landowner (Matthew 20:1–16) focuses on God's grace towards those who entered the vineyard at the last hour of the workday and received the same wages as the rest. But when those who started first see that the last ones receive one denarius for their one hour of work, they feel that they deserve more than the originally agreed amount (see verses 9, 10), yet they too receive one denarius. They start grumbling about the unfairness of the situation (verses 11, 12), just like the older brother in the parable found in Luke 15, who got angry with his father because of his graceful treatment of the prodigal son. The grumblers speak to the landowner with an air of entitlement: "These last men have worked *only* one hour, and you made them *equal to us* who have borne the burden and the scorching heat of the day" (Matthew 20:12). The owner explains to them that he has not violated their agreement and that he can do as he wishes with the undeserving ones; grace is His prerogative. The kingdom's mathematics are not based on *fairness*, but on *grace*. None of us *deserve* salvation. Terms of entitlement or contract are not part of the equation. There are no shorter or longer versions of eternity; *we are all saved by grace*. Let's treat each other as fellow undeserving-yet-saved citizens of God's gracious kingdom!

My Response: _____

---

* "The Good-O-Meter," Central Films, May 12, 2007, https://www.youtube.com /watch?v=XrLzYw6ULYw.

HIS FORGIVENESS

*"And the lord of that slave felt compassion and released him
and forgave him the debt."*

—Matthew 18:27

The man was Oskar Groening, the former SS Sergeant known as the book-keeper of Auschwitz, who was accused (and later found guilty) of being complicit in the murder of 300,000 people. She was Eva Kor, an 81-year-old Hungarian Jew and survivor of the camp where her mother, father, and two older sisters were all gassed to death." She explains why, despite protest from other Holocaust survivors, she has decided to forgive him. " 'Why survive at all if [all] you want to be is sad, angry and hurting?' she says. 'That is so foreign to who I am.' "* She forgave him a debt that he couldn't possibly pay.

In the discourse about the kingdom's community (Matthew 18), Peter comes to Jesus to find out how many times to forgive. "Up to seven?" he asked (verse 21). The rabbis advocated for a "generous" three times. Jesus answered: "Up to seventy times seven" (verse 22). The point of Jesus is not to count four hundred ninety times but to propose an unlimited, exuberant forgiveness. Then He tells a parable in two parts, the second of which we will examine tomorrow. Jesus compares the kingdom of heaven to a king who called his slaves to settle accounts with them. One of the servants owed ten thousand talents (the Greek word *muriōn* can also mean "beyond count"). This was an insurmountable debt, equivalent to billions of dollars today. How could a slave get into such debt? It is believed that this is consistent with servants who collected the taxes of the land and were to bring those proceeds to the king. This man doesn't have the astronomical amount to pay. But instead of mercy, he asks the king for patience, having a completely unrealistic view of himself and his ability to pay (see verse 26). Nevertheless, "the lord of that slave felt compassion and released him and forgave him the debt" (verse 27). Instead of patience, the man found forgiveness of an immeasurably huge debt. Christianity is not a debt payment system. On the topic of forgiveness, the first indispensable part is to understand that we have been forgiven a debt that we could have never been able to pay!

My Response: _____

---

* Joe Shute, "Why I Forgive the Nazis Who Murdered My Family, *Telegraph*, January 20, 2016, 5:45 P.M. GMT, https://www.telegraph.co.uk/history/world-war-two/12111155/Why-I-forgive-the-Nazis-who-murdered-my-family.html.

HIS OVERFLOW

"Should you not also have had mercy on your fellow slave,
in the same way that I had mercy on you?"
—Matthew 18:33

On our ministry's website, www.Jesus101.tv, you can watch a video entitled "Challenged,"* which is part of our TV series "After God's Heart," a study in brokenness from the life of David. In this show, pastor Mike Tucker and I discuss forgiveness: what it is and what it is *not*. Forgiveness is not denial; it's not saying that it didn't hurt or that it didn't matter. It is not justification or condonement of the wrong, and it's not a lack of boundaries, which means that forgiveness does not always lead to reconciliation. Forgiveness is cancelling the debt, releasing the person who has committed the offense, and not holding resentment.

In the second part of Jesus' parable on forgiveness (we studied the first part yesterday), the forgiven slave finds a fellow slave who owes him money; the amount of the debt is about four months' wages (Matthew 18:28). The slave, who had just been forgiven an unfathomable debt, now seizes and starts choking a man who owes him a small debt (verse 28). The fellow slave pleads for patience in almost identical words to those used by the first slave when pleading with the king (verse 29, compare with verse 26), yet the first slave refuses to have patience with his colleague (verse 30). He can't sell a fellow slave but imprisons him for non-payment. He treats his fellow debtor with contempt, refusing to become a conduit of the king's mercy. His fellow slaves were baffled by his lack of compassion and reported him to the master, who revokes the previous debt-cancellation and sends him to prison. "Should you not also have had mercy on your fellow slave, in the same way that I had mercy on you?" (Matthew 18:33). God was willing to forgive the debt but would not stand for an *unforgiving forgiven* servant. By his lack of compassion, the forgiven slave revealed that he had not understood the magnitude of God's mercy towards him. The forgiveness principles of the kingdom of heaven are to produce a chain reaction, in which the mercy we have received overflows through us to our fellow humans. Merciful Jesus, make us true instruments of Your grace!

My Response: _____

---

* "After God's Heart—Challenged," Jesus 101, accessed May 2, 2019, https://jesus101.tv/watch/?media=5969.

HIS REALITY

After the demon was cast out, the mute man spoke;
and the crowds were amazed, and were saying,
"Nothing like this has ever been seen in Israel."
—Matthew 9:33

As I was studying organizational behavior, I learned that we all evaluate and interpret reality through our *perception*, and that we can be quite obstinate about arguing that our interpretive filters are the *right* ones. In my family, we often alluded to a joke about two men involved in an animated argument about an item in the store. One of them believed it was a bar of soap, while the other insisted it was a piece of cheese. They continued to argue until the cheese proponent decided to take a bite to prove his perspective. "It tastes like soap, but it's definitely cheese," he insisted. This is how stubborn we can be.

The miracle of Jesus in Matthew 9:32–34 is the tenth miracle within two chapters. However, it elicits two opposite responses. A man who was mute due to demon possession was brought to Jesus (verse 32). Just as blindness turned to sight in the preceding miracle (9:27–30), the deaf-mute being able to hear and speak was an expectation to be fulfilled by the long-awaited Messiah (see Matthew 11:5; Isaiah 35:5, 6). The double miracle of exorcism and healing is implied in the introduction to the crowd's response to the miracle: "After the demon was cast out, the mute man spoke; and the crowds were amazed" (verse 33). The first response is excitement and amazement, as had been the case with those who witnessed the calming of the storm on the lake (8:27), with an important addition about the newness of Jesus' ministry; "Nothing like this has ever been seen in Israel" (9:33). On the opposite side, there was the shocking response of the antagonistic Pharisees, who issued their most public attack against Jesus so far in this Gospel, stating that "He casts out the demons by the ruler of the demons" (verse 34; see also 12:24–29). We should always ask God to give us a heavenly perspective. Even today, many are amazed and rejoice when confronted with the grace of God in Jesus, while others react negatively, calling it a license to sin. The grace of God is outrageous and scandalous. Let's ask God to give us humility and joy to accept it.

My Response: _____

His Choice

As Jesus went on from there, He saw a man called Matthew,
sitting in the tax collector's booth; and He said to him, "Follow Me!"
—Matthew 9:9

Rejection takes many forms. You might send out invitations to a party and no one shows up, or you might not get picked for either of the two teams being formed in a school PE class until the very end. I have vivid memories of being rejected when I was twelve years old. Having just come to the United States with my family, I distinctly remember the most popular girl in my class and the way she looked down on me because of my accent, skin color, or the hand-me-down clothes I wore. But all of that changed the day when another girl befriended me.

Matthew (called Levi in Mark and Luke) is the perfect example of a rejected person. He was a tax collector (Greek *telōnēs*) and therefore was despised by his fellow countrymen for at least three reasons. First, tax collectors were viewed as traitors because they collected tax for the hated Roman government. Second, the tax collectors were known to abuse their authority for personal gain because the amount of tax was at the collector's discretion. Extortion was the norm for these people, thus making them rich at the expense of the needy and destitute. Third, Jews viewed tax collectors as ritually unclean, as they often compromised the purity laws by dealing with Gentiles and handling their money. Therefore, for socio-religious-political reasons, tax collectors were despised and rejected. That Jesus would choose a tax collector as His disciple (see Matthew 10:3) is more shocking than we can understand. And perhaps just as startling is the fact that Matthew left everything and followed Him (Matthew 9:9). The next scene happens at Matthew's house with a big celebration at which Jesus and His disciples, as well as "many tax collectors and sinners," are guests (Matthew 9:10; see also Luke 5:29). If you have ever been *rejected* by a religious person or group, you must know that this is not the way Jesus treats you. Furthermore, Jesus invites the rejects, the despised, and the marginalized to follow Him. He has a special interest in the captives and the lost. Yes, He has come for all of us, the least of these.

My Response: _____

HIS ACCEPTANCE

"I did not come to call the righteous, but sinners."
—Matthew 9:13

A pastor shared quite an impactful story with me. One morning, he happened to step outside the church during the service and ran into one of his young adults and smelled a strong scent on his breath. The young man was hesitant to come back into the church because the smell betrayed one of his unhealthy habits. The pastor encouraged him to come in anyway, explaining that we are all sinners in need of a Savior. "If all our sins had a smell, the church would be a pretty smelly place," he said. What a true statement!

After Jesus had called Levi Matthew to follow Him (Matthew 9:9), Matthew organized a big celebration in his house, and *"many* tax collectors and sinners came" (Matthew 9:10; see Luke 5:29). These were probably Matthew's former coworkers and acquaintances who were now sharing a meal with Jesus and His disciples. I am sure they were more than curious to meet the One who had accepted a person like Levi Matthew as His disciple. In Greek the word "sinners" denotes people who disregard the Jewish scribal law, even though it can also carry a moral connotation. This crowd of "sinners" was in stark contrast to the Pharisees, who voiced their objections to the disciples of Jesus: "Why is your Teacher eating with the tax collectors and sinners?" (verse 11). Sharing a meal was a sign of acceptance and community, and these guardians of the ritual law resented this outrageous acceptance of "sinners" and had to point it out. Jesus heard them and answered with a symbolic saying about a doctor being needed by those who are physically sick and not by the healthy ones (verse 12), meaning that He had come for those with spiritual illness. Then He quotes (unique to Matthew) Hosea 6:6: "I desire compassion [mercy], and not sacrifice" (Matthew 9:13; see also 12:7). Afterward, Jesus goes on to proclaim His mission: "for I did not come to call the righteous, but sinners" (Matthew 9:13). He was exposing the type of legalistic, pharisaical "righteousness" in which purity trumps mercy. Paradoxically, only those who know they are unworthy/smelly (21:31) receive Jesus' outrageous acceptance!

My Response: _____

HIS BOLDNESS

"Rabbi, look, the fig tree which You cursed has withered."—Mark 11:21

When I was a little girl, my family lived in Buenos Aires, behind an Adventist Publishing House. In spite of living in the city, we had the unusual blessing of having a backyard with fruit trees. Among them, we had a huge fig tree, which bore hundreds of sweet and large figs each year. We monitored the tree closely, looking for the early figs which we called *brebas*, that would appear much earlier than the rest of the crop. They were so sweet!

Coming back to Jerusalem from Bethany, Jesus became hungry (Mark 11:12). "Seeing at a distance a fig tree in leaf, He went to see if perhaps He would find anything on it; and when He came to it, He found nothing but leaves, for it was not the season for figs" (verse 13). We are clearly told that it was not the season for figs, but this particular tree had the *appearance of fruit*; sometimes early figs were found along with the leaves. All of a sudden, "Jesus, meek and mild" seems to turn into "Jesus, mean and wild,"* right in front of our eyes! And He makes a disturbing pronouncement "May no one ever eat fruit from you again!" (verse 14). Jesus appears irrationally angry, but in fact He is using the fig-less tree to enact a parable, to teach something really important to the disciples. In the prophetic utterances of the Jewish Scriptures, the fig tree represented Israel. But when Israel was not fulfilling its purpose to represent Him to the nations, God spoke against them in terms of a dried-up fig tree: "I saw your forefathers as the earliest fruit on the fig tree in its first season. But . . . their root is dried up, They will bear no fruit (Hosea 9:10, 16). The cursing of the fig-less tree was an enacted parable of judgment on the system's fruitlessness and hypocrisy. After this, Jesus cleansed the temple (Mark 11:15–18), judging what they had done with it. The following day, as they passed by, Peter said "Rabbi, look, the fig tree which You cursed has withered" (verse 21), thus completing the enacted parable. The temple had become like the barren fig tree, a fruitless institution. In this way, Jesus announced that God will not tolerate exclusivity, religious pride, and hypocrisy among His people.

My Response: _____

_____

---

* Mark Galli uses this phrase as the title of his book that studies troubling passages in the Gospel of Mark.

HIS ZEAL

He entered the temple and began to drive out those who were buying and selling in the temple, and overturned the tables of the money changers.—Mark 11:15

In His righteous indignation, Jesus positioned himself in the temple court: "And He would not permit anyone to carry merchandise through the temple" (verse 16). Can you imagine Jesus with His hand up, prohibiting people from carrying goods through the temple courts? Maps of ancient Jerusalem shed light into what is going on. A shortcut, which went through the temple court of the Gentiles, had been created between the Mount of Olives and the city. If this route was not available, merchants would have to go around the temple, which was quite a big structure.

After cursing the fig tree (Mark 11:12–14; see yesterday's devotional), Jesus entered the temple. This time the fraud covered by the appearance of piety was too much for Him. In the only violent demonstration in all His public ministry, "He entered the temple and began to drive out those who were buying and selling in the temple, and overturned the tables of the money changers, and the seats of those who were selling doves; and He would not permit anyone to carry merchandise through the temple" (verses 15, 16). Everyone is astounded! It seems that up to approximately the year A.D. 30, the markets for the sacrificial animals were located on the Mount of Olives, and they were under the control of the Jewish ruling group. But around this time, the high priest appears to have authorized the setting up of markets in the outer courts of the temple, creating a competitive, businesslike atmosphere. Jesus drove out all who were buying and selling, and the money changers. The very place that God had designed to reveal His grace and welcome the contrite-hearted had become a sacrilegious, self-centered, crooked, businesslike, and proud institution. The ultimate blasphemy is an empty, self-sufficient, hypocritical religious system with the appearance of piety. And His authority took over. His disciples remembered that it was written, "Zeal for Your house will consume me" (John 2:17). Just imagine a parent defending his children, and you get the picture. God always defends the oppressed!

My Response: _____

His Comparison

*"And forgive us our debts, as we also
have forgiven our debtors."*

—Matthew 6:12

R *eader's Digest* tells the touching story of a woman who met her husband's killer and forgave him. While riding his bike, her husband
was struck by a drunk driver. Two years later, the woman's young
daughter made a card for the driver, who was in prison. That simple card
propelled the family on an amazing journey of forgiveness that ended up
transforming the murderer's life. The conclusion is surprising: "Helping her
husband's killer transform himself, Patty [the wife] explains, 'was my form of
vengeance. I got a life for a life.' "*

Sometimes forgiveness seems out of reach, especially when tragedy
strikes. That's why a little word in the Lord's Prayer gives us trouble. Both
in the original language and in English, the word has only two letters, yet it
makes all the difference in the world. "Forgive us our debts, *as* we also have
forgiven our debtors" (Matthew 6:12). When Jesus instructed His disciples
in prayer, He taught them to request forgiveness *in the same manner* as they
forgave. This comparison phrase is addressing moral debtors, meaning those
who trespass against us. It's a paradigm given by Jesus, who calls His Father "our" Father; it's for us who have forgiveness through Jesus. Others can
never owe us as much as we owe God (see Matthew 18:23–35). If we are not
willing to forgive our neighbor from our hearts, Jesus says that His Father
will not forgive us either (see Matthew 18:35). Forgiveness does not mean to
stay in harmful situations; it does not remove the accountability of the debtor
nor does it necessarily restore a relationship. Forgiveness is to release in *our
hearts* the other person's moral debt to us, and it is often a process. Jesus died
for us, and He died for them. "We are not forgiven *because* we forgive, but *as*
we forgive. The ground of all forgiveness is found in the unmerited love of
God, but by our attitude toward others we show whether we have made that
love our own."† So how can we possibly extend this forgiveness to others?
Those who have been forgiven by grace, are given the grace to forgive. It's *all
a divine gift of grace!*

My Response: _____

_____

* Kenneth Miller, "Patty O'Reilly Came Face to Face With Her Husband's Killer—And
Forgave Him, *Reader's Digest,* https://www.rd.com/true-stories/inspiring/how-i-forgave
-my-husbands-killer/.
† Ellen G. White, *Christ's Object Lessons* (Washington, DC: Review and Herald®, 1941), 251.

HIS DELIVERANCE

*"This woman . . . whom Satan has bound for eighteen
long years, should she not have been released
from this bond on the Sabbath day?"*

—Luke 13:16

When writing my book *I Will Give You Rest,** I wanted to find an image for the cover, depicting full rest in Jesus. And I did! I found a piece of artwork in which every detail touches my heart: Jesus embracing the little girl as she rests in His arms. His passionate expression as He is reunited with His child. The girl's facial expression as she is safe in her Rescuer's embrace; her hand grabbing His shoulder, never to let go, resting in complete trust and assurance.

And this is how I imagine the woman who started glorifying God after Jesus released her from her sickness (Luke 13:13). Only Luke records the healing of this woman on the Sabbath (Luke records five healing miracles on the Sabbath, more than any of the Gospel writers; Luke 4:31–35, 38, 39; 6:6–10; 13:13–16; 14:1–6). As Jesus was teaching in a synagogue on the Sabbath, He saw a woman who was bent and could not straighten up; she had been afflicted with this condition for eighteen years (Luke 13:11). He took the initiative to call her to Himself and announced her deliverance before He laid hands on her: "Woman, you are freed from your sickness" (verse 12). As He performed the miracle, she began glorifying God (verse 13). I am startled by the contrast of the responses of the audience: she is glorifying God while the synagogue official is indignant because Jesus healed on the Sabbath. And in the conclusion, the opponents of Jesus are humiliated while the entire crowd is rejoicing. Jesus used the rabbinical argument style "how much more" (*qal wahomer*) to expose the hypocrisy of the religious leaders of the time. If they would untie their own donkey to get water on the Sabbath, *how much more* should this woman be released from her eighteen years of bondage on the Sabbath, the divine day of remembrance and restoration! Our release from bondage is God's priority, specifically typified on the Sabbath day! May our religious gatherings reflect the Redeemer's mission: to preach the gospel to the poor, *to proclaim release to the captives, to set free those who are oppressed!* (Luke 4:18).

My Response: _____

* Elizabeth Talbot, *I Will Give You Rest* (Nampa, ID: Pacific Press®, 2015).

HIS FORESIGHT

Jesus said to him [Peter], "Truly I say to you, that this very night, before a rooster crows twice, you yourself will deny Me three times."
—Mark 14:30

I confess that I am embarrassed about what I am about to tell you, but it was an important lesson for me, so here we go. After finishing a master's degree in organizational behavior, I enrolled in a master's degree in biblical studies. I had done well in my first graduate degree, and I got a little self-confident. I thought that my second graduate degree would be a breeze, especially because I was born in a pastor's home and had studied the Bible since childhood. *What are they really going to teach me?* I thought. Oh boy! Was I in for a surprise! God humbled me big-time! I felt like I was back in kindergarten! I realized that I knew so little!

Unhealthy self-confidence results in a dark pit. The disciple Peter always knew better than everyone else. And when Jesus told His disciples that all of them would abandon Him, Peter protested. Jesus added a revelation of hope: "But after I have been raised, I will go ahead of you to Galilee" (Mark 14:28), yet Peter missed this completely. That Jesus would imply that he, Simon Peter, would abandon Him, well . . . that was offensive! *Maybe some of your weaker disciples might leave you, but not me! I am Peter!* "Even though all may fall away, yet I will not" (verse 29). But Jesus knew what would happen; He knew about Peter's weaknesses more than Peter himself. So, Jesus made it a bit more specific, using the second person singular, explaining unequivocally that Peter would fail: "This very night, before a rooster crows twice, *you yourself* will deny Me three times" (verse 30). Peter kept insisting that he wouldn't. But Jesus knows us intimately; He even has a foreknowledge of our failures. Yet, He always offers us His grace and hope, which sometimes we miss because we are feeling strong. The story of Peter's downward spiral is picked up again in Mark 14:66, and it will only take seven verses to describe one of the most complete failures of a follower of Jesus. If you find yourself at the bottom of a dark pit that you never imagined, remember that Jesus already knew about it and has provided a way out for you through His sacrifice.

My Response: _____

HIS PETITION

"I have prayed for you, that your faith may not fail; and you, when once you have turned again, strengthen your brothers."

—Luke 22:32

The acrobat, Charles Blondin, became famous in the summer of 1859 when he crossed the Niagara Falls on a tightrope. He crossed it several times and in different ways: on stilts, going backwards, and blindfolded; his skills stunned the audience. The story is told that at one point he asked the crowd if they believed he could do it with a wheelbarrow, to which everyone answered with a resounding "Yes!" Then he asked for a volunteer to get into the wheelbarrow and the crowd grew silent. Sometime later he crossed the Falls with his manager on his back.

It's one thing to assert that we have faith in someone's ability to do something, and it's another thing to believe they can do it for us personally. All three synoptic Gospels (Matthew, Mark, and Luke) report that Jesus predicted Peter's upcoming betrayal, but only Luke records two verses where Jesus told Peter that He was praying for Him. "Simon, Simon, behold, Satan has demanded permission to sift you [plural, *you all*] like wheat; but I have prayed for you [singular, *you specifically*], that your faith may not fail; and you, when once you have turned again, strengthen your brothers" (Luke 22:31, 32). Jesus had been praying for Peter! Interestingly, He wasn't pleading that Peter might not betray Him or that Peter might be strong. Instead, He was praying that *Peter's faith* would not fail, and that he would *turn back* when he did fail. Satan not only wants us to fail but tempts us to believe we've gone too far and tries to undermine our faith in the sufficiency of Jesus' sacrifice to save us personally. Grace and faith are gifts from God (see Ephesians 2:8, 9); we can accept them or reject them. Jesus petitioned that Peter might believe that no matter how badly he had failed, God's grace was sufficient for him personally. By faith he could *return*, ready to strengthen his brothers. As with Peter, Jesus intercedes for us; His grace is for all of us who have failed one way or another. And there is a unique ministry awaiting those who *return* from unbelief. Believe! His grace is more than sufficient for you!

My Response: _____

HIS FORBEARANCE

Jesus said to Peter, "Put the sword into the sheath; the cup which the Father has given Me, shall I not drink it?"

—John 18:11

*A*mazing Grace, how sweet the sound, that saved a wretch like me."* I don't know if you have had the experience of facing your own weaknesses, character defects, and failures. It can be disheartening, yet it is absolutely necessary to see ourselves in the true light of our fallen humanity. It is only in this context that we can grasp a glimpse of God's forbearance with us. Our utter need of God is recognized in the place where two realities meet, like a coin with two sides: our wretchedness and His saving grace!

I see God's grace and forbearance in Jesus' treatment of His disciples, who constantly misunderstood Him and kept acting contrary to what He had taught them, and eventually abandoned Him in His darkest hour. Simon Peter, for example, the self-sufficient disciple who thought he had all the answers, eventually had to face his own wretchedness. Having spent three years with Jesus, listening to His teachings and learning from Him, Peter still had a long way to go. In the Gospel of John, we see how Peter reacted when Jesus was betrayed by Judas: "Simon Peter then, having a sword, drew it and struck the high priest's slave, and cut off his right ear; and the slave's name was Malchus" (John 18:10). Was he really that hardheaded? Had he not seen Jesus perform miracles? Didn't he know that Jesus was the Christ? Yet Jesus gracefully told Peter to put the sword away and reminded him that this was the cup that the Father had given Him, and that He would voluntarily drink it. Later on, in the same chapter, Peter denied Jesus (verses 25–27). Yet Jesus patiently endured the failure of His disciples in the midst of His own suffering. It was Jesus who sought out His unsuccessful and deficient disciples after His resurrection and restored Peter and appointed him to ministry (John 21:15–17). When we are painfully confronted by our weaknesses and shortcomings, that's the time to rely and trust in the forbearing grace of our Savior. *"Amazing Grace, how sweet the sound, that saved a wretch like me."*†

My Response: _____

_____

* John Newton, "Amazing Grace."
† Newton, "Amazing Grace."

His Grip

"But go, tell His disciples and Peter, 'He is going ahead of you to Galilee; there you will see Him, just as He told you.' "

—Mark 16:7

My husband Patrick was walking with a friend on a long bridge over a busy high-speed freeway in the city of Buenos Aires. When he had almost crossed over, he looked back and saw a man swinging one of his legs over the railing. Patrick started running back; the man was already on the outer side of the bridge, ready to jump to his certain death. Patrick was able to lock his own hands around the man's chest, preventing him from jumping. The man kept screaming, "Let me go!" But Patrick kept telling him, "God loves you!" And God's love prevailed!

Peter's desire to stay close to Jesus is commendable. While Jesus is beaten and spit upon, Peter follows at a distance (see Mark 14:54). A servant girl recognizes him: "You also were with Jesus the Nazarene"; Peter denies it (verses 67, 68). And he refuses to acknowledge his relationship with Jesus two more times, saying that he definitely *does not know* this Man (verse 71). "Immediately a rooster crowed a second time, And Peter remembered how Jesus had made the remark to him, 'Before a rooster crows twice, you will deny Me three times.' And he began to weep." (verse 72). He had been so sure that he wouldn't fail, but he did. When you hit bottom and realize your true condition, that's when you can allow life-changing help in your life; that's when we realize that we really need a Savior. But what if he had gone too far? Should he jump from a bridge or hang himself, like Judas had done? Mark tells us something about the morning of the Resurrection that no other Gospel writer records. When the women went to the tomb on Sunday morning, they found an angel who told them that Jesus had risen! Then the angel added: "But go, tell His disciples *and Peter*, 'He is going ahead of you to Galilee" (Mark 16:7). Did you catch that? Did you see the two words? Can you imagine Jesus that morning, giving specific instructions to the angel to mention Peter by name? His blood had covered even *his* ransom. Peter was in His grip, and Jesus didn't want to let him go. And *you* are in Jesus' grip, and He is calling you by name!

My Response: _____

His Confirmation

"All that the Father gives Me will come to Me, and the one
who comes to Me I will certainly not cast out."

—John 6:37

Body language is a powerful way of communicating; it is sometimes more convincing than the words we speak. For example,
someone may assure you that they have time to dialogue with
you, yet by constantly looking at their watch, they are sending the opposite message. The same is true when someone says that we are welcome
to visit, yet if we are not gladly received with opened arms, we will feel
unwelcome in spite of the verbal assurances.

Jesus made sure that we understood that He welcomes us, and that
He will never reject us. During His ministry on earth, He was accused
of receiving the sinners, the outcasts, and the marginalized. He often
extended His invitation to come to Him. God took the initiative to save
us and to seek that which was lost. The truth about Him coming down
from heaven is repeated seven times in John 6 (see verses 33, 38, 41,
42, 50, 51, 58). His actions loudly declare His love for the human race.
And just in case someone thought themselves to be the exception, Jesus
confirmed that *anyone* coming to Him will find out that He will *never*
throw them out. The negative used in this pronouncement is emphatic;
it is something like: "He will *not ever* reject, dismiss, repudiate, or turn
down." There is no crime so heinous, no addiction so dark, no shame so
profound, no detour so distant, that would deem a person unwelcome
by the Savior of the world. This extreme confirmation, that everyone
who comes to Him will be accepted, is given even in the context of an
unbelieving crowd (verse 36). Yet Jesus knows that many *will* come to
Him, though not all, and everyone who does will be welcomed with His
open arms. Furthermore, God the Father is in complete agreement with
this salvific rescue: "This is the will of Him who sent Me, that of all that
He has given Me I lose nothing, but raise it up on the last day" (verse 39).
If you ever find yourself in a deep pit, wondering if God will accept you,
come back to Jesus with confidence. He will surely, certainly, without a
doubt, receive you with open arms!

My Response: _____

HEEDING HIS TEACHING

His Deity

*In the beginning was the Word, and the Word
was with God, and the Word was God.*

—John 1:1

Perhaps you remember the 3-D puzzles and pictures that became very popular several years ago. I couldn't see what others claimed to see until my birthday came along, and I received one of those pictures as a gift. Someone took the time to teach me how to focus my eyes, and I will never forget what happened next. Following the instructions, my eyes started to perceive a whole other reality within the picture, and I could now see the things others had insisted they were seeing. It was truly breathtaking!

John introduces Jesus as much more than a prophet from God or just a miracle worker. He wants us to see Jesus beyond His humanity and offers a breathtaking picture of His deity. John's Gospel starts long before the birth of Jesus, at "the beginning," with a deliberate reminder of the first words of the Bible in Genesis 1:1: "*In the beginning* was the Word, and the Word was with God, and the Word was God. He was *in the beginning* with God" (John 1:1, 2). From the start, we step into an eternal picture of a preexisting God. The Word was not created but was God and was with God since the very beginning of the universe. John introduces Jesus as God, who was with God since the beginning but who is distinct from God the Father. This is a bold statement with which to begin his gospel because Judaism was, and is, a monotheistic religion. Christianity is also a monotheistic religion that believes in one God, manifested in Three Persons (Father, Son, and Holy Spirit), which we call the Trinity. But this was a foreign concept for Judaism. John's prologue starts and ends in the same way: Jesus is God! (see John 1:1, 18). When we pray in the name of Jesus, we're not just talking of another powerful prophet or anointed man sent from God, even though Jesus is all of these things. We are praying in the Name of the most powerful Being in the universe, the Omnipotent, the Omniscient, the Creator of heaven and earth, the Redeemer of the human race, and the One God who loved us above and beyond Himself!

My Response: _____

HIS EXPLANATION

Then beginning with Moses and with all the prophets, He explained to them the things concerning Himself in all the Scriptures.

—Luke 24:27

Dan Stevers* is a gifted artist who creates animated video illustrations to explain the deeper, Christ-centered meaning of biblical texts. He has produced one of the best videos that I have ever seen, entitled "True and Better." It is a cartoon designed to show the connection between the best known stories of the Old Testament and their fulfillment in Jesus. It shows how Jesus is the true and better Adam, the true and better Abraham, Moses, David, Joseph, Esther, Job, Passover lamb, et cetera. It is amazing and remarkable for it is all about Jesus!

This is what Jesus explained on the resurrection morning, and it has become the core concept of our Jesus 101 ministry. On this occasion, Jesus explained to his disciples how to interpret Scripture as a whole: "And He said to them, 'O foolish men and slow of heart to believe in all that the prophets have spoken! Was it not necessary for the Christ to suffer these things and to enter into His glory?' Then beginning with Moses and with all the prophets, He explained to them the things concerning Himself in all the Scriptures" (Luke 24:25–27). The verb in the Greek original, *diermēneuō*, "to explain," contains the root word from which we've got the English noun *hermeneutics*, which deals with the interpretation of biblical text. Here Jesus provides the best biblical interpretive tool ever! The Law of Moses and the prophets are about Him! The Passover? The Tabernacle? The kinsman-redeemer concept? All about Him! Jesus later joins the rest of the disciples and repeats this explanation in greater detail: "He said to them, 'These are My words . . . that all things which are written about Me in the Law of Moses and the Prophets and the Psalms must be fulfilled.' Then He opened their minds to understand the Scriptures" (verses 44, 45). The Greek verb, translated as "understand," means to go deeper or to gain insight. It has been suggested that a good way to render it would be *"to connect the dots."* Let's ask God to teach us how to connect the dots, until we understand that the whole Bible is about Jesus!

My Response: _____

---

* www.DanStevers.com.

HIS PERSEVERANCE

"There was a landowner who planted a vineyard
and put a wall around it . . . and built a tower."
—Matthew 21:33

When I was growing up, my family had a vine that covered the whole back patio. This was a rare blessing, since we lived in the city. My parents took good care of it; they were vigilant against anything that could threaten its existence. Every year on the day of the *harvest*, my parents would bring in special equipment to make juice and bottle it. It was amazingly sweet! Later I was surprised to learn that a vineyard was a metaphor for God's people.

Jesus began the second of three parables addressed to the religious leaders using a unique metaphor of Israel as a vineyard (see Matthew 21:33–41). The details alluded to Isaiah's portrayal of Israel:

> My well-beloved had a vineyard . . .
> He dug it all around, removed its stones,
> And planted it with the choicest vine.
> And He built a tower in the middle of it
> And also hewed out a wine vat in it . . .
> (Isaiah 5:1, 2).

Renting out a vineyard and paying rent with the produce was customary, but in the parable, the renters withheld the fruit from the landowner and then beat and killed his servants who were prophets/messengers from God. I am amazed at the perseverance of the landowner (God). Instead of destroying the renters, He kept sending more messengers to the vineyard, who met the same fate. Finally, the landowner sent his son, representing Jesus. The vine growers, wanting the inheritance for themselves, took Him out of the vineyard and killed Him. Eventually God took the vineyard from them and gave it to others. It's not that God ran out of patience, but that He gave all His Resources! Jesus is the Heir and the exact representation of God's nature (Hebrews 1:1–3). In Jesus, God emptied Himself, giving all He had! If a person, or a religious system, rejects the centrality of Jesus, the maximum manifestation of God's love and grace and the *only way to be saved*, what else can God do? May we lift up Jesus and His salvific work as our core belief, because He is the *One and Only Savior!*

My Response: _____

HIS WATER

Now on the last day, the great day of the feast,
Jesus stood and cried out, saying, "If anyone is thirsty,
let him come to Me and drink."

—John 7:37

As I write this, two celebrities have taken their own lives in the last few days. Every time a tragedy like this happens, the news broadcasters bring in professionals to discuss early signs of depression and other mental health issues, and where to find help to prevent a suicide. As friends and families share their thoughts on why this happened, it becomes clear to all of us that all human beings are looking for meaning and purpose in life; we are all born with a spiritual thirst. When we fail in this search, hopelessness sets in.

God gave Israel *festivals of remembrance*, thanksgiving celebrations, which reminded them of their history, their purpose as a people, and the presence and provision of God in their past, present, and future. One of the three major Jewish festivals was the Feast of Tabernacles or Booths. Temporary booths made of branches could be seen everywhere; it was a Jewish family camp meeting celebration. They were reminded that they had been without a roof over their heads while God took care of them during the Exodus (see Leviticus 23:40–43; Deuteronomy 16:13–15). It has been described as the most joyful of all of their festivals. It was also a harvest thanksgiving celebration, which was sometimes simply called "the Feast." This festival was filled with symbols. An impressive visual was the water libation: every day the priest would participate in a procession filling a golden pitcher with water from the Pool of Siloam and carrying it back to the temple while people uttered the words of Isaiah 12:3: "You will joyously draw water from the springs of salvation" and sang the *Hallel* (Psalms 113–118). They remembered how God had provided water for them in the wilderness, and they also prayed for rain. It is said that on the last day, they went around the altar seven times. It was on the last great day of the Feast that Jesus stood up and, in the context of this water celebration, proclaimed in a loud voice: "If anyone is thirsty, let him come to Me and drink" (John 7:37). Yes! Jesus is the *only* One who can quench our deepest thirst.

My Response: _____

HIS CENTRALITY

Jesus said to her, "I am the resurrection and the life; he who believes in Me will live even if he dies. . . . Do you believe this?"
—John 11:25, 26

When I was a little girl, I went to Uruguay, where my parents were from, and marveled at the quartz stones that were found there. Uruguay has some of the world's largest deposits of amethyst, which is a quartz of a deep purple color. Back then we could find some of these in the open. I am not a rock and mineral expert, but I remember the surprising contrast between the grayish, unexceptional outside of the stone and the amazingly beautiful purple quartz center once it was opened. It was breathtaking. This will be today's visual aid.

Lazarus had been dead for four days (John 11:17). The first exchange between Jesus and Martha (John 11:21–27) is one of the most amazing dialogues about faith. To understand it, try to visualize a layered quartz stone or a fruit, like an orange, with three layers. These layers represent the three levels of faith that are developed in this narrative. Martha begins by confirming her belief that God will still hear Jesus and will give Him *whatever things* (plural) He asks, even though Jesus apparently missed this particular healing opportunity (verses 21, 22). She knows that prayers work. Let's call this first level the *how* of belief in Christ. The how of the Christian lifestyle is important. It is composed of belief in prayer, Bible study, and various spiritual disciplines. But there is more. Jesus says: "Your brother will rise again" (verse 23), and Martha responds that she *knows* that her brother will rise on the resurrection day (verse 24). We'll call this second level the *what* of Christianity. *What* we believe. Doctrines are extremely important! But there is more! Jesus said to her: "I am the resurrection and the life. . . . Do you *believe* this?" (verses 25, 26). This is the third and deepest level of faith. It is the *who* of the Christian faith. Jesus wanted Martha to believe in Him! The *how* and *what* of Christianity are a means to an end, which is the *who*. Christian doctrines and disciplines must be used like straws through which we drink the Living Water; they exist for us to access Jesus. Jesus is the beautiful, sweet core. He is the precious center. May He be the center of our lives!

My Response: _____

HIS PRAYER

"Father, I thank You that You have heard Me."

—John 11:41

There are people who seem to have such a deep connection with God, that when they pray all of heaven appears to come closer to listen. My father-in-law was one of those people. His prayers seemed to be so effective, with a child-like faith, that when anyone in the family had a pressing problem, they immediately called him to pray. I believe that we all have direct access to God in prayer, and that we don't need intermediaries. Still, some *prayer warriors* have adopted an intercessory prayer lifestyle that God honors, responds to, and is pleased with.

Jesus prayed at all times and in diverse circumstances. He prayed with thanksgiving (Matthew 11:25), He prayed for the Father's will to be done (Mark 14:36), He prayed for particular people (see Luke 22:31, 32), and He prayed when He gave up His Spirit (Luke 23:46). Jesus prayed in unparalleled intimacy with His Father. But there is a prayer of Jesus that breaks my heart. It is a public prayer that He prayed for the sake of those standing around. The stone from Lazarus' tomb had been removed. "Then Jesus raised His eyes, and said, 'Father, I thank You that You have heard Me. I knew that You always hear Me; but because of the people standing around I said it, so that they may believe that you sent Me' " (John 11:41, 42). Jesus doesn't ask for power or pray for God to hear His request for a resurrection. He thanks His Father that His request has already been heard ahead of time (see verse 42). Jesus *knew* that His Father *always* heard Him. This time Jesus prays that those who are about to witness this climactic sign might *believe in Him*, that they might come to understand that the Father has sent Him. The Jews had the Scriptures, they had the law and the Sabbath, they had dietary rules they followed, but they didn't believe that God had sent Jesus as the Messiah. What would Jesus pray about if we were His audience? Perhaps He would pray that we may believe that His sacrifice was more than sufficient and therefore live without fear of the future. Perhaps He would pray that we may fully rest in His salvific work, filled with the joy of salvation and the assurance of His ultimate victory. In Jesus' name: Amen!

My Response: _____

His Clarity

"Unless one is born again he cannot see the kingdom of God."
—John 3:3

Sometimes we desperately need total clarity. I was sitting with my dad and mom in the oncologist's office, waiting for him to give us the final results of my mother's tests. The doctor showed us a few things on the screen, but we were not quite sure that we fully understood what it all meant. After some more back and forth discussion, we finally had to ask the difficult question: "How long does she have?" The doctor hesitated for a moment and said, "I would be surprised if in six months she is still with us." He was right. And I learned the hard way that in matters of life and death, clarity is indispensable.

Nicodemus was a Pharisee and a ruler of the Jews (John 3:1); as such he kept and taught the law. He was very influence conscious, so he decided to visit Jesus privately at night before endorsing Him publicly. Nicodemus opened the dialogue with a diplomatic assertion: "Rabbi, *we know* that You have come from God as a teacher; for no one can do these signs that You do unless God is with him" (verse 2). Curiously, he spoke in plural, representing the ruling group of educated and religious people. He called Jesus a *teacher*, in other words, a colleague. In the first-century world, the informal principle of reciprocity should have elicited a series of flattering comments from Jesus in return for Nicodemus's praise. But Jesus skipped the expected sweet talk altogether: "Truly, truly, I say to you, unless one is born again he cannot see the kingdom of God" (verse 3). Jesus explained that whatever Nicodemus stood for was not enough for salvation, which is amazing considering who he was. Nicodemus was so baffled that first he interpreted the words of Jesus as referring to a physical birth. When circumcised non-Jews converted to Judaism, they were considered to be spiritual newborns, but why would *he* need to be reborn? But Jesus was crystal clear; he needed something else. Many of us are startled when we realize that our law keeping is not enough for salvation. Jesus calls us to be born again and to accept His death for us as the only way to enter His kingdom. Our acceptance of that invitation is a matter of life and death.

My Response: _____

His Embrace

"Whoever believes will in Him have eternal life."
—John 3:15

In some countries, couples to be married typically send two separate wedding invitations. Because most couples cannot afford a dinner for all the wedding guests, they send one invitation for the wedding ceremony, to many people, and the other one for the reception, to only a few close friends and family. I know of a bride and groom who decided to do something different. They sent out only one invitation, and when the service was over, the officiating pastor invited *all* the guests to the festivities that followed. The menu was scaled down to a bare minimum, but everyone was surprised and had a great time at the reception.

Nicodemus was a renowned person, a ruler of the Jews (John 3:1). He was baffled when Jesus explicitly told him that he had to be born again. But perhaps one of the most radical statements of Jesus in the interaction with Nicodemus was His use of the word *"whoever"* or *"everyone"* (Greek *pas*). "*Whoever* believes will in Him have eternal life. For God so loved the world, that He gave His only begotten Son, that *whoever* believes in Him shall not perish, but have eternal life" (John 3:15, 16). This is a shocking news: God's embrace includes everyone who believes in His Son! How could this be? *Everyone* who looks at the cross and believes in Him has eternal life. *Whoever, everyone, each person* who understands that they cannot save themselves and looks up to the Savior will live. For some reason, this truth is harder for Pharisees to understand than for public sinners (see Matthew 21:31). The latter already know their need, but the Pharisees . . . not so much. The disciples of Jesus also struggled with the reality of God's inclusive embrace for *all*, regardless of race, color, language, et cetera (see Acts 10:28, 34, 35). Is there someone in your circle who needs to know that they are included in the statement of truth that Jesus gave to Nicodemus? Think about specific people— perhaps your teenage grandchild, with his green hair and the belly-button ring. How about your ex-convict neighbor, or the girl in your congregation who got pregnant out of wedlock? Let them know! I am grateful that *whoever* includes even me.

My Response: _____

HIS TREASURE

"If you wish to be complete, go and sell your possessions and give to the poor, and you will have treasure in heaven; and come, follow Me."

—Matthew 19:21

I am often amused by the way little children think about money. In a store you can see children trying to convince their parents to buy a particular toy for them. Sometimes, when the parents refuse, the child self-confidently announces that he will buy it himself and proceeds to empty his pockets, revealing a handful of pennies that amount to nothing when compared with the price of the item. We resemble these little ones when we try to purchase our salvation.

A young man came to Jesus and asked: "Teacher, what good thing shall I do that I may obtain eternal life?" (Matthew 19:16). This question presupposes that he can obtain salvation by doing something good. Jesus reproves this way of thinking by explaining that "there is only One who is good" (verse 17); even the best human attempts cannot be called "good." Still, He meets him where he is and points to keeping the commandments. The young man asks "Which ones?" and Jesus enumerates the second part of the Decalogue, the fifth to the ninth commandment, which concentrate on how to treat others, and summarizes them, quoting Leviticus 19:18, "You shall love your neighbor as yourself" (Matthew 19:19). There was no surprise here; this was a customary Jewish view. The young man proceeds to show "all the pennies in his pocket" and claims to have kept all these things but senses there is more. "What am I still lacking?" Jesus goes deeper this time: "If you wish to be complete . . ." It's time to reveal the heart of the matter. He invites him to give up all his security and be fully dependent on God for provision, and this only as a preparation for discipleship. "Go and sell your possessions and give to the poor, and you will have treasure in heaven; and come, follow Me" (verse 21). The young man went away grieved, for he had many possessions (verse 22). Jesus is the real treasure and the highest priority. Nothing else, as good as it may seem, can purchase eternal life. Our heart follows what we treasure (Matthew 6:21), and Jesus is the *real* treasure.

My Response: _____

HIS DOING

*"With people this is impossible but with God
all things are possible."*

—Matthew 19:26

I t was quite an experience. We had planned the trip to Egypt for a long time, but because my mother had cancer, we were not sure if it would happen. But it did! We were now in front of the pyramids. My mom and I headed for the camels, and we sat on them as they were kneeling. But when the camel stood up … well, I was sitting much higher than I had expected; it was a bit scary. I had never realized how big these animals really are until I got to ride one.

Jesus used these animals, the largest in Palestine, to explain how we are saved. He spoke first of the difficulty, then of the impossibility, of a wealthy person gaining entrance into the kingdom. "It is easier for a camel to go through the eye of a needle, than for a rich man to enter the kingdom of God" (Matthew 19:24). Jesus was using hyperbole, an exaggerated figure of speech. Some have attempted to minimize this teaching by interpreting the eye of a needle as a small gate, but there is no indication of such meaning at the time, and this suggestion undermines the context of the verse.* Jesus addressed the danger of not being aware of our great need. In the Jewish culture, rich people were considered most blessed by God, because they had abundant provision, and could give alms to the poor and devote more time to the study of the Scriptures. The disciples were completely shocked; if it was impossible for such a blessed person to merit the kingdom, who then could be saved? Jesus was teaching that we are not saved by what we have, or by who we are in society. Salvation is His doing, not ours. The rich, the smart, the strong, none of them can earn heaven; the "blessed ones" should be vigilant, not letting their abundance keep them out of the kingdom. For every single human being, no matter the status, salvation is impossible; but for God *all things* are possible.

My Response: _____

* "A needle's eye in Jesus' day meant what it means today; the idea that it was simply a name for a small gate in Jerusalem is based on a gate from the medieval period and sheds no light on Jesus' teaching in the first century." Craig S. Keener, *The IVP Bible Background Commentary: New Testament* (Downers Grove, IL: InterVarsity Press, 1993), 98, https://books .google.com/books?id=5N3fAgAAQBAJ&pg.

HIS PREEMINENCE

"Being full of the Holy Spirit, he [Stephen] gazed intently into heaven and saw the glory of God, and Jesus standing at the right hand of God."

—Acts 7:55

I had a memorable trip to Taiwan. I had a fantastic time, sharing Jesus in that beautiful country. I had been told that evangelical Christianity was at a single digit percent in that country, but I never expected what I saw. I visited a famous temple and was dumfounded by the many idols I saw there. Hundreds of people were bringing offerings to their "gods," and my soul was stirred. Some of these "deities" looked so angry, even with red faces, that it made a lasting impact on me.

When we refer to idolatry, we often think of pagan nations and cultures that worship many different deities. In the Western world, we also talk about *modern* idols: people, things, and behaviors that take preeminence in our lives over the Creator-Redeemer God. In his *history of redemption* sermon, Stephen brought up a different type of idolatry. First, he referred to their fathers' unwillingness to obey and how, "At that time they made a calf and brought a sacrifice to the idol, and were rejoicing in the works of their hands" (Acts 7:41). But then he turned to the tabernacle, and the temple that Solomon built, and noted how, in spite of being *religious*, those in his audience were still being idolatrous by rejecting God's *Righteous One*. "You men who are stiff-necked and uncircumcised in heart and ears are always resisting the Holy Spirit; *you are doing just as your fathers did.* . . . They killed those who had previously announced the coming of the Righteous One, whose betrayers and murderers you have now become" (verses 51, 52). No matter what religious structures they boasted of, they were still behaving as pagans, because they were *uncircumcised in heart and ears*. This is what happens when Jesus is not *superior* to all religious symbols, beliefs, and structures. Jesus is our Redeemer and Advocate, and His righteousness (not ours) is the only reason why we will be saved. Stephen's audience covered their ears (verse 57). Filled with the Holy Spirit, Stephen saw Jesus, standing at the right hand of God, in approval and confirmation of his message (verse 55). May we heed this warning. Jesus is superior to *all* else!

My Response: _____

His Bidding

*He said, "Come!" And Peter got out of the boat, and walked
on the water and came toward Jesus.*
—Matthew 14:29

I was preaching at my church and decided to use a visual aid. We had a baptism that day, so it occurred to me that as an introduction to my sermon, someone could walk on the water, in front of the whole church. The baptistry had a glass wall facing the congregation so we placed two long tables in the water, and a person walked "on water" from one side of the platform to the other. It was quite an effective visualization for the sermon's topic: that *everything* is by grace through faith, both eternal salvation *and* the Christian walk. It's all about Jesus.

After Jesus disclosed His "I am" identity as He approached the disciples walking on the water (Matthew 14:27), Peter had a great idea. "Peter said to Him, 'Lord, if it is You, command me to come to You on the water" (verse 28). Jesus said "Come!" and Peter walked on water. In this story, Peter illustrates both faith and doubt in the power of Jesus. First, at Jesus' bidding, Peter does the impossible, not because of who he was, but because of Jesus' power. Then, when he saw the wind, he was filled with fear (verse 30) and began to sink. He cried for help: "Lord, save me!" (verse 30). The same word "to save" is given as the reason for Jesus' name: "You shall call His name Jesus, for He will *save* His people" (Matthew 1:21). True to His name, Jesus immediately took hold of Peter, and made it clear that it was an issue of lack of faith: "You of little faith, why did you doubt?" (Matthew 14:31). It's all about Jesus and His power to save. We accept this by faith, and even that is a gift from God (see Ephesians 2:8). When Jesus and Peter got into the boat, the wind stopped (Matthew 14:32). "And those who were in the boat worshiped Him, saying 'You are certainly God's Son!' " (verse 33). Can you imagine? A church in the middle of the lake! The disciples realized that they were in the presence of the Son of God and His supernatural power to save. This is the second and last time (the first time was by the Magi in 2:11) that Jesus is *worshiped* before His resurrection in this gospel. He continues to be the only One worthy of our worship. It's all about Jesus!

My Response: _____

HIS VALUE

*"The kingdom of heaven is like a treasure hidden in the field,
which a man found and hid again . . . and sells all that
he has and buys that field."*

—Matthew 13:44

C hildren and adults alike enjoy a good treasure hunt. I live in a gated community where every once in a while there is a popular community garage sale and many participate in the selling and buying. There was a story in the community newsletter about a resident who had found a great bargain in such a garage sale. Later she discovered that this item had a great value and she was able to sell it for approximately a million dollars, most of which she donated to the homeowners association. How is that for finding a treasure?

In the ancient world, it was common to bury coins and valuables in the ground, and sometimes the owner would die without anyone having information about the treasure. In the above-mentioned short parable, the owner of the field is not aware of the treasure, otherwise he would not have sold the property. The man who found it hid it again. Then he *joyfully* sold everything he had and bought the field, becoming the legal owner of the field and the treasure. The kingdom of Jesus is the greatest treasure. Nothing that we must leave in order to possess it comes even close in value. To leave everything else behind and make Jesus the first priority is not a sacrifice but rather a pure joy. The second parable on this topic is similar: "Again, the kingdom of heaven is like a merchant seeking fine pearls, and upon finding *one pearl of great value*, he went and sold all that he had and bought it" (Matthew 13:45, 46). Divers then, as now, sought pearls in different places (Persian Gulf, Indian Ocean, etc.) and some pearls were worth millions in the equivalent of today's dollars. The merchant in the parable sells everything to have the *one pearl of great value*. What things did Matthew's listeners have to "sell?" Other religious systems? World views? Ideas? Behaviors? The gospel of Jesus is worth more than everything we possess. Is God asking you to let go of something in order to embrace the gospel fully? Whatever we give up for Jesus cannot even compare to the joy of having Him! I'd rather have Jesus than anything. . . .

My Response: _____

HIS NEWNESS

*"But no one puts a patch of unshrunk cloth on
an old garment; for the patch pulls away from
the garment, and a worse tear results."*

—Matthew 9:16

When I was a girl, I needed a dress, but the family finances were tight, so my mother got really creative. She found two older items of clothing we no longer used and got busy sewing, creating a beautiful red-and-white dress that I remember to this day. But first, she made sure that both materials were compatible, preshrunk, and could stretch the same so that the dress wouldn't tear when washed.

Jesus used a similar example to explain the incompatibility of the newness of the gospel with the old patterns of thinking and observing traditions. It all started when the disciples of John came to ask Jesus why His disciples didn't ritually abstain from eating on a regular basis, like they and the Pharisees did (Matthew 9:14; Pharisees fasted twice a week, see Luke 18:12). Jesus answered with a metaphor of the bridegroom (Himself) and His disciples as the attendants of the bridegroom, who now were joyful with His presence but would have occasion to fast when He would be taken from them (Matthew 9:15; this is the first indication in this Gospel about the future sudden and unexpected death of Jesus). Jesus then goes on to expose the futility of trying to superimpose the joy of the newness of the Gospel on the old Jewish traditions. *Everything in the Scriptures had to be reinterpreted in the light of the identity and mission of Jesus.* To explain this incompatibility, Jesus uses two examples: a patch of unshrunk cloth placed on an old garment, which tears when shrunk (verse 16), and putting new wine into old wineskins (verse 17). When the new wine goes through the process of fermentation and expands, the new wineskins stretch with it, but the old ones, which are already hardened, fracture instead, and the wine is spilled. Christianity, which started within Judaism, eventually became a separate religious group. This was an event called "the parting of the ways." Jesus did not follow the Pharisaical tradition but proposed a new way that welcomed the unacceptable. The gospel of Jesus Christ is characterized by joy, inclusivity, grace, and acceptance! Join in the celebration!

My Response: _____

241

HIS FOUNDATION

"Everyone who hears these words of Mine and acts on them, may be compared to a wise man who built his house on the rock."

—Matthew 7:24

California is pretty dry, until it's not. When we get rain, there is a great danger of mudslides, especially in the areas previously affected by wildfires. One time we had fourteen straight days of rain, and I was afraid we would become isolated from the outside world, because the only way to get to our home was by crossing a bridge built over a normally dry riverbed. The water under the bridge rose up to the level of the road. When it was all over, the landscape of the area had completely changed, but the bridge was standing due to its firm foundation.

The Sermon on the Mount (Matthew 5–7) concludes with a series of contrasts, the last one being between two men: one called wise, the other called foolish. Both *hear* the words of Jesus (as His audience had been doing in His sermon). But only the wise man *hears* the words of Jesus and *acts* upon them. The phrase "these words of Mine" in the original Greek emphasizes the word "My" because it appears first in the sentence. This is a call to heed, not just a personal opinion or a religious system, but the words of *Jesus*. *Heeding* His words is compared to building on the rock; the foolish man *hears* Jesus' words but ignores them, building on the sand. Some misuse this text to propose that Jesus is emphasizing *works versus faith*. But these forget that both men in the parable build a house, both do something, but only one makes Jesus' words the foundation of his house. The wording is similar for both, which highlights the main difference: both men hear the words of Jesus; both houses are exposed to the same elements; the only difference is the foundation, which is revealed during the storm. Within minutes, the torrential rains in the Near East can turn dry riverbeds into raging rivers. In this parable, such circumstances reveal what kind of foundation each house has. The house built on the rock did not fall (verse 25); the one built on the sand had a great fall (verse 27). To hear and ignore Jesus' words means total collapse. Our choice, often made evident during hard times, carries eternal consequences. Choose the Rock!

My Response: _____

His Repose

"Take My yoke upon you and learn from Me, for I am gentle and humble in heart, and you will find rest for your souls."

—Matthew 11:29

Help me, I'm Amanda Berry.' With one frantic 911 call . . . three women missing for years were found in a Cleveland house. . . . 'I've been kidnapped,' Berry, who disappeared a decade ago, told the dispatcher. 'I've been missing for 10 years and I'm out here. I'm free now.' . . . The break came when Berry summoned the courage to escape. . . . Shocked relatives could hardly believe that their missing family members had been found after so many years."*

You and I were spiritually kidnapped when Adam and Eve sinned, surrendering to the deceiver (see Genesis 3). All of us have felt the sting of pain and loss. We were made for peace and not for anxiety, for abundance and not for pain, for life and not for death! Humans were made in the image of God, and "He has also set eternity in their heart" (Ecclesiastes 3:11). This is why there is this constant nagging feeling in the core of our souls that reminds us that this world is not our home. And we get *restless*. . . . Jesus offers us His rest, a true repose from the burdens and pain of this world. This invitation is only found in Matthew 11:28–30. I spent eight years studying it, as the topic of my PhD dissertation.† This same word for *rest* (*anapausis*) is found 137 times in the Greek Old Testament (LXX), carrying the predominant meanings of *sabbatical rest, the repose of wisdom, and a peaceful dwelling*. Our weekly sabbatical rest is a commemoration of Creation and Redemption, and it is also a celebratory *appetizer* of heaven, where we will have complete rest from pain and suffering and will live eternally in a heavenly repose and in complete peace. Jesus invites us to start experiencing the "age to come" now, in our souls, because He is the one who offers and guarantees the eternal age of rest. I pray that you will accept the invitation of Jesus to rest in His redemption, victory, provision, and restoration. He has made a promise regarding our past, our present, and our future: "You will find rest for your souls" (Matthew 11:29). Accept His offer, take a deep breath, and enter *His rest*!

My Response: _____

---

* "Ohio Woman Missing for Years Has Daughter," NBC News, May 6, 2013, https://www.nbc11news.com/home/headlines/2-women-missing-for-a-decade-found-alive-in-Ohio-206359751.html.
† For further information on the dissertation based on Matthew 11:28–30, contact the author at gospelpastor@Jesus101.tv.

HIS AFFIRMATION

*Jesus said to them, "The Sabbath was made for man,
and not man for the Sabbath."*

—Mark 2:27

Bob Atchison, a man fascinated by the Alexander Palace in Russia, shared an insightful anecdote. "For generations before Alexandra [the last Russian empress] the Russian Imperial family had loved flowers. Catherine the Great treasured her roses in Tsarskoe Selo and had special guards assigned to protect them year-round from the harsh climate and accidents. Once an Imperial order had been given it was followed until rescinded. Over a century after Catherine died Nicholas and Alexandra discovered a guard still stationed to protect a long vanished rose of Catherine's."*

Can you imagine that? Imperial guards, standing there for more than one hundred years, guarding, without reason, a rosebush that no longer existed? Jesus wanted to make sure that this did not happen to His followers. He realized that many were keeping a Sabbath Day of rest but were rejecting Him. (They were just standing there, guarding a tradition while at the same time rejecting the real *Rose of Sharon*!) Others kept talking about Sabbath laws and making the day a burden instead of a celebration of their Creation and Redemption. This was the case with the Pharisees. Rabbinic traditions, with an eventual list of thirty-nine unlawful works, had created man-made restrictions that veiled the real meaning of the Sabbath Day. But this holy day was designed to be a *feast of remembrance and restoration*, reminding us that we are children of the Creator-Redeemer. As the disciples were picking the heads of grain on the Sabbath (Mark 2:23), the Pharisees complained to Jesus that they were doing what was not lawful, interpreting their actions through legalistic lenses (see Deuteronomy 23:25; Exodus 34:21). In response, Jesus affirmed the Sabbath Day and the real reason for the Sabbath: "The Sabbath was made for man, and not man for the Sabbath. So the Son of Man is Lord even of the Sabbath" (Mark 2:27, 28). Our weekly Sabbath rest reminds us *who we are in Jesus*. May we rest in His accomplished work for us!

My Response: _____

---

* Bob Atchison, "A Romanov Passion for Flowers," *Alexander Palace Time Machine* (blog), accessed on April 15, 2019, http://www.alexanderpalace.org/palace/blog .html?pid=1213306016379451.

HIS COMMAND

"Get up, pick up your pallet and walk."

—John 5:8

I admire devotion to God that takes over a person's lifestyle. When I went to Israel, I encountered many Orthodox Jews who practiced their religion openly, whether on the plane, in the streets, or in the common workplace. The culture itself was modified in order to accommodate these religious beliefs. In our hotel there was a Sabbath elevator, that stopped on every floor so that no one had to push the button and violate the Sabbath. I thought these things were extreme, but then I looked at my own life and realized that I too had imposed *burdens* on others.

I am challenged by the story of the paralyzed man healed at Bethesda. After thirty-eight years of a miserable existence, relying on the scraps of resources he may have had, Jesus *commanded* the man to, "Get up, pick up . . . and walk" (John 5:8). The man responded by following these instructions and realized that he had indeed been made well (verse 9). What an indescribable joy! But instead of hearing shouts of praise to God, he was met with censure by the religious folk: "It is the Sabbath, and it is not permissible for you to carry your pallet" (verse 10). How cold! How sad! In their religious fervor, these law keepers could not rejoice at the healing miracle of Jesus. I am sure these made-up regulations had started with a desire to keep God's holy day of rest (see Jeremiah 17:19–27; Nehemiah 13:15–19), but they ended up making it a burden. There were thirty-nine types of work forbidden on the Sabbath, and thousands of nuanced interpretations of what that meant. Could you carry a needle in your tunic or an ornament on your robe? Such were the perpetual arguments at the time. Jesus wanted to restore the creative and redemptive meaning of the Sabbath, especially in the light of His salvific mission, and therefore chose to make this man whole on the Sabbath day. Jesus and the healed man focused on reporting his new condition: cured! (John 5:14, 15), but the Jews emphasized the breach of their made-up rules. Let's ask God to give us the joy of our salvation, to teach us the beauty and simplicity of His commands, and to free us from burdensome, man-made rules!

My Response: _____

HIS PRUNING

"Every branch in Me that does not bear fruit,
He takes away; and every branch that bears fruit,
He prunes it so that it may bear more fruit."

—John 15:2

I n my early twenties, I directed a youth choir that eventually became a young adult choir. One of our favorite songs was "The Refiner's Fire," made popular by the Christian singer Steve Green. Looking back now, I realize that all of us were way too young to even begin to understand the meaning of what we were singing: "No matter what I may lose, I choose the Refiner's fire."* As adults we all eventually experienced brokenness, and these words became real.

Terms such as "refiner's fire" and "divine pruning" make us a bit uncomfortable because we shy away from suffering. But what is the purpose of the pruning? In the Old Testament, Israel was often depicted as a vine (see Isaiah 5:1–7; Jeremiah 2:21; Ezekiel 15; 19; Hosea 10:1; etc.). God frequently observed that this vine (Israel) had become wild and fruitless. Now Jesus declares that He is the *true* Vine, His followers are the branches, and His Father is the vinedresser (John 15:1, 4, 5). The whole purpose of a vineyard is to produce grapes, and it cannot produce fruit without pruning; the purpose of our existence is to give glory to God and invite others to His kingdom, and only God knows how to bring this about. In this vineyard metaphor, there are only two groups of branches: the fruitless ones that are *taken away* and the fruitful ones that are *cleansed or pruned* (verse 2). Note that it is the fruitful branches that are pruned. There is a play of words in Greek between *He takes* (*airei*) and *He prunes or cleanses* (*kathairei*) that cannot be reproduced in English, but we are all either on one group or the other. The next verse (verse 3), makes it clear that we are *cleansed* by His Word. Let's trust that the Vinedresser knows what we need to give Him glory. Our part is to surrender to His able hands. The Vine produces the fruit in the branches; the branches submit to the Vine and to the cleansing of the Vinedresser. Trust that in our brokenness we can give glory to God. And remember the cross, which reminds us of His infinite love; when we don't understand His ways, we can trust His heart!

My Response: _____

---

* Steve Green, "The Refiner's Fire," *The Mission* (Sparrow Records, 1989).

HIS VITALITY

"I am the vine, you are the branches; he who abides in Me and I in him, he bears much fruit, for apart from Me you can do nothing."
—John 15:5

We recently had a problem with our air-conditioning unit, which was still under warranty, and we waited for several days while the new parts were shipped. When the technician found evidence of scorched cables, he made sure that we wouldn't use the unit while waiting. He disconnected it from its source of power, and it stopped working. Not connected to the source of power, the air-conditioner could no longer serve its purpose and was useless until it got reconnected.

Jesus said: "Abide in Me, and I in you" (John 15:4). I have always been intrigued with the word *abide*, which means to remain or stay connected; and this "remaining" has two sides: Jesus abides in us, and we abide in Him. In the Greek, the pronouns "Me" and "I" are next to each other, highlighting both sides of the equation. This intimate union is necessary for productivity, because we do not have the vitality to produce fruit on our own. Jesus explains this in detail: "As the branch cannot bear fruit of itself unless it abides in the vine, so neither can you unless you abide in Me. I am the vine, you are the branches; he who abides in Me and I in him, he bears much fruit, for apart from Me you can do *nothing*" (verses 4, 5). He is the Source, and we are the branches; we shouldn't get confused about these roles. Every day the branches experience the miraculous vitality of the Vine producing fruit in them. Apart from Him, God's followers can do *nothing*. On our own, we lack skills, energy, time, insight, patience, joy, hope, et cetera. Without Jesus' life-giving power, we can't even begin to grow spiritually nor minister to others. I am convicted of the absolute opposites: with Jesus, we can do *everything* (see Philippians 4:13); without Him we can do *nothing*. Both our salvation and our Christian walk are God's doing. By grace we have been saved, and by grace we are His workmanship, created in Christ Jesus to be fruitful (see Ephesians 2:8, 10). He has designed us to live purpose-filled lives for His glory. If you find yourself lacking today, remember the Source of everything! And abide in Him!

My Response: _____

HIS WORK

*"This is the work of God, that you believe
in Him whom He has sent."*

—John 6:29

I've experienced personally the saying, "A picture is worth a thousand words." Having discovered *The Ragamuffin Gospel Visual Edition: Good News for the Bedraggled, Beat-Up, and Burnt Out* by Brennan Manning,* I was astonished. The illustrator had managed to capture deep gospel concepts in art, for example, a homeless man holding a sign, "Will Work for Salvation," as an antithesis of grace.

After the miraculous feeding of the five thousand, Jesus challenged people about their selfish motives for seeking Him (John 6:27). He admonished them, "Do not work for the food which perishes, but for the food which endures to eternal life, *which the Son of Man will give to you*, for on Him the Father, God, has set His seal" (verse 27). The crowd, as some still do, interpreted Jesus' words as having to "do work" in order to gain eternal life, so they asked Him, "What shall we do, so that we work the works of God?" (verse 28). They missed the part where He told them that the Son of Man would give them the unperishable food. It is human nature to want to work in order to earn something. We struggle accepting that even God's "good works" through us, are not meritorious for our salvation; His works in us are for His glory (Matthew 5:16), not ours. He paid our ransom two thousand years ago, and we are saved only by grace, not works (Ephesians 2:8–10). Max Lucado makes an observation about the grace versus works struggle in Acts 15: "It wasn't that the people didn't believe in grace at all. They did. *They believed in grace a lot. They just didn't believe in grace alone.* They wanted to add to the work of Christ. Grace-a-lots believe in grace, a lot. Jesus almost finished the work of salvation, they argue. In the rowboat named Heaven Bound, Jesus paddles most of the time. But every so often he needs our help. So we give it."† To those who asked about works, Jesus answered, *"This is the work of God, that you believe in Him who He has sent"* (John 6:29). This is God's work for us: Believe in Jesus! He takes care of the rest.

My Response: _____

---

* Brennan Manning, *The Ragamuffin Gospel Visual Edition: Good News for the Bedraggled, Beat-up, and Burnt Out* (Colorado Springs, CO: Multnomah Books, 2005).

† Max Lucado, *Grace: More Than We Deserve, Greater Than We Imagine* (Nashville, TN: Thomas Nelson, 2012), 45; emphasis added.

His Analogy

*"Truly I say to you, whoever does not receive the kingdom
of God like a child will not enter it at all."*

—Mark 10:15

W hen my step-grandchild was a baby, she wouldn't go to sleep one afternoon. I took her in my arms and started singing and softly patting her tiny back and she fell fast asleep. She didn't know that she was suspended quite a distance from the floor, and she was trustingly resting in my arms. Right then I started a meaningful conversation with God, asking Him: "Is this what You meant when You asked us to trust You like a child, surrendering completely to Your keeping?" It was a sacred moment.

I'm sure that all of us have been blessed by a child's smile and eagerness, as well as their simplicity and honesty. When some were bringing children to be blessed by Jesus, the disciples rebuked them (Mark 10:13). They figured that Jesus had a kingdom to establish and more important matters to attend to. Mark tells us that Jesus was indignant! (verse 14). He gave His disciples two parallel orders, one stated positively and the other negatively: "Permit the children to come to Me" and "Do not hinder them" (verse 14). Why? *For of such as these is the kingdom of God!* But that's not all. Jesus takes this opportunity to pronounce, through an analogy, the "requirement for entry" into the kingdom of God: "Truly I say to you, whoever does not receive the kingdom of God *like a child* will not enter it at all" (verse 15). Like a child? Really? Some had expected the kingdom to come by strength and military power; others sought to establish it by a scrupulous keeping of the law. Who could assume to enter the kingdom with the impotence of a child? As adults, we naturally want to earn and deserve the kingdom, yet it is *only* a gift. Little ones to Him belong! "The Kingdom may be entered only by one who knows he is helpless and small, without claim or merit. The comparison 'receive . . . as a little child' draws its force from the nature of the child to take openly and confidently what is given. . . . What is specifically in view is the reception of the gospel and of Jesus Himself as the one in whom the Kingdom has come near."*

My Response: _____

---

* William L. Lane, *The Gospel of Mark*, NICNT (Grand Rapids, MI: Eerdmans, 1974), 360–361.

HIS HIERARCHY

"Whoever . . . humbles himself as this child, he is the greatest in the kingdom of heaven."

—Matthew 18:4

I have attended a few kindergarten graduations. Invariably, the children are asked: "What do you want to be when you grow up?" Most answer with professional titles, such as lawyer, doctor, or accountant. But every once in a while, you hear unusual answers, such as: "When I grow up, I want to be happy" or "When I grow up, I still want to be a child." Spiritually speaking, Jesus said that when we "grow up," we should become like children.

The disciples came to Jesus with a question: "Who then is greatest in the kingdom of heaven?" (Matthew 18:1). This section begins the discourse of Jesus regarding the kingdom community. But the disciples are focused on the hierarchy of the kingdom; their minds are filled with questions of status and power. *Who is the greatest? How do you climb the ladder in this kingdom? How do you secure the best position?* This Gospel records more than one instance of these thoughts plaguing the disciples (see Matthew 20:26–28; 23:11, 12). Jesus, who was fond of using illustrations to explain the kingdom's values, called a little child to present a visual aid for His teaching. "Truly I say to you, unless you are converted and become like children, you will not enter the kingdom of heaven" (Matthew 18:3). Children had the lowest position in first-century society; even if loved and cherished by their parents, they had no social status. Jesus explained that the disciples must turn from their ways of thinking and become humble as a child, whose impotence was the very antonym of the disciples' thirst for power. Those who humble themselves and come to God without entitlement or pretense are the recipients of the kingdom of heaven, now and in the future. The utter dependence of children on their caregivers for their very survival exemplifies how Jesus' followers have no meritorious claim to the kingdom of heaven. God's kingdom operates with a reversed value system, an upside-down hierarchy, where those who humbly recognize their low status are considered great, and the last are placed first.

My Response: _____

HIS CENSURE

*"Why do you yourselves transgress the commandment
of God for the sake of your tradition?"*
—Matthew 15:3

I was leaving for Germany in order to preach there. I was waiting for the security agents to go through the luggage, when suddenly one of the agents started yelling my last name: "Talbot!" He said to me: "Are you trying to give me a heart attack?" I had no idea what was happening. He then pointed to a large rubber snake in my luggage which I intended to use as a visual aid for my sermon on John 3:14–16. I understood his fear now; he had thought it was a live reptile!

Jesus revealed that a fake and merciless religion is even more frightening. In one of His sharpest charges against the Pharisees and scribes, Jesus called them *hypocrites* because they invalidated the words of God for the sake of their traditions (Matthew 15:1–20). A *hypocrite* is someone who pretends to be something different than he is; it means to put on a false appearance. The term comes from the Greek word that was used in reference to actors in theater. At the time of Jesus, the traditions of the elders were in oral form, and were later put in writing. In this story, the Pharisees accused the disciples of not washing their hands before eating. The issue was not about hygiene but about ceremonial observance. Jesus answered with a countercharge: they were holding their traditions above the Word of God. They were "acting" piously yet negating the principles of love and mercy. One such practice was that, instead of honoring and taking care of their parents, they could state that their possessions had been set aside as an offering for God (called "Corban," see Mark 7:11), and therefore they had nothing left to help their parents with. God saw right through it. Jesus applied Isaiah's prophecy to them: "This people honors Me with their lips, but their heart is far away from Me" (Matthew 15:8). Jesus often censured people's lack of mercy (see Matthew 12:7), which is a foundational principle in His kingdom. We are all recipients of His mercy! May God teach us to extend mercy to those around us, placing God's principles above our personal interpretations and preferences.

My Response: _____

HIS INSTRUCTION

He said to him [Peter], "Follow Me!"

—John 21:19

I don't know much about horses, but I think they are amazing animals. I have always wondered about the blinders that I often see covering their eyes. I did a little bit of research on this and learned that horses have peripheral vision. Sometimes they need blinders in order to keep focused forward instead of what is on the side, or behind. Blinders help horses stay on-course. Do you ever feel that your own mind needs blinders to remain focused on what matters most?

Our minds can get distracted by hundreds of questions like "what if?" "what about?" "what now?" and many others. Peter, the disciple, contemplated these types of questions too. Having commissioned him to "shepherd His sheep" (John 21:15–17), Jesus reveals to Peter something about his future (verse 18). When the Gospel of John was written, Peter had already become a martyr, and John adds a parenthetical statement, commenting on Jesus' words: "Now this He said, signifying by what kind of death he would glorify God" (verse 19). Previously, Peter had told Jesus that he was ready to go with Him to death (Luke 22:33), and he would get that privilege. After this revelation about his future, Jesus said to Peter: "Follow Me!" Peter should not get distracted by this revelation but focus on following Jesus. Always the eager disciple, Peter's attention was often drawn off-course by his side vision, as was the case with the waves in the storm and his use of the sword at the time of the arrest of Jesus. This time was no exception. When he saw that John was following behind them (John 21:20), he wanted to know what would happen to him! Did Jesus have a word about John's future? "So Peter seeing him said to Jesus, 'Lord, and *what about* this man?' Jesus said to him, 'If I want him to remain until I come, what is that to you? *You follow Me!'* " (verses 21, 22). For a second time, Jesus instructs Peter to focus, to follow Him, and leave the rest to Him. The One who purchased our salvation is also in full control of our life, death, and future, and he is also in charge of our loved ones. We can trust Him! Our existence is in His hands. Let's concentrate on following Him!

My Response: _____

HIS MOTIF

"That they may receive forgiveness of sins and an inheritance among those who have been sanctified by faith in Me."
—Acts 26:18

I have attended many women's retreats over time. Sometimes a particular one stands out because of an activity that stayed with me all these years. On one of those occasions, all the ladies were given little papers to write the initial letter of a sin that was weighing heavily on their hearts and that they wanted to surrender to God, to receive forgiveness by faith in Jesus. Then all of us got up and placed our papers on a cross, to visualize this spiritual yielding of guilt. It was very powerful. Many ladies felt that a burden had been lifted off their shoulders.

Sin is heavy, and many live under a cloud of guilt and shame. On the third occasion in which Paul's conversion and commissioning on the way to Damascus is told in the book of Acts (Acts 26:1–23), Paul explains that the *forgiveness of sins by faith in Jesus* is the central idea of what he was commissioned to proclaim: "to open their eyes so that they may turn from darkness to light and from the dominion of Satan to God, that *they may receive forgiveness of sins* and an inheritance among those who have been sanctified by faith in Me" (verse 18). This is a repeated motif in the words of Jesus recorded by Luke, for the same commission was given by Jesus to His disciples in the last chapter of Luke's gospel: "Thus it is written, that the Christ would suffer and rise again from the dead the third day, and *that repentance for forgiveness of sins would be proclaimed in His name* to all the nations beginning from Jerusalem" (Luke 24:46, 47). Furthermore, Paul highlighted that in addition to forgiveness there is a sure inheritance for those who have been *sanctified by faith in Jesus* (Acts 26:18). Christ highlighted that these are declared as "set apart/holy," not because they are sinless or perfect, but by faith "in Me" (verse 18). This theme of forgiveness of sins through faith in the sacrifice of Jesus is the central proclamation of the Christian church. The result of accepting His forgiveness is an undeserved, yet assured, eternal inheritance. Place your sins upon His cross and live in the light and the joy of your eternal salvation!

My Response: _____

HIS HARVEST

*"Therefore beseech the Lord of the harvest to
send out workers into His harvest."*

—Matthew 9:38

When we arrived in Canada, the canola fields were ready for harvest, and the sight of the yellow fields in full bloom has stuck in my mind. A farmer invited my husband and me to visit his fields. I have photos where you can barely see us standing in the canola fields, because the plants were so tall. He gave us a ride in his new tractor and showed us his harvesting machinery, explaining and demonstrating its many functions. It was an awesome experience! I left amazed at his undivided attention to, and his unreserved investment in, his canola fields, doing absolutely everything necessary for a successful harvest.

As Jesus ministered from city to city, proclaiming the gospel and healing the sick, "He felt compassion for them, because they were distressed and dispirited like sheep without a shepherd" (Matthew 9:36). There was so much to do! So many people to help! So many needs to provide for! So many lost souls to preach to! He said to His disciples: "The harvest is plentiful, but the workers are few" (verse 37). As a minister, I have often felt powerless at the same realization. The work is never done, and there is so much need and pain in this world. This is why I find great comfort in the words of Jesus that follow His observation: "Therefore beseech *the Lord of the harvest* to send out workers into *His harvest*" (verse 38). Did you notice the possessive pronoun? It is His harvest! It is not ours to produce nor to take credit for. He provides what is needed, He knows the right timing, and He provides the workers. The outcome is in His hands! I am the type of person who can easily take on responsibilities that are not mine; sometimes I even try to do the work of the Holy Spirit. I want people to make a decision for Jesus . . . right now! God does empower us for service, as exemplified by the disciples going out in the next chapter (Matthew 10). But He does not give us control over the results, the timing, or the outcome. It is *His* harvest, and rest assured that He is more than invested in it! So invested, in fact, that Jesus died so that the harvest may be plentiful!

My Response: _____

His Perfection

*This was to fulfill what had been spoken by the Lord through
the prophet: "Out of Egypt I called My Son."*
—Matthew 2:15

The young woman was very intelligent, but her family could not pay for her studies. She decided to enroll in medical school and apply for student loans. She became a very successful student, but when she graduated, she wondered how she would ever pay the large student debt that she had accumulated. Then she received a job offer that included the full pay-off of her student debt! She was beside herself! Has someone ever paid a debt that you couldn't pay?

Matthew proposes that Jesus relived Israel's history, becoming victorious where they had failed. Therefore, Matthew sometimes quotes Old Testament verses about Israel and applies them to Jesus. One such case is found in Baby Jesus' return from Egypt, for which Matthew cites Hosea 11:1: "This was to fulfill what had been spoken by the Lord through the prophet: 'Out of Egypt I called My Son" (Matthew 2:15). Hosea 11 is one of the most passionate chapters in the Old Testament, in which God, using a father/son symbolism, explains how He loved Israel as His son, how He took them in His arms and led them with bonds of love. And yet they turned away from Him. The people of Israel (corporately; see Exodus 4:22) and the king of Israel (individually; see 2 Samuel 7:14) are the two Old Testament precursors of the Father/Son relationship between God and Jesus in the New Testament. Now, Jesus would be the perfect kingly representative of God's people. Matthew's proposal that Jesus relived Israel's history and was triumphant in what they had failed in has brought great peace to my soul. That Jesus lived a perfect life and died a perfect death in my place, paying the debt that I couldn't pay, is the source of the assurance of my salvation. When God sees me, He sees Jesus' perfect righteousness in my place. When I accept Jesus as my Savior, the sinful things on my record are covered by His perfection. Matthew proposed to Israel that their history was hidden in Christ, because Jesus rewrote their history. I invite you to believe the same. Your story is His story!

My Response: _____

255

HIS OVERCOMING

*And they overcame him because of the blood of the Lamb
and because of the word of their testimony.*
—Revelation 12:11

Have you seen paintings depicting the reformer Martin Luther throwing his inkwell at the devil? These illustrations sprang from Luther's statement that, while in the Wartburg Castle, he fought the devil with ink. Even though it has been suggested that this was a literal event, there is no doubt that Luther fought the devil most effectively with ink by writing about the gospel and translating the Bible into German so that the common people could understand God's grace.

The Bible teaches that God's adversary is the accuser of God's children. Satan was the one who introduced sin and deception into this world (Revelation 12:9); but he was also the one who continuously brought insistent accusations against God's people to the heavenly council (verse 10). Such was the case with Job (Job 1:6) and the high priest Joshua (Zechariah 3:1). But all of this changed at the Cross: "Now the salvation, and the power, and the kingdom of our God and the authority of His Christ have come, for the accuser of our brethren has been thrown down. . . . And they overcame him because of the blood of the Lamb and because of the word of their testimony" (Revelation 12:10, 11). Ranko Stefanovic explains: "The situation changed with the death of Christ on the cross where Satan's defeat was assured. It was at the cross that it became clear to the entire universe who God was and the character of his rule. In the same manner, Satan's character was revealed at the cross. . . . As a result, Satan was forever excommunicated from the heavenly places."* Jesus has conquered the adversary! Yet until his final destruction, God's enemy will try to entice us to accuse others or to denounce ourselves, even though we have accepted forgiveness for sins. However, he can no longer accuse us in front of God or the heavenly beings. The adversary wants to discourage us until we give up by inducing us with paralyzing shame. Let's remember that the overcoming came through *the blood of the Lamb*, and the testimony, even to the point of death, about His victory on the cross. Satan is a defeated enemy, and his time is short! (verse 12).

My Response: _____

---

* Ranko Stefanovic, *The Revelation of Jesus Christ* (Berrien Springs, MI: Andrews University Press, 2002), 388. See also Ellen G. White, *The Desire of Ages* (Mountain View, CA: 1940), ch.: "It Is Finished," 758–768.

HIS COMMISSION

"Go therefore and make disciples of all the nations, baptizing them in the name of the Father and the Son and the Holy Spirit."
—Matthew 28:19

The Visual Bible: Matthew," featuring Bruce Marchiano, is a word by word rendition of the story of Jesus as told by Matthew (NIV) in a 1993 film. I have watched the ending of this movie dozens of times. Having delivered the Great Commission (Matthew 28:18–20), Jesus, with his back to the camera, starts walking away. Suddenly, he turns around and, with a big smile looking directly into the camera, beckons to the disciples to follow him. This scene has always felt so personal to me, that it continues to bring tears to my eyes.

Having announced that all authority in heaven and on earth had been given to Him (Matthew 28:18), Jesus goes on to speak what has been called *the Great Commission*: "Go therefore and make disciples" (verse 19). The word "therefore" links the commission to the previously stated authority of Jesus; they are to go in *His* authority. The purpose is clearly stated with three verbs that point to a fourth: *go, baptize, teach* . . . in order *to make disciples* of Jesus (verses 19, 20). "Make disciples" is a one-word verb in the original Greek. The word "disciple" means "student" or "pupil." They are to make more disciples by continuing Jesus' teaching ministry, teaching what He taught and commanded (verse 20). They are to go to all nations (verse 19), which was the original covenant with Abraham (see Genesis 12:3): not only the Jews, but all the families of the earth would be blessed! That Jesus was able to redeem persons from every tribe, tongue, people, and nation is highlighted in the worship scenes of the heavenly realms (see Revelation 5:9, 10). The disciples are to baptize in the name (singular) of One God in three Persons: Father, Son, and Holy Spirit (Matthew 28:19). Finally, the last words of Jesus assure them of His Presence until the end of time, whether in their daily life, ministry, or matters of salvation. This assurance of Jesus forms an *inclusio* (narrative sandwich) with the beginning of the gospel, which states that Jesus was Immanuel: God with us (Matthew 1:23). Now Jesus reminds them and us: *I am with you, till the very end!* Amen!

My Response: _____

HIS VALIDATION

*"Therefore if God gave to them the same gift as He gave to us
also after believing in the Lord Jesus Christ, who was
I that I could stand in God's way?"*

—Acts 11:17

I will never forget the testimony of a godly man at a church board meeting. For many years, he had been actively opposing a particular proposal, and on this day he spoke at the board as a witness, being convicted that the Holy Spirit was working through the very thing he opposed. He proceeded to announce that he was surrendering his previously held views, ready to follow God's confirmation.

God gently guides us on profound journeys of understanding. When we stay open to His revelations, we are sure to grow and even change our minds as we become more deeply acquainted with the scope of God's salvific grace. Even after the death and resurrection of Jesus, the disciples did not understand that everyone who called on the name of the Lord would be saved and could be used by God for the proclamation of the good news. In Acts 10, Peter was gently pushed by God through a vision to enter a Gentile's home and to preach Jesus to them. But even then, the newly-formed church was not ready to baptize Gentiles. So, the Holy Spirit got ahead of them, falling upon those who were not yet baptized but were gladly receiving the good news of Jesus. This is when Peter ordered them to be baptized (Acts 10:44–48), but then he had to explain his *out-of-the-box* actions! In Jerusalem, the Jewish-Christians took issue with him (Acts 11:2, 3). Peter proceeded to explain what had happened and added: "Who was I that I could stand in God's way?" (verse 17). As a result, they accepted it and changed their minds because of the validation shown by the Holy Spirit. "When they heard this, they quieted down and glorified God, saying, 'Well then, God has granted to the Gentiles also the repentance that leads to life.' " (verse 18). The work of the Lord then erupted throughout the known world (verses 20–24). What would have happened if Peter stood in the way of God? We are also given the same opportunity. May our minds remain open to God's leading, so that the gospel may be proclaimed in our homes, places of employment, schools, and churches. Then the end will come!

My Response: _____

SHARING
HIS MERCY

HIS WITNESSES

"Behold, the Lamb of God!"

—John 1:36

My colleague and friend, Dr. Ozolins, tells a story about a student he met at the Bugema University in Uganda.* The young man had purchased an air ticket to Pakistan, but on the day of the trip he lost his passport and missed the flight. He was so angry that he did not want to speak with anyone, but then met someone who was so excited about Jesus that eventually he too became a Christian. Now he was a ministerial student, preparing to witness for his new Master. On the day he missed his flight, he was on his way to join a terrorist training-camp in order to become a suicide bomber. What a difference the witness of one person makes!

John, the Baptizer, looked at Jesus and testified: "Behold, the Lamb of God!" (John 1:36). Two of John's disciples decided to follow Jesus; one of the two was Andrew, Simon Peter's brother (verse 40). They spent a day with Jesus, and that was enough for Andrew to become convinced that Jesus was indeed the Messiah. He was so thrilled about having found his new extraordinary Master, that the first thing he did was to look for Simon, his brother "and said to him, 'We have found the Messiah' " (verse 41), and "he brought him to Jesus" (verse 42). Andrew is a behind-the-scenes guy—not one who receives recognition for thousands of baptisms or spectacular sermons. Peter preached sermons and thousands were baptized (Acts 2:41), but Andrew was the one who brought Peter to Jesus. Andrew brought to Jesus one person or a small group at a time. Once some Greeks came to Philip asking to see Jesus. Philip told Andrew, and the two disciples brought these Greeks to Jesus (John 12:20–22). In John 6, when the disciples faced the challenge of having to feed a multitude, it was Andrew who spotted a little boy with a lunch box that contained a very small amount of food. He brought the boy to Jesus, and Jesus performed an astounding miracle, turning this miniscule amount of food into supplies enough to feed thousands. It is our privilege to tell others about our extraordinary Master, and we don't have to worry about our lack of wisdom or skill. Just as with our salvation, He supplies what is needed!

My Response: _____

---

* Elizabeth Talbot and Aivars Ozolins, *Jesus 101: Radical Discipleship* (Nampa, ID: Pacific Press®, 2016), 26.

HIS ACHIEVEMENT

They enclosed a great quantity of fish,
and their nets began to break.

—Luke 5:6

I enjoy documentaries about butterflies, and I am now more amazed at these little creatures than I've ever been. How a caterpillar turns into a butterfly continues to baffle scientists, many of whom use the word *miraculous* when trying to explain this incredible metamorphosis. Hundreds of changes occur in the cocoon, from the formation of a reproductive system to the sense of orientation for migration; all of it continues to be a mystery. It is obviously God's doing!

When Jesus called the first disciples, the first item on His agenda was to convince them that He, not they, would be the one to achieve their mission. Everything that they had and knew how to do would be transformed by God's power into something completely different. They had to learn to trust His way, not theirs. When Jesus finds them, they have been unsuccessfully fishing all night and are now washing their nets, which means they are done for the night (Luke 5:2). Having taught the crowd from Simon Peter's boat, Jesus instructs him to "Put out into the deep water and let down your nets for a catch" (verse 4). Being a professional fisherman, Peter objects to the seemingly senseless command; Peter knew that effective net-fishing in the sea of Galilee happened at night, yet it is broad daylight already. However, he relents: "Master, we worked hard all night and caught nothing, *but* I will do as You say and let down the nets." (verse 5). Oh, the surrendering "but" that we all need so badly! When Peter lets down the nets, a miracle happens, and they catch so many fish that their nets begin to break and their boats begin to sink (verses 6, 7). Yet it was Jesus who achieved these results. They would go through quite a metamorphosis in their personal lives and in their ministry. From then on they would be "catching men" (verse 10); yet it would be God's doing, not theirs. The success of God's mission is not subject to our skills, tools, and know-how. It depends entirely on the presence and action of Jesus. Our salvation and calling are completely His doing, His achievement, and His success. And He delights in saving us, assuring us, and giving us wings!

My Response: _____

HIS EFFECT

"Do not fear, from now on you will be catching men."
—Luke 5:10

I had the privilege of studying under several outstanding scholars, both in the United States and England. They were my professors when I was pursuing my master's and subsequent PhD in biblical studies programs. I felt two mutually opposed, yet coexisting sentiments. On the one hand, in their presence I felt unlearned, uninformed, and therefore humbled, while, in comparison, they seemed so utterly intelligent, knowledgeable, and brilliant. On the other hand, I felt eager to be in their presence, to learn from them and absorb their vast knowledge.

On a much greater scale, this is what happened to Peter in the presence of Jesus. After a fruitless night of fishing, Jesus found them washing their nets (Luke 5:2). Jesus instructed Peter to let down the nets again; he objected but eventually relented. When he did, he experienced a miraculous catch, so great that the nets were about to break and the boats were about to sink (verses 6, 7). Having witnessed this amazing demonstration of power, it suddenly dawned on Peter that he was in the presence of the Divine. And in the Presence of Jesus, Peter's sinfulness became unbearably obvious to him, and *he fell at Jesus' feet*, saying "Go away from me Lord, for I am a sinful man!" (verse 8). Because of his sinfulness, Peter felt totally unworthy to be in the presence of Jesus, yet that very Presence was his only hope. I can imagine Peter holding on to the feet of Jesus, crying out, "Go away from me but please stay. You are all I've got! I am not worthy, but I need you! I am a sinful man, but please don't ever leave me!" This is the effect Jesus has on us: we feel unworthy yet we are eager to receive His infinite love and unmerited redemption. In His presence we never feel righteous, far from it. If someone boasts of their sinlessness, they are surely far away from God. Luke tells us that everyone was amazed at the miraculous catch. Having had an awareness of his own sinful condition, Peter was called to minister. Jesus said to Peter: "Do not fear, from now on you will be catching men" (verse 10). Peter and those with him left everything and followed Jesus. May Jesus have the same effect on us!

My Response: _____

HIS OUTLOOK

"There were many lepers in Israel in the time of Elisha the prophet; and none of them was cleansed, but only Naaman the Syrian."

—Luke 4:27

Henry Tajfel was a social psychologist known for his work on the cognitive side of prejudice. In his experiments, insignificant distinctions between groups, such as the preference for a particular type of art, provoked an impulse to favor one's own group. The "us vs. them" mentality is a verifiable human condition. Belonging to a group provides self-esteem and pride, and one group can easily discriminate against other groups in order to preserve their social identity.

When Jesus visited the Nazareth synagogue (Luke 4:14–30), He found that the "us vs them" mentality was strong there. Jesus knew what they were thinking. "And He said to them, 'No doubt you will quote this proverb to Me, "Physician heal yourself! Whatever we heard was done at Capernaum, do here in your hometown as well" ' " (verse 23). In other words, "Doctor, cure yourself! How can you benefit strangers and not us, your own people? The good news is for us, actually *just for us*!" But Jesus continued: "Truly I say to you, no prophet is welcome in his hometown" (verse 24), and He proceeded to reveal His outlook, His inclusivity, and the scope of His mission. He gave the Nazareth audience two biblical examples of God's favors to outsiders: Elijah was sent to the widow of Zarephath, and Elisha miraculously cured Naaman, the Syrian, from his leprosy (verses 25–27). There were many widows and lepers in Israel, yet God sent His prophets to them. The audience was enraged! *Jesus, are you saying that God bypassed "our" widows and lepers, and chose the "outsiders?"* But it was all too evident. Their rage was overpowering, and, on the Sabbath day, they tried to throw Him off a cliff (verses 28, 29), but it wasn't His time to die yet. Jesus was and is absolutely inclusive. There is no "them vs. us" at the foot of the cross; Jesus paid the highest price for each one of us. Heaven will be more diverse than we can imagine, with every people, nation, color, tongue, and gender (Revelation 5:9). Father, grant us your grace, that as Christians we may display your inclusive outlook, here and now. Amen!

My Response: _____

HIS DESIRE

"If you had known what this means, 'I desire compassion, and not a sacrifice,' you would not have condemned the innocent."
—Matthew 12:7

There is a story about a mother who loved to make a special fruit tart from a family recipe. But she always cut off one end of it before putting it into the oven to bake. When her little daughter asked about it, her mother said that she didn't really know the reason, so they decided to talk to her grandma, who had always done the same thing. But grandma didn't know the reason either, so they visited the great-grandma, who explained that when she had just gotten married, she had a tiny oven that did not fit the full length of her tart! I wonder how many of us have done the same, following a man-made religious tradition without a real purpose.

On one occasion, as they were going through the grain fields on the Sabbath, Jesus' disciples began to pick grain and eat (Matthew 12:1). The Pharisees saw this and challenged Jesus: "Look, Your disciples do what is not lawful to do on a Sabbath" (verse 2). Jesus answered with a three-fold appeal to the Scriptures: from the historic books (verses 3, 4), from the Law/Pentateuch (verses 5, 6), and from the prophetic books (verse 7). This third appeal is from Hosea 6:6: "But if you had known what this means, 'I desire compassion [mercy], and not a sacrifice,' you would not have condemned the innocent" (Matthew 12:7). The principle of interpretation proposed by Jesus is *compassion/mercy*. This word is used three times in Matthew (Matthew 9:13; 12:7; 23:23), and all three times Jesus challenges the Pharisees' interpretation of the law and lack of mercy. All the law, not just the Sabbath laws, must be interpreted through the principles of love and mercy (see Matthew 22:38–40; 23:23). Even though they observed the rituals and sacrifices (Matthew 23:23, 24), they did not understand the principles behind them. Without mercy, the religious system is divinely rejected. Jesus explained that the underlying principles are greater than the rituals themselves. God despises void religiosity and observance of rituals without mercy and without Jesus. God's grace, mercy, and love are at the heart of His character, and are the basis of the plan of redemption on our behalf.

My Response: _____

HIS MINISTRY

He rebuked the unclean spirit, saying to it, "You deaf and mute spirit, I command you, come out of him and not enter him again."
—Mark 9:25

A very gifted violinist was scheduled to give a concert in the city hall. It was advertised that he would be playing a very expensive violin. People came from all over to hear the marvelous music! During the concert, the violinist suddenly stopped and, to everyone's astonishment, smashed the violin on the floor. He then admitted that the violin he had just broken had actually been purchased in a secondhand store for less than a dollar. As he proceeded to play on the expensive violin, only a few people could tell the difference. The violinist had made his point: it was all about the musician and his capability, not about the instrument.

In life and Christian ministry, we must all learn that we are neither the Musician nor the music; we are only humble instruments in the Master's hands. The disciples learned this the hard way when they were not able to drive out a demon. Then Jesus rebuked the evil spirit, and it came out immediately (Mark 9:18–26). They were so confused! Had Jesus not given them power to exorcise demons? Had they not driven out demons before and healed many people? (Mark 6:7, 13). What was going on? In the conclusion, this story explains their inability. When Jesus came into the house, they asked Him, "Why could we not drive it out?" Jesus answered: "This kind cannot come out by anything but prayer" (Mark 9:28, 29). Matthew adds that Jesus pointed out that they were lacking faith, even as small as a mustard seed (see Matthew 17:20). They had lost their connection with the divine Source of power. Perhaps they had started to rely on their own authority over demons or on their talents and experience. They took their ministerial abilities for granted instead of relying on the limitless power of God. All things are possible for the one who believes (Mark 9:23), but that belief is not about our capabilities but about complete reliance on God's power. We are not the Musician nor the music; we are only instruments. Jesus is the Master and has unlimited power to save, to heal, and to restore. He is everything! It's all about Jesus and His ministry!

My Response: _____

265

HIS GRACIOUSNESS

*"Is it not lawful for me to do what I wish with what is my own?
Or is your eye envious because I am generous?"*

—Matthew 20:15

The evil eye is an ancient, superstitious belief, dating back thousands of years. It suggests that someone could alter your good fortune because they are envious of you. To this day, if you visit Greece, you will see thousands of blue-eye amulets in the marketplace that people buy to protect themselves from the evil eye. It has become a very popular souvenir. But what about our own envy or jealousy regarding God's graciousness to those who *seem* less worthy of His goodness?

The parable of the laborers in the vineyard is about God's generous grace. The landowner hires laborers to work for him at different times of the day, and he even hires a group at 5:00 P.M.! But when evening came, the landowner gave all the laborers the same pay, and those who had worked longer grumbled against him, because to them it seemed unfair. This is when the landowner responded: "Is it not lawful for me to do what I wish with what is my own? Or is your eye envious because I am generous?" (Matthew 20:15). The Greek text reads: "or is your eye *evil* because I am *good*?" His response exposes a discrepancy in values between the good, gracious, and generous landowner, and his jealous and envious laborers, demanding justice and fairness. Donald A. Hagner explains: "The spirit of envy, like the insistence on 'justice' reflected in the complaint of the workers who were hired first, stands in sharp contradiction to the reality of grace."* Our ability to share the grace and mercy of God with others is rooted in the understanding that we ourselves do not deserve anything, and that we have received salvation out of God's graciousness and not by the sweat of our brow. Only when we understand that at the foot of the cross we all stand on even ground, that none of us is worthier than the other, that there is only One who is worthy of our praise and glory, only then will we be able to joyfully share God's mercy and grace with *everyone*. The kingdom of heaven is like a landowner whose graciousness was lavished upon us, undeserving sinners. Let's share His grace without reservations!

My Response: _____

---

* Donald A. Hagner, *Matthew 14–28*, World Biblical Commentary, vol. 33b (Nashville, TN: Thomas Nelson Inc., 1995), 572.

HIS IMPARTIALITY

There came a woman of Samaria to draw water.
Jesus said to her, "Give Me a drink."

—John 4:7

Prejudice and discrimination have existed throughout history. Even the church of the first century struggled with these issues. As the Christian church was growing, there arose a racially motivated feeling of discontent: "While the disciples were increasing in number, a complaint arose on the part of the *Hellenistic [Greek] Jews* against the *native Hebrews*, because their widows were being overlooked in the daily serving [*diakonia*] of food" (Acts 6:1). Given that the complaint came from the Hellenistic Jews, the twelve disciples insightfully appointed seven men with Hellenistic names, to help in the serving of tables (verses 2–6).

At the time of Jesus, there was a great enmity between Jews and Samaritans. It was rooted in several events, including their religious differences during the Assyrian/Babylonian captivity, as well as the building and subsequent destruction of the rival Samaritan temple on Mount Gerizim. Aside from these past events, the Jews considered the Samaritans ritually unclean, which meant that they wouldn't use a drinking vessel that had been used by a Samaritan, least of all a woman. When the woman of Samaria came to the well to draw water, Jesus broke all these barriers by talking to her, asking for a favor, and implying that He would drink from whatever cup or bowl of water she was handling: "Give Me a drink" (verse 7). She brings up the issue; maybe Jesus had forgotten the rules. . . . Have you ever felt the pain of being considered a second-class citizen due to your race, social-economic status, accent, color, gender, age, et cetera? "The Samaritan woman said to Him, 'How is it that You, being a Jew, ask me for a drink since I am a Samaritan woman?' " John adds an explanation: "(For Jews have no dealings with Samaritans.)" (John 4:9). But Jesus didn't even respond to her objections; instead, He offered her a *gift*; He said: *ask Me for the Living Water* (see verse 10). The best way to break the barriers of prejudice is to treat others according to the heavenly principle of impartiality, embodied by Jesus Himself.

My Response: _____

HIS AGENDA

*"The water that I will give him will become in him
a well of water springing up to eternal life."*

—John 4:14

Many years ago, during a very difficult time in my life, God provided for me a wonderful mentor. He was a very skilled pastor and counselor and walked with me on the lonely path of self-discovery. He helped me shed many layers of pain, one by one. Once my heart was exposed, I started the longest human journey possible in this world: thirteen inches—from head to heart—that we are all invited to travel. Maybe this is why the story of the Samaritan woman fascinates me so much; the loving and tender words of Jesus, exposing her soul, layer by layer.

The woman of Samaria came to draw water at noon: lonely, filled with shame, and carrying the burdens of her painful past. Her conversation with Jesus constantly switches between the temporal and the spiritual, typical of the stories in the Gospel of John. In this case it is between the water she came to draw from the well and the Water of Life that Jesus offers. But, as most of us do when we have been hurt, she uses various avoidance techniques to distance herself from this Stranger, not to allow Him to touch the many layers of pain that are enveloping her heart. First, Jesus asks *her* for a favor, "Give Me a drink" (John 4:7). She responds by employing five well-developed avoidance techniques that probably had worked well in the past: *prejudice* (John 4:9), religious *superiority* (verse 12), *superficial truth* (verse 15), *religiosity* (verse 20) and *procrastination* (verse 25). She is saying, in effect, "Sir, I don't have to deal with this right now. The Messiah is coming, and He will clarify all these things. I will deal with it then." But Jesus had come to her, and comes to us, with a salvific agenda. He is patient and kind and reaches out to peel layers of hurt off our souls, exposing our hearts to His love, especially when we have been badly hurt. His desire is to get to our heart, no matter how deep it may be buried under the layers of pain. He wants to bring us His Gift of salvation (verse 10). In an unprecedented disclosure, Jesus reveals to her that He is the awaited Messiah! And He wants to do the same for each one of us as well.

My Response: _____

HIS EXCHANGE

So the woman left her waterpot, and went into the city.

—John 4:28

M any years ago, I attended a party to which everyone was to bring a little something for a gift exchange. We all received our mystery gifts. A teenage boy was very excited to open his, but then he discovered that inside the beautifully wrapped package was . . . a showerhead! Immediately his excitement dissipated, his smile vanished, and his body language communicated utter disappointment. When the party was over, one of the adults who had gotten a nice tool approached the teenager and offered him a trade, which was gladly accepted!

The Samaritan woman had come to the well because she needed water. She came because she had to, in spite of her shame and loneliness. Jesus kept offering her a different type of water, and she kept resisting, not understanding His gift. This dialogue is the only place in all four Gospels where Jesus admits, before His trial and crucifixion, that He is the Messiah (John 4:26). Then something amazing happens: "the woman left her waterpot"! (verse 28). She left it! The very same pot she had brought to draw water with. Burdened with layers of hurt and fear, she had finally taken a sip of the Living Water! She had accepted the offer to exchange her burdens for His life-giving water! She went into the city to share what was given to her and became the most successful evangelist in the four Gospels, for many believed in Jesus as the Savior of the world! (verse 42). The gospel of Jesus Christ embodies the *great exchange.* Like the kind person at the gift exchange, Jesus offers us the best trade. We brought death, but Jesus came with eternal life. He offered us the exchange. At the end of the day, we left with the eternal life Jesus had brought, and He went to Calvary with our death sentence and died in our place. Take a moment to look at the pronouns in this passage: "*He* was pierced for *our* transgressions, *he* was crushed for *our* iniquities; the punishment that brought *us* peace was upon *him*, and by *his* wounds *we* are healed" (Isaiah 53:5, NIV). That's the great exchange. Trade in your sorrows, your past, your layers of pain, and your hurts; He already paid for all of that and purchased your healing as well.

My Response: _____

HIS ADMONITION

*"Do you suppose that those eighteen on whom the tower in
Siloam fell and killed them were worse culprits than
all the men who live in Jerusalem?"*

—Luke 13:4

I had just started as an associate minister in a church when the worst terrorist attack on the United States occurred on September 11, 2001. I was in the office, wondering why no one else was showing up for our staff meeting. On the phone someone told me about the tragedy that was unfolding. The next weekend, we were all expectant for what the senior pastor would be preaching about, and I will never forget the topic of the sermon. He preached from the above-mentioned text.

As many still do now, ancient Jewish culture interpreted adversity and misfortune as direct judgment from God upon the most sinful (see John 9:1, 2). When a report was brought to Jesus regarding Galileans "whose blood Pilate had mixed with their sacrifices" (Luke 13:1), which is consistent with Pilate's clashing relationship with the Jews, Jesus called attention to the fact that all human beings are sinful and in need of repentance. He argued that just because these Galileans suffered this way, they were not greater sinners than others (see Luke 13:2). In the event that follows, Jesus also dismissed the interpretation that those who were victims of the falling of the Tower of Siloam (probably at the southeast corner of the Jerusalem walls), were worse people than the others who lived in Jerusalem. Jesus concludes on both events with the same admonition: "I tell you, no, but unless you repent, you will all likewise perish" (verses 3, 5). The use of the word *all* in every verse of His answers shows the generalization of the sinful condition (verses 2, 3, 4, 5). Jesus speaks against assigning degrees of sinfulness according to the level of tragedy and warns against self-approval and considering oneself better than others. Jesus makes it clear that we are all sinners in need of repentance. We *all* need a Savior. Our only two choices are perishing or believing in the One who perished in our place. Jesus wins! And we can choose His victory on our behalf. "For all have sinned and fall short of the glory of God, being justified as a gift by His grace through the redemption which is in Christ Jesus" (Romans 3:23, 24).

My Response: _____

HIS RESTORATION

"So it is not the will of your Father who is in heaven that one of these little ones perish."
—Matthew 18:14

If you google "nobody showed up to my party," you will be surprised to find many heartbroken kids (and adults) who have felt despised by their classmates and friends. One such case recently caught my attention because it was on the news. A boy had a birthday party, and no one came, as can be seen in a photo of him sitting by himself next to the food spread and a Happy Birthday sign. His mother was extremely sad and disappointed. However, some celebrities responded to this news by pledging to come visit him for his next birthday.

To *despise* someone means to undervalue and treat them with disdain; it is the opposite of accepting, welcoming, and cherishing a person. Matthew 18 is the chapter in which Jesus details the way we are to treat each other in His community. Jesus said, "See that you do not despise one of these little ones." (Matthew 18:10). "Little ones" refers not just to children but to those who have humbled themselves and have a child's attitude towards the kingdom of heaven (verse 4). God cares for each and every one of His "little ones." To exemplify concern for each member of the Christian community, Jesus tells the parable of the lost sheep, which is also found in Luke 15, yet in a different setting. In the latter, it is about seeking the lost or the unbelievers, but in Matthew 18:12–14 it refers to members of the "flock" who have gone astray. The shepherd goes after the one that strays and restores it to the fold; the joy that accompanies the restoration shows how each "sheep" is highly esteemed. The conclusion of the parable explains: "So it is not the will of your Father who is in heaven that one of these little ones perish" (verse 14). God does not want any of His "little ones" to cease being part of His family, and each member of a faith community should remember this. Furthermore, the next verse shows the application of this parable: "If your brother sins, go and show him his fault in private; if he listens to you, you have won your brother" (verse 15). The motivation for admonishment is *not* punishment or contempt, but *always restoration*.

My Response: _____

His Goal

*"If your brother sins, go and show him his fault in private;
if he listens to you, you have won your brother."*

—Matthew 18:15

I still remember where we were when my friend spoke to me. She wanted to talk to me about a blind spot of mine, which I didn't even know I had. What was so remarkable was that she did it with such love and care, that I was able to listen and actually hear what she was saying. I knew that she had my best interests in mind and that she was doing it out of kindness, not with an accusing spirit. And that made all the difference in the world. She truly won me over.

After telling them the parable of the lost sheep, Jesus reminded His disciples that "it is not the will of your Father who is in heaven that one of these little ones perish" (Matthew 18:14). Then He gave them a process through which to reach out to a brother in sin: go privately; then go with one or two witnesses; then go through the church. What catches my attention is that little word that expresses the goal of such conversations: to *win* our brother; "If he listens to you, you have *won* [gained] your brother" (verse 15). The intention is not to accuse nor to shame; it is not to make our brother "pay" for his sins; it is not to punish and not to diminish or humiliate. The goal is to *win* our brother over. God doesn't want anyone to perish; His motivation is always to save and redeem. Accusations have a different *source*, and he is a defeated foe: "For the accuser of our brethren has been thrown down, he who accuses them before our God day and night" (Revelation 12:10). If a sin has been committed *against us*, our bringing the issue up with our friend or relative has the same motivation. We are not to bring it up in order to belittle them but to gain them back. *Jesus wins* not only on a cosmic scale, as the Savior of the world, but He wins every time that a brother is won over, redeemed, and reestablished. God's goal is always to save: "God demonstrates His own love toward us, in that while we were yet sinners, Christ died for us" (Romans 5:8). When we didn't want anything to do with Him, Jesus provided for our salvation. And He provided for our brother's redemption as well. May we be instruments of healing and restoration.

My Response: _____

His Inclusivity

"I say to you that many will come from east and west,
and recline at the table with Abraham, Isaac
and Jacob in the kingdom of heaven."

—Matthew 8:11

I had finished preaching and was invited to proceed to the fellowship hall of the church for lunch. The leaders that I had gotten to know were busy, and therefore I got my food and sat down next to people that I had never met. Within a few minutes something incredible happened. We started sharing our lives with each other, and it turned out that we were sitting at the "United Nations" table! We had come from all over the world and with very diverse backgrounds! It was fantastic! Such a table fellowship would have been unheard of in the first century.

Right after Jesus marvels at the centurion's faith (Matthew 8:10), Matthew records a saying of Jesus that is most shocking (this saying is also found in Luke 13:28, 29 in a different context). "I say to you that *many* will come from *east* and *west*, and recline *at the table* with Abraham, Isaac and Jacob in the kingdom of heaven" (Matthew 8:11). In response to the centurion's faith, Jesus announces to His followers that all who believe in Him, both Jews *and* Gentiles, would be present, together with the patriarchs, at the Messianic banquet that had been prophesied for the end of times (see Isaiah 25:6; Revelation 19:9). In the past, the Old Testament prophecies that talked about people coming from the "east and west" (for example, see Isaiah 43:5) had been often interpreted as the Diaspora (dispersed) Jews coming back to Israel. But now Jesus, referring to the centurion, was including the Gentiles! Until then, to be qualified for such a banquet, one had to come from Abrahamic ancestry (see Matthew 8:11) or had to belong to a particular religious group. But Jesus was breaking these barriers. From then on, faith in Jesus would be the only ticket to the eschatological banquet; and some who claimed to be "sons of the kingdom" would be left outside (Matthew 8:12). I am so thankful for this inclusive statement of Jesus! I believe that God will receive a wretch like me and anyone and everyone who comes in the name and through the merits of Jesus. Inclusivity, not exclusivism, will characterize those who will partake at Jesus' banquet!

My Response: _____

HIS CHALLENGE

*"Which of these three do you think
proved to be a neighbor . . . ?"*

—Luke 10:36

There are good Samaritan laws that are designed to legally protect a bystander who assists an individual in an accident or any troublesome situation. The phrase "good Samaritan" has become a synonym of compassion in action. But many do not know the actual parable. During my studies in corporate psychology, one of my classmates was the CEO of the Good Samaritan hospital in the Los Angeles area. I asked him if he knew the parable, and he answered, "What parable?" And even though most people in religious environments are aware of the parable of the good Samaritan, I realize that the same challenge that Jesus gave the expert of Mosaic law back then is more than relevant today.

A lawyer asked: "And who is my neighbor?" (Luke 10:29). Jesus replied with a story. The description of the awful event is detailed and revealing. "A man was going down from Jerusalem to Jericho, and fell among robbers, and they stripped him and beat him, and went away leaving him half dead" (verse 30). A priest was going down on that road, which means he is done with his religious responsibilities in Jerusalem. When the priest saw the man half dead on the road, "he passed by on the other side" (verse 31). The purity laws didn't allow even a shadow to be cast on a corpse, but the mercy laws required one always to help a person in trouble. The mercy laws were considered higher than the purity laws. Given that the man was "half dead," the priest decided to uphold the purity laws, all the while ignoring the mercy laws. He crossed over to the other side of the road, so that his shadow wouldn't touch the potential corpse. The Levite followed suit. Some still do the same: placing mercy laws below purity laws and rejecting the very people who are in need of help. If you have been hurt due to *purity* rules trumping *mercy* rules, may you know that this reversal does not represent God's ways. Jesus challenged the lawyer not to be like the priest or the Levite in this story but to show mercy as the Samaritan did (verse 37). The victory of Jesus on the cross for us was not achieved through His indifference but through His merciful and selfless incarnation.

My Response: _____

HIS CONCLUSION

Then Jesus said to him, "Go and do the same."

—Luke 10:37

Our young adult group went white-water rafting every year. On one of these trips, the more experienced people decided to take a longer and more difficult river run. We were used to all the documentation and the guides' lectures about safety. But that day, when an emergency occurred, more than just talk was needed. One of the rafts turned over in one of the larger rapids, trapping people underneath. The guide acted instantaneously and got the rest of the group out of trouble with firm and clear instructions. Her knowledge and her actions saved their lives. As important as lectures were, the time for action had come.

An expert of the law came to Jesus asking about eternal life. Jesus, in turn, asked him what was written in the law. The lawyer answered, summarizing the law by quoting Deuteronomy 6:5 and Leviticus 19:18—loving God and loving our neighbor (Luke 10:27). Jesus commended him for his answer, but the lawyer then asked: "And who is my neighbor?" (verse 29). In response, Jesus told the parable of the good Samaritan (verses 30 37), which we started to review yesterday. The story is narrated in a crescendo-like series of shocks. First, the level of violence that the man endured: he was robbed, stripped, beaten, and left half dead. The second level of shock is what the religious men, the priest and the Levite, *didn't do*: they didn't help at all; their religion was about talking the talk but not walking the walk. The third shock is what the Samaritan *did do*: he was a despised foreigner, yet he saw the victim, felt compassion, cared for his wounds, loaded him on his own animal, brought him to the inn, took care of him, and paid for his expenses. The fourth level of shock is the conclusion Jesus gives: the expert of the law should imitate the Samaritan! It is hard for us to grasp how this would have astounded His audience. Jesus asks us to show our love in action, just as He did towards us. His love made Him come to die for us, when we didn't want anything to do with Him. Now He empowers us to love our neighbor, which is everyone He died for. He said that His community would be recognized by their love (John 13:35). *And the time to love has come!*

My Response: _____

HIS PURPOSE

"The Son of Man did not come to destroy
men's lives, but to save them."

—Luke 9:56

I n the book *Radical Discipleship*, my colleague and friend, Aivars Ozolins, tells an amusing story from his childhood. He remembers a time when he was quarreling with a neighbor's kid: "In the heat of the argument, as I was running out of good comebacks, I decided to throw in my religion and declared with all the force of my ten-year-old conviction, 'Do you know that God will burn you in fire because you are so bad to me?' Somehow I am pretty sure that my 'missionary venture' did not convert anybody."* I believe that many of us have used such "evangelistic" methods at one time or another.

James and John, the "Sons of Thunder" (Mark 3:17), employed similar tactics when they entered a Samaritan village. The Samaritans had a distinct antipathy to Jews who were traveling towards Jerusalem, usually refusing them hospitality and shelter. This was often a problem for those who embarked on a journey from Galilee to Jerusalem, which was about a three-day journey. Because of this, many Jews, instead of traveling through Samaria, chose rather to cross over to the other side of the Jordan river. But Jesus decided to go into the Samaritan village and sent a messenger to make arrangements for Him (Luke 9:52). When "they did not receive Him [Jesus,] because He was traveling toward Jerusalem" (verse 53), James and John decided that it was time for one of those "missionary" moments. "When His disciples James and John saw *this*, they said, 'Lord, do You want us to command fire to come down from heaven and consume them?' " (verse 54). What were they thinking? They assumed they had been given the divine power to punish and destroy. But Jesus rebuked them sternly: "You do not know what kind of spirit you are of; for the Son of Man did not come to destroy men's lives, but to save them" (Luke 9:55, 56). When we witness about Jesus, we should never do it in order to win arguments, showcase our intelligence, or humiliate people. Let's always remember that *His* purpose is to save, not to destroy.

My Response: _____

---

* Elizabeth Talbot and Aivars Ozolins, *Radical Discipleship: Ordinary People Accepting Extraordinary Grace* (Nampa, ID: Pacific Press®, 2016), 17.

HIS MESSENGERS

"Thus it is written . . . that repentance for forgiveness of sins would be proclaimed in His name to all the nations, beginning from Jerusalem."
—Luke 24:46, 47

Living in a desert area, I have several types of cacti in my backyard. These are very dear to me because they belonged to my mother. The flowers they produce are so gorgeous and colorful, that year after year they take me by surprise. Some cacti produce very large, showy flowers; others bloom with many tiny ones. All of them lovely and breathtaking! It is hard to grasp how these rough-looking, leafless plants with spiny stems are capable of producing such flamboyant beauty. These cacti give me hope that God can use my life for His glory.

After His resurrection, Jesus explained to His disciples what the Scriptures said about Him (Luke 24:45). Jesus said: "Thus it is written, that the Christ would suffer and rise again from the dead the third day, and that repentance for forgiveness of sins would be proclaimed in His name to all the nations. . . . You are witnesses of these things" (Luke 24:46–48). Jesus clearly told the disciples the core proclamation of the Christian church: *forgiveness of sins in His name.* They were His witnesses and His messengers to proclaim the good news. But if we look closer, we see that they were a rough-looking, raglag bunch of people. How could they be God's messengers to a needy world? The followers of Jesus included angry fishermen, violent rebels, a despised businessman, and a woman of shady reputation. They were definitely rough-looking cacti with spiny stems. How could they possibly fulfill their calling to be messengers of forgiveness for their generation? So glad you asked! The grace of Jesus took over their lives, and they were promised power from on high through the Holy Spirit (Luke 24:49). And that's how we find them in Acts 2, when they were baptized with the Holy Spirit, and the desert bloomed and filled the earth with colorful flowers. Let's ask God for the power of His Spirit to fulfill our calling to proclaim the gospel to our generation. For, "we have this treasure in earthen vessels, so that the surpassing greatness of the power will be of God and not from ourselves" (2 Corinthians 4:7).

My Response: _____

HIS SOVEREIGNTY

They came to Jesus and observed the man who had been demon-possessed sitting down, clothed and in his right mind.

—Mark 5:15

B efore and after" pictures are an effective advertising tool. Whether it's an anti-wrinkle face cream or a house remodeling tool, the advertisers make sure that the "after" photo is much more attractive than the "before" picture. Yet these products do not always turn out to be as effective as portrayed in the advertisements. God's "before and after" pictures are always true; they are guaranteed. The Gospels present the miracles of Jesus in a flamboyant "before and after" style. Jesus never left the scene the same as He had found it.

Having stilled the sea, Jesus and His disciples arrived on the *other side*, in the country of the Gerasenes. Here they found a more terrifying scene than the storm itself. The detailed description of the demon-possessed man reminds us of how evil spirits have always sought to destroy the image of God in humans (see Mark 5:3–5). No one had been strong enough to bind him until Jesus arrived. The demons immediately recognized Jesus and called Him "Jesus, Son of the Most High God" (verse 7; in Acts, the demons also called Paul and Silas "bond-servants of the Most High God," Acts 16:17). Jesus said, "Come out of the man, you unclean spirit!" (Mark 5:8), and the demons entered a large herd of swine, and drowned them in the sea (verse 13). In the next scene, we have an "after picture" with the man totally transformed: clothed and in his right mind (verse 15), in radical contrast with the "before" reality. He actually became an evangelist for Jesus in that region! The metamorphosis was staggering! Satan continues to seek the destruction of men and women through addictions, vices, and mind-altering behaviors. Evil spirits seek to separate human beings from their Creator and Redeemer. But Jesus is sovereign over evil forces, and He purchased our healing on the cross. "Satan is humanity's enemy and destroyer while Jesus is humanity's Friend and Savior. This story gives us hope that even those who have been under Satan's control can be changed into messengers of the gospel as they tell what God has done for them."*

My Response: _____

---

* Jerry D. Thomas, *Man of Peace: A Contemporary Adaptation of the Classic Work on Jesus' Life, The Desire of Ages* (Nampa, ID: Pacific Press®, 2008), 98.

His Endeavor

*He said to him, "Go home to your people and report
to them what great things the Lord has done for you,
and how He had mercy on you."*

—Mark 5:19

Following in the footsteps of Paul, we arrived at Philippi; I found this place fascinating. It was in this city that an evil spirit, speaking through a slave-girl, became an obstacle to the preaching of the gospel. In the name of Jesus, Paul commanded the spirit to leave, and it did (see Acts 16:16–21). But her masters did not like it, and they were enraged because they had lost their profitable business because she no longer had the fortune-telling spirit. Then Paul and Silas were imprisoned.

Throughout His ministry, Jesus endeavored to bring salvation, healing, and restoration to everyone He came in contact with, yet not everyone accepted what He offered. Sometimes, as seen above, people chose money and profit over healing and salvation. When faced with an amazing supernatural manifestation of God's grace and power, different audiences responded differently, either with rage, fear, and asking Jesus to leave, or by surrendering to His love and desiring to follow Him. In the exorcism of the Gerasene demoniac, both responses are present. The evil spirits called Jesus by name, "Jesus, Son of the Most High God" (Mark 5:7). "Jesus" means "Yahweh saves" (see Matthew 1:21), and His endeavor was clear: to save and to restore. When Jesus commanded the evil spirits to leave the possessed man, the demons asked permission to enter a large herd of swine. When it was granted, the swine drowned in the sea, exposing the ultimate intention of Satan (Mark 5:10–14). The herdsmen reported what had happened, and that's when the people pressed Jesus to leave, because they chose money over restoration. In contrast to their fear and rejection, the restored man was clothed and in his right mind, and pleaded with Jesus that he might accompany Him (verses 17, 18). The crowd *implored* Him to leave; while the man *implored* to follow Him. Jesus left the place, but His endeavor to save them continued. He commissioned the man to proclaim God's mercy throughout the region. Jesus will never *force* His presence on His creatures, yet He does not give up in His efforts to seek the lost.

My Response: _____

HIS WARNING

"But woe to you, scribes and Pharisees, hypocrites, because you shut off the kingdom of heaven from people; for you do not enter in yourselves, nor do you allow those who are entering to go in."
—Matthew 23:13

To begin our trip in Israel, we arrived in the ancient city of Jaffa (Joppa). Right next to the traditional site of the house of Simon the Tanner, there is a church with a beautiful painting that commemorates Peter's vision (see Acts 10:11–16). Peter would not have entered the centurion's home if God had not communicated with him in this manner, because Jews were not allowed to enter the house of a Gentile. God had to teach His ways to His own flawed disciples.

Up until now, legalistic religious beliefs have frequently gotten in the way of the spreading of the gospel, especially when one group feels superior to another. Jesus was often involved in controversies with the Pharisees and scribes due to their religious traditions and interpretations, which they placed above the commandments of God. Even now, some choose *purity over mercy*, denying access to God for those who don't seem to qualify. Jesus often denounced those who were tithing the mint and dill and yet neglected mercy, exposing the burden of a pharisaical religion (see Matthew 23). If you have felt the pain of pharisaical oppression, may God grant you His healing. Jesus condemned lack of mercy (Matthew 12:7). He even said that publicans and prostitutes were getting into the kingdom of God ahead of those who were not aware of their own need for a Savior (see Matthew 21:31). Matthew uses the word *burden* twice. In Matthew 23:4, talking about the scribes and the Pharisees, Jesus said that they tie up heavy burdens and lay them on men's shoulders. The other occurrence is found in Matthew 11:30, in which Jesus offers us His rest: "For My yoke is easy and My *burden* is light." The Pharisees offered a heavy burden, but the burden of Jesus is light. May our hearts overflow with the joy of our salvation! And may He teach us to share Him with others openly and with compassion and grace, keeping in mind His redemptive purposes. For He came to proclaim liberty to captives and release to the oppressed.

My Response: _____

His People

When the centurion, who was standing right in front of Him, saw the way He breathed His last, he said, "Truly this man was the Son of God!"

—Mark 15:39

For several years, I taught a master's level class on the Gospels, and most of my students were ministers. One semester, a particular student caught my attention; he seemed shy, and wore a hood on his head. After a few weeks, he shared with the class that he had an urban music ministry. I was intrigued and asked him to come up front and perform for us. I will never forget the depth of the gospel content of his music; he definitely could reach many for Christ! Throughout the class, I was amazed at his intelligence! I encouraged him to pursue a PhD.

This experience challenged the way I made assumptions about others. Have you ever asked yourself what the people of God are supposed to look like? If you have, perhaps today's devotional will challenge you as well. In the time of Jesus, the religious elite had stereotypes about what godly people were supposed to look like. They certainly did not resemble centurions, who not only were Gentiles but were also employed by the Roman army to lead at least one hundred men. They were soldiers, pledging allegiance to Caesar, who, incidentally, was called *the son of god*. Perhaps this is why it is so shocking to find that the centurion, who was overseeing the crucifixion of Jesus, makes the most discerning statement about Jesus in the passion narrative! When he saw the manner in which Jesus died, he exclaimed: "Truly this man was the Son of God!" (Mark 15:39). Luke reports that the centurion also declared Jesus a righteous man (Luke 23:47). That this commander recognized Jesus, instead of Caesar, as the Son of God, when no one else showed such piercing insight, emphasizes that God touches and uses people for his glory everywhere and in all circumstances! By the way, only once in the Gospels did Jesus marvel at someone's faith, and that someone was a centurion! (see Matthew 8:10). There is no stereotype of what the people of God *should* look like. All languages, colors, age, social and economic status, worship styles, et cetera are invited and used by God to enlarge His kingdom. And you are included!

My Response: _____

HIS METHOD

"When you give a reception, invite the poor,
the crippled . . . and you will be blessed, since they
do not have the means to repay you."

—Luke 14:13, 14

The costly, non-refundable wedding reception had been booked at the Ritz Charles hotel in Carmel, Indiana, but the wedding got cancelled just a few days before the event. The bride-to-be contacted several homeless shelters in the area, and the surprised impromptu guests were bused in to the posh location for a high-end dinner they would never forget. Local businesses donated clothing for the guests to wear for this occasion. In the midst of her pain, Ms. Cummins made a decision to act selflessly, and to share with those who couldn't repay her.*

The first-century Mediterranean world was an honor/shame-based society. Therefore conventional rules of reciprocity were practiced, especially by the elite. Gifts and invitations were often given with strings attached, leaving the poor and destitute disadvantaged. Jesus frequently challenged these social methods used to secure advantageous relationships. When He realized that some guests had been picking places of honor (Luke 14:7–11), Jesus spoke to them: "When you are invited by someone to a wedding feast, do not take the place of honor, for someone more distinguished than you may have been invited. . . . For everyone who exalts himself will be humbled, and he who humbles himself will be exalted" (verses 8–11). This was a new way of life! But Jesus wasn't done yet. He went on to teach a new way to relate to others, receiving the poor, the crippled, the lame, the blind, and those who couldn't repay (verse 13, 14); in other words, He taught us to welcome the marginalized of society. Who would that be today? The fearful pregnant teenager? The young man who just got out of jail? This is Jesus' method, for He reached out to us and invited us to His banquet table, which we could never repay. May the overflow of the unmerited grace we have received cause us to reach out and gladly receive those who feel alone, diminished, and hopeless.

My Response: _____

---

* Maureen C. Gilmer, "Bride-to-be Calls off Wedding, Invites Homeless to Her Reception," *IndyStar*, November 20, 2017, 9:52 A.M. EST, https://www.indystar.com/story/life/2017/07/13/bride/476828001/.

HIS SURRENDERING

"Father, if You are willing, remove this cup from Me;
yet not My will, but Yours be done."

—Luke 22:42

I was headed to my parents' place with a flask of oil and a prayer in my heart, as it had become obvious that mom's cancer was terminal. I gave her a figurine of a girl holding a large bouquet of forget-me-nots. I told mom that this was to remind her that I would never, ever, forget her; and that when she wasn't around anymore, I would have the forget-me-not figurine close to me. Then I anointed her, praying for a miraculous healing if it was God's will but also saying that we were submitting to His will. She passed away two weeks later, in peace. The figurine is next to me as I write. Today, September 24, is the anniversary of her death.

All of us have prayed such prayers, asking yet submitting to God's will, even if it's contrary to what we have asked. We have such a limited view of God's will, that we would do well to surrender to His view of the circumstances. When my parents faced death, I had to contend with my own will in order to add this sentence to my prayers: "Yet not my will, but Yours be done" (Luke 22:42). When Jesus arrived at the Garden of Gethsemane on the Mount of Olives, He instructed His disciples to pray that they might not enter into temptation (Luke 22:40). Then He withdrew from them and knelt down to pray (verse 41). Luke emphasizes that Jesus prayed three times (verses 41, 44, 45). He brought to His Father a specific request: "Father, if You are willing, *remove this cup from Me*" (verse 42). This was the cup that only a few verses before He had told His disciples about: "This cup which is poured out for you is the new covenant in My blood" (verse 20). Now this cup was trembling in His hands. His humanity was eagerly asking for a different way to save the human race other than this anguish and darkness of His soul, which He felt to the point of sweating blood (verse 44). Still, He added: ". . . yet not My will, but Yours be done" (verse 42). There was no other way. An angel came to strengthen Him. In answer to His prayer, He received strength instead of the removal of the cup. You and I have been saved because He surrendered *His cup* to God's will.

My Response: _____

HIS ASSIGNMENT

"For it is just like a man about to go on a journey, who called his own slaves and entrusted his possessions to them."
—Matthew 25:14

It is hard to believe that the man behind the Apple technology that changed the world and the way we communicate was once given up by his unmarried biological parents. Adopted by Paul and Clara Jobs, Steve grew up to become one of the geniuses of our time, leaving a legacy that will impact generations to come. Steve Jobs passed away on October 5, 2011, one day after the iPhone 4S was introduced, leaving an inheritance worth over ten billion dollars.

If one technology whiz could change the way the world communicates, how much more can the followers of Christ influence the whole world with His redemptive gospel? Today's verse is part of the third parable explaining what Jesus entrusted His disciples to do between His ascension and the Second Coming (Matthew 25:14–30). It would take a long time, and His disciples were to spread the gospel of the kingdom using any and all abilities and gifts that they were given for that purpose. In the parable, the man who is going on a journey entrusts *his* possessions to *his* servants. "To one he gave five talents, to another, two, and to another, one . . . and he went on his journey. . . . Now after a *long time* the master of those slaves came and settled accounts with them" (verses 15, 19). When the master returned, he found that both the servant with the five talents and the one with the two talents had made a 100 percent return for him. Both were commended: "Well done, good and faithful slave. . . . enter into the joy of your master" (verses 21, 23; see also 24:47). But the third servant said: "I was afraid, and went away and hid your talent in the ground" (Matthew 25:25). This slave represents those who have a fear-based religion and are scared to take risks for Christ. God did not intend such a fear-based religious experience for us. He desires that we put it all on the line in order to reach souls for His kingdom; His plan of redemption must be proclaimed. The spreading of the gospel has not been entrusted to the unfallen angels but to us, weak human beings who can testify of the magnitude of the grace of God!

My Response: _____

HIS RULING

"Truly I say to you, to the extent that you did it to one of these brothers of Mine, even the least of them, you did it to Me."

—Matthew 25:40

My family moved to the United States for one year when I was twelve. It was hard for me to adjust without knowing the language, and I felt out of place, even at school. Soon a wonderful girl named Lynell Blazen befriended me and changed my life. We hugged, cried, and laughed when we met again forty years later. I told her what a difference she had made for me, but she kept repeating, "I didn't do anything! I didn't do anything! You were my friend!"

This is the typical response of the blessed ones inheriting the kingdom: they are unaware of their kind deeds and are not counting on them in order to be saved. In Matthew 25:31–46, Jesus is the King on His throne, separating the nations into two groups as He pronounces His verdict. Both the righteous and the unrighteous seem absolutely astonished by the King's ruling. The King informs those on the right that they had ministered to Him in six distinct ways: when He had been hungry, thirsty, a stranger, naked, sick, and in prison. We see astonishment in their response: *When . . . ?* They don't remember doing these things for Him; they were not keeping record. Jesus explains that when they did this for His brothers, even the least of them, they actually did it for Him. The unrighteous feel baffled by the King's decision as well, because they feel that they have done plenty of good deeds to prove their righteousness. *When did we see You, and didn't minister to You? When did we miss You?* But the truth was that by ignoring *the least of these*, they had ignored Him. The kingdom of God is characterized by the selfless spirit that was manifested in Jesus. "It is in unselfish ministry that true happiness is found. And every word and deed of such service is recorded in the books of heaven as done for Christ. . . . Live in the sunshine of the Savior's love. Then your influence will bless the world. Let the Spirit of Christ control you. Let the law of kindness be ever on your lips. Forbearance and unselfishness mark the words and actions of those who are born again, to live the new life in Christ."*

My Response: _____

---

* Ellen G. White, *Testimonies for the Church*, vol. 7 (Mountain View, CA: Pacific Press®, 1948), 50.

HIS GROWTH

*"The kingdom of God is like a man who casts
seed upon the soil . . . and the seed sprouts and grows—
how, he himself does not know."*

—Mark 4:26, 27

The teacher asked us to place a bean in the middle of a jar and secure it with blotting paper. We were to water it, and the blotting paper would absorb the moisture. And it did sprout with no outside help! For me as a child, the whole process of watching the shoots and the roots developing right in front of my eyes was both exciting and mysterious! The power of the seed to sprout and grow is one of the mysteries of nature that carries God's magnificent fingerprint.

Jesus used this example to convey the mysterious power contained within the seed of the gospel. In a very short parable recorded only in the Gospel of Mark (Mark 4:26–29), Jesus explains that the kingdom of God is like a man who scatters seed on the ground, and whether he sleeps or gets up, the seed sprouts on *its own*, and *the man does not know how*. The seed has a mysterious power of its own to sprout and grow, producing crops: "the blade, then the head, then the mature grain in the head" (verse 28). This parable emphasizes how the gospel proclamation contains, within itself, the power of God to germinate and mature. We do well to study and train to share the good news of Jesus, yet ultimately it is the power of God to bring about salvation that will take root and grow in a person's heart. Many parents contact me to share their concern about their adult children, who seem uninterested in spiritual matters. I always point out that God is even more interested than we are in our children's salvation, and that the Holy Spirit has power to grow the gospel seed in their hearts. The same is true for all of us who feel unfit and unqualified to share the treasures of the gospel with others. Always remember that God adds His mysterious power to our feeble human efforts. We can't always see the extent of what is happening, yet great things are fashioning themselves together without our understanding. The proclamation of the gospel of Jesus Christ is never in vain. Trust that the seed of the good news of eternal salvation through His blood will grow, *by itself*, through the power of God's Spirit!

My Response: _____

HIS EMPATHY

*"Do you see this woman? I entered your house; you gave
Me no water for My feet, but she has wet My feet with
her tears and wiped them with her hair."*

—Luke 7:44

Yesterday I witnessed a profound scene. I stopped for gasoline and saw a homeless man sitting close to the entrance of the gas station store. He wasn't asking for money though he was obviously destitute. Suddenly, a man got out of his car and approached him. He handed the man some bills but more importantly took time to connect with him by talking to him for a while. His compassion and gentleness had an impact on me. We are often called to share Jesus' victorious grace through simple acts of kindness, such as approaching people with empathy, not criticism, sharing their feelings, and demonstrating pure love and compassion. In an imperfect world, we will always find reasons to fear and criticize, yet God asks us to find ways to share His unconditional love with gentleness and no strings attached.

A Pharisee invited Jesus to dine with him. Whether his motives were to honor or entrap Him, Jesus accepted the invitation. Then a woman, who was known to be a sinner, entered the house, "and standing behind Him at His feet, weeping, she began to wet His feet with her tears, and kept wiping them with the hair of her head, and kissing His feet and anointing them with the perfume" (Luke 7:38). When the religious man saw this, instead of displaying compassion or empathy, he had harsh critical thoughts about both Jesus and her (verse 39). In response, Jesus asked the Pharisee: "Do you see this woman?" (verse 44). Do you really *see* her? He went on to tenderly explain her actions and made a public statement that her sins had been forgiven, and that she could go in peace (verses 48, 50). Is there someone in your life, work, school, or neighborhood that you need to *see* and share God's mercy with? We share His kindness with others, not because we are perfect, but because we ourselves are in great need of God's grace, and He loves us regardless of our weaknesses. "So, as those who have been chosen of God, holy and beloved, put on a heart of compassion, kindness, humility, gentleness and patience" (Colossians 3:12). May we share His grace freely!

My Response: _____

287

His Extravagance

"Give, and it will be given to you. They will pour into your lap a good measure—pressed down, shaken together, and running over."
—Luke 6:38

When I was a pastor for young adults, we used to hold an Easter art exhibit, inviting everyone to participate by submitting their art. I still remember many amazing items of art. One of them, simple yet so profound, consisted of two elements: a tiny cup with some rice in it and, next to it, a large bucket overflowing with rice that spilled over all around. The label for the tiny cup read: "What we expect from God," while the large bucket's label, which was partially covered by the abundance of rice, said: "What God wants to give us."

The generosity that characterizes the kingdom of God is not *fair*—it is extravagant and outrageous! God lavishes His grace recklessly upon all of us who are so undeserving of His kindness. He desires His followers to exercise the same principle of flamboyant mercy toward others. "But love your enemies, and do good, and lend, expecting nothing in return . . . and you will be sons of the Most High; for *He Himself is kind to ungrateful and evil men*. Be merciful, just as your Father is merciful" (Luke 6:35, 36). These two verses are a summary of the previous section in which Jesus tells His followers to treat others, even those who have wronged them, generously (verses 27–34). The reason to treat others generously comes from recognizing the way God treats us, for He Himself is kind with the ungrateful. "Give, and it will be given to you. . . . pressed down, shaken together, and running over. For by your standard of measure it will be measured to you in return" (verse 38). The illustration of Jesus comes from the marketplace: a generous merchant who, instead of being simply upright or fair, chooses to pour on the outer garment of his customer (used to carry grain) a measure that is pressed down and overflowing. God has loved us extravagantly, even when we were not His friends. He is our bountiful God, who is merciful upon wretched sinners like us. Now, He asks us to be conduits of His overflowing mercy, loving our enemies, forgiving, and giving without expecting anything in return. Let His mercy flow!

My Response: _____

HIS GREATNESS

"It is like a mustard seed, which . . . though it is
smaller than all the seeds . . . it grows up and becomes
larger than all the garden plants."

—Mark 4:31, 32

I don't know much about physics, yet I understand that when the atom was discovered, it was the smallest known particle of matter; but then protons and neutrons were discovered inside the atom's nucleus! Proton therapy is the most precise radiation therapy available to date. I live close to the Loma Linda Medical Center where many people come to be treated for prostate, breast, and lung cancer at the Proton Treatment Center. How is it possible that something so small, which is not visible to the naked eye, can render such great healing power?

In Jewish culture, mustard proverbially had the smallest seed. This is why Jesus chose it as a parable about the "contrasting dimensions"* of the kingdom of God, highlighting its growth. "What can such a *small* seed amount to?" one would think. Yet, placed in the soil, the seed will grow to become the *largest* of the garden plants. So large, in fact, "that the birds of the air can next under its shade" (Matthew 4:32). The baby born in a manger did not measure up to the Messianic expectations of Israel's elite. Even the public teaching and healing ministry of Jesus was so unassuming that it could not in any way meet the Jewish Messianic anticipation. And what about the band of unlikely followers that Jesus chose as the first disciples? Oh, yes, most definitely, the beginnings of God's kingdom looked small and without much potential. And how about Calvary? The cross looked like the end of all kingly hopes! Yet it was exactly in His death and resurrection that the redemptive prophecies of old were fulfilled! Facing His accusers, Jesus pointed to the future greatness of His kingdom: "I am [the Christ]; and you shall see the Son of Man sitting at the right hand of power, and coming with the clouds of heaven" (Mark 14:62, 63). Soon, every knee shall bow at the name of Jesus, both in heaven and on earth (Philippians 2:10). Never underestimate the power of the gospel seed, even if it is planted in the most unlikely of human hearts! Let God be in charge of its growth!

My Response: _____

---

* For a further explanation of the two "contrasting dimensions" in this parable, see Robert A. Guelich, *Mark 1–8:26*, World Biblical Commentary, vol. 34a (Nashville, TN: Thomas Nelson Inc., 1989), 246–253.

EMBRACING HIS ASSURANCE

HIS TREATMENT

"Do not be afraid. Only believe . . ."

—Luke 8:50*

O ur senior pastor, Jon Cicarelli, preached a sermon entitled *Fearless*. To help the congregation visualize *fear*, he introduced his talk by showing several underwater photos of people cautiously swimming next to large whales and sharks. As he developed the topic, he asked the congregation to repeat aloud: *"Do not be afraid, only believe."* He reminded us that God is competent to handle our lives and that He loves us. Fear is like a giant shadow lurking in the deep waters of our minds. Yet most of what we fear never happens, and the rest is not within our control. This is not the "fight or flight" type of fear but a restless anxiety that takes over our lives. But what if we are actually facing our worse fears?

This is what happened to Jairus. He came to Jesus, asking Him to heal his only daughter, who was twelve years old and was dying. On the way to his house, Jesus healed a hemorrhaging woman, who had been sick for twelve years (Luke 8:48). Then Jairus's worst nightmare came true: "While He was still speaking, someone came from the house of the synagogue official, saying, 'Your daughter has died; do not trouble the Teacher anymore' " (verse 49). Jairus must have been very much afraid at that point, because Jesus had to tell him: "Do not be afraid *any longer*; only believe, and she will be made well" (verse 50). Then Jesus proceeded to raise Jairus's daughter from the dead (verse 54). The treatment Jesus prescribes for *fear* has always been to choose *faith over fear*. The Greek words for "To believe" and "faith" share the same root. We are invited to believe in God's sovereignty and to trust that Jesus will make all things right eventually, with no more pain or death (Revelation 21:4). Jesus reminds all of us to *believe* in Him. We don't understand many things, yet we can believe that He is infinitely capable of handling our daily lives, and that He has already secured our eternal life through His sacrifice. We can live fully trusting in Him: "Since we have confidence to enter the holy place by the blood of Jesus . . . let us draw near with a sincere heart in full assurance of faith" (Hebrews 10:19, 22). He has provided for our salvation and now empowers us to trust Him. Do not fear!

My Response: _____

---

* J. D. Douglas, *The New Greek-English Interlinear New Testament*, 4th rev. ed. (Carol Stream, IL: Tyndale House, 1993).

HIS EFFICACY

He . . . took her by the hand and called, saying, "Child, arise!"
And her spirit returned, and she got up immediately.
—Luke 8:54, 55

My young cousin has a big heart for the *untouchables* of society. Carla is in her early twenties; she gets together with a group of church friends her age, and they head to obscure areas of the large metropolitan city where they live to minister to the many people who live in the cold, under dark bridges. They bring blankets, food, and a big smile to the homeless, helpless, and hopeless of society.

Jesus was always attracted to the *untouchables*. Jairus's daughter and the bleeding woman (Luke 8:41–56) have several things in common: both are female in a society that didn't really value women; both are sick and dying; the girl was *twelve* years old, and the woman had been sick for *twelve* years. The woman and the girl's dad both fall at Jesus' feet; Jesus speaks to both of them about believing and being made well (saved). Surprisingly the woman and the girl are both called daughters: the girl is Jairus's daughter (verse 42), and the woman is called Jesus' daughter (verse 48)! One of the strongest links between both stories is the fact that they are both *untouchable*. There were many rules forbidding anybody to touch the sick or the dead. Due to her condition, no one was allowed to come in contact with the bleeding woman in order not to become unclean themselves (see Leviticus 15:19–31). Yet she touched Jesus, and, instead of making Him unclean, He made her whole. By the time Jesus gets to Jairus's house, his daughter has died (verse 49), and once again, Jesus touches the *untouchable*. Taking her hand, which would have made Him unclean, He said " 'Child, arise!' And her spirit returned" (verses 54, 55). Perhaps you are at your wit's end today. Or maybe you have a child or grandchild who is deemed *untouchable* by the rest of society. Amazingly, Jesus specializes in touching the untouchables. You cannot make Him unclean! On the contrary, He will make you (or your child) whole. Don't ever be afraid to come to Jesus *just as you are*, no matter how *unclean, destitute,* or *untouchable* you may feel. This is the efficacy of Jesus: His touch gives life!

My Response: _____

HIS ASSURANCE

"I will not drink of this fruit of the vine from now on until that day when I drink it new with you in My Father's kingdom."
—Matthew 26:29

When I was in my early teens, one day I decided to decline my mother's help and to do my own haircut. Soon I realized that I was in deep trouble; my hair was all uneven, but I had only a few inches of hair left! Finally, I had to swallow my pride and ask for my mother's forgiveness and help. I ended up with a very short haircut and a very profound lesson about her willingness and ability to help. I always had the assurance that she would be there for me. Sometimes our challenges are much greater than a haircut, and we wonder: Will God still help me, or is He going to say, "I told you so?" Can He still save me or have I gone too far?

As Jesus and His disciples were having the last Passover meal together, Jesus took the cup, gave thanks and explained its ultimate meaning: "This is My blood of the covenant, which is poured out for many for forgiveness of sins. But I say to you, I will not drink of this fruit of the vine from now on until that day when I drink it new *with you* in My Father's kingdom" (Matthew 26:28, 29). What an amazing assurance! Not only was Jesus explaining that His blood would be poured out for the forgiveness of sins, but He was also assuring them of the future! He was talking about His everlasting kingdom and eternal life. I can imagine the disciples' excitement: they couldn't wait to be drinking of the fruit of the vine with Jesus in His kingdom! I want to live with that assurance, don't you? But there's more to it, which takes my breath away. Jesus sees the future: "You will all fall away because of Me [abandon Me] this night, for it is written, I will strike down the shepherd, and the sheep of the flock shall be scattered. But after I have been raised, I will go ahead of you to Galilee" (Matthew 26:31, 32). What? Do you mean that Jesus already *knew* about their upcoming failure and *still* gave them the assurance of the kingdom? Yes! Quoting Zechariah 13:7, Jesus let them know the outcome. Even though they would fail Him miserably, they would be in the kingdom if they chose to believe in Him! And so will we!

My Response: _____

His Reversal

*"He has filled the hungry with good things;
And sent away the rich empty-handed."*

—Luke 1:53

Nick Vujicic* was giving his testimony at our church that day. This remarkable young man, born without limbs, encourages people throughout the world to accept and share Jesus. He says: "If God can use a man without arms and legs to be His hands and feet, then He will certainly use any willing heart!" Exceeding all expectations, hundreds of people flocked to the church, and they were a very diverse group. One section of our parking lot was taken over by tough-looking motorcycle riders, who went on to sit in the front pews and worshipped with raised hands and open hearts. There were casually dressed young people, and older folks wearing suits and ties. Somehow all distinctions had disappeared; we were one group, amazed at God's grace.

The Gospel of Luke,† the longest book of the New Testament, is narrated in a way that highlights the inclusivity of God's grace for *all* people. One of the fascinating ways how Luke makes this point is by presenting parallel stories about a man and then about a woman. A few of these men-women pairs are Zacharias and Mary (Luke 1), Simeon and Anna (Luke 2), the widow of Zarephath and Naaman the Syrian (Luke 4), the centurion of Capernaum and the widow of Nain (Luke 7), a man losing a sheep and a woman losing a coin (Luke 15), et cetera. Another way in which Luke portrays the inclusion of every human in the plan of salvation is by presenting the genealogy of Jesus all the way back to Adam (Luke 3:23–38). But perhaps the most radical of all his theological proposals is the fact that salvation includes those who, by society's standards, don't seem to qualify: the poor, the lowly, the outcast, and the marginalized. Story after story ushers in a new era of reversals when it comes to qualifying for eternal life: "He has brought down rulers . . . And has exalted those who were humble. He has filled the hungry with good things" (Luke 1:52, 53). In this reversal you and I find assurance and a new song of deliverance. The Savior has come for such as us!

My Response: _____

---

* For more information about Nick's ministry, go to www.lifewithoutlimbs.org.

† For further insights from this Gospel, see Elizabeth Talbot, *Luke: Salvation for All* (Nampa, ID: Pacific Press®, 2001).

HIS SURETY

*"The stone which the builders rejected,
this became the chief corner stone."*
—Matthew 21:42

We bought our first home before the actual housing development was built, about twenty minutes from where we were living at the time. In our excitement, we were visiting the site quite often, but months went by until they started excavating. One day, we found that the construction crew had just laid the foundation. We wanted to leave a declaration of God's faithfulness towards us, so with a little stick we wrote in the freshly-poured concrete, "1 John 4:19." Later we sold that house, but the love and grace of Jesus continue to be our sure foundation.

At the end of the parable of the vineyard and the vine-growers (Matthew 21:33–41), Jesus quoted Psalm 118:22, 23 about the stone that was the *head of the corner* (Matthew 21:42, Greek text), but that originally had been rejected by the builders. Jesus is the cornerstone, on which everything rests and is secure. That God would set up a stone as a sure foundation had been prophesied by Isaiah: "I am laying in Zion a stone, a tested stone, a costly cornerstone for the foundation, firmly placed. He who believes in it will not be disturbed" (Isaiah 28:16). There would be only two possible responses to the Cornerstone: some would be broken on it (accepting it) and those who would be crushed by it (rejecting it; see Matthew 21:44; 1 Peter 2:3–8). For some He would be an offense; for those who believed, He would be their firm foundation. E. G. White explains: "In infinite wisdom, God chose the foundation stone, and laid it Himself. He called it 'a sure foundation.' The entire world may lay upon it their burdens and griefs; it can endure them all. With perfect safety they may build upon it. Christ is a 'tried stone.' Those who trust in Him, He never disappoints. He has borne every test. He has endured the pressure of Adam's guilt, and the guilt of his posterity, and has come off more than conqueror of the powers of evil. He has borne the burdens cast upon Him by every repenting sinner. In Christ the guilty heart has found relief. He is the sure foundation. All who make Him their dependence rest in perfect security."* Amen!

My Response: _____

---

* Ellen G. White, *The Desire of Ages* (Mountain View, CA: Pacific Press®, 1940), 598, 599.

HIS EXHORTATION

"You will be hearing of wars and rumors of wars. See that you are not frightened, for those things must take place."
—Matthew 24:6

The signs of the second coming of Jesus are like pointers on a map confirming that we are getting closer to our destination. A woman shared with me how her young children had learned different road landmarks to know when they were getting closer to their grandparents' place. As they recognized these signs, they grew more and more excited. Then she said: "This is the role of the signs of the second coming of Jesus. They are there so that we may recognize His closeness and get more and more excited!" I absolutely agree.

The signs of the coming of Christ were never meant to frighten us but to encourage us. The second coming of Jesus is the great hope of the Christian faith. Having died in His first advent in order to pay the ransom for humanity, the risen Christ will come a second time to take us to be with Him forever. It means the end of pain and death. It means that, just like in the beginning, we will be with our Beloved Creator and Redeemer. As we recognize the signs of His coming, we are to grow more and more excited! But Jesus knew that revealing troublesome times preceding His coming, His disciples, and we, could become fearful. Therefore, He gave this exhortation: "See that you are *not frightened*, for those things must take place" (Matthew 24:6). The original word translated as "frightened" may also be translated as *"alarmed"* or *"disturbed."* The reason not to be disturbed is because God is sovereign, and He is in total control of the redemption plan; these things "are necessary"; they must take place before the end. We often respond with fear to things we don't understand. It even happened to John when he saw a vision of Jesus. But Jesus said to him: "Do not be afraid; I am the first and the *last* . . . I was dead and behold, I am alive forevermore" (Revelation 1:17, 18). The word "last" is *eschatos* in Greek, which is the root of *eschatology*, the study of last day events. Jesus reminds us not to fear, because He is the first and the last (*eschatos*); He is the Alpha and the Omega, the Beginning and the End. We will never be alone!

My Response: _____

His Capacity

*"So that you may know that the Son of Man
has authority on earth to forgive sins."*

—Mark 2:10

I was a newly appointed senior pastor and went to church to prepare for that evening's event. I found a singing group, which sometimes used to rent our facilities, rehearsing in the main hall; they claimed someone had given them permission. I answered that we had an event there and that next time they should check availability directly with the pastor. Then a man from the group addressed me, "And who are you, dear?" "I am the pastor," I replied. After an awkward silence, the director introduced me to the group. Sometimes, we still laugh about it.

Has anyone ever questioned your position, role, or capability? In the Gospels, the scribes and Pharisees are constantly second-guessing the identity and capacity of Jesus. When Jesus said to the paralytic: "Son, your sins are forgiven" (Mark 2:5), the scribes started questioning in their hearts: "Why does this man speak that way? He is blaspheming; who can forgive sins but God alone?" (verse 7). This is the first of five consecutive controversy stories between scribes and/or Pharisees and Jesus. Why was this pronouncement not acceptable to the experts of the law? The passive phrase "Your sins are forgiven" would have been used by those who acted as God's representatives when announcing that a person's sins were forgiven; similar phrases were heard at the temple after the person had brought his or her sacrifice and a confession was heard. The priest would say something like "Your sins have been forgiven," because the priests and the teachers of the law often used the passive form to describe God's acts on behalf of the people. But now Jesus has opened up new access to grace, and they don't like it! Jesus, knowing their questions about His authority and capacity, said to them, "So that you may know that the Son of Man has authority on earth to forgive sins," before saying to the paralytic, "I say to you, get up, pick your pallet and go home" (verses 10, 11). And he did. Now, wherever you are, without any other intermediaries or mediators, Jesus has the capacity and the prerogative to forgive you and heal you.

My Response: _____

HIS APPRAISAL

"There will be more joy in heaven over one sinner who repents than over ninety-nine righteous persons who need no repentance."
—Luke 15:7

In studying organizational behavior, I was exposed to the concept of *reification* as used in corporate psychology. The word signifies the added abstract value/meaning of an item that otherwise might not be worth much. If an outside corporate consultant is hired to facilitate change, before suggesting the disposal of certain items such as pictures and decors, these must be first apprised of any special meaning or sentimental value these items may have for the people; in other words, the consultant must consider the *reification* of that item, and preserve it.

There are many items in life that surpass their mathematical or monetary value, such as photos, memories, et cetera. When it comes to people and animals, these are simply irreplaceable. Jesus told a parable of a lost sheep to a group of religious leaders who were complaining that Jesus was eating with sinners (Luke 15:1–7). A similar parable is found in Matthew 18:12–14, but there it is used in the setting of the recovery of someone who has wandered away from the kingdom's community. Luke's setting for this parable is Heaven's eagerness to seek the lost and the joy of their recovery. "What man among you, if he has a hundred sheep and has lost one of them, does not leave the ninety-nine in the open pasture and go after the one which is lost until he finds it?" (Luke 15:4). The parable is one long question that sounds like, "Who among you wouldn't do the same?" If you have five children and one of them gets lost, would you take out the calculator and say, "It's OK, I have eighty percent left?" Of course not! You would search passionately *until* she's found. The point of the parable is not to find out who cared for the ninety-nine while the shepherd was gone but to realize the value the Shepherd places on each one of his sheep. The appraised value of the one sheep is one hundred percent because of what it means to the Shepherd. Your value in heaven's eyes is limitless and infinite. If you were the only one lost, Jesus would have died just for you. You mean too much for Him. He won't give up in His search for you!

My Response: _____

HIS SEARCH

*"Or what woman, if she has ten silver coins and loses
one coin, does not light a lamp and sweep the house
and search carefully until she finds it?"*

—Luke 15:8

Have you ever lost something really valuable to you? I remember several years ago when someone lost their wedding ring. It was a very simple ring, made of an inexpensive material, but it had the couple's names and wedding date engraved on it and meant an awful lot to them. We looked for it in every possible place, including a large trash dumpster. We took all its content out and meticulously combed through every piece of trash. I don't even recall where the ring was ultimately found, but I do remember the intense search.

When the Pharisees were grumbling against Jesus because He was receiving sinners (Luke 15:1, 2), Jesus told them three parables. In Luke's narrative style, the first two parables are a man-woman pair. The man who loses a sheep is followed by the second parable of a woman who loses a coin (Luke 15:8–10). She loses one of her ten *drachmas*, which were silver coins with an approximate value of one day's wage. These coins would have been her savings for a rainy day. Some argue that this was part of her *ketubah*, her dowry, which would be the only money she brought into the marriage and her only financial safety in case of a divorce. In this parable, the woman represents God's passionate search and recovery of sinners; God is the active Agent portrayed in the four stages of recovery in the parable. First, the woman *initiates the search*. Second, she employs *every resource* she has available, such as using a lamp, sweeping the house, and searching carefully. Third, she perseveres, *until* she finds it; not giving up *until* the recovery is successful. Fourth, she has a celebration of joy for the recovery. God passionately searches for us, using infinite resources that we don't know anything about. If you have a wayward child or grandchild, may you find great comfort in knowing that God doesn't give up on us *until* He recovers what is lost. This is the true biblical picture of God: His passionate *search for us*. Our search for God is only a response; His search for us precedes our search for Him.

My Response: _____

HIS DESIGN

He said, "This sickness is not to end in death, but for the glory of God, so that the Son of God may be glorified by it."

—John 11:4

In the life of a Christian there are *unseen certainties*. It seems like an oxymoron, but it is the premise on which the Gospel of John is written. There is a reality that we see, but there is also a deeper and more important reality that we do not see; one that we can access only through belief in Jesus Christ and His design for our lives. Faith is like a pair of glasses through which we perceive an unseen reality that we come to trust above and beyond anything our physical eyes can see.

Lazarus, Martha, and Mary are introduced in John 11:1. The sisters send a message to Jesus with the news that their brother is sick, and it is safe to assume that a plea for help is implied: "So the sisters sent word to Him, saying, 'Lord, behold, he whom You love is sick' " (verse 3). Martha and Mary are relying on Jesus' love for their brother. The name *Lazarus* is a form of the name *Eleazar*, which means "God is my help," and they really need God's help this time. When Jesus hears the news, He tells those who are with Him that there is a plan; this sickness is not to end in death; it is for the Son of God to be glorified (verse 4). Wow! I would love to know the plan, wouldn't you? But we usually don't know the plan, only God does, and we come to trust His design over our own perspective of the situation. The juxtaposition of the next two verses is paradoxical: "Now Jesus loved Martha and her sister and Lazarus. So when He heard that he was sick, He then stayed two days longer in the place where He was" (John 11:5, 6). How strange! It doesn't make sense to say: "He loved—so He delayed," or does it? Obviously, it wasn't that Jesus lacked affection and therefore got delayed! God's timing is part of His design, and He knows what, and when, will bring Him the most glory, giving witness to His love and power. We can learn to trust it, even when we can't understand it. I have made myself a motto: *God's apparent delays are designed to show the magnitude of the miracle.* I love it! When we can't understand God's timing, we can trust His love and His design for our lives.

My Response: _____

HIS EXPANSION

"The kingdom of heaven is like leaven, which a woman took and hid in three pecks of flour until it was all leavened."
—Matthew 13:33

Recently, I had to make some radical changes in my garden. When we moved to this house four years ago, we had chosen some plants for the backyard, along with some rose bushes. Four years later, two of those plants had grown so much that they had completely taken over one side of the garden. I had to hire a professional to extirpate the two plants with their intricate root system, which was almost impossible to remove. This is the type of visualization that Jesus chose in order to explain the surprising expansion of the kingdom of heaven on earth.

In Matthew 13, Jesus told two parables that contrast the undetectable beginnings of the kingdom of heaven and the astonishing growth that no one can disregard. Both portray an almost imperceptible start. The first parable is about the mustard seed: "The kingdom of heaven *is like* a mustard seed, which a man took and sowed in his field" (Matthew 13:31). The mustard seed was the smallest known seed at the time, attested to in extra-biblical sources, and it was used as a symbol of comparatively tiny dimension (see Matthew 17:20 in regards to faith). The kingdom of heaven had begun, but not in the way it was expected. Yet it was to grow larger than anyone could have thought: "But when it is full grown, it is larger than the garden plants and becomes a tree, so that the birds of the air come and nest in its branches" (Matthew 13:32, see Daniel 4:21). The second parable is about a woman who "hides" leaven in a dough "until it was *all* leavened" (Matthew 13:33). The leaven is *incognito*, but Jesus assures us that its influence becomes undeniable. The same is true with the Jesus movement and its humble beginnings, which eventually became a world-wide phenomenon with eternal consequences. We all have family and friends that we would like to see come to the Lord. These two parables are very encouraging because they remind us that we shouldn't ever underestimate the kingdom's growth in a human heart. God works behind the scenes. Give time for the leaven of the gospel to do its work.

My Response: _____

HIS REIGN

"Repent, for the kingdom of heaven is at hand."

—Matthew 3:2

I had not seen my very dear cousin Elena for a very long time. Now she was coming from South America in order to visit me in the USA. Anticipation was building up for both of us as the time was drawing near. She was crossing off the days on her calendar, and I was excitedly getting a room ready for her. And finally, the day arrived when our anticipations became a reality! Can you remember the anticipation you felt while waiting for the arrival of a child or dear friend? There is nothing like the indescribable feeling of the fulfillment of a long-awaited hope.

God's ultimate reign on earth had been prophesied throughout Israel's history, and the announcement of the nearness of the kingdom of heaven resounded with much excitement throughout the Judean territory. Matthew abruptly transitions from Jesus' infancy to his adult ministry by introducing John the Baptist who "came, preaching in the wilderness of Judea" (3:1). The message he brings is unequivocal: "Repent, for the kingdom of heaven is at hand" (3:2; repeated by Jesus in Matthew 4:17). The first verb is an imperative in the present tense, which could be translated as "turn," "return," "have a change of heart," "change your way," et cetera. There was an urgency in his message; a crucial action was needed to prepare for the long-awaited fulfillment. "The kingdom of heaven" is used by Matthew thirty-three times, but it is unique to his Gospel, as it is found nowhere else in the New Testament. Finally, the long-awaited reign of God was beginning on the earth. It had come near; it was about to arrive in the person of Jesus. And it did! The kingdom of heaven is among us, and we can already partake of its blessings of peace and joy, even though it has not yet been fully consummated. This is what we call the "already and not yet" of God's reign on earth. It has *already* started through the ministry, death, and resurrection of Jesus, but it has *not yet* completely eradicated sin and evil, which God will accomplish at the time of the second coming of Jesus. We are living in between those two realities. What a time of exciting expectancy as we wait for our Savior to come back for us!

My Response: _____

His Guarantee

" 'I am the Alpha and the Omega,' says the Lord God."
—Revelation 1:8

It was supposed to be a normal trip, but it wasn't. I made sure my bag had a tag clearly indicating the beginning and the end of my trip: LAX–HSV. We had a weather-related delay on the second leg, which I am quite used to. I arrived in Huntsville close to midnight, only to find that my bag had not made it. I had to conduct my seminars without the props, microphone, and clothes that I had carefully packed. My luggage was delivered to my hotel the day I left. I wondered: what part of *"from LAX to HSV"* didn't the airport scanners understand?

Maybe it is because of experiences like this, and not only in travel but in relationships, jobs, finances, et cetera that most of us become a bit anxious about the future outcome of our lives and the world. God knows that one of the hardest places for us to be is *in-between*, a place where we are neither here nor there. Deep within, we all long to know our final destination and to have a certainty that we are going to reach it. The truth is that we all find ourselves living in this space called *in-between*; between the *already* and the *not yet*. Jesus *already* paid the price and is victorious; but He has *not yet* come for us to end all pain and to recreate this earth. This is why I cherish so much the fact that in the introduction to the book of Revelation, one of the first pictures of Jesus is " 'I am the Alpha and the Omega,' says the Lord God, 'who is and who was and who is to come, the Almighty' " (Revelation 1:8). *Alpha* is the first letter of the Greek alphabet, and *omega* is the last letter. Thus, in our terms, God announces that He is the A and the Z, and whether you look to the past, present, or future, He is there; He is the first and the last (Revelation 1:17; 2:8), and He is the Victor! This portrait is also found in the very last chapter of the Bible: "I am the Alpha and the Omega, the first and the last, the beginning and the end" (Revelation 22:13). Whether you are facing a problem that starts with an A or a Z, or any other letter in between, *you are covered*! He is the beginning, the middle, and the end. He guarantees that there is absolutely no way to get lost *in between* when you follow Him! Hallelujah!

My Response: _____

HIS AUTHORITY

The centurion said, "Lord, I am not worthy for You to come under my roof, but just say the word, and my servant will be healed."
—Matthew 8:8

Having unsuccessfully tried to fix a problem with one of my utility bills, I was almost ready to give up because I had spoken to many different agents, none of whom seemed to be able to resolve the issue. But I decided to try one more time. I asked to speak with someone who actually had authority to fix the problem: a supervisor. Within a few minutes, a year-long problem was resolved. She had a different clearance level and was obviously able to override what others couldn't.

The centurion had a problem that no one could fix, except Jesus. Even though he was a Gentile, the military official came to the renowned Jewish teacher imploring relief and healing for his paralyzed servant (Matthew 8:5, 6; the Greek word may also be translated as son). Luke adds that the Jewish elders were trying to persuade Jesus to help him, saying "He is worthy for You to grant this to him; for he loves our nation and it was he who built us our synagogue" (Luke 7:4, 5). It was not lawful for a Jewish man to enter the home of a Gentile, yet Jesus tells him, "I will come and heal him" (Matthew 8:7). Some scholars translate this sentence as a question: "You want me to come and heal him?" Either way, the centurion answered: "Lord, I am not worthy . . . but just say the word, and my servant will be healed" (Matthew 8:8). He goes on to explain that he understands authority and what it means to receive and give orders while expecting obedience. The one who had been recommended as "worthy" now says "I am not worthy" and goes on to imply that he is certain that Jesus has complete authority over the disease, and that just a word from Him will suffice! Wow! And this statement of absolute faith came from a Gentile! No wonder Jesus was *amazed* at the centurion's faith (verse 10). The servant was healed that very moment (verse 13). I want to remember this all-encompassing authority of Jesus every time there is a problem too big for me to handle. He is in complete control, and we are not. Be assured that He is sovereign, and all authority over our problems has been given to Him (see Matthew 28:18).

My Response: _____

His Conquering

*The tombs were opened, and many bodies of the saints
who had fallen asleep were raised.*

—Matthew 27:52

I have a little sign on my refrigerator. I bought it in a Christian store after my mom passed away from cancer. It reads "For cancer is so limited—It cannot cripple love, shatter hope, corrode faith, destroy peace; it cannot kill friendship, suppress memories, silence courage, invade the soul; it cannot steal God's gift of eternal life, it cannot quench the Holy Spirit, *it cannot lessen the power of the resurrection."* The tomb is not the last word.

There is a striking passage found in Matthew 27:52, 53, which is not found in any other Gospel. After Jesus yielded up His Spirit (verse 50), and the veil of the temple was torn, and the rocks were split, Matthew records the amazing event of the resurrection of many saints, linking their rising from the dead with the power of Jesus over death. From Old Testament times, there was an expectation that when the Messiah came, He would have power over death (see Daniel 12:2; Isaiah 26:19, and Ezekiel 37:13). Matthew points out that this expectation was fulfilled through the death of Jesus; resurrection and salvation are shown as the result of the death of Jesus. His death *conquered* death! When Jesus died, so did death.

Jesus' sacrifice on our behalf was confirmed when He rose from the dead. We have the assurance that death is not permanent for those who believe in Jesus. When mourning the companionship of a loved one you lost, remember that Jesus already conquered death! The resurrection of many saints, which occurred that weekend, foreshadows the upcoming resurrection of *all* believers in Christ at His second coming. This is the blessed assurance that we have, especially at a time when we have lost a loved one, or when we ourselves are facing death. Death is not the end! The resurrection is followed by eternal life, because Jesus conquered death and He has the keys of death (Revelation 1:18). Jesus said: "An hour is coming, in which all who are in the tombs will hear His voice" (John 5:28). Jesus wins! Take heart, and comfort each other with His words of assurance.

My Response: _____

---

* Author unknown

His Capability

Immediately the boy's father cried out and said,
"I do believe; help my unbelief."

—Mark 9:24

When I was a little girl, my aunt sent me a doll. It was every girl's dream; it had built-in functions! She would move her eyes, suck on her bottle, and do other fascinating things. I loved her! But one day the mechanism broke down, and I was distraught. My parents told me that they would *operate* on her, but I couldn't come into the room while the "surgery" was going on. I believed in my parents' capability to do it but still was so nervous that I got a skin rash while waiting!

When it comes to our beloved children in real life, sometimes our faith seems to fail us. We wonder if God is capable of healing their minds and restoring their souls. Perhaps other people have failed us in the past, and now we hesitate to surrender our children to our Father. This is what happened to the father with the demon-possessed child. When Jesus and His three disciples came down from the mount of Transfiguration, they found the rest of the disciples with a crowd (Mark 9:14). Jesus asked them, "What are you discussing with them?" (verse 16). A father explained that he had brought his son, who was afflicted by a mute spirit, to the disciples to be healed, but they had not been able to do it. With great anguish, the father related how this spirit had tormented his son since childhood. For a moment, Jesus allowed the evil spirit to display its power, in order to highlight the magnitude of the miracle that He was about to perform. The father said to Jesus, "*If You can do anything,* take pity on us and help us!" (verse 22). Jesus responded: " 'If You can?' All things are possible to him who believes" (verse 23). At that moment, the father realized that even though he believed, at the same time his faith was lacking, and he cried out: "I do believe; help my unbelief" (verse 24). Jesus rebuked the spirit, and it came out. When we believe in Him, God's infinite capabilities are set in motion, and nothing is impossible for Him! Oh, by the way, my parents did fix my doll. In real life, God is more than capable to save and heal our loved ones. Believe! And turn your loved ones over to Him! Trust His capability to save!

My Response: _____

HIS COMMITMENT

*"When He, the Spirit of truth, comes, He will guide you
into all the truth. . . . He will glorify Me, for He will take
of Mine and will disclose it to you."*

—John 16:13, 14

I lost my mom two years before I lost my dad. When I lost my second parent, I technically became an orphan, yet I never expected this new stage to be so painful. There is something about the unconditional love of godly parents that is irreplaceable. A friend of mine described it as a loving "safety blanket" that you lose and never get back. I am so thankful for the assurance of the resurrection!

Jesus told His disciples that He wouldn't leave them as orphans (John 14:18). When He revealed to the disciples that He was about to go away, they became troubled and He comforted them (see John 14). He encouraged them by disclosing that He would be preparing a place and would be coming back for them. He also promised a Helper, a Comforter, an Encourager—namely the Holy Spirit. Later on, in John 16, Jesus again addressed His commitment to send the Holy Spirit: "But I tell you the truth, it is to your advantage that I go away; for if I do not go away, the Helper will not come to you; but if I go, I will send Him to you. And He, when He comes, will convict the world concerning sin and righteousness and judgment; concerning sin, because they do not believe in Me; and concerning righteousness, because I go to the Father and you no longer see Me; and concerning judgment, because the ruler of this world has been judged" (John 16:7–11). I have always been fascinated with this description of the Holy Spirit's role. He comes to convict us of the sin of disbelief in Jesus. He also convicts us of the righteousness of God in Christ, because Jesus would ascend to heaven, and only the Spirit would be able to convince us that it is only through the perfect life and death of Jesus, and not by our own works, that we are declared righteous in the sight of God (see Romans 3:21–26). Lastly, the Spirit would come to remind us of the outcome, for the adversary of God has already been judged at the cross, and Jesus wins! Yes! We know how the story ends! Come, Spirit, come! Light our hearts on fire with a new understanding of the assurance that we have in Jesus!

My Response: _____

HIS COVENANT

"To show mercy toward our fathers, and to remember His holy covenant, the oath which He swore to Abraham our father."

—Luke 1:72, 73

The events in redemption history do not happen in a vacuum. They are part of the bigger picture and of the plan of salvation designed before the Creation of the world. And we are to connect the dots to interpret the Scriptures accurately. Joel B. Green explains: "From the standpoint of the Lukan narrative, the key to making sense of the death of Jesus lies in construing it within the matrix of 'the scriptures.' . . . What has happened with Jesus can be understood only in light of the Scriptures, yet the Scriptures themselves can be understood only in light of what has happened with Jesus."* Luke takes this very seriously. And not only does he connect the dots between the Old Testament and the death of Jesus (see Luke 24:27, 44) but he does it for all of Jesus' ministry, including His birth.

When Zacharias regained his voice after doubting the angel's message regarding the birth of his son, he praised God with a prophetic hymn (see Luke 1:68–79). This song has been called "Benedictus," after its first words in Latin. In this song, Zacharias praises God for visiting His people to accomplish their redemption. He reaches all the way back to Abraham and the prophets, connecting the upcoming roles of both John the Baptist and Jesus the Messiah, as part of the salvific covenant that God had made from the beginning. This is the only time that the word "covenant" is used in the four Gospels (Luke 1:72), aside from the explanation of Jesus in the Last Supper, that His blood was, in fact, the blood of the covenant (see Luke 22:20; Mark 14:24; Matthew 26:28). Yet Luke, throughout his Gospel, often emphasizes that the life and death of Jesus had been prophesied in the Law, the Prophets, and the Psalms long before. I find great assurance in understanding that God has a detailed plan for our salvation, and that He has been faithful to His redemptive covenant throughout the centuries. And He is faithful in our own individual lives as well, guiding us, and our loved ones, providentially, in order to fulfill His redemptive purposes in us. He is loyal to His salvific covenant!

My Response: _____

———————
* Joel B. Green, *The Gospel of Luke*, NICNT (Grand Rapids, MI: Eerdmans, 1997), 843, 844.

His Certainty

"Everyone who beholds the Son and believes in Him will have eternal life, and I Myself will raise him up on the last day."
—John 6:40

There are moments in life that you never forget. My father's cancer had returned aggressively, and there was nothing more that medicine could do. I went to his house to anoint him with oil, and we surrendered to whatever God's will was for him. It was a very special and profound moment. He had complete peace in his heart. I read John 11:25: "I am the resurrection and the life; he who believes in me will live even if he dies." Then I asked him: "Do you believe this?" and he answered: "Yes! I do!" He passed away a few days later. I will never forget the certainty of his conviction that Jesus will raise him up.

Jesus Himself gave this certainty to those who come to believe in Him: "I Myself will raise him up on the last day" (John 6:40). I have embraced this assurance with all my heart, and it became my anchor when I lost both of my parents within a short period of time. I find a two-fold certainty in this statement of Jesus. First of all, Jesus takes this personally, with an emphatic *"I Myself."* *He Himself* will raise those who believe in Him, which points to the fact that He is taking personal responsibility for the resurrection of His followers. The second part of this amazing certainty is the verbal tense: "I *will* raise up." It is a future reality, not just a possibility. It's not, "I might" or "I may," but "I *will* raise him up." We are living in an age of uncertainty, when everything around us is constantly changing, from technology to politics and economics. Yet in Jesus we find the unchanging Rock of our salvation; He gives us the assurance of the resurrection and eternal life. We still live in this world of sin, with pain, illness and death. But these are temporary realities that soon will be no more (Revelation 21:4)! Jesus died on the cross for us and resurrected on the third day; His death overcame death itself (see Matthew 27:52, 53). When I visit my parents' tomb, I am reminded that this is their temporary place of rest. Jesus has given us the *certainty* that *He Himself* will raise our loved ones. May His certainty comfort you!

My Response: _____

HIS DISPOSITION

"I am the good shepherd; the good shepherd
lays down His life for the sheep."

—John 10:11

My husband met a couple who shared a very moving story. Their daughter needed a bone marrow transplant, and her little brother was a perfect match to be a donor. The parents asked him if he would be willing to save his sister's life by donating his bone marrow. He agreed without hesitation. After the procedure that took place in the hospital, he asked in a tremulous voice, "And how long before I die?" What a display of love! The little boy had agreed to save his sister, mistakenly thinking all along that he would be giving up his own life in the process.

Jesus didn't just *think* that He would give up His life for us; He actually *did*. It wasn't only His willingness but the very act of laying down His life that saved us. Our assurance comes from *who* He is and *what* He has done. Jesus Himself highlighted the contrast between the good shepherd and a hired hand, who, taking care of the sheep for money, would flee when danger arose. But not the shepherd! He would protect them even to the point of losing his life in the process. Jesus said: "I am the good shepherd; the good shepherd lays down His life for the sheep. He who is a hired hand, and not a shepherd, who is not the owner of the sheep, sees the wolf coming, and leaves the sheep and flees, and the wolf snatches them and scatters them. He flees because he is a hired hand and is not concerned about the sheep." (John 10:11–13). *You are the apple of His eye; He places your well-being higher than His own life.* If we find ourselves in want, we can fully trust in the Shepherd's capability to provide what we need, and in His disposition to tenderly care for us. His sacrifice became a reality at the cross. We have assurance for this life and eternity because Jesus has already proven His faithfulness. When danger assails us as a wolf attacking sheep, we can be assured that the Shepherd will never abandon us. On the contrary, it is in our darkest times that we realize that He does for us what the sheep cannot do for themselves!

My Response: _____

His Closeness

*Seeing them straining at the oars . . . He came
to them, walking on the sea.*

—Mark 6:48

As a young girl, Psalm 46 was one of my favorite Scriptures. I was always impressed by the fact that God is both our refuge and strength, a *very present* help, even in the midst of a disaster. This Psalm provided a great comfort to my young soul. Now, as an adult, I continue to rely on God's powerful, comforting Presence, and in His ability to be close to me at all times, especially in the midst of the dark and painful storms of life. Surely, He is our very present help in trouble.

It was the evening after a busy day of ministry. Mark tells us that the disciples were in a boat in the middle of the lake, while Jesus had stayed behind on the land (Mark 6:47). Though physically distant, there was no spiritual separation between them; Jesus was always aware of their whereabouts. This is when the storm hits, and the disciples, apparently left on their own, seem to be losing their battle against the forces of nature. "*Seeing them straining at the oars,* for the wind was against them, at about the fourth watch of the night He came to them, walking on the sea" (verse 48). This is such a comforting verse! Jesus saw them struggling; at no point was Jesus unaware of the location and situation of His beloved followers even though He was not physically with them. He came to aid them in their time of need as a response to His awareness of their struggle. He chose to come to them in the fourth watch of the night (between 3:00 A.M. and 6:00 A.M.), yet at all times He was conscious of their whereabouts. It is in our most difficult hour that we may experience most vividly God's closeness to us. There is no darkness so dense that the Son of God cannot penetrate with His light. Jesus came walking to them *on the water,* which was a unique demonstration of His sovereign power and divinity. Even though His disciples had seen the multiplication of bread, they had not fully understood the depth of the divine identity of Jesus nor His salvific plan. May you be encouraged by the realization that the most powerful Being in the universe is also the closest to you in time of need.

My Response: _____

HIS APPROACH

But when the day was now breaking, Jesus stood on the beach;
yet the disciples did not know that it was Jesus.

—John 21:4

I t is not easy to reach out to a person who is in the midst of a confusing or difficult moment, especially if they feel lost. My father was particularly gifted in this area. When I was a young adult and found myself in trouble, I would speak with my father. Somehow his approach to problems was logical yet tender and loving. Even when I had gotten myself in trouble, his motivation was always to help and to offer hope, not punishment.

I am moved by the tenderness of Jesus as He reached out to His disciples in their darkest moments. One such case is narrated in John 21:1–11. Peter decides to go fishing after Jesus had been crucified; and six other disciples join him. This fishing trip, right after the disconcerting events that had transpired in Jerusalem, portrays a group of men who were confused and lacked direction. We are not told if they went fishing simply to try to forget about their troubles or due to a financial need. Whatever the reason, the futility of their attempt, after a nightlong effort, is summarized in one sentence: "That night they caught nothing" (verse 3). At dawn, the risen Jesus *stood* on the beach (verse 4). He appeared in the midst of their frustration and confusion. God *always* comes to us in our distress, approaching us tenderly and compassionately, bringing hope and miraculous help. He comes to save, not to punish. They did not recognize Him, just like in other appearances of the risen Christ to Mary Magdalene (John 20:14) and on the way to Emmaus (Luke 24:16). He then addressed them with the most tender expression: *"Children . . ."* (John 21:5). He calls them children! (The NIV translates it as *friends*). How thoughtful of Jesus to approach these tough fishermen as a loving father approaches a child. Then He asked them a question and performed a miracle to fulfill their need (see tomorrow's devotional). God reveals Himself to us in powerful ways during our darkest times of confusion and frustration. He comes to us as our Father, with affection, compassion, and the assurance of His saving love for us.

My Response: _____

HIS ATTENTIVENESS

They saw a charcoal fire already laid and fish placed on it, and bread. . . .
Jesus said to them, "Come and have breakfast."
—John 21:9–12

When we are concerned about a loved one who is in need of help, peace, or guidance, it is crucial to remember that God is even more interested in their well-being than we are! When Abraham had to send Hagar and Ishmael away, he was greatly distressed because of his son (Genesis 21:9–21). As they wandered about in the wilderness, God heard the lad crying, and He provided water and all they needed. God is always attentive to all our needs and those of our loved ones.

Yesterday we started studying the third manifestation of the risen Christ to a group of His disciples in the Gospel of John. He appeared to them by the Sea of Galilee (Sea of Tiberias). After they had unsuccessfully tried to catch fish all night, He addressed them: " 'Children, you do not have any fish, do you?' They answered Him, 'No.' And He said to them, 'Cast the net on the right-hand side of the boat and you will find a catch.' So they cast, and then they were not able to haul it in because of the great number of fish." (John 21:5, 6). That's when they realized that it was the Lord, and Peter threw himself into the sea (verse 7). They brought in one hundred fifty-three large fish (verse 11). This miraculous catch was reminiscent of a similar event at the beginning of the disciples' call to public ministry (Luke 5:1–11), when they had left everything to follow Him. Now they were reminded of their calling, after the death and resurrection of Jesus. And I am extremely touched that Jesus, knowing that they had a hard and unfruitful night, prepared a hot breakfast for them! When they got out of the water, they found a charcoal fire lit and some fish and bread. And, evocative of the Lord's Supper, Jesus, "took the bread and gave it to them" (John 21:13). Later, Jesus restored Peter, who had denied Him, back to ministry. Jesus supplied them with a great miracle, a warm breakfast, and a restoration to ministry, all in the same morning. The same God who has saved us, is *attentive* to *all* of our needs. I invite you to submit yourself and your loved ones into His loving and vigilant care.

My Response: _____

HIS MESSAGE

He [Paul] went to them. . . explaining and giving evidence that the
Christ had to suffer and rise again from the dead.
—Acts 17:2, 3

I took a trip called "In the Footsteps of Paul." Most cities on the tour were located in Greece, with the exception of Ephesus (Turkey). It was quite exciting to see signs on the highways pointing to Thessalonica, Corinth, Athens, et cetera as if history had become alive in front of my eyes! Aside from the amazing sites we visited, I also became much more aware of the opposition Paul had met when proclaiming the message of Jesus. The believing brethren had to send him from one town to another because of the agitation caused by unbelieving Jews.

Jesus gave His disciples the assurance of His presence (Matthew 28:18–20), but He never promised that they wouldn't encounter fierce opposition when preaching the gospel. Jesus said that we should rejoice when people insult and persecute us because of His name, "for your reward in heaven is great; for in the same way they persecuted the prophets who were before you" (Matthew 5:12). Paul must have been a very joyful person . . . because he was persecuted quite a bit! When Paul arrived in Thessalonica, he went to the synagogue to reason with the Jews about Jesus from the Scriptures, which he did for three Sabbaths (Acts 17:2). The core of his message is found in today' devotional text: *he gave evidence that Jesus had to die and rise again,* and that He was the Christ (verse 3). Some believed, but the Jews became jealous and formed a mob and, "set the city in an uproar" (verse 5). They even followed him to Berea! (verse 13). The fiercest opponents of Jesus during His public ministry were the Jews, God's chosen people; and they were the most violent opponents of Paul as well. It's astonishing that the most intense opposition to the gospel came from those who were devoted students of the Scriptures. You have the assurance of God's Presence even in the midst of hostility against a Christ-centered message. Opposition is not a sign that you are on the wrong path. Like Paul, you may be called to stand alone with God, even in law-keeping, Bible-studying, or church-attending environments. May you stand in full assurance of faith.

My Response: _____

HIS ENCOURAGEMENT

And the Lord said to Paul in the night by a vision, "Do not be afraid any longer, but go on speaking and do not be silent."
—Acts 18:9

The ancient city of Corinth is an impressive place to behold. The archaeological sites include, among other things, the marketplace and traces of small shops along the main street, as well as remnants of public baths. As we were walking down the main street, someone in our group pointed out that it was very possible that we could be walking in front of Paul's tent-making place of business. It felt as if we were walking through the pages of the Bible, specifically the eighteenth chapter of Acts. Surely Paul walked this street and preached in this city!

The city of Corinth was a commercial trade center on a land bridge. It was accessible by sea routes from east and west, and by land from north and south. In Acts 18, we read about Paul's arrival to Corinth from Athens, and how he stayed with Aquila and Priscila, fellow leather workers from Italy, who had also come to Corinth, "because Claudius had commanded all the Jews to leave Rome" (verse 2). Paul, as was his custom, went to the synagogue every Sabbath to reason with the Jews to convince them that "Jesus was the Christ" (verse 5), the Messiah, whom they had been waiting for throughout the centuries. Can you imagine Paul, a Jew of Jews, trying to convince the Jews that in Jesus all of the redemption promises of God had come true? Oh, how much I would have liked to hear his gospel presentations! But the audience resisted and blasphemed so much that he had to leave and go to the Gentiles . . . which, by the way, was next door to the synagogue, in the house of Titius Justus (verse 7). Every once in a while, we all need strong encouragement. Paul received a vision in Corinth. The Lord appeared to him with a fivefold message (verses 9, 10): (1) Do not be afraid; (2) Be bold for the gospel; (3) I am with you; (4) The opposition will not prevail against you; (5) I have many people in Corinth (He knows *where His people are*). The same Christ who had redeemed the world was with him personally! Perhaps you are needing encouragement today. Do not be afraid. Go on! Jesus Christ is on your side!

My Response: _____

HIS OWN

"I am with you, and no man will attack you in order to harm you, for I have many people in this city."

—Acts 18:10

When I was in my twenties, my aunt, who loves to talk about Jesus, had invited her young hairdresser to study the Bible, with me as the Bible teacher. My aunt was there, bringing a tasty breakfast to every meeting. We concluded the series and the young lady didn't make a decision for Christ. It seemed like a futile endeavor. Many years went by, and one day my aunt saw her again, and was happily surprised to learn that she had been baptized, was attending church, and had become a zealous missionary, bringing dozens of her relatives to the feet of Jesus! God knows where His own people are and will not leave us in the darkness, even if it takes a little while for us to accept the Light!

The Lord encouraged Paul in a vision, after the apostle found fierce opposition in the Corinthian synagogue: "Do not be afraid any longer, but go on speaking and do not be silent; for I am with you, and no man will attack you in order to harm you, for I have many people in this city" (Acts 18:9, 10). Having been persecuted by the Jews in Thessalonica and Berea, Paul had come to Corinth with "fear and in much trembling" (1 Corinthians 2:3), determined to preach nothing among them *except* Christ and Him crucified (verse 2). The Lord met him in the vision, assuring him of His presence, encouraging him to preach the gospel boldly, and reminding him that *He had many people in that city*. With renewed strength, Paul ended up staying there eighteen months. The opposition had erupted at the synagogue, and that's when Paul moved next door, to the house of Titius Justus (Acts 18:7). "Crispus, *the leader of the synagogue,* believed in the Lord with all his household" (verse 8). Who would have imagined! Well . . . God knew because He always knows where His own are to be found. I have an app on my iPhone called "Find Friends." When I open it, I see the location of my friends and loved ones at that very moment. God has a giant *"Find Friends app."* He knows exactly where His people are! He knows where you are, and He calls you His own!

My Response: _____

HIS TENACITY

"This Paul has persuaded and turned away a considerable number of people, saying that gods made with hands are no gods at all."
—Acts 19:26

When I saw ancient Ephesus for the first time I was stunned. I couldn't believe my eyes! It has impressive structures, a large marketplace, and a theater that could seat twenty-five thousand people! It boasted one of the seven wonders of the ancient world: the temple of Artemis, four times the size of the Parthenon in Athens! It was in this prosperous city that the dramatic events of Acts 19 took place.

I am overwhelmed by God's tenacity to reach cultures, societies, and people who are hostile toward the gospel. This gives me great assurance that God is reaching out to my friends and loved ones who are not walking in the way of the Lord. God doesn't give up, no matter how lost they may seem. When Paul preached the gospel in Ephesus, many extraordinary miracles occurred (see Acts 19:11–20). But there was also a fierce opposition. People oppose the gospel for various reasons: for religious, social, political, and, as in this case, financial considerations. Being that the pagan temple of Artemis was one of the seven wonders of the ancient world, visitors came from all over to see it and were buying souvenirs and amulets. Demetrius was a silversmith who made silver shrines of Artemis and had quite a lucrative business (verse 24). He was concerned with Paul's preaching. He gathered workers of the same trade, and said: "Not only in Ephesus, *but in almost all of Asia,* this Paul has persuaded and turned away a considerable number of people. . . . Not only is there danger that this trade of ours fall into disrepute, but also that the temple of the great goddess Artemis be regarded as worthless and that she whom *all Asia and the world worship* will even be dethroned from her magnificence" (Acts 19:26, 27). These statements caused a great crowd to assemble in the theater (read the outcome in verses 29–41). They devised one plot after another against Paul and the gospel he preached, yet God enabled him to continue proclaiming the good news in pagan cities. Be assured that God's tenacity to save continues to be the reality in our present day.

My Response: _____

His Certitude

Having said this, he took bread and gave thanks to God in the presence of all, and he broke it and began to eat.

—Acts 27:35

My mother and my aunt were on board a ship off the coast of South Africa when a fierce storm hit. The rocking was so violent that they thought they wouldn't make it, and it lasted for quite some time. The next day, to their surprise, they noticed a huge dent in the front of their large ship, and no one knew what they had collided with in the middle of the ocean. My mom never forgot that storm.

It was supposed to be a short trip along the shore of Crete, between Fair Havens and the intended port of Phoenix. But the violent wind, called "the Northeastern" came rushing down on them. "Since neither sun nor stars appeared for many days, and no small storm was assailing us, from then on *all hope of our being saved was gradually abandoned*" (Acts 27:20). Storms are scary because we don't know how or when they are going to end, and this was the situation for Paul. Yet in the middle of the storm an angel appeared to Paul and brought a message of certitude from God: "God has granted you all those who are sailing with you" (verse 24). Paul tried to encourage everyone because he knew they would be saved, but they were still in the storm. I refer to this as the in-between time: when we have been given the assurance of the future, but we are not yet there. After being in the storm for fourteen days, Paul encouraged them to eat (as they had not eaten for days). And Luke records what Paul did next: "He took bread and gave thanks to God . . . and he broke it and began to eat" (verse 35). These words are reminiscent of Jesus during the Lord's Supper (Eucharist), when He told His disciples to remember Him and His sacrifice until He comes. Now Paul offered them God's assurance even when they were still in the storm. The truth is that we are all in an in-between storm. Jesus has *already* conquered death, but He has *not yet* destroyed evil. Still, we can go through the storms of life with the certitude of salvation, because Jesus secured our destiny on the cross. So, take the bread. His broken body provides assurance for the future, even in the middle of the storm!

My Response: _____

HIS OPPORTUNITIES

And he [Paul] stayed two full years . . . preaching the kingdom of God and teaching concerning the Lord Jesus Christ.
—Acts 28:30, 31

A Christian pastor had been imprisoned for his faith. Even his family had rejected him due to his beliefs. In jail he was lacking many things, still he shared Christ with his cellmates and many of them were converted! Instead of becoming resentful, he took his circumstances as an opportunity to let others know about the gospel. Is it possible that what seems like a tragic misfortune is used by God as a divine opportunity to share Jesus?

We have the assurance that no trial is ever *wasted* if we let God use it for His glory and the growth of His kingdom. In the final chapters of the book of Acts, Paul encounters all kinds of difficulties, including a conspiracy to kill him, imprisonment, a violent storm, a shipwreck, and a poisonous viper, just to name a few. You would think that when he arrived in Rome to appear before Caesar, he would have been exhausted, resentful, and doubting God's protection and direction. Yet the gospel of Jesus Christ had completely taken over his life, and he used every trial and difficulty as an opportunity to write, preach, teach, sing, and testify about Jesus and what He had accomplished on the cross. When he got to Rome, it was no exception. He was put under house arrest with a soldier to guard him in his own rented lodging (see Acts 28:16, 30). And Paul did not waste any time! After three days, he called for the leaders of the Jews and tried to persuade them about Jesus (verse 23)! He also let them know that the salvation achieved by Christ was also for the Gentiles (verse 28). The Jews departed when they heard this, but this wasn't going to deter Paul, not now, not ever! The book of Acts ends with a victorious note about how he stayed there for two years, "welcoming all who came to him, preaching the kingdom of God and teaching concerning the Lord Jesus Christ with all openness, unhindered" (verses 30, 31). Like Paul, let's allow God to turn our disappointments into divine appointments to share the gospel of grace with those around us! Be assured that this will yield eternal results!

My Response: _____

HIS LONGING

*"How often I wanted to gather your children together,
the way a hen gathers her chicks under her wings,
and you were unwilling."*

—Matthew 23:37

When I was a little girl, I couldn't have dogs or cats as pets due to my asthma. We lived in the city, yet we had a good-sized backyard, so my parents got me a colorful pygmy hen and a rooster. Soon I was excitedly expecting little chicks that were about to hatch. About that time, we experienced a strong and long storm. The hen, with her motherly instincts, tried so hard to save her eggs in the chicken coop, yet the weather affected the development of the chicks and only one survived. She then focused all her tender care on that one. It was beautiful to watch!

In one of the most tender visualizations of God's efforts to save His children, Jesus uttered a heartfelt lament: "Jerusalem, Jerusalem, who kills the prophets and stones those who are sent to her! How often I wanted to gather your children together, the way a hen gathers her chicks under her wings, and you were unwilling" (Matthew 23:37). Jesus had previously exposed the Pharisees and scribes for killing the prophets (verses 29–32), and now He laments over the whole city. This longing of Jesus to reach those who were refusing God's plan of salvation, by killing the prophets and stoning the messengers, has touched my heart. The metaphor of His longing is filled with warmth and affection. He wanted to gather the *children* of Jerusalem as a hen gathers her brood. In the words of Donald Hagner: "The image of a mothering bird who gathers her young under her wings suggests such things as security, nurture, and well-being (cf. Ruth 2:12; Psalm 17:8; 36:7; Isaiah 31:5 among many OT examples). In the message of the dawning of the kingdom, this salvation had been offered repeatedly to the Jews."* But they were *unwilling*. They chose to reject Him. The reason why this passage brings me assurance is that in the words of Jesus, I find a glimpse of how God views us. Not only is He always ready to reach out to us, but He actually *longs* for us to become willing to be saved. He *longs* to place you under His redemptive wings. Are you willing?

My Response: _____

* Donald A. Hagner, *Matthew 14–28,* World Biblical Commentary, vol. 33b (Nashville, TN: Thomas Nelson, Inc., 1995), 680.

HIS SELECTION

"Make disciples of all the nations."

—Matthew 28:19

A lready serving in a ministerial capacity, I happened to see one of the supervisors of my geographical area. He asked me what graduate schools I had attended so far. My answer prompted this response, "That's too bad; if you had attended such and such a school, you could become a member of our new committee, because we are looking for someone just like you." I felt like an outsider, judged by something that had nothing to do with me as a person.

In the first century, many people felt like that. They were not of Jewish descent, and therefore not part of the "select" group of people that claimed to be God's own. On the other hand, some of the Jews pointed to their ancestry as a qualification to enter the kingdom. Matthew, who wrote to a predominantly Jewish audience, challenges the idea of God's *selective exclusivity* by ancestry, pedigree, nationality, background, or even institutional affiliation. The genealogy of Jesus in Matthew reminds us that there are no outsiders in the kingdom of God. Everyone is blessed through the sacrifice of Jesus: Abraham's descendants and foreigners, men and women, young and old, even those of us who have taken great detours away from the path of righteousness and are now totally dependent on God's grace, which is greater than our detours. Even though people may have told us that we do not qualify, the divine GPS reroutes our path. That all the nations and families of the earth would be blessed through *Abraham's Descendant*, had already been prophesied in Genesis 12:1–3, as part of God's covenant with him. Matthew starts his Gospel by reminding us that Jesus is the descendant of Abraham (Matthew 1:1), and ends his Gospel with Jesus reminding His followers of the inclusivity of His covenant, which says to make disciples of *all the nations* (Matthew 28:19), not just of the Jews, which would have been quite a shock for His followers. Some call this an *Abrahamic inclusio* (Matthew 1:1; 28:19), a narrative sandwich that reminds us that all the nations, all the families of the earth, people from every color and tongue, are included in God's selection for salvation. And that includes you and me! Hallelujah!

My Response: _____

PRAISING HIS WORTHINESS

His Title

*Jesus went out . . . to the villages of Caesarea Philippi;
and . . . He questioned His disciples, saying to them,
"Who do people say that I am?"*

—Mark 8:27

When I visited the ancient city of Caesarea Philippi, I encountered a really interesting background for today's text. This city, also named Paneas, after the pagan god Pan, was located at the base of Mount Hermon. It had a beautiful spring of water and a large cave that was known as the cave of Pan. There were several niches carved out of the rock next to it, where statues of gods were placed. This was an important center of pagan worship showcasing images of several pagan deities.

Seeing those pagan shrines carved in the rock, I could visualize Jesus in that place, asking His disciples: "Who do people say that I am?" (Mark 8:27). Throughout the first half of Mark, people had asked "Who is this man?" Now Jesus asked them the same question. "They told Him, saying, 'John the Baptist; and others say Elijah; but others, one of the prophets' " (verse 28). Then He asked His own disciples directly: "But who do *you* say that I am?" (verse 29). Peter answered, "You are the Christ" (verse 29). The first half of Mark emphasizes the authority of Jesus as *Son of God,* but now Jesus revealed that there was more to Him than His power. "He began to teach them that the Son of Man must suffer many things and be rejected by the elders and the chief priests and the scribes, and be killed, and after three days rise again" (verse 31; see also 9:31; 10:33). He was also the suffering Servant, the *Son of Man,* who would, "give His life a ransom for many" (10:45). "Son of Man" is the title that Jesus most often used when referring to Himself in the Gospels. It is a veiled messianic title from the Old Testament (see Daniel 7:13), and it is the title that most closely identifies Him with the human race. And who do *you* say that He is? He is not one of many deities, or a god who is aloof and distant. He is the Creator-Redeemer God, our Kinsman-Redeemer, who died to set us free. He is the One who knows us intimately; He guides us and provides what we need. He is worthy of our praise because of *who* He is, and what He has done!

My Response: _____

HIS APPROVAL

*"Let her alone, so that she may keep it
for the day of My burial."*

—John 12:7

Nick was born in Melbourne, Australia, without arms and legs. But that didn't stop him from becoming a worldwide evangelist.* Refusing to be resentful about his condition, he has consecrated his life to preaching about Jesus in response to God's love for him, and he is granted access to countries and groups of people forbidden to most of us. I personally experienced the power of his testimony and his heart for Christ, when he shared his journey at our church. Truly, the place was filled with the fragrance of the perfume of his devotion.

Mary, the sister of Lazarus, is usually found at the feet of Jesus (see Luke 10:39; John 11:32; 12:3); His love had truly captured her heart and she wanted to honor Him with the best she had to offer. In Bethany, a supper is prepared for Jesus and His disciples (John 12:2). Lazarus is there, Martha is serving, and suddenly Mary enters the scene with an exuberant and unconventional act of devotion. "Mary then took a pound of very costly perfume of pure nard, and anointed the feet of Jesus and wiped His feet with her hair; and the house was filled with the fragrance of the perfume" (John 12:3). The fragrance made it evident to all. With all eyes on her, she first took the position of a servant, anointing Jesus' feet, the lowliest of tasks in the festivities. Then, she offered her costly possession, appraised by Judas at a year's wages (three hundred denarii; verse 5). Third, she displays a spontaneous, unrestrained show of devotion by wiping Jesus' feet with her hair, something women wouldn't do in public. As is often the case, flamboyant acts of worship make someone else uncomfortable. Judas, who was dishonest and would betray Jesus, complained publicly (verse 4). Jesus defended Mary, publicly approving her selfless act of devotion and associating it with His upcoming burial (verse 7). Jesus was about to pour out the most precious liquid in the universe: His blood. The intrinsic motivation inspired by God's grace and love far exceeds the extrinsic motivation produced by fear, and elicits true and unrestrained devotion to Christ. May our lives be a fragrance that points to His love!

My Response: _____

---

* For more information on Nick's ministry, go to www.lifewithoutlimbs.org.

HIS SUPREMACY

"This is My beloved Son . . . listen to Him!"
—Matthew 17:5

Our ministry, Jesus 101 (www.Jesus101.tv), started a children's section, and our first resource was a coloring book entitled *Discovering Jesus in the Bible*,* designed to teach children about Jesus from well-known Old Testament stories. Every page contains two pictures to color: on the left side there is a visualization of an Old Testament story (Abraham, Moses, David, etc.), and on the right side is a visualization of how Jesus fulfilled that story. In the middle of the two there is an arrow, from left to right. When I was reviewing the design, I thought, *How appropriate! The Law and the Prophets are arrows pointing to Jesus!*

Matthew's Gospel emphasizes that Jesus is the new and greater Moses. This is highlighted in the Transfiguration narrative (Matthew 17:1–8), in which Jesus takes Peter, James, and John up on a high mountain. This account includes many words that remind us of the experience of Moses when he went up the mountain to meet with God and receive the commandments for His people in their renewed covenant with Him. Back then, the face of Moses had been shining, and now the face of Jesus is shining too. Moses and Elijah appear in the scene and are talking with Jesus (verse 3). This setting seems so perfect that Peter has an idea: "Lord, it is good for us to be here; if You wish, I will make three *tabernacles* here, one for You, and one for Moses and one for Elijah" (verse 4). The Greek word for *tabernacle* used here is the same word used in the Greek translation of the Old Testament (LXX) for the tent of meeting (Exodus 29:42). Peter wanted to create three equal tents (shrines). But God didn't think this was a great idea. While Peter "was still speaking," God interrupts him. "This is My beloved Son, with who I am well-pleased; listen to Him!" (Matthew 17:5; see Deuteronomy 18:15). God's revelation of Himself and His salvific plan through the Old Testament is important and not to be dismissed. Nevertheless, God's revelation through Jesus supersedes all previous revelations. If you ever struggle about who God is and how He views us, remember that in Jesus we have God's supreme revelation. Worship Him!

My Response: _____

---

* Elizabeth Talbot, *Discovering Jesus in the Bible Coloring Book,* (Nampa, ID: Pacific Press®, 2017).

HIS EXODUS

Moses and Elijah, who, appearing in glory, were speaking of His departure which He was about to accomplish at Jerusalem.

—Luke 9:30, 31

When I visited Greece, I found many exciting things there, from the magnificent archaeological excavations of ancient buildings to amazing sculptures and a wide variety of artifacts. But there was something unexpected that really caught my attention: the word *"Exodos,"* which in Greek means *"exit."* I could see it everywhere—in public buildings, on freeway exits—signs in Greek: EXODOS. As you can imagine, I took many photos of them.

I've always been fascinated by the fact that the Exodus of the Hebrews from Egypt is a symbol of our ultimate redemption and journey to the Promised Land. It is only possible through the blood of the Lamb, as seen in the blood of the Passover lamb on Hebrew doorposts (Exodus 12:21, 22). This theological theme runs from the beginning to the end of the Bible. I became even more captivated with the topic when I realized something amazing in the Transfiguration account, when Moses and Elijah came to discuss with Jesus His upcoming death. The literal translation of the words from the Greek are incredibly striking: "And behold, two men were conversing with Him, who were Moses and Elijah, who having appeared in glory were speaking of the *Exodus* of Him which He was about to fulfill in Jerusalem" (Luke 9:30, 31).* Did you see that? Jesus fulfilled the Exodus in Jerusalem! I can imagine Moses encouraging Jesus, saying, "Hang in there; I will never forget the elated look on the faces of the Hebrew slaves after the crossing of the sea; You are about to accomplish the *ultimate Exodus*, redeeming the whole world from slavery to sin!" Jesus is the Passover lamb (see 1 Corinthians 5:7), and His blood is the assurance that we are His own people, whose freedom He purchased. Yes! We are on our way! This is not our home; we are just passing through. Whenever the realities of this world become unbearable, remember that Jesus has purchased our freedom. How about we start praising Him from now until eternity? "Redeemed, how I love to proclaim it! Redeemed by the blood of the Lamb!"†

My Response:_____

---

* J. D. Douglas, *The New Greek-English Interlinear New Testament*, 4th rev. ed. (Carol Stream, IL: Tyndale House, 1993).

† Fanny Crosby, "Redeemed," 1882, public domain.

HIS INVOLVEMENT

"The very hairs of your head are all numbered."

—Matthew 10:30

I am a visual learner. Therefore, in my prayer journal, I sometimes draw a particular scriptural idea; thereby it makes a lasting impact on my mind. One day I was studying the concept of today's verse, and I drew my head with a few hairs. Then I started placing numbers next to each hair: 1, 2, 3. And all of sudden a realization hit me: I am worth so much to God, that He is fully aware and engaged in every detail of my life. He knows much more about me than I do. And this is the reason why I should never be afraid (Matthew 10:31).

With this realization, praise and thanksgiving started to flow freely. I thanked God for taking care of me and for loving me just as I am, with all my thoughts, emotions, joys, and pains. Who can count our hairs? We can't, but God can. That He has numbered *the hairs on our head* is an expression that denotes both God's care and protection, as in "not a hair of your head will perish" without His knowledge (Luke 21:18). He is fully aware of what is going on in our lives. Furthermore, His love and involvement are constant and continuous. The hairs of our head are (present tense) all numbered today; they were five years ago and they will be five years from now. Some people only talk about God's love and care as events in the past or in the future. The greatest manifestation of God's love occurred on the cross, when Jesus died. And our deliverance will be accomplished when He returns for us in His second coming. Yet it is imperative that we recognize that the same love that nailed Him to the cross is active in our daily lives today. In this passage, we are reminded three times to "not fear" (Matthew 10:26, 28, 31), because God knows us, and we are valuable to Him. Take a moment to thank God for His direct involvement in your life and for His powerful hand that protects and guides you. After all, His care in our personal lives has been the focus of beautiful psalms, such as: "You know when I sit down and when I rise up; You understand my thought from afar . . . And are intimately acquainted with all my ways . . . Such knowledge is too wonderful for me" (Psalm 139:2–6).

My Response: _____

HIS EVIDENCE

*When they came up out of the water, the Spirit of the Lord
snatched Philip away; and the eunuch no longer saw him,
but went on his way rejoicing.*

—Acts 8:39

No one or anything can take away the joy that we experience when we accept Jesus as our Savior. When I started my ministry as a pastor for young adults, a young woman in our group was diagnosed with Parkinson's. I saw her go through several surgeries as the disease slowly progressed over twenty years, yet she never lost her joy and trust in the Lord. On the contrary, she became a beacon of bright light and continues to live out her powerful testimony.

Luke continuously emphasizes, both in his Gospel and in Acts, that true joy is powerful evidence that someone has accepted the good news of Jesus. In the first two chapters of the Gospel of Luke, we find four hymns of praise and thanksgiving; joyful praises continue to flow throughout this Gospel. When we get to the book of Acts, joy is associated with accepting salvation as well (see Acts 8:39; 16:34). In today's biblical story, God sent Philip to explain the good news of Jesus to an Ethiopian man who was reading Isaiah 53 while traveling in his chariot (Acts 8:31–35). And as soon as the man understood the gospel, he wanted to respond and asked to be baptized! "As they went along the road they came to some water; and the eunuch said, 'Look! Water! What prevents me from being baptized?' " (verse 36). Immediately after the Ethiopian man understood the gift of God, he wanted to accept it and give a public testimony about his decision. "And he ordered the chariot to stop; and they both went down into the water, Philip as well as the eunuch, and he baptized him. When they came up out of the water, the Spirit of the Lord snatched Philip away; and the eunuch no longer saw him, but went on his way *rejoicing*" (verses 38, 39). Joy, joy, joy! True inner joy, praise, and gratitude are the result of accepting by faith our salvation in Christ. Whatever your situation, pause a moment to joyfully praise the Lord for His gift of eternal life through Jesus! If you have not been baptized, I invite you to make that decision as soon as possible!* Only in His Presence can we find fullness of joy! (Psalm 16:11).

My Response: _____

---

* For a free set of Bible studies, entitled *Amazing Grace*, please contact us at www.Jesus101.tv, and we will be delighted to mail it to you free of charge.

HIS LONGANIMITY

"You will all fall away, because it is written, 'I will strike down the shepherd, and the sheep shall be scattered.' "

—Mark 14:27

I have witnessed the type of love that patiently endures long hardships. I know a mother who continues to visit her son in jail for many long years and never stops loving and encouraging him. I met a man whose wife became extremely ill and ended up bedridden, yet week after week he brought her to church on a gurney. But what about love that endures rejection and offense?

Jesus is worthy of our praise for many reasons: His love, His grace, His power; the list is limitless. And today I want to add one more: His longanimity. His patient endurance in the face of opposition, rejection, provocation, and offense. How many times did my mind oppose His plans and my soul reject His ways? How many times was He blamed for evil in this world, or His sacrifice rejected by a pharisaical religion? Yet He continued to love, to knock on the door of our hearts, and to save. Jesus revealed to His disciples that the Passover meal was really pointing to His own sacrifice (Mark 14:22–25), and explained that the cup was His, "blood of the covenant, which is poured out for many" (verse 24). Then they sang a hymn and went out to the Mount of Olives. At this time Jesus made the announcement: "You will *all* fall away, because it is written, 'I will strike down the shepherd, and the sheep shall be scattered' " (verse 27). This prediction of Jesus really stunned His followers who listened in disbelief, unable to comprehend the poignancy of His words. What kind of God is this? Who makes a covenant to give His life as a ransom for people that He knows are going to fail Him? Jesus is saying that His blood of the covenant would be poured out and that His own disciples would abandon Him. Then He goes on, "But . . . ." I love God's "buts." They give us a way out; they extend grace for the lost; they offer another chance. "But after I have been raised, I will go ahead of you to Galilee" (verse 28). What? You still want to see us? Even after we failed You? Seriously, what kind of God is Jesus? A patient God, worthy of our praise!

My Response: _____

HIS READINESS

*"For your heavenly Father knows that
you need all these things."*

—Matthew 6:32

Bestselling author David Jeremiah shares his experience. Having been very energetic since his childhood, he had not really understood physical weakness, until he was diagnosed with stage four lymphoma. The treatments left him severely weak and fatigued. When he went back to preach for the first time after his treatment, he began to cry when the choir sang "Total Praise," which praises God for His strength. He writes: "I knew God was the One who had strengthened me in my recovery from cancer. Almighty God was the source of my strength. He was the strength of my life."*

I am sure that you, like me, sometimes feel overwhelmed by certain circumstances, whether financial, relational, emotional, or physical. We realize that we can't face them on our own because we have exhausted our resources, vitality, and strength. I find great comfort in knowing that God is intimately aware of all my needs and is ready to supply them: "Do not worry then, saying, 'What will we eat?' or 'What will we drink?' or 'What will we wear for clothing?' . . . for *your heavenly Father knows that you need all these things. But seek first His kingdom and His righteousness, and all these things will be added to you.*" (Matthew 6:31–33). There are many parts of verse 32 that give me hope. First, the phrase *"Your heavenly Father,"* which highlights His relationship with us as a Father and the fact that He is *our* Father; we are His children, and we are not on our own! What would you do for your kids? Everything! Exactly! Then the verb: He *has known* (Greek tense); He is not guessing; He already *knows*. What does He know? Our *needs*; all of them. And you can expand the list of food, drink, and clothing to whatever else you are needing that you can't supply for yourself. When we focus on Christ, His righteousness, and the salvation that He has already provided, we realize that He is also ready to supply all our other needs. He will surely provide strength, wisdom, peace, and hope. Let's praise God for His knowledge and readiness to provide for all of our needs in Christ Jesus! (Philippians 4:19).

My Response: _____

---

* David Jeremiah, *Overcomer: 8 Ways to Live a Life of Unstoppable Strength, Unmovable Faith, and Unbelievable Power* (Nashville, Tennessee: W Publishing, 2018), 27.

HIS REPLY

"For everyone who asks receives, and he who seeks finds,
and to him who knocks it will be opened."

—Matthew 7:8

My husband opened his wallet to look for his credit card, but it wasn't there. We looked everywhere but couldn't find it. We prayed about it and tried to retrace our steps; and that's when I received a phone call. It was the administration office of our gated community. Someone had found his card on one of our hiking trails and brought it to the office. We were so thankful! It was such a fast and immediate answer from God! We didn't even have time to worry about it!

Wouldn't it be great if all of our prayers were answered like that? But all of us know that from our human perspective, it is not always that way. Perhaps you, like me, sometimes feel stuck between the first part: "everyone who asks" and the second part: "receives." The three Greek present participles, "asks . . . seeks . . . knocks," imply ongoing and constant actions (Matthew 7:8). Furthermore, there are two present tense promises: "receives" and "finds." We might think: *I have been asking constantly and have not received! Am I really part of "everyone"?* Well, four elements, highlighted in verse 11, provide helpful insights for us: "If you then, being evil [sinful], know how to give good gifts to your children [see verses 9, 10], how much more will your *Father* who is in heaven give *what is good to those who ask Him*!" (verse 11). Therefore: (1) Even though we give good gifts to our children, we are *sinful*: we don't always have a heavenly perspective. (2) God is not a distant deity; He is our heavenly *Father*, replying to us, who are His children. (3) He gives *good things* to His children, but we won't always know or understand how something is good for us. (4) He *gives* good things to those *who ask* Him! He hears our ongoing petitions, and always gives us an answer that is good for us.

How important it is to remember that this is the same Father who has given us His Son in response to our need for salvation, so that *everyone* who believes in Him may have eternal life! Let's praise God for His greatest gift of redemption, and for all the good things that He gives us that we don't always understand.

My Response: _____

HIS ESSENCE

"For this I have come into the world, to testify to the truth.
Everyone who is of the truth hears My voice."
Pilate said to Him, "What is truth?"

—John 18:37, 38

I f you look for the meaning of the word "truth," you will find such descriptions as *actuality, fact, reality*; connotations like *fidelity* and *sincerity*, and even definitions of the word as "God."* The question was asked by Pilate as Jesus stood before him: "Pilate said to Him, 'What is truth?' " (John 18:38), and he asked this right after Jesus had revealed that He had come to testify to the truth!

We all want to know what "the truth" is, especially when we are facing pivotal and uncertain moments in our lives. In his Gospel, John uses the words "truth" and "true" forty-seven times (in English), more than any other book in the New Testament. From the very beginning, John describes truth as the essence of who Jesus is: "full of grace and truth" (John 1:14); "grace and truth were realized through Jesus Christ" (verse 17). In contrast, the devil is described as the ultimate liar: "There is no truth in him. Whenever he speaks a lie, he speaks from his own nature, for he is a liar and the father of lies" (John 8:44). Satan, God's adversary, has been telling lies since the beginning, when he tempted humans in the Garden of Eden (Genesis 3). He lied to Adam and Eve that they would not be facing adverse consequences for their disobedience. Well, we all know how that turned out! When he can't succeed in tempting us on that side, he lies about us being able to merit salvation by our good works/pedigree, or by telling us that we have gone too far, and that there is no more redemption for people like us. On the other hand, Jesus introduced Himself as the *Truth*: "I am the way, and the *truth*, and the life; no one comes to the Father but through Me" (John 14:6). There is no other way of salvation than through Jesus, for He *is* the Truth, and there is no lie in Him. He said: "You will know the truth, and the truth will make your free. . . . So if the Son makes you free, you will be free indeed" (John 8:32–36). He is the ultimate Voice of truth and you can trust Him: His sacrifice on your behalf, His promises, His Word, His salvation, His freedom, and His eternal life. Because Truth is who He is.

My Response: _____

---

* *Merriam-Webster*, s.v. "Truth (n.)," accessed April 17, 2019, https://www.merriam-webster.com/dictionary/truth.

HIS AMBASSADORS

And the brethren, when they heard about us, came . . . to meet us; and when Paul saw them, he thanked God and took courage.

—Acts 28:15

9/11, a documentary film by the Naudet brothers that captured first-hand the events of the horrific terrorist attacks, made a profound impact on me. Among many scenes, I especially remember the one at the firehouse, just after the first plane had hit the North Tower of the World Trade Center. The retired Chief Larry Byrnes arrives to the Battalion 1 quarters because he just could not stay home. He had trained all his life for this and *had* to come to help those in need.

Today I praise God for the people He has sent in my life to encourage and help me as His ambassadors. People who dropped everything they were doing and came to my aid as emissaries of God's hope and assurance. Perhaps you, too, want to pause and thank God for His representatives on earth, whom He sends to encourage you during dark times. The community of believers is there to spread the good news, *and* to encourage each other in times of pain and need. It is hard to imagine that Paul needed encouragement, but he did! After going through many hardships, he arrived in Rome. The believers, having heard of his approach, went out to welcome him. The Greek language seems to imply that they escorted him, walking with him along the road. The text says that they "came from there as far as the Market of Appius and Three Inns" (Acts 28:15). F. F. Bruce explains: "Some of them got as far as Tres Tavernae ('the Three Taverns'), a halting place on the Appian Way about thirty-three miles from Rome; others walked ten miles farther and met him at Appii Forum ('the marketplace of Appius')."* "When Paul saw them, *he thanked God and took courage*" (verse 15). We all need to be comforted from time to time. That's why God gave us brothers and sisters in Christ. Perhaps today God is impressing you to encourage someone who needs to be reminded of His love and care, of Jesus' all-sufficient sacrifice that covers their sin completely, and of His soon coming to take us to a pain-free eternal home. We praise you and thank you Lord, for your ambassadors of grace and hope!

My Response: _____

---

* F. F. Bruce, *The Book of the Acts,* rev. ed., NICNT (Grand Rapids, MI: 1988), 502, 503.

His Wedding

"Blessed are those who are invited to the marriage supper of the Lamb." And he said to me, "These are true words of God."
—Revelation 19:9

He did what any husband would have done for his wife," reported an online news service recounting an emotional event that took place on January 13, 2012, as the *Costa Concordia* cruise ship was sinking. When Francis Servel and his wife Nicole realized that the ship was going down, they decided to jump into the water, but they had only one life jacket between the two of them. Francis, a strong swimmer, handed the jacket to his wife and said, "Swim ahead, darling, I'll survive." She never saw him again. He gave his life for his wife of forty years.*

God chose to describe His incredible love for us using the metaphor of a husband who loves his wife to the point of dying for her. In surrendering his life, Jesus said "Go ahead, darling, I'll catch up," and He went to the cross and died in our place so that we may have eternal life. At the end of the Bible, in the book of Revelation, we are assured not only of God's final and complete victory over evil, but of the joining of Jesus, the Lamb, with His bride, the church, whom He has purchased with His life. The text for today is the fourth of seven beatitudes in the book of Revelation: "Blessed are those who are invited to the marriage supper of the Lamb" (Revelation 19:9). What an encouraging blessing! Ranko Stefanovic adds, "John was instructed to write this beatitude to remind God's people that even though they might be experiencing hardship and suffering, they are blessed because of the call to the wedding supper of the Lamb. . . . This joining of Christ with the people whom He has purchased on the cross is the focus of the entire book of Revelation. Everything in the book moves toward that climactic triumph."† I am so thankful to Jesus for the assurance of a future with Him! He gave us His lifejacket and died in our place. Take a moment to write a joyful acceptance of the invitation to attend the marriage supper of the Lamb!

My Response: _____

_____

* "Costa Concordia Cruise Disaster: Husband Sacrifices Life Jacket for Wife, Disappears Into Water," Huffpost.com, updated January 16, 2012, https://www.huffpost.com/entry/costa-concordia-cruise-disaster_n_1208773.

† Ranko Stefanovic, *The Revelation of Jesus Christ,* 2nd ed. (Berrien Springs, MI: Andrews University Press, 2009), 559, 545.

HIS REPOSSESSION

And He will wipe away every tear from their eyes;
and there will no longer be any death . . . or crying,
or pain; the first things have passed away.

—Revelation 21:4

When Adam and Eve rejected the moral umbrella of the Creator, sin entered the world. Then they tried to "fix the problem" themselves. Victor Hamilton explains: "The couple's solution to this new enigma is freighted with folly. Having committed the sin themselves, and now living with its immediate consequences, i.e., the experience of shame, the loss of innocence . . . they attempt to alleviate the problem themselves. Rather than driving them back to God, their guilt leads them into a self-atoning, self-protecting procedure: they must cover themselves."*

But they couldn't fix it. Beside sin-induced fear, shame, and blame (see Genesis 3), they would also experience pain and death (verses 16, 19). Our story would be the saddest and most hopeless story in the universe if the Bible had ended here. But that is not where it ends! It's where it only begins, because in Genesis 3:15, God makes a covenantal promise that brings hope to humanity; He makes the divine announcement that this was not the end. God told the tempter:

> "I will put enmity
> Between you and the woman;
> And between your seed and her seed;
> He shall bruise you on the head,
> And you shall bruise him on the heel" (Genesis 3:15).

God promised recovery for His children, and the rest of the Bible is the story of redemption. We couldn't fix it ourselves, we needed a Savior to defeat the serpent. Jesus carried our sin to the cross and won victory over evil and its consequences. I am so thankful that in the new earth the consequences of the Fall will no longer exist: "*He* will wipe away every tear from their eyes; and there will no longer be any death . . . mourning, or crying, or pain . . ." (Revelation 21:4). If you are in pain, or mourning, join me in praising Jesus for achieving the victory that will remove all the consequences of sin. We know the end of the story! And Jesus wins!

My Response: _____

---

* Victor P. Hamilton, *The Book of Genesis: Chapters 1–17*, NICNT (Grand Rapids, MI: Eerdmans, 1990), 191.

335

HIS VOW

"I will come again and receive you to Myself,
that where I am, there you may be also."

—John 14:3

A vow is a serious and solemn promise. Perhaps you have heard the story of Robertson McQuilkin and his wife Muriel. He was the president of a seminary when Muriel started forgetting things, and it became evident that she had Alzheimer's disease. He left his position to take care of her and stated that this decision had been made forty-two years before, when he had taken his marriage vows, "in sickness and in health, till death do us part." Their story, now a book,* inspires us in this age of broken vows and dishonored promises.

Jesus made a solemn vow to us. When life's circumstances seem to hide His face, we can stand on His firm promises, for He is faithful. His second coming is not just a possibility but a certainty. Jesus assures us that He *will* be with us. His declarations about the future sustain me in dark times, when I don't seem to see the light at the end of the tunnel: "Truly I say to you today with me you *will* be in Paradise" (Luke 23:43; Greek-English Interlinear NT); "This Jesus, who has been taken up from you into heaven, *will* come in just the same way as you have watched Him go into heaven" (Acts 1:11); "He [God] *will* dwell among them, and they *shall* be His people, and God Himself *will* be among them, and He *will* wipe away every tear from their eyes" (Revelation 21:3, 4). These promises (add a few of your favorites) assure us that Jesus *will* be coming again, that evil *will* be permanently destroyed, and that God *will* dwell with us eternally. These statements do not suggest that He *might* come back but that He *will* return for us. In the Greek text, today's verse adds another dimension to His promise. It reads: "And if I go and prepare a place for you, again I am coming and *will receive you to myself,* that where I am also you may be" (John 14:3, Greek-English Interlinear). He is coming back, and He *will receive us,* to be with Him forever. Jesus died in order to keep His vow to us. He is more than trustworthy, and He is worthy to be praised! Whenever things seem to fall apart, stand on the sure bloodstained promises of Jesus, your Savior!

My Response: _____

---

* Robertson McQuilkin, *A Promise Kept* (Carol Stream, IL: Tyndale House Publishers, 1998).

HIS INSISTENCE

"Now my soul has become troubled; and what shall I say,
'Father, save Me from this hour'? But for this purpose
I came to this hour."

—John 12:27

One of the admirable aspects of Jesus was His restraint. Having the power to free Himself from death, He did not. He restrained Himself. Fully capable of destroying this sinful world in order to start anew, He chose the way of sacrificial love, dying for the race that crucified Him. He insisted on the path of love versus the display of power. As Philip Yancey points out: "God made himself weak for one purpose: to let human beings choose freely for themselves what to do with him."*

Instead of exercising His power and forcing us into compliance, He chose the way of meekness, deciding to die for us. In Gethsemane Jesus expressed His anguish of soul, as He faced the hour of His suffering: "Now My soul has become troubled; and what shall I say, 'Father, save Me from this hour'? But for this purpose I came to this hour" (John 12:27). Surely, He could have saved Himself from the cross! But He did not. Instead, He submitted to the salvific purpose that His death would achieve. " 'Now judgment is upon this world; now the ruler of this world will be cast out. And I, if I am lifted up from the earth, will draw all men to Myself.' But He was saying this to indicate the kind of death by which He was to die" (verses 31–33). His death on the cross ensured His triumph over the evil one and paid the penalty for our sin. His sacrificial love elicits our allegiance. Yancey explains: "Satan's power is external and coercive. God's power, in contrast, is internal and noncoercive. . . . Such power may seem at times like weakness. In its commitment to transform gently from the inside out and in its relentless dependence on human choice, God's power may resemble a kind of abdication. As every parent and every lover knows, love can be rendered powerless if the beloved chooses to spurn it."† God chose sacrificial love to draw us to Himself. *Dear Jesus: we praise You for Your submission to die in our place, and for choosing the power of love instead of coercion. It wasn't the nails that kept You on the cross. It was Your love for us!*

My Response: _____

---

* Philip Yancey, *The Jesus I Never Knew* (Grand Rapids, MI: Zondervan, 1995), 1010, Kindle.
† Yancey, *Jesus*, 1003, Kindle.

HIS CHRONOLOGY

So they were seeking to seize Him; and no man laid his hand
on Him, because His hour had not yet come.

—John 7:30

Where is the safest place on earth? A well-traveled person offered a good answer, which has stuck in my mind: "The safest place on earth is *wherever* God wants us to be," he said. Whether on a plane, a ship, a car, or on foot, when I submit my life to God's will, nothing can happen to me unless God permits it for His redemptive purposes. I am not in control of my own life, death, and mission. He is. And His purposes obey a divine timetable.

During His life and ministry, the opponents of Jesus tried to capture Him many times, but they could not, because the great heavenly clock had not yet marked *His hour*. In the temple Jesus emphatically stated His identity, and His relationship to the Father: "You both know Me and know where I am from; and I have not come of Myself, but He who sent Me is true, whom you do not know. I know Him, because I am from Him, and He sent Me" (John 7:28, 29). In response to this amazing revelation, "they were seeking to seize Him; and no man laid his hand on Him, because *His hour had not yet come*" (John 7:30). God was in control of the redemptive mission of Christ, and nothing could harm Him until it was time. Commenting on verse 30, Leon Morris adds: "His enemies sought to arrest him. But God is over all. His purpose is worked out. People cannot prevent it. The time for Jesus' death was not yet, and his enemies could not bring that time forward no matter how they might try."* In the Gospel of John, the "hour" of Jesus points to the cross specifically. Jesus had come to die. Several times the narrative highlights that His hour/ time had not yet come (2:4; 7:6, 8, 30; 8:20), and afterwards it announces that His hour was coming and had come (12:23, 27; 13:1; 16:32; 17:1). Jesus died at the appointed time, for a predesigned purpose. Praise be to God for His indescribable plan of salvation! Let's submit ourselves to the One who holds the divine chronology and timetable in His hands, and let's live our lives without fear of the future, resting in His design *and* timing.

My Response: _____

———————————
* Leon Morris, *The Gospel According to John*, rev. ed., NICNT (Grand Rapids, MI: Eerdmans, 1995), 367.

HIS TRIUMPH

*"Hosanna to the Son of David; Blessed is He
who comes in the name of the Lord."*

—Matthew 21:9

There are many things that I will never forget about the Holy Land. Among them is the experience we had as our bus started the gradual ascent to the city of Jerusalem. Our guide surprised us by playing a jubilant song of praise through the audio system of the bus. I will treasure this moment forever. As we imagined the joy of the pilgrims on their journey to Jerusalem and their flamboyant expressions of jubilation in song, we all started to sing and clap.

It is hard for us to imagine the reality of the triumphal entry of Jesus into Jerusalem. We are told that Jesus and His disciples were entering the city from the Mount of Olives (Matthew 21:1), a place that was prophetically linked to Messianic expectations: "In that day His feet will stand on the Mount of Olives" (Zechariah 14:4). The Mount of Olives was a significant site: Jesus gave His eschatological (end-times) discourse there (Matthew 24:3), and He also ascended to heaven from there (Acts 1:9–12). Now, in fulfillment of Zechariah 9:9, Jesus was riding a colt into Jerusalem and encountering a reception fit for a king. The participants of the flamboyant crowd were spreading their coats and palm branches on the road in front of Him, no doubt understanding the symbolism of the moment (see 1 Kings 1:38–40). They welcomed Him with jubilant expressions from the Hallel Psalms (113–118): "Hosanna to the Son of David! 'Blessed is He who comes in the name of the LORD!' " (Matthew 21:9, NKJV; compare with Psalm 118:26). The long-awaited Davidic king had arrived! Only, this was not the conquering military leader they had been expecting but a peaceful, humble, *gentle, and meek* Messiah (see Matthew 21:5; 11:29) who would triumph through His sacrifice on the cross. A few days later, the same crowd that praised Him now would demand His death. Yes! Jesus Wins! *But not in the way we expect Him to,* whether in our daily lives or in our eternal salvation. God's ways are not our ways. Jesus triumphed in a way no one expected: through suffering and death. Hallelujah to the Son of David!

My Response: _____

HIS REVELATION

"I praise You, Father, Lord of heaven and earth,
that You have hidden these things from the wise and
intelligent and revealed them to infants."

—Matthew 11:25

Sometimes, as adults, we really complicate things. Children are able to perceive profound truths in a simple way and accept them at face value. For example, I often find that children easily understand the core message of the book of Revelation: they know that the dragon is bad, that the King is good, and that the King wins! Children are trusting and discerning, and their honesty is unsurpassed.

Today's devotional verse starts with a *Todah*. These were prayers of praise or thanksgiving, often used in the Jewish Scriptures (for example, see 2 Samuel 22:50; Psalm 9:1). What is striking about this passage is the content of the praise of Jesus. It is the only time in the New Testament where the reason for the praise is *revelation*. Jesus praises His Father, who is Sovereign over heaven and earth, for *concealing* and *revealing*: "You have *hidden* these things from the wise . . . and *revealed* them to infants" (Matthew 11:25). "These things" refers to the previous context, about understanding and accepting Jesus' identity and mission. God conceals the mysteries of the gospel from those who are proud and wise in their own eyes. The concept of God "depriving" the understanding of those who think highly of themselves is present in the Old Testament as well (see Job 12:24, 25). Yet God is eager to reveal (Greek *apokaluptō*) the good news of Jesus to those who become teachable and know themselves lacking understanding. In the time of Jesus, the theologically learned and religious elite were considered wise, yet they missed Jesus. On the other hand, the infants (see the same word used in Matthew 21:15) possessed understanding about Jesus that the theologically wise were lacking. This is not an attack on those who devote themselves to learning, but is an important reminder of why we need to be teachable and without entitlement, like children, to receive the revelation of the gospel. Have you ever felt like you are not wise enough to enter the kingdom? Welcome! Remember that God gives a revelation of the gospel to those who seem unworthy of such knowledge!

My Response: _____

HIS MIGHT

"He who is coming after me is mightier than I."
—Matthew 3:11

There is a healthy sense of humility and unworthiness that comes over us when we encounter someone whose knowledge or abilities surpass ours. That was my constant experience throughout my academic career, studying under the supervision of distinguished Bible scholars. To this day, if someone compliments me on Bible knowledge, I respond with: "You should meet so and so . . . he knows so much more about biblical studies; I don't even come close."

I can't imagine how John the Baptist felt when he was describing the One who was coming after him. John was sent to prepare the way for Jesus, yet he was fully aware that a mightier, stronger One than he was about to enter the scene. His statement is striking, especially in the light of Jesus' tribute to John: "Truly I say to you, among those born of women there has not arisen anyone greater than John the Baptist!" (Matthew 11:11). Jesus, the Stronger One, cannot be compared with any other prophet, for He is supreme! And John goes on to describe himself as not even being worthy to carry out the lowliest of tasks for Him, like removing or carrying His sandals, a task normally performed by a slave for his master. The mission of Jesus was so much greater than John's. John was given the preparatory mission, but the Stronger One would have the unsurpassed salvific task. When interpreting the Scripture, establishing the supremacy of Jesus over any other prophet is of utmost importance, because the law and the prophets point to Him. There are many who study the Scriptures and miss Jesus as the central figure in redemption history. Jesus himself pointed out this sad reality: "You search the Scriptures because you think that in them you have eternal life; *it is these that testify about Me*; and you are unwilling to come to Me so that you may have life" (John 5:39, 40). Jesus is mightier than Abraham, Moses, David, Isaiah, and John the Baptist. He is our Savior and the Lord of our lives. We are not worthy of Him, and yet we have the assurance of the salvation that He has provided for us. Let's make Him the focus of all our devotion, praise, and worship. It's all about Jesus!

My Response: _____

HIS RIGHTEOUSNESS

"In this way it is fitting for us to fulfill all righteousness."
—Matthew 3:15

Since my childhood, I have been fascinated by the story about the little slave-girl from Israel who was a servant of Naaman's wife (2 Kings 5). Through her witness, the captain of the army of the king of Aram was healed from leprosy when he followed the prophet's directions and immersed himself in the river Jordan for seven times. What I didn't know then is that the story of Naaman's healing in the waters of the river Jordan is the only instance in the Greek Old Testament where the notion of baptism by immersion is mentioned.*

It is with amazement that I see how this story continues to unfold centuries later, when Jesus arrives at the same river in order to be baptized by John (Matthew 3:13). Initially, John tried to dissuade Jesus from doing it because he understood that Jesus was greater than him and would baptize His followers with the Holy Spirit (verse 14; see verse 11). In this exchange, recorded only by Matthew, Jesus answers John that it must be so, "for in this way it is fitting for us to fulfill all righteousness" (verse 15). Jesus was baptized not because He was sinful but because He was, and is, our Representative and Substitute. He came to fulfill the law and the prophets (see Matthew 5:17) through his perfect life, death, and resurrection in our place. It is through His righteousness, not ours, that we are assured of salvation. Through Jesus' fulfillment of the law we find grace, peace, and healing, as Naaman did. We all have things that we wish were not part of our biography. We all know that we don't deserve salvation. If you find yourself, or your loved ones, in a season of despair about mistakes/sins of the past (or present), remember that Jesus lived a perfect life in our place. When we accept Him as our Savior, His perfect life is credited to us; we are declared righteous on account of His righteousness, not ours. Isn't that the best news ever? This is what we call "Righteousness by Faith": "The righteousness of God through faith in Jesus Christ for all those who believe" (Romans 3:22; see verses 23–26). Thank and praise the Lord for His perfect righteousness, accredited to us as His gift!

My Response: _____

---

* 2 Kings 5:14, LXX. *Baptizō.*

HIS OBEDIENCE

*Then Jesus was led up by the Spirit into the wilderness
to be tempted by the devil.*

—Matthew 4:1

Have you ever had the amazing experience of someone doing for you what you couldn't do for yourself? Several years ago, when I was studying for my PhD, I was short one thousand dollars for that year's tuition. When my birthday came along, my parents handed me a gift bag with all kinds of fun little things that they knew I would like. But then I touched a little wooden box at the bottom of the bag. When I opened it, I found a little roll of ten one-hundred-dollar bills. I cried with gratitude, knowing their sacrifice. My debt was paid by my parents' loving efforts!

In his Gospel, Matthew propositions that Jesus relives Israel's history, and is victorious where they have failed. Jesus is the Representative and Substitute of the new Israel. The same Spirit of God that descended on Jesus at His baptism (Matthew 3:16), now leads Him into the wilderness "to be tempted by the devil" (Matthew 4:1). In his introduction to this event, Matthew reminds us of Israel's journey: "Then Jesus was led up by the Spirit into the wilderness to be tempted by the devil. And after He had fasted forty days and forty nights, He then became hungry" (Matthew 4:1, 2). Let's compare that with Deuteronomy 8:2, 3, as it relates to Israel: "You shall remember all the way which the LORD your God has led you in the wilderness these forty years, that He might humble you, testing you. . . . He humbled you and let you be hungry, and fed you with manna which you did not know . . . that He might make you understand that *man does not live by bread alone, but man lives by everything that proceeds out of the mouth of the LORD.*" This last part is cited by Jesus to answer the first temptation (Matthew 4:4). All three answers of Jesus come from the parallel account of Israel's history in Deuteronomy 6–8. This is a most important truth to understand: When we accept Jesus as our Savior, not only His death, but also His perfect life is placed in our account, paying it in full. His obedience and His death are counted as ours. Our assurance of salvation comes from His achievements, not ours. And that is truly good news! Amazing Grace!

My Response: _____

HIS FAITHFULNESS

*And at once his mouth was opened . . . and he
began to speak in praise of God.*

—Luke 1:64

Having spent many hours with my mouth shut, now it was open, and I wanted to talk to everyone around me. It happened years ago, on the day my dad had a major surgery to remove a cancerous tumor from his stomach. We had been waiting for many hours, more than we expected. We didn't talk much during that time. Then we saw the doctor approaching us, and I only remember his first words: "The cancer is out." Then he went on to explain many other things, but all I wanted to do was to announce to everyone in that waiting room: "The cancer is out!!"

Due to his unbelief, Zacharias had been silent for at least nine months (see Luke 1:20). When he wrote on a tablet that the name of the newborn would be John, as the angel had said, then his mouth was opened and "he began to speak *in praise of God*" (verse 64). It is so different when we open our mouths in gratitude and praise instead of doubt and unbelief! And the Holy Spirit came upon him and he prophesied in a beautiful psalm of praise (Luke 1:67–79) that we call "Benedictus," referring to the first word in Latin: "*Blessed* be the Lord God of Israel, for He has visited us and accomplished redemption for His people" (verse 68). The hymn is divided into two parts. In the first section (verses 68–75), Zacharias recounts how God has been faithful to His covenant with Abraham by bringing redemption as promised. He uses many beautiful metaphors and images from the Old Testament. When we recall the way God has led us in our past, we will always find encouragement for the future. In the second part of the song (verses 76–79), the person and tense change, and Zacharias speaks to his son: "And you, child, will be called the prophet of the Most High; for you will go on before the Lord to prepare His ways" (verse 76). He goes on to tell of the salvation that would be coming in the near future through Jesus. Let's join Zacharias in praising God for His covenantal faithfulness towards us in the past, present, and future. God's faithfulness provides the only true assurance for our future!

My Response: _____

His Replenishment

"I [Paul] did not prove disobedient to the heavenly vision, but kept declaring . . . that they should repent and turn to God."
—Acts 26:19, 20

Due to his beliefs, Desmond Doss (Medal of Honor recipient) refused to carry weapons and became a combat medic. In the battle of Okinawa, he saved many lives, carrying one soldier at a time while putting his own life on the line. When asked how he had found enough strength to keep going back for more, he replied that each time he prayed: "Lord, please help me get one more."

When we trust in Jesus for our salvation, we are also promised the strength needed to share His mercy with others, even under the most adverse circumstances. As we join in His salvific rescue efforts, He provides resources that we do not possess on our own. When Paul became a prisoner, God enabled him to keep sharing the gospel, even when he was in chains. Instead of being overcome by discouragement, Paul kept sharing the gospel with Jews and Gentiles, kings and governors. In Acts 24, Paul became a prisoner of Felix, the governor. After two years of Paul being in this condition, Felix was succeeded by Festus, who was left in charge of Paul's case. After Paul appealed to Caesar (Acts 25:11, 12), Festus was confused as to what charges to bring against Paul, since he had found no wrongdoing (verses 25, 26). When King Agrippa (Herod Agrippa II) visited Festus, they arranged an audience for Agrippa to hear Paul speak. And even then, Paul tried to evangelize *the king*! " 'King Agrippa, do you believe the prophets? I know that you do.' Agrippa replied to Paul, 'In a short time you will persuade me to become a Christian' " (Acts 26:27, 28). It seems as if Paul's motto was: "Lord, please help me get one more." When it comes to sharing God's mercy, each of us may have our own distinct "one more": one more hour of taking care of a chronically-ill loved one; one more day of kindness towards an unkind person; forgiving the same offense one more time; sharing Jesus with one more person, in spite of being ridiculed in the process. Praise God, for He miraculously replenishes our souls, so that we may be able to continue sharing Jesus through words and actions.

My Response: _____

HIS MERIT

"Worthy are You . . . for You were slain and purchased for God with Your blood men from every tribe and tongue and people and nation."

—Revelation 5:9

When I was a little girl, I used to be obsessed with heaven. (By the way, I still am.) One of the things I was curious about was the lyrics of the songs we'll be singing for Jesus in heaven. I needed to know because I didn't want to miss the opportunity to sing for Him myself. I know it sounds a little strange, but as a child I wondered how people would know the words of totally new songs that they would have never sung before. I really wanted to know the songs!

In Revelation 5, a *new song* erupts in heaven! So many things are new in the book of Revelation: a new name, a new heaven, and a new earth, because God makes all things new. (I can't wait for that newness!) The appropriate response to what was accomplished by the Lamb's sacrificial death, is a new song of worship, flamboyant and startlingly marvelous, a song that has never been sung before because the magnitude of His redemption has never been fully understood before. It is recorded in Revelation 5:9, 10; please take a moment to read it. I am amazed at the details of the song, as it answers all of the main questions about why the Lamb merits everyone's praise, honor, and worship forever. (1) When did the Lamb come to be victorious? He became victorious when He died. (2) What did the Lamb accomplish? He purchased humanity! (3) How did He achieve it? He accomplished it through His blood. He paid a very high price—that's why He is worthy! (4) Who did He redeem? He purchased people from every tribe and tongue and people and nation. No group is excluded! (5) For whom did He purchase them? For God! He reestablished the relationship designed at Creation. He made them a kingdom and priests to our God! When I read this song, I feel loved by God, appreciated, valued, included, and I start getting a glimpse of how much Jesus gave up for me! Yes! I want to sing His praises! Will you join me in heralding His redemptive victory, the everlasting gospel? May our lives be a song of praise to the Lamb, from now until eternity!

My Response: _____

HIS REMEMBRANCE

"This is My body which is given for you;
do this in remembrance of Me."

—Luke 22:19

Thanksgiving became a federal holiday in the United States in 1863, when president Lincoln proclaimed it a day of, "Thanksgiving and Praise to our beneficent Father who dwelleth in the Heavens."* I have a personal memory that accompanies this holiday. Back in 2016, as we sat at the Thanksgiving table, my dad, in the other room, was too ill to join us, therefore his plate stayed empty at the table. He passed away that very night. During Thanksgiving meals, I always remember that day, and thank God for my parents' godly lives and unconditional love. Today is the anniversary of my dad's death.

In the Scriptures, God often told His people to "remember." They were to *remember* to keep the Sabbath day holy, in honor of their Creator and Redeemer (Exodus 20:9–11; Deuteronomy 5:12–15). When they entered the Promised Land and became afraid, they were to *remember* what the Lord had done for them in Egypt, and how God had led them (Deuteronomy 7:17, 18; 8:2). Yearly, the people of Israel celebrated a meal of remembrance, a memorial of redemption called Passover, in which they recalled how they had been delivered through the blood of the Passover lamb (Exodus 12:21–27). It was this yearly meal that Jesus and His disciples were eating, when Jesus took the bread and, instead of reciting the regular Passover story, told them to eat from now on in memory of Him: "This is My body which is given for you; do this in remembrance of Me" (Luke 22:19). A greater deliverance, foreshadowed by the original Passover, was about to take place. Jesus wanted us to remember Him, to eat the bread and drink the cup in memory of Him and His sacrifice for us. If we ever become afraid of the future, we are to remember the past. Every time we take the bread and the cup as emblems of His sacrifice, we do this in His memory, accepting the assurance of our salvation in Him. Let us remember the price He paid for our ransom, until that Day when He will come to take us to our heavenly Home! Do not be afraid . . . remember Him!

My Response: _____

---

* Wikipedia, s.v. "Thanksgiving (United States)," last modified on March 27, 2019, 12:30 A.M. UTC, https://en .wikipedia.org/wiki/Thanksgiving_(United_States).

HIS MERCY

*"Were there not ten cleansed?
But the nine—where are they?"*

—Luke 17:17

There are certain places in this world where social and ethnic barriers tend to break down and disappear because a greater reality takes over. One of those places is hospitals. Due to my parents' cancer treatments over the years, I have been to several surgery waiting rooms, cancer centers, and emergency rooms, and I realized how we all stand on even ground when it comes to pain and sickness. Somehow, we all become united in our humanity, praying for a positive outcome.

In the time of Jesus, it was leprosy that thus broke down social barriers among the victims of the disease. When Jesus entered a village, ten leprous men stood at a distance (Luke 17:12). The law required lepers to live separately from the rest of society (Leviticus 13:45, 46; Numbers 5:2). The ten men raised their voices, saying, "Jesus, Master, have mercy on us!" (Luke 17:13). Jesus never ignores such a plea. But instead of pronouncing a healing, He told them to show themselves to the priests. "And as they were going, they were cleansed" (verse 14). The healing occurred on their way to show themselves clean. "Now one of them, when he saw that he had been healed, turned back, glorifying God with a loud voice, and he fell on his face at His feet, giving thanks to Him" (verses 15, 16). Amazing! When he saw that he was healed, the man turned back and did three things: glorified God with a *loud voice*, in Greek *phones megales*, two words that make up our English word *"megaphone"*! Second, he fell at Jesus' feet, in reverence and submission, recognizing the source of his healing. Third, he thanked Jesus. Only then the reader is given a shocking fact: the one who came back was a Samaritan, a foreigner! (verse 16). All ten had been healed, because God is merciful even with the ungrateful (see Luke 6:35, 36). But only this foreigner, who recognized the mercy of Jesus, was not just *healed* but *saved* (Luke 17:19). Being a Samaritan, he probably wouldn't have been allowed into the temple, but the real Temple had come by to heal him! Jesus has broken down barriers. May our lives be a *megaphone*, glorifying, praising, and thanking God for His mercy bestowed upon *all* of us, through Jesus!

My Response: _____

HIS MOTIVATION

"Today salvation has come to this house."

—Luke 19:9

A s a child, I was deeply impressed by the story by O. Henry "The Gift of the Magi." A young couple loved each other very much. There were two things they cherished: she had beautiful long hair; he had a pocket watch, inherited from his father. They wanted to give each other a Christmas gift but had no money. On Christmas day, they discovered the magnitude of each other's love when they exchanged their gifts: he had sold his pocket watch to buy her a beautiful set of combs for her hair, and she had cut and sold her hair to buy an exquisite chain for his pocket watch. Love is definitely the most powerful motivator.

God's love is the greatest intrinsic motivator for the human heart and exceeds by far the extrinsic motivation produced by fear. This is exemplified in the story of Zaccheus, a wealthy leader of tax collectors (Luke 19:2). A tax collector was synonymous with *sinner*, attested by the crowd's comment later in the story (verse 7). Zaccheus climbed a tree in order to see Jesus over the crowd. As He was passing by, Jesus stopped, looked up, and spoke to him: "Zaccheus, hurry and come down, for today I *must* stay at your house" (verse 5). The verb utilized by Jesus ("must") implies a need, an action fundamentally indispensable. Jesus *had* to go to his house that day. It is imperative for us to understand that God's grace and love *precede* repentance and transformation. A person must be exposed to God's grace *before* he can be motivated to repent and be restored. Only then, can that person respond positively, just as Zacchaeus did; not *in order* to be loved but *because* he already is loved. Zacchaeus responded with amazing hospitality, welcoming Jesus with joy, which is in stark contrast to the crowd that is grumbling: "He has gone to be the guest of a man who is a sinner" (verse 7). His response was flamboyant! "Lord, half of my possessions I will give to the poor, and if I have defrauded anyone of anything, I will give back four times as much" (verse 8). Fear is not a permanent or intrinsic motivator; *love is*. Let God lavish you with His love and grace! Only then will we be enabled to respond in love (1 John 4:19).

My Response: _____

HIS KINGDOM

*Pilate also wrote an inscription and put it on the cross. It was written,
"Jesus the Nazarene, the king of the Jews."*

—John 19:19

The Palace of Versailles offers visitors a glimpse of the lavishness enjoyed by those who lived and reigned there. Its impressive architecture, the magnificent never-ending gardens, the hall of mirrors, the art collection, and many other things witness to the opulent lifestyle of kings and queens. This, the largest of the chateaus in France, was built as a statement of the power of France at the time.

Even in the time of the New Testament, kings and rulers were surrounded by opulence. That's why Jesus did not fit the popular notion of a king. "Pilate entered again into the Praetorium, and summoned Jesus and said to Him, 'Are You the King of the Jews?' " (John 18:33). "Jesus answered, 'My kingdom is not of this world. If My kingdom were of this world, then My servants would be fighting so that I would not be handed over to the Jews; but as it is, My kingdom is not of this realm" (verse 36). This inscription, "The king of the Jews" (19:19), became the official charge that was placed on the cross, and John adds that it was written in three languages: Hebrew, Latin, and Greek; which means that everyone who could read could understand it. This title made the chief priests of the Jews very uncomfortable, and they asked Pilate to clarify that this was His claim, not a fact. Pilate did not agree. Yet what was meant as a charge and a mockery, helped create the most profound scene in the universe: the King of kings had left His heavenly palace to come and die as a criminal on a cross in order to save His people. F. F. Bruce adds, "So now John sees a deeper meaning in the 'title' on the cross than either Pilate or the chief priests could appreciate. 'The hour has come for the Son of Man to be glorified.' The Crucified One is the true king, the kingliest king of all; because it is he who is stretched on the cross, he turns an obscene instrument of torture into a throne of glory and 'reigns from the tree.' "* Let's praise our King, who is worthy of all glory, for He considered our salvation higher than all heavenly riches and honor (Revelation 5:12).

My Response: _____

---

* F. F. Bruce, *The Gospel of John* (Grand Rapids, MI: Eerdmans, 1983), 369.

His Jurisdiction

*"All authority has been given to Me
in heaven and on earth."*

—Matthew 28:18

One encounters issues of jurisdiction in many spheres of life, such as courts of law, geographical divisions, economics, and even cyberspace. Jurisdiction is defined as: "The authority of a sovereign power to govern or legislate," and "the limits or territory within which authority may be exercised."* I am so thankful that Jesus starts His last recorded statement in the Gospel of Matthew by announcing the comprehensive jurisdiction of His authority: "*All* authority has been given to Me in *heaven and on earth*" (Matthew 28:18). Any questions? *All* of heaven and *all* of earth; *all* are under His authority.

The last scene in Matthew occurs when the eleven disciples go to Galilee "to the mountain which Jesus had designated" (Matthew 28:16). There they worshipped Him, but "some were doubtful" (verse 17). Jesus came towards them (verse 18). He gets a little closer; this is their farewell, and His last words will be remembered forever. Matthew highlights the momentous occasion by utilizing two verbs to introduce Jesus' words: "[He] *spoke* to them, *saying* . . ." (verse 18). I can imagine the disciples feeling the seriousness of the moment, earnestly listening to the words of the resurrected Christ: "All authority has been given to Me in heaven and on earth. Go therefore and make disciples of all the nations, baptizing them in the name of the Father and the Son and the Holy Spirit" (verses 18, 19). The commission of Jesus to go proclaim Him to all the nations is preceded by His assurance that all of creation, the whole universe, is under His authority. This is to be the disciples' surety. Jesus had already stated during His ministry that the Father had handed *everything* over to Him (see Matthew 11:27), but now His perfect life and death had been validated by the resurrection, and, in fulfillment of prophecy, all dominion would be His (see Daniel 7:13, 14). Pause for a moment to meditate on what this means: Jesus has complete authority over all angels and principalities, sickness and health, life and death, the past, present, and future, good times and bad times. He is sovereign over *all*! And nothing can separate us from Him! (Romans 8:38, 39).

My Response: _____

---

* *Merriam-Webster,* s.v. "Jurisdiction (n.)," accessed April 18, 2019, https://www.merriam -webster.com/dictionary/jurisdiction.

HIS SONG

"Great and marvelous are Your works, O Lord God, the Almighty; Righteous and true are Your ways, King of the nations!"
—Revelation 15:3

My major in college was music, and I've always been fascinated with the biblical narratives containing songs. Israel was the nation that went out into battle with musicians along with the army. There are many flamboyant worship scenes in the Bible, including the final events in the book of Revelation, that contain many beautiful songs of worship. But let's start with the book of Exodus.

The Israelites had been waiting for hundreds of years to be delivered from their oppressors. Following the last plague and the Passover lamb, we find the opening of the sea, the miraculous way in which God delivered His people and took them to the Promised Land. After the parting of the waters, there is a wonderful celebration. This deliverance song, recorded in Exodus 15, in most Bibles is entitled "The Song of Moses," but it highlights the mighty hand of the Lord (Yahweh), who was able to redeem His people. We find this song once again at the end of the Bible, but the beauty and newness of the narrative in Revelation 15 is that even though the plagues are still to happen, John first contemplates the celebration of the redeemed! The Exodus is in the background, and the redeemed sing the song of Exodus 15. John describes it like this: "I saw something like a sea of glass mixed with fire, and those who had been victorious over the beast and his image . . . standing on the sea of glass . . . *And they sang the song of Moses,* the bond-servant of God, and the *song of the Lamb,* saying, 'Great and marvelous are Your works' " (Revelation 15:2, 3). Now we understand! The song of Moses is *also* the song of the Lamb. Jesus is the triumphant Redeemer, the greater Moses! He made a way when there was no way. The Promised Land is at hand! May our lives become a celebration of the Lamb's work. No matter what we are going through, may we live from now on with an *attitude of gratitude* that is contagious. How about if we already start singing this song, now until eternity? "Redeemed, how I love to proclaim it! *Redeemed by the blood of the Lamb!"**

My Response: _____

---

* Fanny Crosby, "Redeemed."

WELCOMING HIS PRESENCE

His Goodwill

"What do you want Me to do for you?" And he said,
"Lord, I want to regain my sight!" And Jesus said to him,
"Receive your sight."

—Luke 18:41, 42

We all need to know that we are loved and valued. I know a couple who decided to visit a nursing home for Christmas and requested all the names of the residents who didn't have any family that would be coming to visit. Then they prepared gift baskets and personally brought them to the people on their list. The responses were amazing! Those lonely people felt loved and valued. There have been times in my life when I felt alone, empty, needing assurance, and guidance, and I learned that God is ready and willing to supply all my needs, often in surprising ways. I can bring him my lack and trade it for His unlimited resources.

Bartimaeus was a blind man, who used to beg by the roadside (Luke 18:35). When Jesus was passing by, he started calling out to Him, saying, "Jesus, Son of David, have mercy on me!" (verse 38). Since he was a beggar, asking for mercy could simply mean a request for money. But this particular cry pointed to the "Son of David," the expected Messiah. The angel had announced Jesus as the long-awaited Son of David who would bring rest and healing (Luke 1:30–33; 2:4; see Ezekiel 34:15, 23, 24), but this is the first time since the birth narratives in the Gospel of Luke that this title of Jesus is stated publicly. "Those who led the way were sternly telling him to be quiet; but he kept crying out all the more, 'Son of David, have mercy on me!' " (Luke 18:39). In contrast to all the people who tried to silence the man, Jesus stopped, called for him, and questioned him: "What do you want Me to do for you?" (verse 41). The man requested his sight, and he received it. The goodwill of God to supply our needs is still the same today. All the miracles in the Gospels point to the ultimate salvation available in Jesus. Until He comes to take us home, let's bring our lack to Him. Let's trade our weakness for His strength, our weariness for His rest, our ignorance for His wisdom, our fear for His peace, our loneliness for His presence, and our neediness for His riches. "My God will supply all your needs according to His riches in glory in Christ Jesus" (Philippians 4:19).

My Response: _____

HIS DWELLING

"Behold, the tabernacle of God is among men,
and He will dwell among them, and they shall be His people,
and God Himself will be among them."
—Revelation 21:3

Visiting the Temple Mount in Jerusalem was a very memorable experience. I went to the Western Wall on Friday evening, as the Sabbath festivities were starting, and the joy of the worshippers was flamboyant! This wall was part of the enlargement of the Second Jewish Temple. Until now, devout believers still place petitions between the stones of the wall, praying and meditating there, trying to be as close as possible to the place where God's Presence was manifested.

When humanity sinned, God continued His relationship with the race. He designed a way in which His people would experience His presence. He designed vivid symbolism in the tabernacle/sanctuary of the wilderness and eventually in the temple. God manifested the glory of His presence as well as His redemption plan in these sacred structures. He dwelt with His people, and His Presence was palpable in their midst. When Jesus became flesh, He *tabernacled* among us (John 1:14). This is the same word as the one used for *tabernacle* in the wilderness, only in a verb form, which is usually translated as "dwelt." Jesus was the ultimate representation of God's glory, and God's presence dwelt with humans through Him. In the new earth, the *tabernacle* (same word as in the wilderness, LXX) of God will be among humans, and He will dwell with us forevermore (Revelation 21:3). He has always been with us and will be with us eternally. He will *tabernacle* with His children, and in His presence, there won't be any death, mourning, crying, or pain (verse 4). And there will be no more temple there, because God Himself will be among us: "I saw no temple in it, for the Lord God the Almighty and the Lamb are its temple" (Revelation 21:22). God will be permanently back with His children who were lost in Eden. God's presence with us is the greatest promise that we have on this earth. God's Spirit dwells with us right now. Jesus came as Immanuel, God with us; He dwelt among us and died on the cross in our place so that we may always be with Him! May you find comfort in God's covenantal promise to always dwell with you!

My Response: _____

His Intent

Abraham was the father of Isaac,
Isaac the father of Jacob, . . .

—Matthew 1:2

When visiting Dublin, I asked my host if he could take me to see the Malahide castle, to which he gladly agreed. I have visited larger and more impressive castles, but this one was of particular interest to me for one simple fact: it had been the home of the Talbot family for eight hundred years. Frankly, that was the main reason why I wanted to go, and it was a great experience. The tour guide kept calling me "Lady Talbot," the title of the women who had inhabited the castle.

Finding out about the whereabouts of possible family ancestors seems to add something to our lives. In the first century, it was much more than that. For the Jewish people, names such as Abraham and David reminded them of their bloodline *and* that they were part of God's chosen people. Often their claims to being descendants of Abraham were uttered as a claim to a religious pedigree. Matthew starts his "book of genesis" (genealogy) by mentioning that Jesus, the Messiah, was the son of David and the son of Abraham (Matthew 1:1), which were big names for the Jews. He goes on from Abraham through Isaac, Jacob, et cetera (verse 2). But if we take a closer look at all these heroes of faith, we realize two things: first, they were all flawed people, and second, God's mercy is greater than our mistakes. Consider Abram (later called Abraham), who was promised a son and offspring as numerous as the stars (Genesis 15:5). He believed, and it was accounted to him as righteousness (verse 6; this is the first clear biblical instance of being declared righteous by faith). Yet in the next chapter (Genesis 16), as he is getting old and his wife Sarai is barren, he tries to *help* God by having a son with Hagar, the Egyptian maid. *Yet God didn't go back on His original intent* of giving Abram the son of the promise (Isaac). Even though Abram lacked faith and took a detour, God *still* brought about His promise. Have you made mistakes that you thought would disqualify you? All of us have. That's why the Cross was necessary. God's original intent of saving us and giving us a divine purpose still stands. Abraham's presence in the genealogy of Jesus reminds us of God's redeeming ability!

My Response: _____

His Ancestry

Judah was the father of Perez and Zerah by Tamar.
—Matthew 1:3

Many years ago, I taped a television program about the great-great-great-grandmothers of Jesus. In it we analyzed Matthew's genealogy of Jesus, and his surprising addition of four women, four mothers among all the fathers, which was not a common practice. The most startling fact is that not one of the four would have been chosen for the "Israelite Woman of the Year" award. We will study each one of them in order to find out more about the plan of salvation.

Genesis 38 seems to be an interlude in the story of Joseph. Yet it provides key information regarding the ancestry of Jesus. Judah, the fourth son of Jacob, left his brothers and took a Canaanite wife. She conceived and bore him three sons: Er, Onan, and Shelah. Judah obtained a wife for his eldest son Er; her name was Tamar; she was most likely a Canaanite. Er was evil, and he died without offspring. The laws of levirate marriage (Deuteronomy 25:5–10) required that offspring be secured through the brother-in-law and, in accordance to those standards, Judah told Onan, his second son, to perform these duties to secure a descendant for his dead brother. Even though Onan had intercourse with Tamar, he prevented conception (see Genesis 38:9). This displeased the Lord, and he also died. Judah did not fulfill his promise to give Tamar his third son Shelah. So one day, Tamar, knowing Judah's whereabouts and desiring to secure a descendant for the family, posed as a harlot. Judah slept with her, leaving his seal, cord, and staff as a pledge, not realizing who she was. Tamar got pregnant with twins! When Judah was told that his daughter-in-law was pregnant, he wanted to burn her (verse 24), yet Tamar produced his seal, cord, and staff, and it became evident who the father was! And he declared her more righteous than him, which was pretty evident! And the twins were born. It is hard to imagine the shock her name would have created in the genealogy of a Jewish Messiah. Yet there she is! Jesus came through the line of Judah, Tamar, and their dysfunctional family. And Matthew makes a point to mention her, that we may know that heaven's doors are open to flawed people, just like us!

My Response: _____

His Emancipation

Salmon was the father of Boaz by Rahab.
—Matthew 1:5

In a Honolulu coffee shop, at 3:30 A.M., Tony Campolo overheard a young lady, who was obviously a prostitute, telling a friend that the next day was her birthday, and that she'd never had a birthday party. Tony organized one. The following morning, everyone was waiting for Agnes when she came in at 3:30 A.M. She was overwhelmed! Tony prayed for her, and the man behind the counter asked him what church he belonged to. "I belong to a church that throws birthday parties for prostitutes at 3:30 A.M.," Tony replied. The man answered: "No, you don't! If a church like that existed, I'd join it!"*

Why in the world would Matthew add the name of a prostitute to the genealogy of Jesus (Matthew 1:5)? Does God's grace reach out so flamboyantly into the darkness? The story of Rahab, the harlot, is told in the book of Joshua, chapters 2 and 6. Joshua had sent two spies to Jericho who, being afraid to stay outside, found Rahab and hid in the stalks of flax on the roof of her house. She lied to the king of Jericho about their whereabouts and gave the spies advice on how to escape. And she, of all people, uttered one of the most profound confessions about the God of Israel. It recounted God's acts in the past, and provided a prophecy for the future and a pronouncement about the true God: "I know that the LORD has given you the land. . . . For we have heard how the LORD dried up the water of the Red Sea before you when you came out of Egypt. . . . for the LORD your God, He is God in heaven above and on earth beneath" (Joshua 2:9–11). The spies gave her a guarantee that if she tied a scarlet cord to the window, whoever was in the house with her would be spared (verse 18). And, just like those who were delivered by the blood of the Passover lamb applied to the doorposts, she was spared. She joined Israel and became one of the ancestors of Jesus; she is mentioned in Matthew 1:5, and is mentioned later as a faith hero: "By faith Rahab the harlot did not perish" (Hebrews 11:31). We serve a God who emancipates everyone willing, whether a prostitute or a tax collector, a criminal or an addict—and gives them a divine purpose for His glory!

My Response: _____

---

* Tony Campolo, *Let Me Tell You a Story* (Nashville, TN: Thomas Nelson, Inc., 2000), 216.

His Lineage

Boaz was the father of Obed by Ruth, and Obed the father of Jesse.
Jesse was the father of David the king.
—Matthew 1:5, 6

Both of my parents were born in Uruguay. I knew that my mother's side was Swiss-German, and my father's side was probably Spanish-Portuguese. When I was a young woman, my parents visited a *Charrua* native Indian cemetery in Uruguay, and to their surprise they found that many of the tombstones had my paternal grandmother's last name! I was so excited about the possibility of having a little bit of *Charrua* blood! Someday I will have to take an ancestry test. . . .

The lineage of Jesus was very important for Matthew's audience, especially His "royal blood" through the Davidic line. But there were a few surprises in the lineage of Jesus that Matthew highlights. And, unlike me, his audience wouldn't have been too excited about them. Ruth, the great-grandmother of David, lived in Bethlehem with her second husband, Boaz. But Ruth was a Moabite and didn't really *belong* to the people of Israel. The Moabites came from Moab, and the Ammonites came from Ammon; both forefathers were the product of two incestuous relationships between Lot and his daughters (see Genesis 19:37, 38). Their descendants were not friends of Israel and were not allowed to enter the assembly of the Lord (see Numbers 22; 23; Deuteronomy 23:3). Ruth came to Bethlehem with her mother-in-law Naomi, after Naomi's husband and two sons died in the land of Moab. She refused to leave Naomi, no matter what the cost, and promised to stay with her even until death: "Your people shall be my people, and your God, my God. Where you die, I will die" (Ruth 1:16, 17). In Bethlehem she married Boaz, one of Naomi's kinsman-redeemers, and they had a son named Obed, who became the grandfather of David. That a Moabite would be mentioned in the *legal* lineage of Jesus points to the Messiah who was coming to tear down walls of separation that had existed for generations. Do you ever feel like you don't *belong* because of your background, painful experiences, or past record? Remember that Jesus is proud to be your Brother! You are accepted! You are loved! You are His!

My Response: _____

His Nobility

Jesse was the father of David the king. David was the father of Solomon by Bathsheba who had been the wife of Uriah.

—Matthew 1:6

One day I was searching on the internet about the geographical location of my ancestors, when I clicked on a website that opened up all kinds of data about my maiden name. It included sections such as the average lifespan, census records, immigration records, draft cards, and much more. And then a question caught my attention: "Is anyone famous hiding in your family tree?"

This would have been an important question at the time of Jesus. The Davidic *royal nobility* of Jesus, as the much-awaited Messiah, appears in the first verse of Matthew's Gospel, where the title "the son of David" is given prominence in His genealogy. But when we get to verse 6, we find that David was not only a famous king, but he had also sinned famously. Perhaps this is the reason why Bathsheba is not mentioned by name in the Greek original. The Greek text reads: "And Jesse fathered David the king. And David fathered Solomon by the [wife] of Uriah" (verse 6). So David fathered a child with someone else's wife? Yep! Which brings us to the famously treacherous story of David's great sin. Take a moment to read 2 Samuel, chapters 11 and 12. David spotted Uriah's wife bathing and, even though he had many other wives, he sent for her and committed adultery with her. She got pregnant, and David tried to cover this up by trying to make it look like this was Uriah's child. But when it didn't work, David had him placed in a dangerous spot in battle where he was sure to be killed, and he was. God reached out to David through a prophet, and he repented and was forgiven, even though there were dire consequences. They had another son: Solomon, who was the ancestor of Jesus. Adultery and murder—the story behind this verse in the genealogy of Jesus. So, why put it there? Because humans, even the most famous ones, are famously sinful and dysfunctional. And Jesus was coming as our Savior because we desperately needed one. His pedigree included foreigners, sinners, and famously dysfunctional families, including all of us. Aren't you thankful for *our* inclusive Savior?

My Response: _____

HIS ANSWER

"Do not be afraid . . . for your petition has been heard."
—Luke 1:13

I have a little prayer box that is really special to me because I made it for my mother when she was battling cancer. I wrote the words of Isaiah 41:10 on the outside of the box. I remember with great tenderness and admiration how my mom would write her prayer requests on little pieces of paper and place them in the box when her days were difficult. God was so faithful in granting her strength, peace, assurance, and even a sense of humor to the very end. Now, as I use the same box, I am amazed at the varied and unexpected ways in which God answers my prayers, usually with immeasurably more than what I ask or imagine!

If we could ask Zacharias, he would have much to say about the surprising ways in which God answers prayers. Elizabeth, his wife, was barren; they probably prayed for a son for decades. Now they were advanced in years, and Zacharias was chosen by lot to enter the temple and burn incense (Luke 1:9). This was a great honor, one to which all priests aspired. The people stayed outside praying as he entered the temple. When the angel Gabriel appeared to him (see verse 19), Zacharias was so troubled that he missed the fact that the angel was standing to the right of the altar (see verse 11), which meant that the heavenly messenger was bearing good news. The angel then said to him: "Do not be afraid, Zacharias, for your petition has been heard, and your wife Elizabeth will bear you a son" (verse 13). Isn't it great to know that our petitions are heard? But which petition was heard? What petition was the angel referring to? I would have thought that Zacharias had stopped petitioning for a son long before that day. Obviously, the people of Israel and the priest representing them would have been praying for the redemption of Israel. Leave it up to God to answer *both* petitions at the same time: one lifelong (their petition for a child), and the other centuries long (for the upcoming Messiah)! Yes, Zacharias's son would be the forerunner of the Messiah! Let's trust God's viewpoint and His surprising answers to our prayers. He accomplishes much more than we imagine, and He always has our redemption in mind!

My Response: _____

HIS FULFILLMENT

"These things . . . will be fulfilled in their proper time."
—Luke 1:20

My mother-in-law was an eager student of the Scriptures and, as she studied verse by verse, she used to record her observations in a journal. I had to smile when I read her observations on Zacharias losing his ability to speak. She wrote: "Thank God Zacharias became mute, that way he couldn't talk about his doubts and unbelief!" I think her comment is funny, true, and profound! Given the fact that he was having a hard time believing that God would fulfill His promise, his speaking would not have been very edifying.

Many times when confronted with something that is humanly impossible, just like Zacharias, our default mode is unbelief and doubt. It was humanly impossible for his wife Elizabeth, who was barren and advanced in years, to conceive a child, the forerunner of the Messiah. When Zacharias asked how he would know these things for certain, the angel answered: "I am Gabriel, who stands in the presence of God, and I have been sent . . . to bring you this *good news*. And behold, you shall be silent and unable to speak until the day when these things take place, because you did not believe my words, which will *be fulfilled in their proper time*" (Luke 1:19, 20). In contrast, when Mary received the news that she would be pregnant of the Holy Spirit, for "nothing will be impossible with God" (verse 37), she responded with submission: "May it be done to me according to your word" (verse 38). The similarities between Zacharias and Mary are striking: both were visited by the angel Gabriel, both had obstacles for child bearing and were wondering how this could happen, both were told to "fear not," both received the promise of a miracle child, both were told what role the child would have in redemption history, and both were given a sign before the angel departed. But the difference between the two was that Mary believed that the impossible would be fulfilled according to God's word! May we believe the *good news* we've received, because, humanly speaking, our salvation is impossible. Yet our salvation has been purchased and everything will be fulfilled . . . according to God's Word!

My Response: _____

HIS EXCEPTIONALISM

*And coming in, he [the angel Gabriel] said to her,
"Greetings, favored one! The Lord is with you."*
—Luke 1:28

We had received many holiday cards from family and friends, but there was one that stood out: a digital card from a relative which had a picture of two Christmas ornaments. The center of the first ornament showcased the face of her little daughter. The second one looked like a regular ornament, until I realized that it was a picture of a baby's sonogram! It was an announcement of her pregnancy! And just like that it became much more than a regular holiday card.

Have you ever experienced how a simple announcement, a realization, or some good news can turn your day from ordinary to extraordinary? In the Bible, the redemptive announcements of God always turn an ordinary moment into an extraordinary experience. To this day, when we personally get a glimpse of God's redeeming love, our life becomes exceptionally different. Mary lived in the unremarkable city of Nazareth, in the region of Galilee. She was probably having a common, ordinary day, going about her tasks at home, until the visit of the angel Gabriel, who brought her exceptional news. Gabriel's salutation to Mary gave her a double assurance of both God's *favor* and *presence* with her: "Greetings [or rejoice], favored one! The Lord is with you" (Luke 1:28). Similar assurances were used in the Old Testament when individuals were chosen by God for a purpose, and He assured them of His presence to aid in accomplishing it (for examples, see Genesis 26:24; Exodus 3:12; Judges 6:12). Mary had been chosen to be the mother of the much-awaited Messiah (Luke 1:30–33); she would give birth to the Savior of the world! And from there on, nothing about Mary's life was ordinary or common. You, too, have been chosen by God for the extraordinary experience of salvation. You are also assured of both His *favor* and His *presence*. You are so favored that God Himself died in your place, securing eternal life for you. And He is with you at this very moment. Yes! God offers you an exceptional life of joy, peace, and purpose, in spite of difficulties. Rejoice, favored one! *The Lord is with you!*

My Response: _____

HIS LIMITLESSNESS

"For nothing will be impossible with God."

—Luke 1:37

This week I had a spiritual experience in an unexpected way. I had an echocardiogram, and it was the first time in my life that I could listen to my heart beat and see its valves in motion. It took me by surprise, not that I hadn't known that it was working . . . but the sounds and visuals highlighted the miraculous. Here is an engine inside my body running on its own for more than five decades, without any outside source of power. I became even more aware that every second we live is a true miracle.

When the angel Gabriel announced to Mary that she would conceive and a miraculous Baby would be born, Mary wondered how was this possible, because she was a virgin. The angel replied that the Holy Spirit would come upon her, and that the holy Child would be called the Son of God (Luke 1:35). Then he told her that her older and barren relative, Elizabeth, was in the sixth month of her pregnancy and added that "nothing will be impossible with God" (verse 37). The Greek words in this sentence may be translated as, "not any word, thing, event, or matter" will be impossible with God. Nothing is impossible for God; *all things are possible* for Him. The Lord gave a similar response to Abraham, when Sarah laughed when she heard that she would conceive in her old age. "Is anything too difficult for the LORD?" (Genesis 18:14). God's covenantal line came through this old, barren woman to show God's design and limitlessness. Then, in the Gospel of Luke, the same root word used by Gabriel with Mary is used by Jesus when explaining salvation: "They who heard it said, 'Then who can be saved?' But He said, 'The things that are impossible with people are possible with God' " (Luke 18:26, 27). Our God is not limited by human limits. God, "gives life to the dead and calls into being that which does not exist" (Romans 4:17). By His Word the universe was created, and by His Word made flesh we have been saved. His divine limitlessness stands in opposition to our powerlessness. Be assured that your salvation, which is impossible for you, has been made possible through Christ! Hallelujah!

My Response: _____

His Direction

"Behold, the bondslave of the Lord; may it be done to me according to your word."

—Luke 1:38

My parents had just moved to another state to continue their ministry. They bought a new townhouse, but when the date arrived to close the escrow, something happened to the foundation, and they couldn't purchase it. They chose another house with the same company, and that one caught fire before the delivery date. They chose a third unit, and that's where they lived until retirement. Even under those unusual circumstances, I watched them trust that God was directing them.

There are many things in life that we don't fully understand, and most of them are outside of our control. Even though Mary was a virgin, when the angel Gabriel announced to her that she would supernaturally conceive the Son of God, she surrendered to the plan, though not because she understood it fully. God's ways are not our ways, and we can't always make sense of God's direction for our lives. Still we can trust Him fully and surrender to His plan instead of following ours. In the Lord's Prayer, Jesus taught His disciples to pray: "Your kingdom come. *Your will be done*, on earth as it is in heaven." (Matthew 6:10). We all want God's will to be done on earth, don't we? But there is a small Greek word that sometimes gives us trouble; it is the word *moi*, which is translated "to me." Mary's response was: "May it be done to *me* according to your word" (Luke 1:38). At some point, God's direction for our lives becomes personal and often unfathomable. When we face perplexing circumstances, we might question how a particular situation could turn out for God's glory. But most of these answers await us on the other side of eternity. As in Mary's case, we are called to submit to God's plan, and by His grace fulfill our part in that plan. "A person's steps are directed by the LORD. How then can anyone understand their own way?" (Proverbs 20:24, NIV). In those situations, it is imperative to trust in God's goodness, love, and grace towards us. He who gave His life so that we may live also directs our steps. "Trust in the LORD with all your heart . . . and He shall direct your paths" (Proverbs 3:5, 6, NKJV).

My Response: _____

365

HIS PLAN

"Joseph, Son of David, do not be afraid."

—Matthew 1:20

It took me a while to start using a GPS. Whenever I traveled for speaking engagements, I was used to printing my maps and going over my route ahead of time. But then I realized that the GPS has the ability to guide me securely to my destination and even recalculate my route whenever I find myself on a detour. My life is like that, because God has His own GPS. Yet all of us sometimes struggle with God's GPS day by day directions, because we don't always understand His ways, even though we believe that God knows best.

I find great comfort in Matthew 1:18–25, in which a righteous man is struggling with his plans versus God's plans. Joseph is the only person, aside from Jesus, in this Gospel to be called "son of David" (verse 20), thereby establishing the legal royal family line for his son whom he would name Jesus (verse 25). He is a righteous and compassionate man. Learning that his fiancée is pregnant, not by him, he decides to divorce her (necessary to break the "husband-wife" engagement at that time), without demanding that she be stoned or even publicly humiliated. Joseph *"planned* to send her away secretly" (verse 19). Yes, he had plans and was pondering how to make them happen; and that's when God decided to take the initiative to communicate with him and turned his plans upside down.

"But when he had considered this [the divorce], behold, an angel of the Lord appeared to him in a dream, saying, 'Joseph, son of David, *do not be afraid* to take Mary as your wife; for the Child who has been conceived in her is of the Holy Spirit' " (verse 20). Did you notice that? Joseph was afraid. He had made other plans, according to his understanding of the situation. Yet God was giving him a completely new perspective, informing him that this Child was conceived by the Holy Spirit (a fact mentioned twice in this section; see verses 18, 20). I am so thankful for God's GPS. So many times, I make my own plans according to my viewpoint, and then God overturns them. I invite you to trust God's viewpoint. He knows more than we do. He who found a way to save us, will surely find a way to guide us!

My Response: _____

HIS SALVATION

"You shall call His name Jesus, for He will save."

—Matthew 1:21

I am sure you have heard the saying "It's *who* you know." Well, that day it was more than true. My plane had just landed when I found the following text message: "Your dad is at the emergency room, come quickly." At the hospital, I learned that he had been fainting, and that they wanted to run some extensive tests. I asked the doctor to transfer him to a much larger hospital where he had been receiving treatment for cancer, but they told me that the ER of that hospital wouldn't take him because he had been already admitted to the local hospital. This was a big problem due to his ongoing cancer treatments! So, it was time to make *that* phone call, to *the person* who could make it happen. After a little while the doctor entered my dad's room and said: "I don't know *who* you know over there, but they are sending medical transportation to transfer him."

When it comes to salvation, it's all about *who* you know. The angel announced that the Savior's name would be Jesus, for "He will save His people from their sins" (Matthew 1:21). Jesus is the Greek version of the name Joshua or Yeshua; it means "Yahweh saves" or "the Lord saves." In Bible times, names had great meaning, and the name of Jesus encompasses His mission: to save. During His ministry most people didn't address Jesus by His first name; usually they would call Him Master, Teacher, Rabbi, Son of David, Son of God, et cetera. But we have a few exceptions, such as the thief on the cross who addressed Him as *"Jesus,* remember me when You come in Your kingdom!" (Luke 23:42). In other words: "The Lord saves: remember me . . . ." The name of Jesus itself provides an assurance for the evildoer hanging next to Him. Jesus came to save us; this was, and is, His primary and core mission. He fulfills many other roles: He is our friend, our advocate, our priest, our king, our Lord, and much more. Yet the primary reason why He came as a baby was to be our Savior. He was born to die. If you ever wonder whether God is willing to forgive you for a particular sin, whisper the name of Jesus, and you will remember: Oh, yes! He came to save!

My Response: _____

His Name

"She will bear a Son; and you shall call His name Jesus."
—Matthew 1:21

Some time ago we were taping TV shows based on the book of Acts, and we got to the program titled "The Name," in which we discussed Acts 3; 4. These two chapters emphasize the fact that there is salvation only in Jesus' name (see Acts 4:12). A musician named Don Singh composed a song for that show titled "The Name of Jesus" that starts with these words: "What's in a name in time, that can save a life like mine . . ." It is a great song, and a great question. The words go on to describe who Jesus is and what He has done.

So, what's in a name? In Bible times names contained even more meaning than they do now. The character and mission of the person were embedded in their name; thus, the name of the child revealed the expectations of the parents. God chose and revealed Jesus' name when He was still in Mary's womb. It was a common name at that time; *Iesous* (Jesus) is the Greek counterpart to the Hebrew *Joshua*. The name means "Yahweh is salvation / Yahweh saves." God's choice of this name reveals the primary purpose and mission of the Child: to save!

The angel of the Lord goes on to explain the reason why He will be called *Jesus*: "For He will save His people from their sins" (Matthew 1:21). The pronoun "He" is emphatic, which carries the meaning of "He Himself will save His people . . . ." He saves; we cannot save ourselves, no matter how hard we try. As discussed yesterday, He fulfills many roles on our behalf: He is a Friend, an Example, a Counselor, et cetera. But *above all*, His mission is to save us because we cannot save ourselves. The idea that He would save His people *from their sins* was contrary to popular anticipations because most people were expecting the Messiah as a religious and political figure, who would deliver them from the power of their oppressors. Yet Jesus came to save us from the curse of sin and alienation from God by carrying our sins so that we may be reconciled with God. Be assured that there is no sin, no matter how dark, that His bloodstained name cannot cover. When we pray in Jesus' name, let's remember who He really is: our Savior!

My Response: _____

HIS PRESENCE

*"They shall call His name Immanuel," which translated
means, "God with us."*

—Matthew 1:23

When my mom realized that we had taken the wrong bus, we got off at the next bus stop. It was night time, and we found ourselves in an industrial area of town; there were no residential homes where we could ask for help. My mom and I just kept walking, reciting Bible verses. Yet for me there was one most important assurance: my mom was with me, and therefore I was safe; her presence was all my young heart needed. She would find a way home—and she did. Only now, as an adult, do I realize how difficult this experience must have been for my mom.

Matthew describes the dismay Joseph felt after receiving the news that Mary was pregnant (Matthew 1:18, 19). He was so dismayed that an angel of the Lord had to appear to him in a dream to let him know that Mary's pregnancy was the work of the Holy Spirit, and that the Son she would bear would be called Jesus (verses 20, 21). After Joseph's dream, the author of this gospel adds two verses that are only found in Matthew; it's an Old Testament prophecy applied to Jesus (Matthew 1:22, 23). The quotation comes from Isaiah 7:14, and the context of the prophecy is most enlightening. In Isaiah chapter 7, Ahaz, king of Judah, is in real trouble. The kings of Aram and Israel are coming to fight against him, and Ahaz and his people are extremely afraid (Isaiah 7:2). Isaiah brings Ahaz the promise of God's *presence* and tries to prevent him from making alliances with other military powers, but Ahaz refuses to ask the Lord for help. Nevertheless, God decides to give Ahaz a sign so that he would always remember that God had offered His presence in this difficult time. A maiden would bear a son who would be called *Immanuel*, which literally means "with us God." God offers us the same assurance: His Presence. Matthew highlights that Jesus was the ultimate fulfillment of that prophecy. We are never alone, because Jesus came to be our all-sufficient Savior. We have the assurance of His Presence no matter how dark it may be around us, how lost we may feel, or how threatening the future may look. God is with us!

My Response: _____

HIS WAY

"Blessed is she who believed."

—Luke 1:45

My dad told this story countless times, always with great emotion. When I was a baby, our tiny car broke down on a desolate road, far away from any possible help. My dad got out of the car to discover that a part had broken, which made it impossible for the car to start. With the broken part in his hand, he got into the car, and right there in the middle of nowhere, my parents asked God for a miracle: for the car to start even though it was mechanically impossible. Our survival, especially mine, depended on it. My dad turned the key . . . and the car started! It kept running for several miles until we got to the main road; then it stopped. We got help and the rest is history. This is one of the explicit miracles my family experienced.

Throughout the Gospels there are blessings pronounced over those who believe in God's pronouncements, even when His ways seem impossible, and they can't fully understand them. We usually call these blessings "beatitudes." Elizabeth, who had conceived in her old age, pronounced two beatitudes over Mary, the mother of Jesus. The first one is found in Luke 1:42: "Blessed are you among women, and blessed is the fruit of your womb!" The first blessing relates to Mary's motherhood. The second beatitude that Elizabeth pronounces relates to Mary believing in the word of the Lord: "Blessed is she who believed that there would be a fulfillment of what had been spoken to her by the Lord" (Luke 1:45). Mary knew that it was impossible for her to conceive without knowing a man, yet she believed in the impossible because God said so. God's way is different than our way, and we often can't understand or explain it. Still we are invited to believe in what God has promised. It is interesting to note that Elizabeth's first blessing on Mary is in the second person "blessed are *you* . . . ," yet the second blessing is in the third person "blessed is *she* . . ." Some scholars suggest that the third person is used as an invitation for others to believe as well.* Surely, we are all invited to believe the unbelievable. It's God's way versus our way. Even our salvation is by faith! Blessed are you . . . who believed!

My Response: _____

---

* Joel B. Green, *The Gospel of Luke,* NICNT (Grand Rapids, MI: Eerdmans, 1997), 97.

HIS FAVOR

"The Mighty One has done great things for me."

—Luke 1:49

The family gathered around as I was about to dedicate to God one of my precious step-grandchildren. She was, and continues to be, a bundle of joy and tenderness. What Bible text could appropriately express such happiness about God's gift of a child? Two biblical mothers came to mind, both with exuberant songs of praise to God for His favor bestowed upon them. As we read these songs, our hearts were filled with thanksgiving.

The first song comes from the heart of Hannah, a misunderstood woman who wasn't able to conceive (see 1 Samuel 1:2). Her husband's second wife constantly provoked her because of her barrenness. She wept, refused to eat, and could not be comforted. When her family went to Shiloh, she brought her request for a son to the tabernacle. But even there she was misunderstood! Eli, the priest, mistook her for a drunk woman and rebuked her, yet Hannah humbly explained that she was pouring out her heart to God, requesting His favor. Eli pronounced a blessing upon her, and Hannah conceived! Her exuberant song of thanksgiving is recorded in 1 Samuel 2:1–10. "My heart exults in the LORD . . . I rejoice in Your salvation" (1 Samuel 2:1). Her son, the prophet Samuel, would eventually anoint King David.

More than one thousand years later, we find the second song. Mary, the mother of Jesus, is greeted by an angel: "Greetings, favored one!" (Luke 1:28). She is then told that she will conceive a child through the Holy Spirit. He will be the Son of the Most High and have the throne of His father David (verse 32). Mary erupts in a song of thanksgiving that is based on Hannah's song: "My soul exalts the Lord, and my spirit has rejoiced in God my Savior. . . . The Mighty One has done great things for me" (Luke 1:46–49). This song is called the "Magnificat" after its first word in Latin. This is the first of four songs found in the first two chapters of Luke! Songs of thanksgiving always overflow from our grateful hearts when we get a glimpse of the magnitude of His favor in the plan of redemption!

My Response: _____

HIS NEARNESS

"Blessed be the Lord God of Israel, For He has visited us and accomplished redemption for His people."

—Luke 1:68

My father was a church administrator in South America during perilous political times. An anonymous letter was sent to his office stating that he had to leave his job at once, or his only child (yours truly) would be kidnapped. Years later another pastor told me that he had asked me at the time of the threat if I was afraid of being kidnapped, to which I had responded: "No! God is with me!" Have you noticed that often children are more aware of the *nearness* of God than adults? What obscures this perception later in life? Perhaps we gain awareness of our sinfulness, or maybe our fears get in the way.

God's presence with His people is a core theme of the whole Bible. He's not a distant deity, but the Creator God who is utterly involved in the affairs and salvation of the human race; and His redemption covenant is evident throughout the biblical story. When Adam and Eve sinned, God promised that a descendant of the woman would crush the serpent's head (Genesis 3:15). In the flood, God continued His covenant with Noah, providing a way of salvation (6:18). He promised Abraham the preservation of his descendants and the ultimate fulfillment of the promise for all nations (12:3; 15; see Galatians 3:16). And so, it continued with Moses (the Passover lamb, the tabernacle, the Day of Atonement, etc.) and David (covenant, temple, etc.). A holy God dwelt with an unholy people through the blood of the sacrifices that pointed to the coming Savior. Finally, in the Gospels, God visits His people and provides the promised Redeemer. In the prophetic words of Zacharias, God *visited* His people and accomplished their *redemption* (Luke 1:68, see also verse 78). God has always been near, even when we sinned and rebelled. The greatest manifestation of His *nearness* was the birth, life, and death of Jesus, God made flesh. Through His Spirit, God continues to dwell with us until that day when He will live with us eternally (Revelation 21:3). As you welcome His presence into your daily life, may His *nearness* become a reality that you experience and trust.

My Response: _____

HIS ORCHESTRATION

While they were there [Bethlehem], the days were completed for her to give birth. And she gave birth to her firstborn son.
—Luke 2:6, 7

When my parents passed away, Ana, a wonderful, godly woman who used to work for our ministry, asked me to send her my favorite photo of my parents and me. I didn't know why she was requesting it, but I soon found out, because I received from her a thoughtful and meaningful gift. She had my favorite picture made into a puzzle; the pieces of the puzzle were placed inside a beautiful box that has the complete photo of the three of us on it. I like puzzles, but I *love* this particular puzzle because every piece reminds me of my beloved parents.

Luke is the only Gospel writer who gives us the last piece of the puzzle about Jesus' birth. Many prophecies in the Old Testament had foretold His birth: A Savior would come to crush Satan's head (Genesis 3:15); the blessings of salvation would be for all the nations of the earth (Genesis 12:3); the Savior would come through the Davidic line (2 Samuel 7:12–16); et cetera. But there was one piece of the puzzle that was missing: the prophecy about the place where the Messiah would be born pointed to Bethlehem (Micah 5:2), but Joseph and Mary lived in Nazareth! Luke unveils the mysterious last piece by telling us that "a decree went out from Caesar Augustus, that a census be taken of all the inhabited earth. . . . Joseph also went up from Galilee, from the city of Nazareth, to Judea, to the city of David which is called Bethlehem, because he was of the house and family of David." (Luke 2:1–4). God had orchestrated this last piece of the puzzle hundreds of years before and revealed it to His prophet. God was behind every detail. It looked like it was Caesar Augustus who was calling for a census (verses 1–5), but in reality there was a whole divine plan behind it. David had been born in Bethlehem one thousand years earlier, and now His awaited descendant was to be born there as well, as part of the master plan. God has orchestrated our lives in detail as well. There is much that we don't understand, but one day Jesus will show us the view from above. Until then, let's trust that He has orchestrated our lives for salvation.

My Response: _____

HIS PREFERENCE

There were some shepherds staying out in the fields. . . .
And an angel of the Lord suddenly stood before them.

—Luke 2:8, 9

You've probably heard of Ted Williams, the so-called "Golden Voice," who alternated between homelessness and being a radio/sportscast personality. Having worked in radio up to 1994, he became homeless because of alcoholism, drug addiction, and criminal behavior. One day he was interviewed by a videographer who posted online the dialogue with him, and suddenly, in 2011, his voice was rediscovered and he received multiple job offers. He even wrote a book, telling the story about his journey from the streets to finding himself and his faith again.*

Who does God choose to be His "voices" to spread the gospel? I'm glad you asked! That God continually chooses the humble and lowly is a Lukan theme. God much rather prefers the ordinary who are meek over the learned ones who are proud. In the first century, there were two groups of people that were not allowed as witnesses in a court of law due to their low social status: women and shepherds. And in his Gospel, Luke points out that the first witnesses of Jesus' birth were shepherds (Luke 2:8–10), and the first witnesses of His resurrection were women (Luke 24:1–12)! Shocking, isn't it?! God has always revealed Himself to those who are socially marginalized, because the only thing that recommends us to God is our great need. Even though society had placed the shepherds at the very bottom stratum of power and privilege, they were highly favored by heaven. The angels bypassed the temple and came to the fields instead, where these lowly people were watching their flocks. An angel appeared, bringing the best news: "Today in the city of David there has been born *for you a Savior*, who is Christ the Lord" (Luke 2:11). A Savior, for them! And just like that, they found their "voice." After finding the baby in the manger, "the shepherds went back, glorifying and praising God for all that they had heard and seen" (verse 20). And they became the first post-birth evangelists. Do you see yourself as *discarded* by society? Let me give you the best news ever: *you* have a Savior, and He wants to give you a voice for Him!

My Response: _____

---

* Wikipedia, s.v. "Ted Williams," last modified April 7, 2019, 8:37 A.M. UTC, https://en.wikipedia.org/wiki/Ted_Williams_(voice-over_artist).

HIS JOY

The angel said to them, "Do not be afraid; for behold, I bring you good news of great joy which will be for all the people."
—Luke 2:10

Elizabeth Smart experienced a horrible ordeal. She was kidnapped on June 5, 2002 and was found only on March 12, 2003. I was deeply touched by the emotional response of Elizabeth's father to her rescue. He described how he was sitting in a police car, with Elizabeth in his arms, when he called his wife: "You are not going to believe this [he was sobbing as he retold the story], Elizabeth is alive! And she is here in my arms!" The greatest news a parent could ever receive is that his kidnapped child has been found alive! Truly good news of great joy!

Perhaps this helps us get a glimpse of God's excitement when sending angels to announce the "good news of great [*mega* in Greek] joy" (Luke 2:10). Back in Genesis 3, God's children had been kidnapped, and right away a Savior had been promised (Genesis 3:15), who would pay their ransom and reunite them with their Father. And the time had come for the Savior to be born! The Greek word for "good news" (*euangelion*) was used to convey a ruler's victory on the battlefield (see Isaiah 52:7), and the messengers who carried the good news were called *evangelists*. Now the angels came with the greatest news ever! God would be victorious through the Savior's salvific work on behalf of the human race. When the shepherds saw the angel, they were terrified (Greek: *mega fear*) (Luke 2:9). "But the angel said to them, 'Do not be afraid . . . I bring you good news of great joy [Greek: *mega joy*], which will be for all the people; for today in the city of David there has been born for you a Savior, who is Christ the Lord" (Luke 2:10, 11). When we accept the good news that we have a Savior, we experience a heavenly *mega joy*, that the world cannot take away. No matter what we encounter in our lives, the *joy* of the reality of salvation through the sacrifice of Jesus trumps all the sadness and pain we may meet in this world. This is why Paul could write from a prison cell, "Rejoice *in the Lord* always; again I will say, rejoice!" (Philippians 4:4). When we choose faith over fear, we find out that the *mega fear* is swallowed up by the *mega joy!*

My Response: _____

His Worthiness

The shepherds went back, glorifying and praising God for all that they had heard and seen, just as had been told them.

—Luke 2:20

Camp meetings are statewide retreats where thousands of people gather for several days to be inspired through the study of God's Word and to worship without distraction; many stay in tents and RVs. Over the years I have attended several such gatherings throughout North America and have many memories. In one of the camp meetings something unusual happened that I will never forget. Every night, after the evening meeting, dozens of people would spontaneously gather to sing praises to God. Without any planning, people brought their musical instruments, and we just sang for about an hour. This had a profound impact on me.

In the Gospel of Luke, the common response to the good news is to *praise* the Lord. Jesus is *worthy* to be praised, and the news of salvation contains intrinsic motivation to sing and glorify God for His grace. When you realize what God has done for you, I don't think you can help it! Joy and praise fill your heart and overflow through hymns and songs. If you are having a difficult day, practice praising the Lord and focusing on His goodness, and you will see how your perspective changes and your day gets better! In Luke, people respond with flamboyant expressions of praise and joy. For example, John the Baptist is leaping for joy in his mother's womb (1:44), and the shepherds respond with praise, glorifying God for seeing Baby Jesus; they are the first evangelists! There are four songs registered in the first two chapters of Luke; each of these hymns became known by their first words in Latin: "Magnificat," sung by Mary (Luke 1:46–55); "Benedictus," sung by Zechariah (1:68–79); "Gloria in Excelsis," sung by the angels (2:14); and "Nunc Dimittis," sung by Simeon (2:29–32). We will be singing and praising the Lamb for eternity! The heavenly beings praise Him as well: "And they sang a *new song*, saying, 'Worthy are You [the Lamb] . . . for You were slain and purchased for God with Your blood men from every tribe and tongue and people and nation' " (Revelation 5:9). Let's start praising the Savior now!

My Response: _____

HIS PEACE

*"Glory to God in the highest, and on earth
peace among men."*

—Luke 2:14

Octavian, better known as Caesar Augustus, was the adoptive heir of Julius Caesar. He was in power from approximately 31 B.C. to 14 A.D. During his rule there was a great emphasis on peace; he established what became known as the *Pax Romana* (the Roman peace), and the increased safety made empire-wide travel possible, which led to prosperity. He was venerated for this achievement.

When the angels came to the shepherds, announcing the good news of the birth of the Savior of the world (Luke 2:8–10), the heavenly choir sang about the *peace* that the Messiah was bringing (Luke 2:14), not just for Rome, but for the whole world! This is not the type of *peace* that merely means "no war," or "no trouble;" it is the inner *peace* of knowing ourselves as reconciled with God.

This is the reason why the word *peace* becomes such a key word in the Gospel of Luke. Having healed or vindicated a person, Jesus doesn't just say "Goodbye!" Instead, He tells them: "Go in peace!" Such is the case with the sinful woman who anointed Jesus' head with oil and whose sins were forgiven (Luke 7:50), and the hemorrhaging woman who touched Jesus' robe and was healed and saved (Luke 8:48). Even when meeting with His disciples after the resurrection, Jesus greeted them with "Peace be to you" (Luke 24:36). Paul, Luke's traveling companion, also spoke often of the peace we have with God through Jesus Christ (see Romans 5:1). When the angels appeared to the shepherds, the song of the heavenly choir provided the answer to one of the most important questions for human beings: how can we live in peace, when there is so much trouble around us? Are you in need of inner peace? Jesus is the answer. There is nothing more paralyzing than a soul in turmoil, and I am so thankful that the Savior offers the ultimate alternative: peace with God. Years ago, I read a beautiful adage (I don't know the author) that became very much a part of my faith walk: *Peace is not the absence of trouble, but the presence of Christ.* May the assuring Presence of the Savior of the world bring peace to your heart today, and every day.

My Response: _____

His Incarnation

And the Word became flesh, and dwelt among us, and we saw
His glory . . . full of grace and truth.

—John 1:14

The Kalaupapa peninsula of the paradisiacal island of Molokai, Hawaii, is the site of a leprosy colony where, over the years, thousands lived out their lives with the dreaded disease. Jozef De Veuster, better known as Father Damien, gave his life to touch the untouchable, becoming one with them. Providing physical, spiritual, and emotional support, he served the afflicted in whatever way needed, dressing their wounds, feeding them, and making coffins for them. After eleven years of tending the sick, he contracted leprosy and died on April 15, 1889. He has been called a "martyr of charity" for his work in Kalaupapa, where his compassion remained unshaken by the risks involved.*

When we talk about Jesus coming as a Baby in a manger, we are actually discussing a mystery called the *Incarnation*. When God humbled Himself to become human, He did it in order to redeem us. Amazing! He walked among us, and we saw God in the flesh. And even though He never sinned, He died the death of a criminal and took our sins upon Himself (see 2 Corinthians 5:21). The words used in John 1:14 are of the utmost importance. For example, the word "dwelt" means that He encamped or, in Old Testament language, *tabernacled* among us. This is a key word derived from the root word used for the *tabernacle* in the wilderness, where God showed His glory and His Presence resided with His people (see Exodus 40:34, LXX). Now the tabernacle is Jesus Christ, and we see God's glory through Him; He is the fullest revelation of the glory of God! He is filled with grace and truth! (John 1:14). That God would love us so much as to become one of us, and *camp* and dwell in our neighborhood, is a mystery that we will ponder for eternity! That He would come from His heavenly throne, become a human being, settle here on this earth, and die in our place, well, it's an event that we will celebrate forever. And even though we are not able to fully comprehend it all, one thing we know: we are *very special* to God! And He definitely loves us!

My Response: _____

---

* Wikipedia, s.v. "Father Damien," last modified April 5, 2019, 5:47 A.M. UTC, https:// en.wikipedia.org/wiki /Father_Damien

HIS ROLE

*Jesus was born in Bethlehem of Judea
in the days of Herod the king.*

—Matthew 2:1

I still remember my excitement as we approached the town of Bethlehem. So much to see! We visited the traditional sites of the birth of Jesus and the shepherd's fields. I noticed some fascinating names of local businesses—signs that read: *Ruth Restaurant and Boaz Field Souvenir Shop.* The romantic story of Boaz and Ruth takes place in the town of Bethlehem, and it plays a fundamental role in the ancestry of Jesus and in the understanding of His redeeming mission.

Throughout redemption history, God acted in certain patterns, both geographically and historically, so that we would not miss the Messiah when He came. And this brings us to the concept of *go'el*, one of the most fascinating themes in the Scriptures. I truly believe that once we understand it, we start to comprehend the plan of salvation on quite a different level. *Go'el* is a Hebrew word meaning "kinsman-redeemer" or the "closest of kin." The *go'el* performed several roles for his relative that no one else could do. For example, the *go'el* could redeem a relative who was sold into slavery (see Leviticus 25:47–54), setting them free! Also, the *go'el* could redeem property that was given up by a poor relative (verses 25–34). And the *go'el* was the one who would marry the widow of a close relative to ensure that the family lineage was not interrupted, thus removing the shame from the kin. The book of Ruth is written with this concept in mind. When Naomi and Ruth returned to Bethlehem as destitute widows, they discovered that Boaz was their *go'el* (Ruth 2:20). Eventually, Ruth asked him to take her under his protection and provision as a "close relative (*go'el*)" (Ruth 3:9). They got married and had a son, whose name was Obed, who became king David's grandfather (see Ruth 4:17). King David was also born in Bethlehem, and that's why Mary and Joseph, descendants of David, went there for the census (Luke 2:4). Many prophecies foretold the coming of the Redeemer (*go'el*), and Jesus fulfilled all the roles of the *go'el*,* setting us free and taking our shame away. Yes! You have a Redeemer!

My Response: _____

---

* For an in-depth study on this topic, see Elizabeth Talbot, *Surprised by Love* (Nampa, ID: Pacific Press®, 2010). For a fascinating study of this topic in relation to the Sabbath, see Elizabeth Talbot, *I Will Give You Rest* (Nampa, ID: Pacific Press®, 2015).

His Guidance

*"We saw His star in the east and have come
to worship Him."*

—Matthew 2:2

Once, when I was going through a troublesome time, I looked outside and saw a thick fog through my window. I could barely make out the treetops and everything was shrouded in a dense haze. I realized that this phenomenon matched the landscape of my heart: I couldn't see anything, and I didn't know where I was heading. Still, I felt God speaking to me in my heart, "I will guide you through the fog; just don't let go of my hand." Knowing that God would lead me brought great peace into my heart, even though I didn't have all the answers. Two decades have gone by, and God has guided my steps all along, especially when I felt absolutely blind in my journey.

Matthew tells the story about the wise men who came from the east (Matthew 2:1–12). A core teaching of this story, which is unique to Matthew, is that God initiates communication with these foreigners through a bright and unusual star (which was the way that they could understand), and thus guides them towards Jesus. That God would communicate with these "Magi from the east" was an alien and challenging concept for Matthew's predominantly Jewish audience. The Magi were a priestly caste of astronomers and magicians from Persia or Babylon, who were often trusted advisors to the king (see Daniel 1; 2). Yes, God guided *them*! As in the times of the Old Testament, when God communicated the future through dreams to Pharaoh and Nebuchadnezzar, king of Babylon, God continues to communicate with all who would heed His voice. And God desires to guide *us* to a deeper revelation of Jesus. He is the greatest expert in communication and guidance! He knows how to reveal His path to all of us, no matter how spiritually and emotionally distant we may think ourselves to be. He is able to reach us, as well as our children and grandchildren, friends and family. And He doesn't give up! Be assured that whenever we choose to do God's will, He will surely reveal it to us! And that is one of the most comforting thoughts we could end this year with. May this be our testimony: We saw . . . and came to worship Him!

My Response: _____

His Communication

*Behold, an angel of the Lord appeared
to Joseph in a dream.*

—Matthew 2:13

I was sitting in my parked car, about to go into a place where I would make one of the most pivotal and consequential decisions in my life. Having prayed, seeking God's counsel for months, I was now asking Him to reveal to me if this was His will. As I prayed, a sudden peace came upon me, and I became keenly aware that God is truly able to communicate with us. If we want to do His will, it becomes His responsibility to reveal it, and He has countless ways to do it.

This is a most important principle. We serve a God who not only desires but initiates communication with His people. In the Gospel of Matthew narratives about the infancy of Jesus, God is constantly communicating through supernatural means: there is a special star, and He sends dreams five times (1:20; 2:12, 13, 19, 22). His communication is direct and sometimes urgent: "Get up! Take the Child and His mother and flee to Egypt, and remain there until I tell you; *for Herod is going to search for the Child to destroy Him*" (Matthew 2:13). Joseph obeyed immediately, "while it was still night" (verse 14). Just as at the time of Moses, when the king of Egypt gave the command to kill the male babies (Exodus 1:16), Jesus, the long awaited New and Greater Moses (Deuteronomy 18:15, 18), had to be protected from another evil ruler who was trying to cut short the life of God's appointed Deliverer. The original language reveals that Herod wanted to "kill" the Child, and the same word is used in Matthew 27:20, when the chief priests and elders persuaded the crowds to demand that Jesus be killed. Evil forces were trying to destroy Jesus from the beginning to the end. But even though humans may delay the plans of God, they cannot frustrate them. And God communicated everything that was necessary for the safety of the Savior. When God provided a Savior to die in our place, He clearly communicated His love for us. He continues to communicate with us through His Word, His Spirit, godly mentors, and so many other means. If you want to do God's will, be assured that He will communicate it clearly, and in a way that you can understand it! He truly guides His children!

My Response: _____

HIS PLEDGE

"A voice was heard in Ramah, weeping and great mourning,
Rachel weeping for her children."

—Matthew 2:18

One of the most painful funerals I ever preached at was that of a thirty-seven-year-old woman, who was a member of the church I used to pastor. She and her husband had three young children. I brought one of her young boys to where the casket was, explaining that his mom was in there, sleeping until Jesus would come to wake her up. I will never forget the child's bright eyes as he asked me: "When?" This is a question we all have: "When will God eradicate pain and death?"

King Herod, whose upcoming death is announced prior to the horrible massacre he orders (see Matthew 2:15, 16), was enraged when he realized that the Magi had not returned to inform him about the whereabouts of the new King (see 2:12, 16). And in a fit of madness, he ruthlessly "sent and slew all the male children who were in Bethlehem and all its vicinity, from two years old and under" (verse 16). Matthew denounces the king's cruelty and maniacal abuse of authority. Herod was known for such atrocities in order to secure his throne, ordering the execution of members of his own family, including his mother-in-law, wife, and three sons. This awful event painfully reminds us that we live in a world of abuse and death, where innocent victims are killed by drunk drivers, and children are abused or die of cancer. On this occasion, Matthew recalls a prophecy from Jeremiah 31:15, that portrays Rachel, depicted as the mother of Israel's children, weeping for Jacob's descendants as they are led away into Babylonian exile: "And she refused to be comforted, because they were no more" (Matthew 2:18; Jeremiah 31:15). However, Jeremiah 31 is a chapter that also offers hope in the midst of tragedy. " 'There is hope for your future,' declares the LORD, 'And your children will return to their own territory' " (verse 17). I am so thankful that we know how the world's history ends. And Jesus wins! God has pledged to eradicate evil: "He will wipe away every tear from their eyes; and there will no longer be any death . . . any mourning, or crying, or pain." (Revelation 21:4). May His pledge bring you comfort in times of sickness and mourning.

My Response: _____

HIS SOLICITUDE

Then after being warned by God in a dream,
he left for the regions of Galilee.

—Matthew 2:22

I had been to the lake before, but this time I drove right up to the water and loved it! But when I tried to leave, I realized that it was going to be a challenge. The wheels were spinning, but the car was not moving until it was completely stuck, its undercarriage resting on the sand. I had to admit that I was unable to deal with the situation on my own. Suddenly a man who had witnessed my ordeal came to the rescue. And he came with a solution! He tied a rope to my car and pulled it out in no time with his four-wheel drive jeep.

I don't think we fully grasp God's tender solicitude towards His children, and maybe that's why we often try to figure things out on our own. It is at the point where we are the weakest and most fearful that God's presence is manifested most powerfully, even though He is with us all along. Even Adam and Eve tried to figure things out on their own after the Fall, but there was no way out, and God stepped in to save humanity. God knows our every move, and He understands our powerlessness. His great solicitude for each one of us is unparalleled. I am fascinated by the detailed way in which God guided Joseph in the infancy of Jesus in order to preserve the life of our Savior. Matthew records five infancy narratives, the last of which is about Joseph and Mary returning from Egypt, as Herod had already died. They arrived in the land of Israel, "but when he [Joseph] heard that Archelaus was reigning over Judea in place of His father Herod, he was afraid to go there" (Matthew 2:22). Archelaus! He was reported to have started his reign with a massacre of three thousand people!* No wonder Joseph was afraid! Was he supposed to find a way out on his own? Where should they go? Yet God was there, with His ever-vigilant and powerful presence. Joseph was "warned by God in a dream" (verse 22), and they headed towards Galilee instead, settling in Nazareth. Whenever you feel stuck in the "sand," remember that you are *never* alone. Your saving God is at your side with His solicitous presence!

My Response: _____

---

* Josephus, *Antiquities,* 17.213–218.

HIS CONSTANCY

"I am with you always, even to the end of the age."

—Matthew 28:20

M y father was approaching the end of his life. His body was no longer responding to treatment. I made a large poster in a bright color and taped it to the wall of his hospital room, so that he could see it at all times. "Do not fear, for *I am with you*; do not be dismayed, for I am your God. I will strengthen you and help you; I will uphold you with my righteous right hand" (Isaiah 41:10, NIV). He told me how much this sign meant to him, reassuring him of God's presence with him during his final days.

God's presence is the most encouraging promise we have on our earthly journey. God promises to be with us on good and bad days, in sickness and in health, in comfort and in want. Matthew highlights God's presence with us both at the beginning and at the end of his Gospel. In Matthew 1:23 we are told that Jesus is Immanuel, which means "God with us." And at the conclusion of this Gospel, Jesus Himself reminds us that He is with us until the end! (Matthew 28:20). In the original Greek, the verse reads in this order: "I with you (I) am *all the days* until the completion of the age." In Greek, the emphasis is found in the middle of the sentence; "all the days" is found at the center of His assurance. I am comforted by the *constancy* of God's presence with me each and every day, and *all* the days until this world is no more. In the Old Testament, God's presence was promised to His people to empower them for a particular task or endeavor. When Moses was overwhelmed with his commission, he asked God "Who am I, that I should go to Pharaoh, and that I should bring the sons of Israel out of Egypt?" (Exodus 3:11). God answered: "Certainly I will be with you" (verse 12). The same promise is given to Joshua, because he was to lead Israel into the Promised Land (see Joshua 1:5). And the promise is given directly by the risen Jesus to His disciples, following the Great Commission. He who has conquered death and possesses authority over all things in heaven and on earth, is the same One who promises: *I am with you all the days until the end.* Be assured, my friend, for the eternal God and Savior is with you!

My Response: _____